FOUNDATIONS OF TQM:
A READINGS BOOK

FOUNDATIONS OF TQM: A READINGS BOOK

JOSEPH G. VAN MATRE
University of Alabama at Birmingham

THE DRYDEN PRESS
Harcourt Brace College Publishers

Fort Worth   Philadelphia   San Diego   New York   Orlando   Austin   San Antonio
Toronto   Montreal   London   Sydney   Tokyo

Acquisitions Editor: **Scott Isenberg**
Developmental Editor: **Tracy Morse**
Project Editor: **Doug Smith**
Art Directors: **Jeanette Barber, Terry Rasberry**
Production Managers: **Erin Gregg, Rob Wright**
Electronic Publishing Coordinator: **Ellie McKenzie**
Product Manager: **Scott Timian**
Marketing Assistant: **Kathleen Sharp**
Permissions Editor and Photo Researcher: **Shirley Webster**

Copy Editor: **Larry Bromley**
Indexer: **Leslie Leland Frank**
Compositor: **Electronic Publishing**
Text Type: **10/13 Galliard**
Cover Image: **Lamberto Alvarez**

Address for orders:
The Dryden Press
6277 Sea Harbor Drive
Orlando, FL 32887-6777
1-800-782-4479 or 1-800-433-0001 (in Florida)

Address for editorial correspondence:
The Dryden Press
301 Commerce Street, Suite 3700
Fort Worth, TX 76102

ISBN: 0-03-007866-0

Library of Congress Catalog Card Number: 94-68601

Printed in the United States of America.

4 5 6 7 8 9 1 2 3 067 9 8 7 6 5 4 3 2 1

The Dryden Press
Harcourt Brace College Publishers

Photo Credits: UPI/Bettmann, p. 58; Bettmann, p. 59; The Bettmann archive, p. 64; Photo courtesy of Motorola, Inc., p. 352.

DEDICATION

To the family:

Mother
Mama and Daddy
W. H. V., Jr. (Sonny)
Mindy and Kelly
Paulette
Alex and Sarah

THE DRYDEN PRESS SERIES IN MANAGERIAL SCIENCE AND QUANTITATIVE METHODS

THE HARCOURT BRACE COLLEGE OUTLINE SERIES

LAPIN
Business Statistics

PENTICO
Management Science

ROTHENBERG
Probability and Statistics

TANIS
Statistics I: Descriptive Statistics and Probability

TANIS
Statistics II: Estimation and Tests of Hypothesis

PREFACE

Kaoru Ishikawa refers to total quality management (TQM) as "a thought revolution in management, therefore the thought processes of all employees must be changed. To accomplish this, education must be repeated over and over." This book was developed to help people learn about TQM, to provide knowledge that will facilitate useful change in the way we think and manage, and thereby to make us more productive, more secure, and more satisfied in our work. Whether you study this material in a classroom or as part of your personal continuing education and self-improvement, I think you will find the readings interesting, informative, and relevant.

My personal interest in TQM began about 10 years ago, following the completion of my formal academic work by several years. My curiosity developed from some thought-provoking articles I encountered (particularly one by Brian Joiner in *The American Statistician*), so, it is quite natural that herein I seek to engage you in the same fashion. My growing interests, plus some timely sabbaticals, allowed me to study at The University of Wisconsin–Madison, The University of Tennessee, and The Rochester Institute of Technology. These experiences (the time, the people, e.g. George Box, the resources, e.g. extensive written and audo-visual materials at U.W., and seminars/meetings such as Brian Joiner's "Executive Overview of Statistical Thinking") gave me an extraordinary opportunity to learn about the quality movement. The readings in this book, plus the supplemental information given in the Instructors' Manual, allow me to share my experiences with others who have not been so fortunate as to have had both sabbaticals *and* the freedom to "leave home." (The younger of my two daughters was in college when this all began.)

My experiences in teaching "the quality course" have led me to the belief that a set of readings is indispensable. Yes, I use a textbook, but I have found readings provide the invaluable breadth and depth needed for an important, complex subject such as TQM. TQM is a difficult subject for one author (or even two or three co-authors) to capture entirely. Perhaps this difficulty reflects the broad, integrative nature of TQM, and thus the problems that a statistician has when writing on the subject of teams or service quality, or, conversely, a management type has writing on the topic of the tools of quality. The readings book allows one to have, for example, former Motorola CEO Bob Galvin discussing leadership and USC professor Ed Lawler reviewing empowerment. Altogether we have gathered together 30-plus authors' work, so that each subject receives first-rate treatment. The readings were selected from the following sources:

Periodicals and Reports:
Benchmark

Business Week
California Management Review
Cornell Hotel and Restaurant Administration Quarterly
Harvard Business Review
Journal of the American Health Information Management Association
Journal of Marketing
Journal of Quality and Participation
Organizational Dynamics
Quality Progress
Report Series of the Center for Quality and Productivity Improvement
   (University of Wisconsin)
Sloan Management Review
Smithsonian

Books:
Contemporary Business Statistics
A World of Quality: The Timeless Passport

This book brings together, in one convenient source, some of the best writings of the quality management literature.

Many individuals were very helpful during my visits, and I wish to identify them and thank them for their kindness:

Center for Quality and Productivity Improvement, University of Wisconsin–Madison: **George Box, Judy Pagel, Soren Bisgaard, Conrad Fung, Mark Finster, Bruce Ankenman, Neil Diamond, Klaus Kristensen, and Ian Hau.**

Management Development Center, Institute for Productivity Through Quality, University of Tennessee: **Mary Sue Younger, C. Warren Neel, David L. Sylwester, James L. Schmidhammer, and Kenneth Gilbert.**

Center for Quality and Applied Statistics, Rochester Institute of Technology: **Edward Schilling, Diann Feeley, Thomas Barker, Joe Voelkel, Hubert D. Wood, and Nicholas A. Zaino, Jr.**

Of the above I especially want to express my appreciation to **Mary Sue Younger** for her friendship and hospitality, **George Box** for opening his home for the Monday night seminars, and **Judy Pagel** for her help on numerous matters during my two semesters in Madison.

Next, I would like to thank a few others who have been helpful in the development and production of this book. First, thanks to **Betty Thorne** of Stetson University and **Uly Knotts** of Georgia Southern University for their review of an early version of the manuscript. I also thank **Brian and Laurel Joiner** for allowing me to use the library of Joiner Associates Inc., and to attend the firm's seminars. At the University of Alabama in Birmingham's School of Business, thanks to **Dean M. Gene Newport** and **David Lewis** for help with my sabbaticals, and to **Jim Dilworth** for reviewing this project's possibilities with me. I also want to thank frequent collaborator **Donna Slovensky** of U. A. B.'s Health Information Management faculty for suggestions on material concerning the learning organization. My secretary, **Rose McCoy,** was invaluable for her timely and creative help, especially on the Instructor's Manual. At The Dryden Press, thanks to **Scott Isenberg, Tracy Morse, Terry Rasberry, Jeanette Barber, Doug Smith, Rob Wright, Scott Timian, Erin Gregg, Kathleen Sharp,** and **Shirley Webster** who made this book a reality. I am grateful for the several authors and organizations who gave permission for their material to be reproduced herein. And, finally, thanks to my students for the opportunity to work with you on TQM and for the feedback you've provided me on the utility of the readings, individually and as a set. To all of you above, thanks again and again.

Joseph G. Van Matre
November 1994

The editor would like to honor the following four individuals, who made major contributions to the development of total quality management, with these biographical sketches that will also help the reader's appreciation of the movement.

W. Edwards Deming (1900–1993)   was born in Iowa, but grew up in Wyoming, first in Cody (named for Buffalo Bill Cody) and then in Powell. He attended the University of Wyoming, the University of Colorado, and Yale. Although not the "father" of quality control (that distinction belongs to his early mentor, Walter Shewhart). Deming is internationally known for his achievements. He very early recognized the key role of management in sustaining a firm's quality progress and addressed this in his "14 Points for Managers."

His quality-related visits and lectures to Japan began in 1950, and many leading Japanese firms subsequently adopted the Deming philosophy. In his honor the Japanese established the Deming Prize, a highly competitive and prestigious award for quality achievements. Corporate winners have included Toyota, Ricoh, and NEC. In 1960, Deming was honored with the Second Order of the Sacred Treasure, the highest honor a foreigner can attain in Japan.

Deming was not, however, widely know in the United States until "discovered" by desperate American industry in the early 1980s. Many books and articles have been written about the Deming management philosophy. His 1993 *The New Economics* is especially recommended as an introduction to his thinking. Deming had a long, fruitful career and conducted the last of his four-day seminars in Los Angeles only two weeks before his death at his Washington, D.C., home on December 20, 1993.

Joseph M. Juran (1904—)   is the other major figure in the development of quality management. Juran was born in 1904 in Romania, but his family immigrated to America in 1912. He earned a B.S. in electrical engineering from the University of Minnesota in 1924 and a J.D. from Loyola University in 1935.

After graduation from Minnesota, Juran began his career at the Hawthorne plant of Western Electric, then the manufacturing arm of AT&T. At AT&T, Juran had the opportunity to learn from Walter A. Shewhart, the Bell Lab physicist responsible for developing the control chart and the PDCA cycle (see Readings 7–9).

After World War II, Juran began a consulting practice that eventually spawned the Juran Institute, Inc. in Wilton, Connecticut, (1979). Juran's work with the Japanese began in 1954 when he conducted seminars for top- and mid-level managers. In 1980, he was awarded the Second Order of the Sacred Treasure in recognition of his contributions to quality management in Japan.

Juran retired in 1994 at age 89. His many books cover a wide range of quality topics, but *Juran on Leadership for Quality* (1989) is especially valuable to managers.

Kaoru Ishikawa (1915–1989) is perhaps the most important of the Japanese contributors to TQM. Ishikawa was born in Tokyo and received both his applied chemistry degree (1939) and his doctorate in engineering (1958) from the prestigious University of Tokyo.

His quality activities began when he joined the Quality Control Research Group of the Union of Japanese Scientists and Engineers (JUSE) in 1949. Ishikawa met with Deming and Juran during their 1950 and 1954 visits, respectively, and highly praised their contributions in his book *What Is Total Quality Control?* (1985).

Ishikawa developed the cause-and-effect diagram, a basic tool of quality improvement (see Reading 5), and played a primary role in the development and spread of quality circles, a form of employee involvement very popular in Japan. His honors in Japan include the Deming Prize and the Second Order of the Sacred Treasure. In the United States he has received the Grant Award and the Shewhart Medal from the American Society for Quality Control (ASQC).

Philip B. Crosby (1926—) is also a well-known figure in quality management. Although he does not appear to be as highly regarded as Deming and Juran by academics and quality professionals, he is clearly admired by American management and is a sought-after consultant.

Crosby was born in 1926 in West Virginia. He earned a degree in podiatry (his father's profession), but then elected to follow a career in industry. He began as an inspector, but advanced within several companies and eventually was named vice-president for quality at ITT in 1965. In 1979, he left ITT to form Philip Crosby Associates and its Quality College in Winter Park, Florida. Crosby's clients have included firms such as General Motors, IBM, Johnson & Johnson, and Xerox. He has written several books—his first, *Quality Is Free* (1979), sold some one million copies. In 1991, he retired from Philip Crosby Associates to begin a new firm, Career IV, Inc.

CONTENTS

PART ONE

INTRODUCTION

Reading 1
Quality on the Line

David Garvin, of the Harvard Business School, spent several years on a very ambitious project studying Japanese and American manufacturers of room air conditioners. His initial research was first published in 1983 in this article from the *Harvard Business Review*. Other aspects of his work were published in a host of leading journals: *Business Horizons, Sloan Management Review,* and the *Academy of Management Journal*. His 1988 book, *Managing Quality* provides a comprehensive account of his findings and recommendations.

This article is particularly useful in two regards. First, it is the product of an objective, academic researcher and reports hard data as opposed to unsupported anecdotal information. Second, the article was published at a low point of domestic product quality. Garvin's study helped send a "wake-up call" that alerted American management to both the problems and opportunities for quality improvement. His timely study did much to foster the U.S. adoption of Total Quality Management (TQM).

READING 1
QUALITY ON THE LINE

BY DAVID A. GARVIN

When it comes to product quality, American managers still think the competitive problem much less serious than it really is. Because defining the term accurately within a company is so difficult (is quality a measure of performance, for example, or reliability or durability?), managers often claim they cannot know how their product quality stacks up against that of their competitors, who may well have chosen an entirely different quality "mix." And since any comparisons are likely to wind up as comparisons of apples with oranges, even a troubling variation in results may reflect only a legitimate variation in strategy. Is there, then, a competitive problem worth worrying about?

I have recently completed a multi-year study of production operations at all but one of the manufacturers of room air conditioners in both the United States and Japan (details of the study are given in the insert, *Research methods*). Each manufacturer uses a simple assembly-line process; each uses much the same manufacturing equipment; each makes an essentially standardized product. No apples versus oranges here: the comparison is firmly grounded. And although my data come from a single industry, both that industry's manufacturing process and its managers' range of approaches to product quality give these findings a more general applicability.

The shocking news, for which nothing had prepared me, is that the failure rates of products from the highest-quality producers were between *500* and *1,000* times less than those of products from the lowest. The "between 500 and 1,000" is not a typographical error but an inescapable fact. There is indeed a competitive problem worth worrying about.

MEASURING QUALITY

Exhibit I presents a composite picture of the quality performance of U.S. and Japanese manufacturers of room air conditioners. I have measured quality in two ways: by the incidence of "internal" and of "external" failures. Internal failures include all defects observed (either during fabrication or along the assembly line) before the product leaves the factory; external failures include all problems incurred in the field after the unit has been installed. As a proxy for the latter, I have used the number of service calls recorded during the product's first year of warranty coverage because that was the only period for which U.S. and Japanese manufacturers offered comparable warranties.

Measured by either criterion, Japanese companies were far superior to their U.S. counterparts: their average assembly-line defect rate was almost 70 times lower and their average first-year service call rate nearly 17 times better. Nor can this variation in performance be attributed simply to differences in the number of minor, appearance-related defects. Classifying failures by major functional problems (leaks, electrical) or by component failure rates (compressors, thermostats, fan motors) does not change the results.

More startling, on both internal and external measures, the poorest Japanese company typically had a failure rate less than half that of the best

EXHIBIT I	**QUALITY IN THE ROOM AIR CONDITIONING INDUSTRY 1981–1982***							
	INTERNAL FAILURES				**EXTERNAL FAILURES**			
	Fabrication: coil leaks per 100 units	**Assembly-line defects per 100 units**			**Service call rate per 100 units under first-year warranty coverage**			
		Total	Leaks	Electrical	Total	Compressors	Thermostats	Fan motors
Median								
U.S.	4.4	63.5	3.1	3.3	10.5†	1.0	1.4	.5
Japan	< .1	.95	.12	.12	.6	.05	.002	.028
Range								
U.S.	.1-9.0	7–165	1.3–34	.9–34	5.3–26.5	.5–3.4	.4–3.6	.2–2.6
Japan	.03-.4	.15–3.0	.0015–.5	.0015–1.0	.04–2.0	.002–.1	0–.03	.001–.2

* Although most companies reported total failure rates for 1981 or 1982, complete data on component failure rates were often available only for earlier years. For some U.S. companies, 1979 or 1980 figures were employed. Because there was little change in U.S. failure rates during this period, the mixing of data from different years should have little effect.

†Service call rates in the United States normally include calls where no product problems were found ("Customer instruction" calls); those in Japan do not. I have adjusted the U.S. median to exclude these calls; without the adjustments, the median U.S. service call rate would be 11.4 per 100 units. Figures for the range should be adjusted similarly, although the necessary data were not available from the U.S. companies with the highest and lowest service call rates.

U.S. manufacturer. Even among the U.S. companies themselves, there was considerable variation. Assembly-line defects ranged from 7 to 165 per 100 units—a factor of 20 separating the best performer from the worst—and service call rates varied by a factor of 5.

For ease of analysis, I have grouped the companies studied according to their quality performance (see the *Appendix*). These groupings illustrate an important point: quality pays. *Exhibit II*, for example, presents information on assembly-line productivity for each of these categories and shows that the highest-quality producers were also those with the highest output per man-hour. On the basis of the number of direct labor hours actually worked on the assembly line, productivity at the best U.S. companies was five times higher than at the worst.

Measuring productivity by "standard output" (see *Exhibit II*) blurs the picture somewhat. Although the Japanese plants maintain a slight edge over the best U.S. plants, categories of performance tend to overlap. The figures based on standard output, however, are rather imperfect indicators of productivity—for example, they fail to include overtime or rework hours and so overstate productivity levels, particularly at the poorer companies, which devote more of their time to correcting defects. Thus, these figures have less significance than do those based on the number of hours actually worked.

EXHIBIT II	**QUALITY AND PRODUCTIVITY**			
GROUPING OF COMPANIES BY QUALITY PERFORMANCE	**UNITS PRODUCED PER ASSEMBLY-LINE DIRECT LABOR MAN-HOUR ACTUAL HOURS***		**UNITS PRODUCED PER ASSEMBLY-LINE DIRECT LABOR MAN-HOUR STANDARD OUTPUT†**	
	Median	Range	Median	Range
Japanese manufacturers	NA††	NA	1.8	1.4–3.1
Best U.S. plants	1.7	1.7†††	1.7	1.4–1.9
Better U.S. plants	.9	.7–1.0	1.1	.8–1.2
Average U.S. plants	1.0	.6-1.2	1.1	1.1–1.7
Poorest U.S. plants	.35	.35†††	1.3	.8–1.6

*Direct labor hours have been adjusted to include only those workers involved in assembly (i.e., where inspectors and repairmen were classified as direct labor, they have been excluded from the totals).

†Computed by using the average cycle time to derive a figure for hourly output, and then dividing by the number of assembly-line direct laborers (excluding inspectors and repairmen) to determine output per man-hour.

††NA = not available

†††In this quality grouping, man-hour data were only available from a single company.

Note carefully that the strong association between productivity and quality is not explained by differences in technology or capital intensity, for most of the plants employed similar manufacturing techniques. This was especially true of final assembly, where manual operations, such as hand brazing and the insertion of color-coded wires, were the norm. Japanese plants did use some automated transfer lines and packaging equipment, but only in compressor manufacturing and case welding was the difference in automation significant.

The association between cost and quality is equally strong. Reducing field failures means lower warranty costs, and reducing factory defects cuts expenditures on rework and scrap. As *Exhibit III* shows, the Japanese manufacturers incurred warranty costs averaging 0.6% of sales; at the best American companies, the figure was 1.8%; at the worst 5.2%.

In theory, low warranty costs might be offset by high expenditures on defect prevention: a company could spend enough on product pretesting or on inspecting assembled units before shipment to wipe out any gains from improved warranty costs. Figures on the total costs of quality, however, which include expenditures on prevention and inspection as well as the usual failure costs of rework, scrap, and warranties, lead to the opposite

EXHIBIT III	**QUALITY AND COSTS**			
GROUPING OF COMPANIES BY QUALITY PERFORMANCE	**WARRANTY COSTS AS A PERCENTAGE OF SALES***		**TOTAL COST OF QUALITY (JAPANESE COMPANIES) AND TOTAL FAILURE COSTS (U.S. COMPANIES) AS A PERCENTAGE OF SALES†**	
	Median	Range	Median	Range
Japanese manufacturers	.6%	.2–1.0%	1.3%	.7–2.0%
Best U.S. plants	1.8	1.1–2.4	2.8	2.7–2.8
Better U.S. plants	2.4	1.7–3.1	3.4	3.3–3.5
Average U.S. plants	2.2	1.7–4.3	3.9	2.3–5.6
Poorest U.S. plants	5.2%	3.3–7.0%	>5.8%	4.4–>7.2%

*Because most Japanese air conditioners are covered by a three-year warranty while most U.S. units are covered by a warranty of five years, these figures somewhat overstate the Japanese advantage. The bias is unlikely to be serious, however, because second- to fifty-year coverage in the United States and second- to third-year coverage in Japan are much less inclusive—and therefore, less expensive—than first-year coverage. For example, at U.S. companies second- to fifty-year warranty costs average less than one-fifth of first-year expenses.

†Total cost of quality is the sum of all quality-related expenditures, including the costs of prevention, inspection, rework, scrap, and warranties. The Japanese figures include expenditures in all of these categories, while the U.S. figures, because of limited data, include only the costs of rework, scrap, and warranties (failure costs). As a result, these figures understate total U.S. quality costs relative to those of the Japanese.

conclusion. In fact, the total costs of quality incurred by Japanese producers were less than one-half the failure costs incurred by the best U.S. companies.

The reason is clear: failures are much more expensive to fix after a unit has been assembled than before. The cost of the extra hours spent pretesting a design is cheap compared with the cost of a product recall; similarly, field service costs are much higher than those of incoming inspection. Among manufacturers of room air conditioners, the Japanese—even with their strong commitment to design review, vendor selection and management, and in-process inspection—still have the lowest overall quality costs.

Nor are the opportunities for reduction in quality costs confined to this industry alone. A recent survey[1] of U.S. companies in 10 manufacturing sectors found that total quality costs averaged 5.8% of sales—for a $1 billion corporation, some $58 million per year primarily in scrap, rework, and warranty expenses. Shaving even a tenth of a percentage point off these costs would result in an annual saving of $1 million.

Other studies, which use the PIMS data base, have demonstrated a further connection among quality, market share, and return on investment.[2] Not only does good quality yield a higher ROI for any given market share (among businesses with less than 12% of the market, those with inferior product quality averaged an ROI of 4.5%, those with average product quality an ROI of 10.4%, and those with superior product quality an ROI of 17.4%); it also leads directly to market share gains Those businesses in the PIMS study that improved in quality during the 1970s increased their market share five to six times faster than those that declined—and three times faster than those whose quality remained unchanged.

The conclusion is inescapable: improving product quality is a profitable activity. For managers, therefore, the central question must be: What makes for successful quality management?

SOURCES OF QUALITY

Evidence from the room air conditioning industry points directly to the practices that the quality leaders, both Japanese and American, have employed. Each of these areas of effort—quality programs, policies, and

[1]"Quality Cost Survey" *Quality,* June 1977: 20.
[2]Sidney Schoeffler, Robert D. Buzzel, and Donald F. Heany, "Impact of Strategic Planning on Profit Performance," *Harvard Business Review,* March-April 1974: 137, and Robert D. Buzzell and Frederik D. Wiersema, "Successful Share-Building Strategies," *Harvard Business Review,* January-February 1981: 135.

attitudes; information systems; product design; production and work force policies; and vendor management—has helped in some way to reduce defects and lower field failures.

PROGRAMS, POLICIES & ATTITUDES

The importance a company attaches to product quality often shows up in the standing of its quality department. At the poorest performing plants in the industry, the quality control (QC) manager invariably reported to the director of manufacturing or engineering. Access to top management came, if at all, through these go-betweens, who often had very different priorities from those of the QC manager. At the best U.S. companies, especially those with low service call rates, the quality department had more visibility. Several companies had vice presidents of quality; at the factory level each head of QC reported directly to the plant manager. Japanese QC managers also reported directly to their plant managers.

Of course, reporting relationships alone do not explain the observed differences in quality performance. They do indicate, however, the seriousness that management attaches to quality problems. It's one thing to say you believe in defect-free products, but quite another to take time from a busy schedule to act on that belief and stay informed. At the U.S. company with the lowest service call rate, the president met weekly with all corporate vice presidents to review the latest service call statistics. Nobody at that company needed to ask whether quality was a priority of upper management.

How often these meetings occurred was as important as their cast of characters. Mistakes do not fix themselves; they have to be identified, diagnosed, and then resolved through corrective action. The greater the frequency of meetings to review quality performance, the fewer undetected errors. The U.S. plants with the lowest assembly-line defect rates averaged 10 such meetings per month; at all other U.S. plants, the average was four. The Japanese companies reviewed defect rates daily.

Meetings and corrective action programs will succeed, however, only if they are backed by genuine top-level commitment. In Japan, this commitment was deeply ingrained and clearly communicated. At four of the six companies surveyed, first-line supervisors believed product quality—not producing at low cost, meeting the production schedule, or improving worker productivity—was management's top manufacturing priority. At the other two, quality ranked a close second.

The depth of this commitment became evident in the Japanese practice of creating internal consumer review boards. Each of the Japanese producers had assembled a group of employees whose primary function was to act as typical consumers and test and evaluate products. Sometimes the products came randomly from the day's production; more frequently, they represented new designs. In each case, the group had final authority over product release. The message here was unmistakable: the customer—not the design staff, the marketing team, or the production group—had to be satisfied with a product's quality before it was considered acceptable for shipment.

By contrast, U.S. companies showed a much weaker commitment to product quality. At 9 of the 11 U.S. plants, first-line supervisors told me that their managers attached far more importance to meeting the production schedule than to any other manufacturing objective. Even the best performers showed no consistent relationship between failure rates and supervisors' perceptions of manufacturing priorities.

What commitment there was stemmed from the inclusion (or absence) of quality in systems of performance appraisal. Two of the three companies with the highest rates of assembly-line defects paid their workers on the basis of total output, not defect-free output. Is it any wonder these employees viewed defects as being of little consequence? Not surprisingly, domestic producers with low failure rates evaluated both supervisors and managers on the quality of output—supervisors, in terms of defect rates, scrap rates, and the amount of rework attributable to their operations; managers, in terms of service call rates and their plants' total costs of quality.

These distinctions make good sense. First-line supervisors play a pivotal role in managing the production process, which is responsible for internal failures, but have little control over product design, the quality of incoming materials, or other factors that affect field performance. These require the attention of higher level managers, who can legitimately be held responsible for coordinating the activities of design, purchasing, and other functional groups in pursuit of fewer service calls or reduced warranty expenses.

To obtain consistent improvement, a formal system of goal setting is necessary.[3] Only three U.S. plants set annual targets for reducing field failures. Between 1978 and 1981, these three were the only ones to cut their service call rates by more than 25%; most of the other U.S. plants showed little or no change. All the Japanese companies, however, consistently improved their quality—in several cases, by as much as 50%—and all had elaborate companywide systems of goal setting.

From the corporate level at these companies came vague policy pronouncements ("this year, let the customer determine our quality"), which were further defined by division heads ("reduced service call rates are necessary if we are to lower costs") and by middle managers ("compressor

---

[3]For a summary of evidence on this point, see Edwin A. Locke et al., "Goal Setting and Task Performance: 1969-1980," *Psychological Bulletin*, vol. 90, no. 1: 125.

failures are an especially serious problem that must be addressed"). Actual quantitative goals ("improve compressor reliability by 10%") were often set by foremen or workers operating through quality control circles. The collaborative nature of this goal-setting process helped these targets earn wide support.

At the final—or first—level of goal setting, specificity matters. Establishing an overall target for an assembly-line defect rate without specifying more detailed goals by problem category, such as leaks or electrical problems, is unlikely to produce much improvement. A number of U.S. plants have tried this approach and failed. Domestic producers with the lowest defect rates set their overall goals last. Each inspection point along the assembly line had a target of its own, which was agreed on by representatives of the quality and manufacturing departments. The sum of these individual targets established the overall goal for the assembly line. As a result, responsibility for quality became easier to assign and progress easier to monitor.

INFORMATION SYSTEMS

Successful monitoring of quality assumes that the necessary data are available, which is not always true. Without specific and timely information on defects and field failures, improvements in quality are seldom possible. Not surprisingly, at the poorest U.S. companies information on defects and field failures was virtually nonexistent. Assembly-line defects and service call rates were seldom reported. "Epidemic" failures (problems that a large proportion of all units had in common) were widespread. Design flaws remained undetected. At one domestic producer, nearly a quarter of all 1979-1981 warranty expenses came from problems with a single type of compressor.

Other companies reported more extensive quality information—daily and weekly defect rates as well as quarterly and, occasionally, monthly service call rates. These variations in the level of reporting detail correlated closely with differences in quality performance. Among average U.S. performers, for example, quality reports were quite general. Data on assembly line defects gave no breakdowns by inspection point; data on field failures were for entire product lines, not for separate models. Without further refinement, such data cannot isolate quality problems.

A 10% failure rate for a product line can mean a number of things: that all models in the line fail to perform 10% of the time, with no single problem standing out; that several models have a 5% failure rate and one a 30% rate, which suggests a single problem of epidemic proportions; or anything in between. There is no way of distinguishing these cases on the basis of aggregate data alone. What is true of goal setting is equally true of reporting systems: success requires mastering the details.

RESEARCH METHODS

This article is based mainly on data collected in 1981 and 1982 from U S. and Japanese manufacturers of room air conditioners. I selected that industry for study for a number of reasons: it contains companies of varying size and character, which implies a wide range of quality policies and performance; its products are standardized, which facilitates inter-company comparisons; and it employs a simple assembly-line process, which is representative of many other mass production industries.

Nine of the ten U S. companies in the industry and all seven of the Japanese companies participated in the study. They range in size from small air conditioning specialists with total sales of under $50 million to large home appliance manufacturers with annual sales of more than $200 million in this product line alone. Taken together, they account for approximately 90% of U.S. industry shipments and 90% of Japanese industry shipments. I have collected data separately for each plant (two of the American companies operate two plants apiece, otherwise, each company employs only a single plant). Of the 18 plants studied, 11 are American and 7 Japanese.

Once U.S. companies had agreed to participate in the study, I sent them a questionnaire requesting background information on their product line, production practices, vendor management practices, quality policies, and quality performance. I then visited them all in order to review the questionnaire results, collect additional data, tour the factories, and conduct interviews with key personnel. The interviews were open-ended and unstructured, although I posed similar questions at each company. A typical visit included interviews with managers in the quality, manufacturing, purchasing, engineering, and service departments, as well as several hours spent walking the production floor.

Preliminary analysis of the interviews and questionnaires showed that companies neither employed the same conventions in reporting data nor answered questions in the same degree of detail. I therefore sent each company its own set of follow-up questions to fill in these gaps and to make the data more comparable across companies. In addition, I requested each company to administer a brief questionnaire on quality attitudes to each of its first-line production supervisors.

I followed a similar approach with the Japanese manufacturers, although time constraints limited the amount of information that I could collect. All questionnaires were first translated into Japanese and mailed to the participating companies. Six of the seven companies completed the same basic quality questionnaire as did their American counterparts; the same companies also administered the survey on quality attitudes to a small number of their first-line supervisors. With the aid of a translator, I conducted on-site interviews at all the companies and toured six of the plants.

The best U.S. companies reported defect rates for each inspection point on the assembly line and field failure rates by individual model. The Japanese not only collected information that their U.S. counterparts ignored, such as failure rates in the later years of a product's life; they also insisted on extreme precision in reporting. At one company, repairmen had to submit reports on every defective unit they fixed. In general, it was not unusual for Japanese managers to be able to identify the 30 different ways in which Switch X had failed on Model Y during the last several years. Nor did they have to wait for such information.

Service call statistics in the United States took anywhere from one month to one year to make the trip from the field to the factory; in Japan, the elapsed time averaged between one week and one month. Differences in attitude are

EXHIBIT IV	**QUALITY AND PRODUCT STABILITY**			
GROUPING OF COMPANIES BY QUALITY PERFORMANCE	**MEDIAN NUMBER OF DESIGN CHANGES PER YEAR**	**MEDIAN NUMBER OF MODELS**	**MEDIAN NUMBER OF DESIGN CHANGES PER MODEL***	**MEDIAN PERCENTAGE THAT PEAK PRODUCTION EXCEEDED LOW PRODUCTION†**
Japanese manufacturers	NA††	80	NA	170%
Best U.S. plants	43	56	.8	27
Better U.S. plants	150	81	1.9	63
Average U.S. plants	400	126	3.2	50
Poorest U.S. plants	133	41	3.2	100

*Column 1 divided by column 2

†The figures in this column were derived by dividing each plant's largest daily output for the year by its smallest (non-zero) output for the year.

††NA = not available.

part of the explanation. As the director of quality at one Japanese company observed, field information reached his company's U.S. subsidiaries much more slowly than it did operations in Japan—even though both employed the same system for collecting and reporting data.

PRODUCT DESIGN

Room air conditioners are relatively standardized products. Although basic designs in the United States have changed little in recent years, pressures to improve energy efficiency and to reduce costs have resulted in a stream of minor changes. On the whole, these changes have followed a common pattern: the initiative came from marketing; engineering determined the actual changes to be made and then pretested the new design; quality control, manufacturing, purchasing, and other affected departments signed off; and, where necessary, prototypes and pilot production units were built.

What did differ among companies was the degree of design and production stability. As *Exhibit IV* indicates, the U.S. plants with the lowest failure rates made far fewer design changes than did their competitors.

Exhibit IV conveys an important message. Variety, at least in America, is often the enemy of quality. Product proliferation and constant design change may keep the marketing department happy, but failure rates tend to rise as well. By contrast, a limited product line ensures that workers are more familiar with each model and less likely to make mistakes. Reducing the number of design changes allows workers to devote more attention to each one. Keeping production level means less reliance on a second shift staffed by inexperienced employees.

The Japanese, however, have achieved low failure rates even with relatively broad product lines and rapidly changing designs. In the room air conditioning industry, new designs account for nearly a third of all models offered each year, far more than in the United States. The secret: an emphasis on reliability engineering and on careful shakedowns of new designs before they are released.

Reliability engineering is nothing new; it has been practiced by the aerospace industry in this country for at least 20 years. In practice, it involves building up designs from their basic components, determining the failure probabilities of individual systems and subsystems, and then trying to strengthen the weak links in the chain by product redesign or by incorporating more reliable parts. Much of the effort is focused up front, when a product is still in blueprint or prototype form. Managers use statistical techniques to predict reliability over the product's life and subject preliminary designs to exhaustive stress and life testing to collect information on potential failure modes. These data form the basis for continual product improvement.

Only one American maker of room air conditioners practiced reliability engineering, and its failure rates were among the lowest observed. All of the Japanese companies, however, placed considerable emphasis on these techniques. Their designers were, for example, under tremendous pressure to reduce the number of parts per unit; for a basic principle of reliability engineering is that, everything else being equal, the fewer the parts, the lower the failure rate.

Japanese companies worked just as hard to increase reliability through changes in components. They were aided by the Industrial Engineering Bureau of Japan's Ministry of International Trade and Industry (MITI), which required that all electric and electronic components sold in the country be tested for reliability and have their ratings on file at the bureau. Because this information was publicly available, designers no longer needed to test components themselves in order to establish reliability ratings.

An emphasis on reliability engineering is also closely tied to a more thorough review of new designs before units reach production. American manufacturers usually built and tested a single prototype before moving to pilot production; the Japanese often repeated the process three or four times.

Moreover, all affected departments—quality control, purchasing, manufacturing, service, and design engineering—played an active role at each stage of the review process. American practice gave over the early stages of the design process almost entirely to engineering. By the time other groups got their say, the process had gained momentum, schedules had been established, and changes had become difficult to make. As a result, many a product that performed well in the laboratory created grave problems on the assembly line or in the field.

PRODUCTION & WORK FORCE POLICIES

The key to defect-free production is a manufacturing process that is "in control"—machinery and equipment well maintained, workplaces clean and orderly, workers well trained, and inspection procedures suited to the rapid detection of deviations. In each of these areas, the Japanese were noticeably ahead of their American competitors.

Training of the labor force, for example, was extensive, even for employees engaged in simple jobs. At most of the Japanese companies, preparing new assembly-line workers took approximately six months, for they were first trained for all jobs on the line. American workers received far less instruction (from several hours to several days) and were usually trained for a single task. Not surprisingly, Japanese workers were much more adept at tracking down quality problems originating at other work stations and far better equipped to propose remedial action.

Instruction in statistical quality control techniques supplemented the other training offered Japanese workers. Every Japanese plant relied heavily on these techniques for controlling its production process. Process control charts, showing the acceptable quality standards of various fabrication and assembly-line operations, were everywhere in general use. Only one U.S. plant—the one with the lowest defect rate—had made a comparable effort to determine the capabilities of its production process and to chart the results.

Still, deviations will occur, and thorough and timely inspection is necessary to ferret them out quickly. Japanese companies therefore employed an inspector for every 7.1 assembly-line workers (in the United States the ratio was 1:9.5). The primary role of these inspectors was to monitor the production process for stability; they were less "gatekeepers," weeding out defective units before shipment, than providers of information. Their tasks were considered especially important where manual operations were common and where inspection required sophisticated testing of a unit's operating characteristics.

On balance, then, the Japanese advantage in production came less from revolutionary technology than from close attention to basic skills and to the reduction of all unwanted variations in the manufacturing process. In practice, this approach can produce dramatic results. Although new model introductions and assembly-line changeovers at American companies boosted defect rates, at least until workers became familiar with their new assignments, Japanese companies experienced no such problems.

Before every new model introduction, Japanese assembly-line workers were thoroughly trained in their new tasks. After-hours seminars explained the product to the work force, and trial runs were common. During changeovers, managers kept workers informed of the models slated for production each day, either through announcements at early morning meetings or by sending assembled versions of the new model down the line 30 minutes before the change was to take place, together with a big sign saying "this model comes next." American workers generally received much less information about changeovers. At the plant with the highest defect rate in the industry, communication about changeovers was limited to a single small chalkboard, listing the models to be produced each day, placed at one end of the assembly line.

The Japanese system of permanent employment also helped to improve quality. Before they are fully trained, new workers often commit unintentional errors. Several American companies observed that their workers' inexperience and lack of familiarity with the product line contributed to their high defect rates. The Japanese, with low absenteeism and turnover, faced fewer problems of this sort. Japanese plants had a median turnover of 3.1%; the comparable figure for U.S. plants was two times higher. Even more startling were the figures on absenteeism: a median of 3.1% for American companies and *zero* for the Japanese.

In addition, because several of the U.S. plants were part of larger manufacturing complexes linked by a single union, they suffered greatly from "bumping." A layoff in one part of the complex would result in multiple job changes as workers shifted among plants to protect seniority rights. Employees whose previous experience was with another product would suddenly find themselves assembling room air conditioners. Sharp increases in defects were the inevitable result.

VENDOR MANAGEMENT

Without acceptable components and materials, no manufacturer can produce high-quality products. As computer experts have long recognized, "garbage in" means "garbage out." Careful selection and monitoring of vendors is therefore a necessary first step toward ensuring reliable and defect-free production.

At the better U.S. companies, the quality department played a major role in vendor selection by tempering the views of the engineering ("do their samples meet our technical specifications") and purchasing ("is that the best we can do on price") departments. At the very best companies, however, purchasing departments independently ranked quality as their primary objective. Buyers received instruction in the concepts of quality control; at least one person had special responsibility for vendor quality management; goals were set for the quality of incoming components and materials; and vendors' shipments were carefully monitored.

Purchasing departments at the worst U.S. companies viewed their mission more narrowly: to obtain the lowest possible price for technically acceptable components. Site visits to new vendors were rarely made, and members of the purchasing department seldom got involved in the design review process. Because incoming inspection was grossly understaffed (at one plant, two workers were responsible for reviewing 14,000 incoming shipments per year), production pressures often allowed entire lots to come to the assembly line uninspected. Identification of defective components came, if at all, only after they had been incorporated into completed units. Inevitably, scrap and rework costs soared.

In several Japanese companies incoming materials arrived directly at the assembly line without inspection. New vendors, however, first had to pass rigorous tests: their products initially received 100% inspection. Once all problems were corrected, sampling inspection became the norm. Only after an extended period without a rejection were vendors allowed to send their products directly to the assembly line. At the first sign of deterioration in vendor performance, more intensive inspection resumed.

In this environment, inspection was less an end in itself than a means to an end. Receiving inspectors acted less as policemen than as quality consultants to the vendor. Site visits, for example, were mandatory when managers were assessing potential suppliers and continued for as long as the companies did business together. Even more revealing, the selection of vendors depended as much on management philosophy, manufacturing capability, and depth of commitment to quality as on price and delivery performance.

CLOSING THE GAP

What, then, is to be done? Are American companies hopelessly behind in the battle for superior quality? Or is an effective counterattack possible?

Although the evidence is still fragmentary, there are a number of encouraging signs. In 1980, when Hewlett-Packard tested 300,000 semiconductors from three U.S. and three Japanese suppliers, the Japanese chips had a failure rate one-sixth that of the American chips. When the test was repeated two years later, the U.S. companies had virtually closed the gap. Similar progress is evident in automobiles. Ford's Ranger trucks, built in Louisville, Kentucky, offer an especially dramatic example. In just three years, the number of "concerns" registered by the Louisville plant (the automaker's measure of quality deficiencies as recorded at monthly audits) dropped to less than one-third its previous high. Today, the Ranger's quality is nearly equal that of Toyota's SR5, its chief Japanese rival.

But in these industries, as with room air conditioners, quality improvement takes time. The "quick fix" provides few lasting gains. What is needed is a long-term commitment to the fundamentals—working with vendors to improve their performance, educating and training the work force, developing an accurate and responsive quality information system, setting targets for quality improvement, and demonstrating interest and commitment at the very highest levels of management. With their companies' futures on the line, managers can do no less.

Classifying Plants by Quality Performance

To identity patterns of behavior, I first grouped U.S. plants into categories according to their quality performance on two dimensions—internal quality (defect rates in the factory) and external quality (failure rates in the field).

Table A presents the basic data on external quality. I measured field performance in two ways: by the service call rate for units under first-year warranty coverage (the total number of service calls recorded in 1981 divided by the number of units in the field with active first-year warranties) and by the service call rate for units under first-year warranty coverage less customer instruction calls (only those service calls that resulted from a faulty unit, not from a customer who was using the unit improperly or had failed to install it correctly).

The second measure was necessary because companies differed in their policies toward customer instruction calls. Some reimbursed repairmen for these calls without argument; others did their best to eliminate such calls completely. An accurate assessment of product performance required the separation of these calls from problems that reflect genuinely defective units.

I classified plants on the basis of their rankings on the second of the two measures in *Table A*, and then grouped them according to their actual levels of field failures. In most cases, the dividing lines were clear, although there were some borderline cases. Plant 8, for example, had a total service call rate well above the industry median, yet after subtracting customer instruction calls, its failure rate differed little from the other average performers. Because this second figure more accurately reflects the rate of product malfunction, I treated Plant 8 as having average, rather than poor, external quality. A number of companies with high failure rates did not break out customer instruction calls. I have treated them as having poor external quality because their customer instruction calls would have to have been two or three times as frequent as the highest rate recorded in 1981 for them to have warranted an average ranking.

I followed a similar procedure in classifying plants on internal quality. Because companies differed in how they defined and recorded defects (some noted every single product flaw; others were interested only in major malfunctions), I employed several indexes to ensure consistency. The results are displayed in *Table B*. I ranked companies first by their total assembly-line detect rates (every defect recorded at every station along the assembly line divided by the number of units produced) and then by the number of defects requiring off-line repair. The second index compensates for the different definitions just noted, for it more accurately reflects the incidence of serious problems. Minor adjustments and touch-ups can generally be made without pulling a unit off the line; more serious problems normally require off-line repair. Measured on this basis, the high total defect rates of Plants 1 and 9 appear to be much less of a problem.

TABLE A	FIELD PERFORMANCE FOR U.S. PLANTS IN 1981			
PLANT	**SERVICE CALL RATE, FIRST YEAR WARRANTY COVERAGE**		**SERVICE CALL RATE LESS "CUSTOMER INSTRUCTION" CALLS**	
	Percentage	Rank	Percentage	Rank
1	5.3%	1	<5.3%	1
2	8.7	2	<8.7	2,3
3	9.2	3	5.6	2,3
4	10.5	4	9.8	5
5	11.1	5	9.3	4
6	11.4	6	10.5	6
7	12.6	7	10.5	6
8	16.2	8	11.8	8
9	17.5	9	13.8	9
10	22.9	10	<22.9	10
11	26.5%	11	<26.5%	11

	Ranking of plants on field performance external quality		
	Good	Average	Poor
Plant number	1, 2, 3	4, 5, 6, 7, 8	9, 10, 11

Because several companies had to estimate the off-line repair rate, I used a third index, the number of repairmen per assembly-line direct laborer to measure defect seriousness. The proportion of the work force engaged in repair activities, including workers assigned to separate rework lines and to rework activities in the warehouse, is likely to correlate well with the incidence of serious defects, for more serious problems usually require more time to correct and necessitate a larger repair staff. This measure provides important additional information, confirming the conclusions about Plant 1 (its high total defect rate appears to include a large number of minor problems) but contradicting those about Plant 9 (its large number of repairmen suggests that defects are, in fact, a serious problem, despite the small proportion of units requiring off-line repair).

I assigned plants to groups using much the same procedure as before. I first computed a composite ranking for each plant by averaging together the three rankings of *Table B*. Dividing lines between groups followed the absolute levels of the indexes for each plant. Once again, some judgment was involved, particularly for Plants 4, 5, and 9. Plants 5 and 9 were borderline cases, candidates for ranking as either average or poor internal quality. I classified the former as average, even though its overall rank was low, because its absolute scores on the first two measures were quite close to the median. I classified the latter as poor because its absolute scores on both the first and the third measures were so high. Plant 4 presented a different problem, for it provided no information at all on assembly-line defects. Rather than classifying the plant on the basis of the third index alone. I employed supplementary data. Based on its defect rate at the end-of-the-line quality audit and its rework and scrap costs as a percentage of sales, both of which were quite close to figures reported by other companies with average internal quality. Plant 4 showed up as an average performer.

Table C combines the results of the previous two tables. Overall quality rankings appear for each plant. In most cases, success on internal quality implied success on external measures, although the correlation is not perfect, as Plants 1, 7, and 8 demonstrate. The Japanese plants are in a category of their own, for on both internal and external measures they are at least twice as good as the best U.S. plant.

TABLE B	**INTERNAL QUALITY FOR U.S. PLANTS IN 1981**					
PLANT	**ASSEMBLY-LINE DEFECTS PER 100 UNITS**		**ASSEMBLY-LINE DEFECTS PER 100 UNITS REQUIRING OFF-LINE REPAIR**		**REPAIRMAN PER ASSEMBLY-LINE DIRECT LABORER**	
	Number	**Rank**	**Number**	**Rank**	**Number**	**Rank**
1	150	9	34	5,6	.06	3
2	7	1	7	1	.05	2
3	10	2	10	3	.04	1
4	NA*	NA	NA	NA	.09	8
5	57	5	47	7	.13	9
6	70	6	67	8	.06	3
7	26	4	7	1	.08	6
8	18	3	11	4	.08	6
9	>100	7	>30	5,6	.16	11
10	165	10	165	10	.13	9
11	135	8	>68	9	.07	5

*NA = not available

	Ranking of plants on internal quality		
	Good	**Average**	**Poor**
Plant number	2, 3, 7, 8	1, 4(?), 5, 6	9, 10, 11

TABLE C	CLASSIFICATION OF PLANTS ON INTERNAL AND EXTERNAL QUALITY

Internal quality	External quality			
	Poor	Fair	Good	Excellent
Poor	Plants 9, 10, 11			
Fair		Plants 4, 5, 6	Plant 1	
Good		Plants 7, 8	Plants 2, 3	
Excellent				All Japanese plants

Poor
U.S. plants

Average
U.S. plants

Better
U.S. plants

Best
U.S. plants

Mr. Garvin is the Robert and Jane Cizik Professor of Business Administration at the Harvard Business School. A previous HBR article, "Managing As If Tomorrow Mattered" (May-June 1982), which he wrote with Robert Hayes, won the McKinsey Award.

READING 2
ZERO DEFECTIONS:
QUALITY COMES TO SERVICES

ZERO DEFECTS IS OFTEN A GOAL ASSOCIATED WITH MANU-
FACTURED GOODS; ZERO DEFECTS MEANS NO ITEMS ARE
PRODUCED THAT DO NOT MEET SPECIFICATIONS. (THIS IDEA
WILL BE DISCUSSED FURTHER IN READING 7.) REICHHELD
AND SASSER TAKE THIS MANUFACTURING IDEAL AND TRANS-
FORM IT INTO A GOAL FOR SERVICE INDUSTRIES: ZERO
DEFECTIONS, I.E. NO LOSS OF CUSTOMERS.

THIS ARTICLE, THOUGH DIRECTED AT SERVICES, IS JUST AS
RELEVANT FOR THE MANUFACTURING SECTOR. THE SUREST
ROUTE TO *KEEPING* ANY CUSTOMER IS *SATISFYING* THE CUS-
TOMER, AND CUSTOMER SATISFACTION IS A BASIC TENET OF
TQM. PERHAPS THE MAJOR POINT OF THE ARTICLE IS THAT
ZERO DEFECTIONS (I.E. SATISFYING CUSTOMERS) IS NOT
SOME ALTRUISTIC ORGANIZATIONAL CONCERN; IT HAS A REAL
PAYOFF FOR THE FIRM. THE AUTHORS REPORT RESEARCH
THAT DEMONSTRATES THE *ECONOMICS* OF CUSTOMER
RETENTION: PROFITS INCREASE DRAMATICALLY AS THE
DEFECTION RATE DECREASES.

READING 2
ZERO DEFECTIONS:
QUALITY COMES TO SERVICES

BY FREDERICK F. REICHHELD AND W. EARL SASSER, JR.

The *real* quality revolution is just now coming to services. In recent years, despite their good intentions, few service company executives have been able to follow through on their commitment to satisfy customers. But service companies are beginning to understand what their manufacturing counterparts learned in the 1980s—that quality doesn't improve unless you measure it. When manufacturers began to unravel the costs and implications of scrap heaps, rework, and jammed machinery, they realized that "quality" was not just an invigorating slogan but the most profitable way to run a business. They made "zero defects" their guiding light, and the quality movement took off.

Service companies have their own kind of scrap heap: customers who will not come back. That scrap heap too has a cost. As service businesses start to measure it, they will see the urgent need to reduce it. They will strive for "zero defections"—keeping every customer the company can profitably serve—and they will mobilize the organization to achieve it.

Customer defections have a surprisingly powerful impact on the bottom line. They can have more to do with a service company's profits than scale, market share, unit costs, and many other factors usually associated with competitive advantage. As a customer's relationship with the company lengthens, profits rise. And not just a little. Companies can boost profits by almost 100% by retaining just 5% more of their customers.

While defection rates are an accurate leading indicator of profit swings, they do more than passively indicate where profits are headed. They also direct managers' attention to the specific things that are causing customers to

---

How Much Profit a Customer Generates over Time

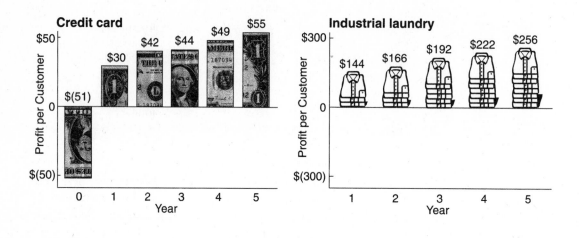

leave. Since companies do not hold customers captive, the only way they can prevent defections is to outperform the competition continually. By soliciting feedback from defecting customers, companies can ferret out the weaknesses that really matter and strengthen them before profits start to dwindle. Defection analysis is therefore a guide that helps companies manage continuous improvement.

Charles Cawley, president of MBNA America, a Delaware-based credit card company, knows well how customer defections can focus a company's attention on exactly the things customers value. One morning in 1982, frustrated by letters from unhappy customers, he assembled all 300 MBNA employees and announced his determination that the company satisfy and keep each and every customer. The company started gathering feedback from defecting customers. And it acted on the information, adjusting products and processes regularly.

As quality improved, fewer customers had reason to leave. Eight years later, MBNA's defection rate is one of the lowest in its industry. Some 5% of its customers leave each year—half the average rate for the rest of the industry. That may seem like a small difference, but it translates into huge earnings. Without making any acquisitions, MBNA's industry ranking went from 38 to 4, and profits have increased sixteenfold.

THE COST OF LOSING A CUSTOMER

If companies knew how much it really costs to lose a customer, they would be able to make accurate evaluations of investments designed to retain customers. Unfortunately, today's accounting systems do not capture the value of a customer. Most systems focus on current period costs and revenues and ignore expected cash flows over a customer's lifetime. Served correctly, customers generate increasingly more profits each year they stay with a company. Across a wide range of businesses, the pattern is the same: the longer a company keeps a customer, the more money it stands to make. (See the bar charts depicting "How Much Profit a Customer Generates over Time.") For one auto-service company, the expected profit from a fourth-year customer is more than triple the profit that same customer generates in the first year. When customers defect, they take all that profit-making potential with them.

It may be obvious that acquiring a new customer entails certain one-time costs for advertising, promotions, and the like. In credit cards, for example, companies spend an average of $51 to recruit a customer and set up the new account. But there are many more pieces to the profitability puzzle.

To continue with the credit card example, the newly acquired customers use the card slowly at first and generate a base profit. But if the customers stay

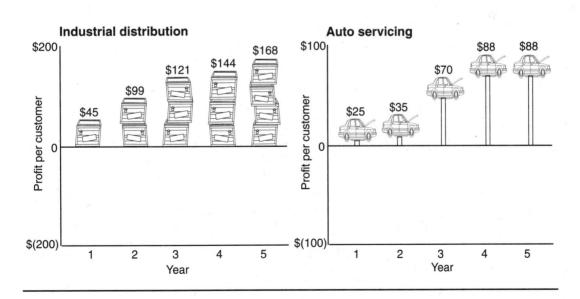

WHY CUSTOMERS ARE MORE PROFITABLE OVER TIME

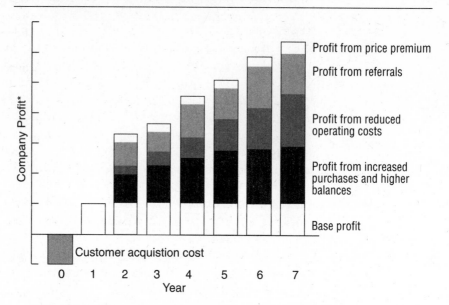

*This pattern is based on our experience in many industries.

a second year, the economics greatly improve. As they become accustomed to using the credit card and are satisfied with the service it provides, customers use it more and balances grow. In the second year—and the years thereafter—they purchase even more, which turns profits up sharply. We found this trend in each of the more than 100 companies in two dozen industries we have analyzed. For one industrial distributor, net sales per account continue to rise into the nineteenth year of the relationship.

As purchases rise, operating costs decline. Checking customers' credit histories and adding them to the corporate database is expensive, but those things need be done only once. Also, as the company gains experience with its customers, it can serve them more efficiently. One small financial consulting business that depends on personal relationships with clients has found that costs drop by two-thirds from the first year to the second because customers know what to expect from the consultant and have fewer questions or problems. In addition, the consultants are more efficient because they are familiar with the customer's financial situation and investment preferences.

Also, companies with long-time customers can often charge more for their products or services. Many people will pay more to stay in a hotel they know or to go to a doctor they trust than to take a chance on a less expensive competitor. The company that has developed such a loyal following can charge a premium for the customer's confidence in the business.

Yet another economic boon from long-time customers is the free advertising they provide. Loyal customers do a lot of talking over the years and drum up a lot of business. One of the leading home builders in the United States, for example, has found that more than 60% of its sales are the result of referrals.

These cost savings and additional revenues combine to produce a steadily increasing stream of profits over the course of the customer's relationship with the company. (See the chart "Why Customer's Are More Profitable over Time.") While the relative importance of these effects varies from industry to industry, the end result is that longer term customers generate increasing profits.

To calculate a customer's real worth, a company must take all of these projected profit streams into account. If, for instance, the credit card customer leaves after the first year, the company takes a $21 loss. If the company can keep the customer for four more years, his or her value to the company rises sharply. It is equal to the net present value of the profit streams in the first five years, or about $100.

When a company lowers its defection rate, the average customer relationship lasts longer and profits climb steeply. One way to appreciate just how responsive profits are to changes in defection rates is to draw a defection curve. (See the graph, "A Credit Card Company's Defection Curve.") This shows clearly how small movements in a company's defection rate can produce very large swings in profits.

The curve shows, for example, that as the credit card company cuts its defection rate from 20% to 10%, the average life span of its relationship with a customer doubles from five years to ten and the value of that customer more than doubles—jumping from $134 to $300. As the defection rate drops another 5%, the average life span of a customer relationship doubles again and profits rise 75%—from $300 to $525.

The credit card business is not unique. Although the shape of defection curves vary across industries, in general, profits rise as defection rates fall. Reducing defections by just 5% generated 85% more profits in one bank's branch system, 50% more in an insurance brokerage, and 30% more in an auto-service chain. (See the chart "Reducing Defections 5% Boosts Profits 25% to 85%.") MBNA America has found that a 5% improvement in defection rates increases its average customer value by more than 125%.

Understanding the economics of defections is useful to managers in several ways. For one thing, it shows that continuous improvement in service quality is not a cost but an investment in a customer who generates more profit

A CREDIT CARD COMPANY'S DEFECTION CURVE

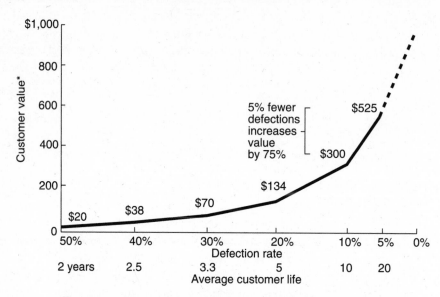

*The net present value of the profit streams a customer generates over the average customer life. At a 10% defection rate, for example, the average customer life is ten years (1 divided by the defection role); the customer value is the net present value of the profit streams for ten years.

than the margin on a one-time sale. Executives can therefore justify giving priority to investments in service quality versus things like cost reduction, for which the objectives have been more tangible.

Knowing that defections are closely linked to profits also helps explain why some companies that have relatively high unit costs can still be quite profitable. Companies with loyal, long-time customers can financially outperform competitors with lower unit costs and high market share but high customer churn. For instance, in the credit card business, a 10% reduction in unit costs is financially equivalent to a 2% decrease in defection rate. Low-defection strategies can overwhelm low-cost strategies.

And understanding the link between defections and profits provides a guide to lucrative growth. It is common for a business to lose 15% to 20% of its customers each year. Simply cutting defections in half will more than double the average company's growth rate. Companies with high retention rates that want to expand through acquisition can create value by acquiring low retention competitors and reducing their defections.

DEFECTIONS MANAGEMENT

Although service companies probably can't—and shouldn't try to—eliminate all defections, they can and must reduce them. But even to approach zero defections, companies must pursue that goal in a coordinated way. The organization should be prepared to spot customers who leave and then to analyze and act on the information they provide.

WATCH THE DOOR.

Managing for zero defections requires mechanisms to find customers who have ended their relationship with the company—or are about to end it While compiling this kind of customer data almost always involves the use of information technology of some kind, major investments in new systems are unnecessary.

The more critical issue is whether the business regularly gathers information about customers. Some companies already do. Credit card companies, magazine publishers, direct mailers, life insurers, cellular phone companies, and banks, for example, all collect reams of data as a matter of course. They have at their disposal the names and addresses, purchasing histories, and telephone numbers of all their customers. For these businesses, exposing defections is relatively easy. It's just a matter of organizing the data.

Sometimes, defining a "defection" takes some work. In the railroad business, for instance, few customers stop using your service completely, but a customer that shifts 80% of its shipments to trucks should not be considered "retained." The key is to identify the customer behaviors that both drive your economics and gauge customer loyalty.

For some businesses, the task of spotting defectors is challenging even if they are well defined, because customers tend to be faceless and nameless to management. Businesses like retailing will have to find creative ways to "know" their customers. Consider the example of Staples, the Boston-based office products discounter. It has done a superb job of gathering information usually lost at the cashier or sales clerk. From its opening, it had a database to store and analyze customer information. Whenever a customer goes through the checkout line, the cashier offers him or her a membership card. The card entitles the holder to special promotions and certain discounts. The only requirement for the card is that the person fill out an application form, which asks for things like name, job title, and address. All subsequent purchases are automatically logged against the card number. This way, Staples can accumulate detailed information about buying habits, frequency of visits, average dollar value spent, and particular items purchased.

Even restaurants can collect data. A crab house in Maryland, for instance, started entering into its PC information from the reservation list. Managers can now find out how often particular customers return and can contact those who seem to be losing interest in the restaurant.

WHAT ARE DEFECTORS TELLING YOU?

One reason to find customers who are leaving is to try to win them back. MBNA America has a customer-defection "swat" team staffed by some of the company's best telemarketers. When customers cancel their credit cards, the swat team tries to convince them to stay. It is successful half of the time.

But the more important motive for finding defectors is for the insight they provide. Customers who leave can provide a view of the business that is unavailable to those on the inside. And whatever caused one individual to defect may cause many others to follow. The idea is to use defections as an early warning signal—to learn from defectors why they left the company and to use that information to improve the business.

Unlike conventional market research, feedback from defecting customers tends to be concrete and specific. It doesn't attempt to measure things like attitudes or satisfaction, which are changeable and subjective, and it doesn't raise hypothetical questions, which may be irrelevant to the

REDUCING DEFECTIONS 5% BOOSTS PROFITS 25% TO 85%

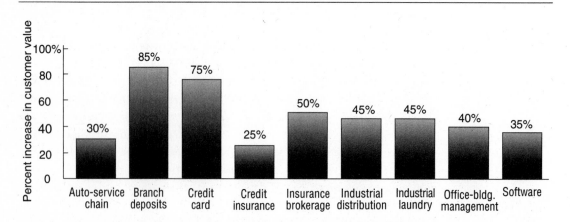

*Calculated by comparing the net present values of the profit streams for the average customer life at current defection rates with the net present values of the profit streams for the average customer life at 5% lower defection rates.

respondents. Defections analysis involves specific, relevant questions about why a customer has defected. Customers are usually able to articulate their reasons, and some skillful probing can get at the root cause.

This information is useful in a variety of ways, as the Staples example shows. Staples constantly tracks defections, so when customers stop doing business there or don't buy certain products, the store notices it immediately and calls to get feedback. It may be a clue that the competition is underpricing Staples on certain goods—a competitive factor management can explore further. If it finds sufficient evidence, Staples may cut prices on those items. This information is highly valued because it pinpoints the uncompetitive products and saves the chain from launching expensive broad-brush promotions pitching everything to everybody.

Staples's telemarketers try to discern which merchandise its customers want and don't want and why. The company uses that information to change its buying stock and to target its catalogs and coupons more precisely. Instead of running coupons in the newspaper, for instance, it can insert them in the catalogs it sends to particular customers or industries that have proved responsive to coupons.

Defections analysis can also help companies decide which service-quality investments will be profitable. Should you invest in computerized cash registers or a new phone system? Which of the two will address the most frequent causes of defection? One bank made a large investment to improve the accuracy of monthly account statements. But when the bank began to study defectors, it learned that less than 1% of its customers were leaving because of inaccurate statements.

A company that is losing customers because of long lines can estimate what percentage of defectors it would save by buying new cash registers, and it can use its defection curve to find the dollar value of saving them. Then, using standard investment-analysis techniques, it can compare the cost of the new equipment with the benefit of keeping customers.

Achieving service quality doesn't mean slavishly keeping all customers at any cost. There are some customers the company should not try to serve. If particular types of customers don't stay and become profitable, companies should not invest in attracting them. When a health insurance company realized that certain companies purchase only on the basis of price and switch health insurers every year, for example, it decided not to waste its efforts seeking their business. It told its brokers not to write policies for companies that have switched carriers more than twice in the past five years.

Conversely, much of the information used to find defectors can point to common traits among customers who stay longer. The company can use defection rates to clarify the characteristics of the market it wants to pursue and target its advertising and promotions accordingly.

THE ZERO DEFECTIONS CULTURE

Many business leaders have been frustrated by their inability to follow through on their public commitment to service quality. Since defection rates are measurable, they are manageable. Managers can establish meaningful targets and monitor progress. But like any important change, managing for zero defections must have supporters at all organizational levels. Management must develop that support by training the work force and using defections as a primary performance measure.

Everyone in the organization must understand that zero defections is the goal. Mastercare, the autoservice subsidiary of Bridgestone/Firestone, emphasizes the importance of keeping customers by stating it clearly in its mission statement. The statement says, in part, that the company's goal is "to provide the service-buying public with a superior buying experience that will encourage them to return willingly and to share their experience with others." MBNA America sends its paychecks in envelopes labeled "Brought to you by the customer." It also has a customer advocate who sits in on all major decision-making sessions to make sure customers' interests are represented.

It is important to make all employees understand the lifetime value of a customer. Phil Bressler, the coowner of five Domino's Pizza stores in Montgomery County, Maryland, calculated that regular customers were worth more than $5,000 over the life of a ten-year franchise contract. He made sure that every order taker, delivery person, and store manager knew that number. For him, telling workers that customers were valuable was not nearly as potent as stating the dollar amount: "It's so much more than they think that it really hits home."

Mastercare has redesigned its employee training to emphasize the importance of keeping customers. For example, many customers who stopped doing business with Mastercare mentioned that they didn't like being pressured into repairs they had not planned on. So Mastercare now trains store managers to identify and solve the customer's problem rather than to maximize sales. Videos and role-playing dramatize these different definitions of good service.

Mastercare's message to employees includes a candid admission that previous, well-intentioned incentives had inadvertently caused employees to run the business the wrong way; now it is asking them to change. And it builds credibility among employees by sharing its strategic goals and customer outreach plans. In the two target markets where this approach has been used, results are good. Employees have responded enthusiastically, and 25% more customers say they intend to return.

Senior executives at MBNA America learn from defecting customers. Each one spends four hours a month in a special "listening room" monitoring routine customer service calls as well as calls from customers who are canceling their credit cards.

Beyond conveying a sense of urgency, training should teach employees the specifics of defections analysis, like how to gather the information, whom to pass it on to, and what actions to take in response. In one company's branch banking system, retention data is sent monthly to the regional vice presidents and branch managers for review. It allows the regional vice presidents to identify and focus on branches that most need to improve service quality, and it gives branch managers quick feedback on performance.

Employees will be more motivated if incentives are tied to defection rates. MBNA, for example, has determined for each department the one or two things that have the biggest impact on keeping customers. Each department is measured daily on how well performance targets are met. Every morning, the previous day's performance is posted in several places throughout the building. Each day that the company hits 95% of these performance targets, MBNA contributes money to a bonus pool to pay yearly bonuses of up to 20% of a person's salary. The president visits departments that fall short of their targets to find out where the problem lies.

Great-West Life Assurance Company of Englewood, Colorado also uses incentives effectively. It pays a 50% premium to group-health-insurance brokers that hit customer retention targets. This system gives brokers the incentive to look for customers who will stay with the company for a long time.

Having everyone in the company work toward keeping customers and basing rewards on how well they do creates a positive company atmosphere. Encouraging employees to solve customer problems and eliminate the source of complaints allows them to be "nice," and customers treat them better in return. The overall exchange is more rewarding, and people enjoy their work more. Not just customers but also employees will want to continue their relationship with the business. MBNA is besieged by applicants for job openings, while a competitor a few miles away is moving some of its operations out of the state because it can't find enough employees.

The success of MBNA shows that it is possible to achieve big improvements in both service quality and profits in a reasonably short time. But it also shows that focusing on keeping customers instead of simply having lots of them takes effort. A company can leverage business performance and profits through customer defections only when the notion permeates corporate life and when all organizational levels understand the concept of zero defections and know how to act on it.

Trying to retain all of your profitable customers is elementary. Managing toward zero defections is revolutionary. It requires careful definition of defection, information systems that can measure results over time in comparison with competitors, and a clear understanding of the microeconomics of defection.

Ultimately, defections should be a key performance measure for senior management and a fundamental component of incentive systems. Managers should know the company's defection rate, what happens to profits when the rate moves up or down, and why defections occur. They should make sure the entire organization understands the importance of keeping customers and encourage employees to pursue zero defections by tying incentives, planning, and budgeting to defection targets. Most important, managers should use defections as a vehicle for continuously improving the quality and value of the services they provide to customers.

Just as the quality revolution in manufacturing had a profound impact on the competitiveness of companies, the quality revolution in services will create a new set of winners and losers. The winners will be those who lead the way in managing toward zero defections.

Frederick F. Reichheld is a vice president in the Boston office of Bain & Company and leader of the firm's customer-retention practice. W. Earl Sasser, Jr. is a professor at the Harvard Business School.

PART TWO

TQM AND DEMING

READING 3
THE D*A*T* APPROACH TO
TOTAL QUALITY MANAGEMENT

THE FIRST TWO READINGS INTRODUCED THEMES THAT ARE A MAJOR PART OF TODAY'S TOTAL QUALITY MANAGEMENT (TQM). GARVIN, FOR EXAMPLE, EMPHASIZED THE IMPORTANCE OF MANAGEMENT COMMITMENT, INFORMATION SYSTEMS/DATA, AND U.S.-JAPANESE QUALITY DIFFERENTIALS AS MEASURED BY PRODUCT DEFECTS AND FAILURES. MEANWHILE, THE SECOND ARTICLE EMPHASIZED CUSTOMER SATISFACTION AND THE ECONOMICS OF CUSTOMER RETENTION. HOWEVER, TQM IS ALL OF THE ABOVE PLUS MORE, AND SOMETIMES IT IS DIFFICULT TO SEE THE FOREST FOR THE TREES.

THE D*A*T MODEL WAS DEVELOPED TO PROVIDE A SIMPLE BUT EFFECTIVE FRAMEWORK FOR CONCEPTUALIZING THE BASIC IDEAS OF TQM AND THEIR INTERRELATIONSHIPS. THE MODEL VIEWS TQM AS *REQUIRING* THE PRESENCE AND INTEGRATION OF THREE ELEMENTS: DATA, ATTITUDES, AND TOOLS. KAORU ISHIKAWA WROTE THAT THE AMERICAN ZERO DEFECTS (ZD) QUALITY MOVEMENT FAILED BECAUSE IT OVERLY EMPHASIZED MOTIVATION, IT WAS A "MERE MOVEMENT OF WILL. *IT WAS A MOVEMENT WITHOUT TOOLS.* IT WAS NOT SCIENTIFIC." AND TOM PETERS NOTES THAT "MOST QUALITY PROGRAMS FAIL FOR ONE OF TWO REASONS: THEY HAVE SYSTEM WITHOUT PASSION, OR PASSION WITHOUT SYSTEM. YOU MUST HAVE BOTH." SUCCESSFUL ORGANIZATIONS WILL UNDERSTAND THE INTEGRATED NATURE OF TQM; THE D*A*T MODEL CAN BE A USEFUL REFERENCE.

READING 3
THE D*A*T APPROACH TO
TOTAL QUALITY MANAGEMENT

BY JOSEPH G. VAN MATRE

Total quality management (TQM) is the capstone of the quality movement that began at AT&T in the early 1930s. Although initiated by Americans such as Walter Shewhart, W. Edwards Deming, and Joseph Juran, it is the Japanese who brought the quality movement to international attention. Their widespread success in the global marketplace led their competitors to adopt similar strategies. In the US, firms leading the way in the 1980s were primarily manufacturers such as Motorola, Ford, and Xerox. Their experiences coupled with the success of "Japanese management" with American labor in Ohio (Honda), Kentucky (Toyota), Tennessee (Nissan), and California (Sony), further increased the credibility of TQM as a major managerial development. Now many firms, service as well as manufacturing, are experimenting with the new philosophy. This article reviews the essential elements of TQM using a conceptually simple but effective framework: the D*A*T approach.

HISTORICAL DEVELOPMENT OF TQM

W. Edwards Deming "is the one who introduced quality control to Japan" in a series of seminars to managers and engineers that began in 1950.[14] Deming's lectures included material that forms much of the foundation of TQM: (1) production is viewed as a process, with (the then unusual) emphasis on supplier partnerships, and feedback from consumers; (2) a "chain reaction" which shows that improvements in process quality leads to

CREDIT: Joseph G. Van Matre, "The D*A*T Approach to Total Quality Management," *Journal of American Health Information Management Association* (November 1992).

lower, not higher, costs; and (3) the Shewhart cycle which evolved into the idea of continuous improvement.[5]

The principles were largely ignored in the U.S. following WWII; the post-war consumer demand encouraged managers to emphasize quantity not quality. Even later (say the '70s), when Japan's success was clearly evident, "conventional" management wisdom contradicted many of TQM's principles. For example, U.S. managers still equated higher quality with higher costs brought on by increasingly stringent inspection practices. They did not see lower costs brought on by improved process quality that produced less rework and scrap.

The Japanese inculcated the ideas of Deming and, beginning in 1954, those of Joseph M. Juran. Not unexpectedly, the Japanese further improved and extended the quality principles, led by, among others, their guru Kaoru Ishikawa. TQM has many synonyms: total quality control (TQC), company-wide QC (CWQC), and continuous quality improvement (CQI), the term often used by the Joint Commission on Accreditation of Healthcare Organizations. The first of these terms TQC, was originated in a 1957 article by another American, Armand V. Feigenbaum, who was then with General Electric.[14] The Japanese made TQC truly company wide, and, in the '60s, began promoting quality circles to increase the participation of all employees.

A number of events in the early '80s helped focus attention on the U.S.-Japan quality gap. First, the NBC documentary "If Japan Can... Why Can't We?" in 1980 publicized the "quality problem," but also showed the success a domestic firm, Nashua Corp., was having with Deming's guidance as a consultant. Demand for his services soared following the program.[20] Several other reports followed which further detailed the problems domestic manufacturers were having in competing with Japan. For example, in 1980 Hewlett-Packard tested memory chips from three domestic and three Japanese producers. They found remarkable differences in failure rates after 1000 hours of use: the best U.S. producer had a failure rate three times higher than the worst Japanese producer.[8] In 1983 Garvin began reporting the findings of his study on the U.S.-Japanese room air-conditioning industry, and his findings were equally dramatic. For example, the service call rate (for warranty coverage) for the best U.S. producer was more than 250 percent higher than for the worst Japanese producers. But finally, in the mid '80s, a few key U.S. firms truly adopted the quality philosophy, and their well-documented successes paved the way for others to follow, and many (mostly manufacturing) did.

Despite the example of such firms as Federal Express, Paul Revere Insurance Co., and Florida Power & Light, the service industry has moved even more cautiously. In fact, *Business Week* reported in 1991 that "a scant 10 percent of American service companies today have any kind of quality pro-

FIGURE 1   THE D*A*T MODEL FOR TQM

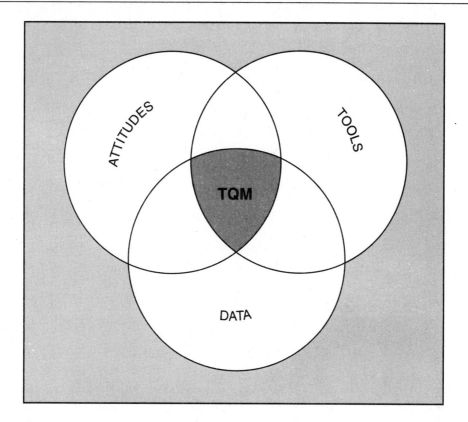

gram." But, they further reported that some 70 percent of service firms with more than 500 employees are predicted to have "formal quality initiatives" by the year 2000, led by financial services providers, healthcare, and government.[1] There are two reasons for optimism if one focuses on the healthcare industry. First, the National Demonstration Project (NDP) on Quality Improvement in Health Care has shown that the methods of quality improvement can be successfully applied in healthcare. As others learn of the NDP (see *Curing Health Care: New Strategies for Quality Improvement,* 1990) and emulate their projects, perhaps local quality champions will emerge at many organizations.

Finally, hospitals must address these issues to comply with the accreditation standards established by the Joint Commission on Accreditation of Healthcare Organizations. The 1992 *Accreditation Manual for Hospitals* (AMH) cites the '92 AMH as "beginning a carefully planned transition to standards that emphasize continuous quality improvement," a transition that will continue in 1993 and 1994.[15] The standards clearly draw upon the theory and methods of today's quality model: TQM. Perhaps the Joint Commission can affect healthcare in the way Japanese competitors affected Ford, Xerox, and Motorola.

OVERVIEW OF TQM

As we have seen, TQM evolved over a period of time with significant developments from both Americans and Japanese. What exactly is TQM today? What are its essential characteristics? A very succinct description of TQM comes from George Box (former director, Center for Quality and Productivity, University of Wisconsin): "TQM is the democratization of the scientific method." This one sentence beautifully describes the essence of TQM. And, lest we have forgotten, the scientific method is "a systematic process in which a problem is identified, data are collected and analyzed, and valid conclusions are drawn from the analysis."[6]

TQM, when reviewed in detail, sometimes appears as a complexity of rather unrelated elements. To provide focus and comprehension, the D*A*T model was developed.

The D*A*T model views TQM as the intersection/simultaneous interaction of three elements: data, attitudes, and tools. The * is the usual software symbol for multiplication, and thus TQM is the product of the three elements. And, if one element is absent, or has a value of zero, TQM is also absent. This is not to say that tools and data alone are not useful; it is to say tools and data alone, without proper attitudes, are not TQM. If your organization attempts to implement TQM and fails, look for the missing element.

Several distinguished authors have previously commented on the failure of TQM programs when a key element is neglected. Garvin noted "many companies... provide training in the tools of quality control but have failed to emphasize quality's connection with basic business objectives. The resulting programs have been long on technique, but lacking in motivation and purpose" [attitudes].[8] And Deming says that if he had only brought statistical quality control (namely, tools) to Japan, "all the statistical methods taught there would have withered away in a few years, and the new economic age created by Japan would never have evolved."[9] Tom Peters observed that "most quality programs fail for one of two reasons: They have system without passion, or passion without system. You must have both."[18] The D*A*T model emphasizes the interdependencies among the three main elements.

Now we turn to develop a more complete description of TQM by reviewing in detail each of the following three elements. The discussion will begin with attitudes, probably the "first among equals." (The order of D*A*T was selected to form the acronym rather than some implied priority scheme.)

ATTITUDES

Most successful TQM organizations exhibit a similar set of attitudes. What do we mean by attitudes? The beliefs, convictions, philosophy, corporate culture, and environment that define the mindset, and the expectations of the organization. A representative, but not exhaustive, list of the more important characteristics is given below.

ATTITUDES:

- Top Management Commitment
- Customer Focus
- Continuous Improvement
- Process Thinking
- Teamwork
- Employee Involvement
- Drive Out Fear/Intimidation
- Data-based Decision Making

Perhaps the most critical element of TQM is commitment at the highest levels of the organization. Total means involving all functions, all employees; corporate change of this magnitude will require new policies, new procedures, changes in the compensation/reward system, changes in the agenda of management meetings that show action by a management committed to quality. Garvin noted "Perhaps the biggest difference between U.S. and Japanese... was the depth of their commitment to quality... [in Japan] the commitment was deeply ingrained and clearly communicated. It was visible everywhere: in statements of company philosophy, policy manuals, and charts and banners on the wall."[8] He also noted that from the beginning "high level Japanese executives have been personally involved in quality activities. They have attended and taught training programs; mastered the rudiments of statistical quality control; stressed the importance of quality in policy directives and statements of company philosophy; and set strong examples for their employees."[8] It is management that must lead the organization to focus on customer satisfaction, instill the notion of continuous improvement, adopt process thinking, drive out fear... all of these are interdependent; the effectiveness of each is contingent upon the presence/degree of the others.

Consider "drive out fear." This idea is a major theme of Deming, who made it one of his "Fourteen Points for Managers,"[5] but it is also noted by others. Kanter tells of a company president who told his division managers "repeatedly [to pursue new opportunities]—generally at the end of monthly operations review meetings in which deviations from budget and failure to meet shipping deadlines and other operational details were attacked rather venomously by the financial officers. Then he claimed that his managers never took risks, never brought him new ideas. . . ."[17] Would not fear discourage change inherent in continuous improvement? In a recent incident, Sears received immense negative publicity when charged with defrauding auto-repair customers. The management had instituted a compensation scheme that set quotas for certain jobs (such as installing shock absorbers), and employee failure meant reduced work hours or transfer.[7] Did fear encourage employees to disregard customer needs in order to remain employed? The scientific method (data-based decision making) requires data. Yet, "there are many false data being used in industries and in society."[14] Why? Superiors who do not understand variation, and when the data vary, become angry. Subordinates then lie and write false reports. David Halberstam reported on an auto executive (later U.S. Secretary of Defense): "Deviations bothered him. Numbers should be true . . . mpg varied from test to test. He was enraged." Company reaction? False production reports, false inventory reports, rigged gauges, namely false data.[10] (And later in Vietnam, false Viet Cong body counts.)

Teamwork is especially important in healthcare organizations where processes are complex and typically involve many units/individuals. Whether called a task force or project team, only cross-functional groups can effectively address the improvement of cross-functional processes. Otherwise, the result is suboptimization: "a group optimizing its own subgoals but losing sight of the larger goals to which they are supposedly contributing."[16] The Joint Commission notes "the processes of delivering care and services cross departmental lines, and so should approaches to improving quality. Up to now, the analysis of quality has often been dissected within the confines of individual departments, thus failing to fully address the cross-departmental and and cross-disciplinary manner in which care is actually delivered. In 1994 and thereafter, standards that promote appropriate cross-departmental attention to quality will replace most if those that now refer only to departmental review."[15]

Kanter identifies what she terms the segmented organization as one "concerned with compartmentalizing actions, events, and problems and keeping each piece isolated from the others. . . . Segmentalist approaches see problems as narrowly as possible, independently of their connections to any other problems . . . . Segmentalism assumes that problems can be solved when they are carved into pieces and the pieces assigned to specialists who work in isolation."[16] Her prescription includes process thinking, employee involvement, and teamwork.

"Proper" attitudes and beliefs are appropriate, indeed required, whether in manufacuring or service. In fact, the Joint Commission identifies the "new" quality approach as CQI, and the 1992 standards reflect what has been reviewed here: "The leaders undertake education concerning... CQI... [they] set priorities for organization wide quality improvement activities... facilitate the collection, management and analysis of data needed for quality improvement." And subsequent standards to be phased in over the next three years will address customer focus, process thinking, and teamwork (cross-departmental or cross-functional teams to address and improve the "manner in which care is actually delivered").[15]

TOOLS

The TQM organization uses various tools to facilitate the realization of continuous improvement, data-based decision making, and effective teamwork (as noted earlier tools alone are inadequate if applied in an alien environment).

TOOLS

- Flow Chart
- Ishikawa's Seven Tools
    Stratification
    Scatter Diagram
    Histogram
    Pareto Chart
    Cause and Effect Diagram
    Check Sheets
    Control Charts
- Nominal Group Technique/Brainstorming
- Problem Solving Process/Scientific Method
- Benchmarking
- Suggestion Systems

Flowcharts are particularly useful in service organizations where processes are less formally developed than manufacturing operations where many processes were designed by industrial engineers. A flowchart is a graphic representation of the steps of a process, and an early step in process improvement is to understand how the process actually works. The flowchart is invaluable in cross-functional processes so the team members can see how things connect outside of their own departments.

Employee involvement on a wide scale also leads to simple tools that can be learned and used by all employees. Ishikawa's seven tools consist of basic analytical methods used in the quality improvement process. In many Japanese companies, everyone from top management to line workers is trained in the use of these methods. Their popularity stems from Ishikawa's belief that "From my past experience, as many as 95 percent of all problems within a company can be solved by means of these tools."[14] Their successful use in this country has also been reported by quality leaders like Motorola who, in some plants, reported "getting a $33 return for every dollar spent, including the cost of wages paid while people sat in class."[23]

Ishikawa's seven tools are so called not because he developed them, but because he pulled them together as a basic set of indispensable tools for process improvement. He did, however, develop one of the seven: the cause and effect diagram, also known as the fishbone chart or Ishikawa diagram. The seven tools were named after the seven weapons of the Japanese warrior Benkei. These tools enabled Benkei to triumph in battle. So too, the seven QC tools, if used skillfully, will enable 95 percent of workplace problems to be solved.[14] Two of the tools are particularly valuable when used by teams. The Pareto chart because it identifies graphically what is important/vital/of first priority and thus encourages consensus-building. And the cause and effect diagram needs the perspectives of several people from different places of the organization in order to ensure that all causes have, in fact, been enumerated. To be most useful, it should be developed by a cross-functional team.

Continuous improvement requires ideas. What exactly is to be improved (changed)? To pursue this we often need what George Box refers to as "inspirational statistics." The goal here is the generation of hypotheses or ideas rather than the testing of hypotheses using inferential statistics. Three items on our list of tools deal with generating ideas for process improvement: the nominal group technique (NGT)/brainstorming, benchmarking, and suggestion systems. Brainstorming was developed around 1940, and a modified version, NGT, was introduced later. Both procedures are used with groups (teams) to produce large numbers of ideas, and both try to maximize the creativity of the participants. (In order to encourage participation criticism of ideas is not allowed.)

Benchmarking is the use of another unit's achieved results as a standard/target for our unit. Benchmarks may come from within or without the organization; in the extreme, the search is for "worldclass" performance: any country, any industry. Xerox, the first major user of benchmarking, identified L.L. Bean's distribution system as world-class and used it to show Xerox where opportunities for improvement existed. Although not discussed by Garvin, his data can be used to show a real improvement opportunity. The worst domestic firm has a customer instruction call (CIC) rate six times larger than the CIC rate of the best domestic firm (a CIC results from when a customer uses a unit improperly or fails to install it correctly).[8] Perhaps an opportunity exists for improvement in the instructions/operating manual or installation instructions?

Finally, a team needs a systematic procedure for executing process improvement; a team needs to be familiar with a problem-solving process. There are many problem solving processes, ranging from a four-step model to an eight-step model. But they are all quite similar as they are basically variations on the scientific method. One is needed, but which one will not be pursued here. Now that the prerequisite attitudes and tools of TQM have been reviewed, turn now to data.

DATA

TQM stresses the importance of data to the improvement of processes. Ishikawa says "Data are the basis of QC."[14] Of course, data are indispensable to the scientific method, as data guide decision making and action. In their book, *Hearing the Voice of the Market,* Barabba and Zaltman say, "Data are the stimuli that make us curious and provide the building blocks—the thinker toys—for our creativity. Data are the stuff from which decisions are fashioned"[2] Without data, decisions are made by rank or position, by force of personality, by political alignments, by hunches or guesses.

It is important to remember that the mere acquisition of data is not what we are about, it is the integration of data into the decision-making process. Remember too that not all data are informative. Management guru Peter Drucker has pointed out that information is data endowed with relevance and purpose. It is in this optimistic sense that we refer to data, assuming it is useful and timely, and a significant improvement opportunity may lie in the elimination of useless data. (In his seminars, Deming reserved an especially disparaging tone when he spoke of "figures," data that no sophisticated analyses could ever make useful.)

DATA

- Source
    - Secondary
    - Internal
    - External
    - Primary (Original)
- Type
    - Qualitative (Attribute)
    - Quantitative (Variables)
    - Time/Sequence
    - Cross-sectional/Panel
- Variation in Data

Common Cause
Special Cause

Where are these relevant data found? In a sense, three broad sources exist. First, the organization itself has developed databases; its management information system (MIS), health records, and the accounting department all maintain databases. Second, various external agencies (HCFA, the Census Bureau, professional associations) gather and report data. But, cross-functional teams working on process improvement may require data that is not available. The requisite data simply do not exist in the organization's computers, the university library, anywhere; and the information must be gathered for the first time. The need for original or primary data is recurring in the TQM organization. Note again the interrelatedness of the elements of the D*A*T model. What data are needed may follow a brainstorming session or the development of a Pareto chart. How original data are gathered may well involve some version of a check sheet and will likely utilize the stratification principle. Further, are the data trustworthy—were the data obtained with a sense of trust and cooperation or in an environment of fear and intimidation?

The technical concepts of data will not be reviewed here, but both the producer and consumer of data need to be familiar with such basic ideas as the "nature" or type of data: quantitative versus qualitative data, the time element... The type dictates which analytical tools are appropriate to "query" the data, to learn what the data have to tell. For example, control charts require time series or sequence data, and scatter diagrams require two quantitative variables. An understanding of variation is also important. The ability to distinguish between common cause and special cause variation is a very important skill that will help guide process improvement. Deming says "The central problem of management in all its aspects... is to understand better the meaning of variation, and to extract the information contained in variation."[5] Deming's famous bead experiment is designed to teach participants about variation, and his *Out of the Crisis* has a lengthy chapter on "Common Causes and Special Causes of Improvement. Stable System."

CONCLUSIONS

The D*A*T model is a simple but effective framework for conceptualizing the basic elements of TQM and their interrelationships. Improvement of quality of process and quality of product/service for the whole organization requires the integrated system of TQM. Successful implementation changes the segmentalist/hierarchical view of the organization to one emphasizing processes and horizontal relationships. It stresses teamwork and customer focus as opposed to functional unit goals. It facilitates continuous improvement. It wars with such attitudes[2] as:

> Ignorance is bliss.
> What you don't know won't hurt you.
> Curiosity killed the cat.
> No news is good news.
> A little knowledge is a dangerous thing.
> Don't be a know-it-all.
> Silence is golden.
> Let sleeping dogs lie.
> Messengers with bad news lose their heads.

as well as others: the not-invented-here (NIH) syndrome, "If it ain't broke, don't fix it," and the famous "That's not my job." Contrast the latter three with benchmarking, continuous improvement, and customer focus.

The TQM revolution has progressed more rapidly in manufacturing firms than in service organizations, but now thanks to the Joint Commission and the successes in the manufacturing sector, healthcare's time has come. (Two very useful readings here are (1) Reichheld and Sasser and (2) Schlesinger and Heskett.) Unfortunately, not all firms will successfully implement TQM. Some will succumb to Deming's obstacles, of which two are particularly relevant here. First, the hope for "instant pudding" or immediate benefit from the moment of proclaiming TQM; patience will be required. Second, "our problems are different." Yes, service industries, and especially healthcare, are different, but the principles, the theory, the models of TQM are applicable. The NDP on Quality Improvement in Health Care provided preliminary evidence of success; more will follow. Successful organizations will understand the integrated nature of TQM; the D*A*T model can be a useful reference.

REFERENCES

[1]Armstrong, Larry, and William C. Symonds. "Beyond May I Help You." *Business Week* (October 25, 1991): 100-103.

[2]Barabba, Vincent P. and Gerald Zaltman. *Hearing the Voice of the Market.* Boston: Harvard Business School Press, 1991.

[3]Berwick, Donald M., A. Blanton Godfrey, and Jane Roessner. *Curing Health Care: New Strategies for Quality Improvement.* San Francisco: Jossey-Bass Publishers, 1990.

[4]Box, George and Soren Bisgaard. "The Scientific Context of Quality Improvement." Madison, WI: Center for Quality and Productivity Improvement, University of Wisconsin, 1987.

[5]Deming, W. Edwards. *Out of the Crisis.* Cambridge, MA: MIT Center for Advanced Engineering Study, 1986.

[6]Evans, James R. *Creative Thinking in the Decision and Management Sciences.* Cincinnati: South-Western Publishing, 1991.

[7]Fisher, Lawrence M. "Sears Auto Center to Halt Commissions." *New York Times* (June 23, 1992): C1.

[8]Garvin, David A. *Managing Quality.* New York: The Free Press, 1988.

[9]Hahn, Gerald J. and Thomas J. Boardman. "The Statistician's Role in Quality Improvement." *AmStat News* (March, 1985): 5.

[10]Halberstam, David. *The Reckoning.* New York: William Morrow, 1986.

[11]Imai, Masaaki. *Kaizen.* New York: Random House, 1986.

[12]Ishikawa, Kaoru. *Guide to Quality Control.* 2nd ed. White Plains, NY: Unipub-Kraus International Publications, 1982.

[13]Ishikawa, Kaoru. *Introduction to Quality Control.* Tokyo: 3A Corporation, 1990.

[14]Kaoru, Ishikawa. *What Is Total Quality Control? The Japanese Way.* Englewood Cliffs, NJ: Prentice-Hall, Inc., 1985.

[15]Joint Commission on Accreditation of Healthcare Organizations. *Accreditation Manual for Hospitals.* Chicago: JCAHO, 1992.

[16]Kanter, Rosabeth Moss. *The Change Masters.* New York: Simon & Schuster, Inc., 1983.

[17]Kanter, Rosabeth Moss. *When Giants Learn to Dance.* New York: Simon & Schuster, Inc., 1989.

[18]Peters, Tom. *Thriving on Chaos.* New York: Alfred A. Knopf, 1987.

[19]Reichheld, Frederick F. and W. Earl Sasser, Jr. "Zero Defections: Quality Comes to Services." *Harvard Business Review* (September-October, 1990): 105-111.

[20]Schlesinger, Leonard A. and James L. Heskett. "The Service-Driven Service Company." *Harvard Business Review* (September-October, 1991): 71-81.

[21]Senge, Peter M. *The Fifth Discipline.* New York: Doubleday, 1990.

[22]Walton, Mary. *The Deming Management Method.* New York: Dodd, Mead & Company, 1986.

[23]Wiggenhorn, William. "Motorola U: When Training Becomes an Education." *Harvard Business Review* (July-August, 1990): 71-83.

READING 4
ED DEMING WANTS BIG CHANGES,
AND HE WANTS THEM FAST

W. EDWARDS DEMING IS PROBABLY THE INDIVIDUAL MOST ASSOCIATED WITH "THE QUALITY MOVEMENT" BY PEOPLE AROUND THE WORLD. JAPANESE QUALITY GURU KAORU ISHIKAWA SAYS "DR. DEMING... IS THE ONE WHO INTRODUCED QUALITY CONTROL TO JAPAN." DEMING DID NOT, HOWEVER, BECOME WIDELY KNOWN IN THE UNITED STATES UNTIL 1980, 30 YEARS AFTER HIS INITIAL QUALITY LECTURES IN JAPAN. HIS DISCOVERY HERE FOLLOWED THE NBC TV DOCUMENTARY *IF JAPAN CAN, WHY CAN'T WE?*, A FILM THAT CHRONICLED THE SUCCESS THE NASHUA CORPORATION HAD FOLLOWING DEMING'S ADVICE AS A CONSULTANT. THE WRITER AND NARRATOR OF THE DOCUMENTARY WAS LLOYD DOBBINS, THE AUTHOR OF THIS ARTICLE FROM THE *SMITHSONIAN* MAGAZINE.

DEMING WAS BORN IN IOWA IN 1900, BUT GREW UP IN WYOMING, FIRST IN CODY (NAMED FOR BUFFALO BILL CODY) AND THEN IN POWELL. HE ATTENDED THE UNIVERSITY OF WYOMING, THE UNIVERSITY OF COLORADO, AND YALE. ALTHOUGH NOT THE "FATHER" OF QUALITY CONTROL (THAT DISTINCTION BELONGS TO WALTER SHEWHART), DEMING IS INTERNATIONALLY KNOWN FOR HIS ACHIEVEMENTS. HE VERY EARLY RECOGNIZED THE KEY ROLE OF MANAGEMENT IN SUSTAINING A FIRM'S QUALITY PROGRESS AND HAS ADDRESSED THIS IN HIS 14 POINTS FOR MANAGERS, WHICH ARE REPRODUCED FOLLOWING THIS READING. HIS MANY VISITS AND LECTURES TO JAPAN BEGAN IN 1947, AND MANY LEADING JAPANESE FIRMS HAVE ADOPTED THE DEMING PHILOSOPHY. IN HIS HONOR THE JAPANESE ESTABLISHED THE DEMING PRIZE, A HIGHLY COMPETITIVE AND PRESTIGIOUS AWARD FOR QUALITY ACHIEVEMENTS WHOSE WINNERS HAVE

INCLUDED TOYOTA, RICOH, AND NEC. IN 1960, DEMING WAS HONORED WITH THE SECOND ORDER OF THE SACRED TREASURE, THE HIGHEST HONOR A FOREIGNER CAN ATTAIN IN JAPAN. DEMING DIED AT HIS HOME IN WASHINGTON, D.C., ON DECEMBER 20, 1993.

READING 4
ED DEMING WANTS BIG CHANGES, AND HE WANTS THEM FAST

BY LLOYD DOBYNS

He has always looked younger than he is, but even with that he is clearly old. He moves slowly through the hotel lobby, preceded by his ample stomach, leaning forward slightly and looking straight ahead through his glasses. From a distance, he appears to be completely bald, but as he gets closer, you see that his hair is white and cropped close to his skull. There are hearing aids in both ears. He is, as always, dressed in a custom-made suit. All of his jacket pockets are stuffed—clippings, a calculator, scraps of paper, a little magnifier, file cards, a small notebook, a pocket diary and whatever else he's picked up—and the pocket of his white shirt holds no fewer than a half-dozen pens and markers. On the lapel of his jacket there is a round, thick, gray pin about the size of a dime. The only thing about him other than his age that attracts anyone's attention this morning is that his assistant, an intern and doctoral candidate in business management, is an attractive, well-dressed woman young enough to be his daughter's daughter, and they are walking through the lobby holding hands. You get a sense that for him, it's partly for support and partly for the hell of it.

His business card reads "W. Edwards Deming, Ph.D., Consultant in Statistical Studies." It would be more accurate if it added, "and Capitalist Revolutionary." He wants changes, and not little ones, in everything—business, industry, education, how we live, how we teach our children and how we deal with one another. Deming wants something better for us all, and for most of his 89 years he's been fighting to get it. He knows from experience that what Machiavelli wrote is true: "There is nothing more difficult to take in hand, more perilous to conduct, or more uncertain in its success than to take the lead in the introduction of a new order of things."

CREDIT: Lloyd Dobyns, "Ed Deming wants big changes, and he wants them fast," *Smithsonian* (August, 1990).

W. Edwards Deming, one of the pioneers of the TQM movement, first introduced the concept to Japan.

He initiated a new order of things in Japan. It was a 49-year-old Ed Deming, tall and crew-cut as shown above, who in 1950 started teaching Japanese managers, engineers and scientists how to manufacture quality. An important step was to teach them to use statistics to find out what any system would do, then design improvements to make that system yield the best results. That idea sounds so logically simple that the tendency is to say, "Everyone knows that." No, everyone doesn't.

Americans have a penchant for solutions that are easy to understand, easy to do, aimed at a specific goal and fast—10 non-threatening steps to nirvana in 30 days. When it comes to improving what we do, there seems almost to be a flavor-of-the-month approach with each new, highly touted technique stepping on the heels of the one that went before—management by objective, management by results, management by problem report and resolution. Those are the cookbook methods, where you blend the worker and the machine, stir in a pinch of raw material, add a promise of a bonus (or a threat of dismissal), half-bake for 30 minutes and declare a dividend. It's easy to explain, easy to understand, and it doesn't work.

Deming teaches that the more quality you build into anything, the less it costs. That, too, sounds self-evident, but it's not. Maryann N. Keller, an automotive industry analyst and managing director of a brokerage firm, believes that the most profound change in the American auto industry in the past 10 years was the realization that "quality can cost less because you design it in rather than inspect it in." The traditional American idea of quality is, as Keller says, to inspect it in; that is, you build a whole lot of widgets, inspect them and separate the good from the bad. The bad can't be sold, but they cost a lot. Not only must all those inspectors be paid, but a

Early in his career, Deming recognized the important role of management in maintaining a company's quality progress.

bad widget takes the same amount of raw material, machinery, work time and attention as does a good widget. That explains why, typically, about 25 percent of any manufacturing plant's budget goes for repair and rework. That's why so many manufacturers think quality costs more, but what actually costs is a lack of quality.

Vernay Laboratories in Yellow Springs, Ohio, makes small, precision-molded rubber parts for the automotive, home appliance, pharmaceutical and medical industries. Before the company heard of Deming in 1983, there was one inspector for each employee molding parts, and to ensure quality, those inspectors checked everything that was produced. Think of that: nearly half of the production workers were paid to check what the other half did. In five years, doing what Deming taught it, Vernay cut its ratio of inspectors to molders by 75 percent. In the same five years, the plant's scrap and returned-product rates were cut by three-quarters, and productivity in the plant was up 30 percent. Quality was up, costs were down and the savings could be given to the customers. "One of the great pleasures I've had over the last five years," says Dale Piper, national sales manager, "was walking into the purchasing office of one of our larger customers and telling them that we were going to be giving them a price reduction, a completely unsolicited price reduction."

The basics of Deming's method are contained in a list of objectives he calls "the 14 points." These managerial imperatives are more philosophical than mechanical. The first of them is to "create constancy of purpose." You have to decide what business you're in and how you can stay in that business. It sounds deceptively simple, until you try it. Buggy whip makers undoubtedly believed they were in the business of making buggy whips, which explains why they are no longer in business at all. They were actually in the business of vehicle acceleration; just making buggy whips, even the world's finest-quality buggy whips, wasn't enough. Part of constancy of purpose is staying ahead of the customer, not only meeting present needs, but planning for future needs, as well.

The Ford Motor Company began consulting with Deming in 1981, and one of the first questions he asked was about constancy of purpose. Top management began to think about it. *Eighteen months later* Ford had a 350-word statement of its missions, values and guiding principles. By now, there can't be a Ford employee, supplier or dealer anywhere in the world who does not know that "Quality is Job 1." Donald Petersen, Ford's recently retired chairman and chief executive officer, says, "I am a Deming disciple." And he adds, "Those enterprises that don't adopt a quality culture simply are not going to succeed."

The issue is even broader than that. Improving quality, Deming says, automatically increases productivity, one of the measures economists use to judge how the economy is doing. Ours is improving, but not at a pace with Japan's. At current rates, the United States' productivity will double in 120 years, Japan's in a generation, meaning its children's standard of living will double while our children's will stay about the same.

When he first went to Japan, Deming was certain he could teach the Japanese how to join the leading industrial nations by improving quality. "I think that I was the only man in 1950," he says, "who believed that the Japanese could invade the markets of the world and would within five years." The lapel pin that few in this country could recognize represents Japan's Second Order Medal of the Sacred Treasure, awarded to him by the late Emperor Hirohito. The citation says the Japanese people attribute the rebirth of Japanese industry and its worldwide success to Ed Deming.

As famous as Deming is in Japan, he was comparatively unknown in the United States until June 1980, when he appeared in a network television documentary titled, *If Japan Can, Why Can't We?* It compared industrial productivity in Japan and the United States. I was the writer and narrator. Cecelia S. Kilian, Deming's secretary since 1954, and known almost universally as Ceil, said that starting the next morning, "Our phones rang off the hook.... Dr. Deming's mail quadrupled, and beyond." Petersen at Ford was one of the eventual callers. By late 1987 he told an interviewer, "We are running well over 50-percent-better levels of quality in our products today, and I dare say that I would not have predicted that much improvement in this short time." That same year, 1987, General Motors called Deming. The word was spreading in the industry: building quality drives costs down and profits up.

At an age that most American men will never reach, Deming continues trying to transform (his word) the United States, to make it possible for us to join what he calls "the new economic age." To teach corporate managers how that can be done, he works six days a week and is booked into 1991. Ceil is his whole staff.

Deming is never quite satisfied, so any attempt to chisel what he says into stone is frustrated by his insistence on constantly trying to improve or clarify his thoughts. But that continual improvement is at the heart of his teaching. It is one of his 14 points: "Improve constantly and forever the system of production and service, to improve quality and productivity, and thus constantly decrease costs." To get to that point, Deming says, you not only need constancy of purpose, you also have to recognize that we're in a new economic age with a single global market, that mass inspection does not produce quality, and that buying from the lowest bidder is costly. To get good supplies, Deming says, you work with a single supplier to improve his quality and lower his costs, cultivating a long-term relationship in which both of you will profit.

CHEAPER IS NOT ALWAYS BETTER

That last one leaves people in purchasing departments almost in shock, since it is a basic tenet of American industry that you play one supplier against another, demanding and getting lower prices, and if one supplier won't cut his price, another one will. That's the way you cut costs and improve profits, and everyone in business knows that. And like a great many other things that everyone knows, it's wrong. Deming tells the story of a shoe manufacturing company where productivity dropped like a rock in a well, and a consultant was called in. The first thing the consultant did was what the typical American manager would rather die than do: the consultant went on the factory floor and asked the workers what went wrong. Shoes are sewn together, and it takes an enormous quantity of thread. Sewing machine operators said the thread kept breaking, so they spent half their day rethreading the machines. You know the end of this story. Some time earlier, some genius in purchasing found a company that would sell thread a penny a bobbin cheaper than their regular supplier, and to save a penny a bobbin, the company's productivity was cut in half.

The rest of Deming's 14 points basically deal with management and labor and their relationship. He says quality is made in the boardroom, but everyone must have a part in changing the company. Management must learn about the responsibility for quality, must learn how to lead, instead of giving orders, and must make it possible for everyone to work together for the good of the company.

Everyone already knows that? If, in the typical American firm, everyone is working for the good of the company, then why are different divisions within that company competing? Why is it necessary to give employees annual ratings or performance appraisals? What's more important to you, getting a good rating for yourself, or helping another person improve so that the whole company will prosper? Why are there numerical goals or work standards? Are we trying to make quality, or are we satisfied to make daily quotas?

If you want to make quality, management leads in the design of product and service, but everyone has to understand where they're going. If you tell someone to wash a table, the order doesn't mean anything unless the worker knows why. Is it being washed to serve lunch? Simple enough and quickly done. Is it being washed as an emergency operating table? Not easy, but it can be done. Is it being washed to go into a computer "clean room"? Can't be done.

Job training alone, Deming says, is not enough; the company has to help with employee education in a more general way, too. At Ford there are joint company-union education programs, everything from helping you brush up on your high school math to studying for your college degree. College courses are taught at no cost to employees in learning centers at Ford facilities or at the local union hall. The idea is this simple: the smarter everyone gets, the more everyone will be able to help the company.

W. Edwards Deming is an unlikely capitalist revolutionary. Had he become a Marxist, it would be more understandable. If he ever saw a silver spoon as a kid, it belonged to someone else. He was born in Sioux City, Iowa, on October 14, 1900. With his mother and father, he and younger brother Robert went to Wyoming seven years later. Wyoming was the frontier, and his father had staked a land claim there. Sister Elizabeth was born in a four-room tar-paper shack in Powell. In winter, snow blew through cracks in the walls and around the windows. Deming remembers kneeling in the shack with his mother and brother and praying for enough to eat. "I think I had a job when I was eight years old or nine," Deming says. "Worked in a hotel, night and morning, before and after school, a job that wouldn't exist today." He carried in kindling and coal, emptied washbasins, tended the boiler. "A dollar and a quarter a week, but those were gold dollars."

In the fall of 1917, his saved money in his pocket, Deming took a train to the University of Wyoming at Laramie. "I studied engineering," he says, "but I really didn't know what engineers did. The course appealed to me—mathematics, thermodynamics, electrical circuits." To stay in college, he worked at anything that paid; after four years, he left Laramie with about the same amount of money he'd arrived with.

Deming taught and finished work on his Ph.D. in mathematical physics at Yale in 1927, then went to work for a research laboratory affiliated with the Department of Agriculture in Washington, D.C. He had other offers, good ones in private industry, he recalls, but he decided on this one and, he says now, "That was no mistake.... There were great men there." (And at least one great woman, Lola E. Shupe, his assistant and coauthor of several papers, whom he married in 1932. She died in 1986.)

Deming had learned to use statistical theory while studying physics. At the Fixed Nitrogen Lab, he devised statistical methods to replace some experiments, saving time and money. Impressed, one of his bosses introduced him to Walter Shewhart, then at the firm now known as AT&T Bell Laboratories, who was working to improve the quality of telephone equipment. Shewhart wanted the expression "as alike as two peas in a pod" to be replaced by "as alike as two telephones." He believed that could be accomplished with statistical analysis.

During World War II, it was largely through Deming's efforts that 35,000 American engineers and technicians were taught to use statistics to improve the quality of war material. That work brought him to the attention of the Union of Japanese Scientists and Engineers (JUSE). When the war was over, Japan was little more than a pile of rubble and its industrial capacity was severely crippled. JUSE asked Deming to help its members increase productivity. In July 1950 he met with the top management of Japan's leading companies, and he gave eight daylong lectures titled "Elementary Principles of the Statistical Control of Quality" to 230 Japanese managers. It was, essentially, the same course he had taught Americans during the war.

Why did his teachings catch on in Japan but not here? Because, Deming says, the Japanese knew they were in an economic and industrial crisis and we don't. Yet here we are in 1990, the world's most indebted nation, borrowing heavily from, of all people, the newly wealthy Japanese. Deming tells students at a four-day seminar in Texas that we can recover. Then he adds, "Nobody's sitting here *predicting* that we'll survive. We may not. There's no regulation saying we must survive. Purely voluntary." And he tells a group in Ohio, "We can rise from the ashes like a phoenix, but it will take a transformation to do it."

By transformation, he means adoption of his quality philosophy. It is not so much a recipe of dos and don'ts, although there are some, as it is a method of continual improvement that involves reducing variation. American manufacturers say that they are already doing that, that they have strict specifications for every part. A quick story. An American car company was having trouble with transmissions made at one of its plants here, and warranty costs were enormous, a drain on profits. The same transmission, built to the same specifications at a plant in Japan, was not causing problems. Engineers carefully examined 12 American transmissions; variations existed,

Deming remained active as a consultant and a lecturer until his death in 1993 at the age of 93.

but all were well within specifications. A quality-control inspector would have been delighted with every one. When the 12 Japanese transmissions were tested, an engineer reported that the measuring equipment had broken. It hadn't; in those transmissions, there simply was too little variation to measure. They didn't just satisfy the specs; for any practical purpose, they were identical.

STAYING CLOSE TO WHAT IS BEST

That story's true; this one's made up. Assume that we all work in a room together, and we know by statistical analysis that we produce our best work when the temperature is 68 degrees F. But if it's 67 or 69, the loss in terms of the quality of our work is so imperceptible that it simply doesn't matter. Now, should the temperature fall to 58 or rise to 78, the loss will be enormous. Take that same idea and apply it to specifications. Everything inside a given set of specifications is not the same. Some are worse than others, and the farther away you get from what is best, the worse it is and the greater the loss in quality will be.

Statistics alone cannot assure reduced variation, Deming says; it takes everyone, management and labor, working together. To get that kind of cooperation you have to throw out much of what is currently accepted as good management practice. Not only do you have to do away with bonuses and incentive pay because they create competition; once you adopt the Deming method little else stays the same.

Ben Carlson, executive vice president at Vernay and chairman of its Deming Steering Committee, says the Deming method "changes the relationship with your customers; it changes the relationship with your suppliers; it changes the relationship you have with your employees." Customers become the most important people in your business. Unless the customer is so delighted that he's not only willing to come back but eager to bring his friends, you can close the door now and save time. Suppliers can no longer be played off one another for lower prices. They become your partners, and you have to help them improve so they can give you continually improving supplies for lower prices. And if you and your employees don't work together in mutual respect toward the same goal, how good the supplies are won't matter. Corny as it sounds, Deming wishes work could be nicer, more satisfying.

In teaching people to be nicer, he himself can be abrasive. Polite to the point of courtliness in social situations, he can be short-tempered and intolerant at work. He always tells people at his seminars that the object is "to have fun," but when one person he is raking over the coals complains, "Dr. Deming, I'm not having fun," he leans back in his chair, smiles broadly and says, "I am."

Deming works as a consultant to private companies, but more people probably know him through his public seminars, most of which are run by Nancy Mann, who has a Ph.D. in biostatistics. People are standing in line to get in. Deming mentions one seminar—500 vacancies, 3,000 applicants. There are 14 of these seminars a year in this country and England, with 500 to 600 students each, and a waiting list of about 100 for each seminar.

"Students" is perhaps misleading. At a seminar I attended in Dallas, the people were mostly in their 30s and 40s—managers, engineers and technicians from major corporations in all types of business, defense contractors, officers of the Armed Forces, health-care insurers. Deming lectures morning and afternoon for the four days, sometimes from notes, sometimes from memory, but with a good teacher's sense of when the lecture is becoming too intense, as it did at one seminar when he tried to make the class understand that there is no true value of anything, that whatever number you get depends on how you count, and if you change the way you count, the number will change. People think the speed of light is a true value, Deming says, but it isn't; there were ten different published figures for the speed of light between 1874 and 1932. Then in his best professorial voice, which is deep and impressive, Deming quotes Galileo as saying, "If the speed of light is not infinity, then it's awfully damned fast." The class roars. The point is unforgettably made.

Deming wants American business and industry to prosper. "All I have to offer is to improve profit," he says, but his method is not easy to understand. The standard American corporate questions about quality improvement are, "What do we do? (But keep it simple)" and "How long will it take? (But keep it short).” With Deming what you do is continually improve, not in great leaps forward, but a little here, a little there, and it never gets any easier. You change the way you think, unlearn everything about management you've been taught, and develop an understanding of statistics and psychology, an understanding of how people learn and what makes them change, and an understanding of people's need to take pride and joy in their work. How many steps are there? No one knows. How long will it take? The rest of your life, but—here's the good news—you should start to see results in three to five years. Why should you do that? Because the people who have tried it say that it works. And not much does these days.

At the hotel, it's early evening, and his lecture is over. Deming is going to his room to rest before dinner, a rare concession to his age. He comes down the hallway, the same attractive, welldressed young woman holding one hand, and a tall, striking woman, a seminar coordinator, holding his other hand, and they are skipping. Skipping! Three kids home from school. W. Edwards Deming, Ph.D., Consultant in Statistical Studies and Capitalist Revolutionary, wears a smile of the most childlike pleasure and delight.

THE 14 POINTS FOR MANAGEMENT

1. Create constancy of purpose toward improvement of product and service, with the aim to become competitive and to stay in business, and to provide jobs.
2. Adopt the new philosophy. We are in a new economic age. Western management must awaken to the challenge, must learn their responsibilities, and take on leadership for change.
3. Cease dependence on inspection to achieve quality. Eliminate the need for inspection on a mass basis by building quality into the product in the first place.
4. End the practice of awarding business on the basis of price tag. Instead, minimize total cost. Move toward a single supplier for any one item, on a long-term relationship of loyalty and trust.
5. Improve constantly and forever the system of production and service, to improve quality and productivity, and thus constantly decrease costs.
6. Institute training on the job.
7. Institute leadership (see Point 12). The aim of supervision should be to help people and machines and gadgets to do a better job. Supervision of management is in need of overhaul, as well as supervision of production workers.
8. Drive out fear, so that everyone may work effectively for the company.
9. Break down barriers between departments. People in research, design,

sales; and production must work as a team, to foresee problems of production and in use that may be encountered with the product or service.

10. Eliminate slogans, exhortations, and targets for the work force asking for zero defects and new levels of productivity. Such exhortations only create adversarial relationships, as the bulk of the causes of low quality and low productivity belong to the system and thus lie beyond the power of the work force.

11a. Eliminate work standards (quotas) on the factory floor. Substitute leadership.

b. Eliminate management by objective. Eliminate management by numbers, numerical goals. Substitute leadership.

12a. Remove barriers that rob the hourly worker of his right to pride of workmanship. The responsibility of supervisors must be changed from sheer numbers to quality.

b. Remove barriers that rob people in management and in engineering of their right to pride of workmanship. This means, *inter alia*, abolishment of the annual or merit rating and of management by objective.

13. Institute a vigorous program of education and self-improvement.

14. Put everybody in the company to work to accomplish the transformation. The transformation is everybody's job.

(Reprinted from W. Edwards Deming's *Out of the Crisis.*)

Lloyd Dobbins is a freelance writer who has written books and television documentaries on TQM.

PART THREE

THE TOOLS
OF QUALITY

READINGS 5 AND 6
THE TOOLS OF QUALITY

GEORGE BOX HAS DEFINED TQM AS "THE DEMOCRATIZATION OF THE SCIENTIFIC METHOD." HIS DEFINITION IMPLIES THE ORGANIZATIONAL-WIDE USE OF TOOLS FOR THE IDENTIFICATION OF PROBLEMS, THE COLLECTION AND ANALYSIS OF RELEVANT DATA, AND DECISIONS BASED ON THE DATA. OF COURSE, ANY SIZEABLE ORGANIZATION WILL HAVE A WIDE VARIATION IN THE PROBLEM-SOLVING/ANALYTICAL SKILLS OF ITS EMPLOYEES; THUS, THE TOOLS THAT ARE TAUGHT TO *ALL* EMPLOYEES SHOULD BE RELATIVELY FEW AND SIMPLE SO THAT *ALL* CAN MASTER THEIR USE, YET POWERFUL ENOUGH TO PROVE USEFUL IN THE PROCESS OF CONTINUOUS IMPROVEMENT. ALTHOUGH WHAT DEFINES THE BASIC SET OF QUALITY TOOLS VARIES SOMEWHAT FROM PLACE TO PLACE, A VERY POPULAR COLLECTION IS REFERRED TO AS *ISHIKAWA'S SEVEN TOOLS* (OR THE SEVEN BASIC QC TOOLS).

KAORU ISHIKAWA IS PROBABLY THE MOST FAMOUS OF THE JAPANESE QUALITY GURUS. HE WAS AWARDED THE DEMING PRIZE AND THE SECOND ORDER OF THE SACRED TREASURE IN JAPAN, AND THE GRANT AWARD AND THE SHEWHART MEDAL IN AMERICA. HIS MANY ACCOMPLISHMENTS INCLUDE INITIATING QUALITY CIRCLES IN 1962. ALTHOUGH ISHIKAWA *DEFINED* A COLLECTION OF BASIC TOOLS, HE ACTUALLY DEVELOPED ONLY ONE OF THEM: THE CAUSE-AND-EFFECT DIAGRAM. THE FOLLOWING PAIR OF READINGS DISCUSS THE CAUSE-AND-EFFECT DIAGRAM AND THE CHECK SHEET. A SUBSEQUENT READING WILL INTRODUCE CONTROL CHARTS. THE OTHER FOUR TOOLS (HISTOGRAM, SCATTER DIAGRAM, STRATIFICATION, AND PARETO CHART) ARE ALREADY FAMILIAR TO MANY READERS AND ARE REVIEWED IN MOST BASIC STATISTICS TEXTS.

READING 5
THE TOOLS OF QUALITY:
CAUSE-AND-EFFECT DIAGRAMS

BY J. STEPHEN SARAZEN

"Quality begins with education and ends with education." These words, attributed to the late Kaoru Ishikawa, sum up a principle philosophy of quality. To improve processes, you must continuously strive to obtain more information about those processes and their output.

One unique and valuable tool for accomplishing this goal is the cause-and-effect diagram. This tool was first developed in 1943 by Ishikawa at the University of Tokyo; he used it to explain to a group of engineers from the Kawasaki Steel Works how various factors could be sorted and related.

The cause-and-effect diagram is a method for analyzing process dispersion. The diagram's purpose is to relate causes and effects. It is also known as the Ishikawa diagram and the fishbone diagram (because the completed diagram resembles the skeleton of a fish). Whatever it's called, the tool is certainly one of the most elegant and widely used of the so-called seven QC tools.

It has been my experience that this tool is not only invaluable for virtually any issue requiring attention, but can be easily learned by people at all levels of the organization and applied immediately. There are three basic types of cause-and-effect diagrams: dispersion analysis, production process classification, and cause enumeration. Figure 1 depicts the basic format for the cause-and-effect diagram. Note the hierarchical relationship of the effect to the main causes and their subsequent relationship to the sub-causes. For example, Main Cause A has a direct relationship to the effect. Each of the sub-causes is related in terms of its level of influence on the main cause.

While a cause-and-effect diagram can be developed by an individual, it is best when used by a team. (Considering how well-suited this tool is for team applications, it is not surprising that Ishikawa is the father of quality circles.)

CREDIT: J. Stephen Sarazen, " The Tools Of Quality: Cause-and-Effect Diagrams," *Quality Progress* (July, 1990) pp. 59-61.

| **FIGURE 1** | THE BASIC CAUSE-AND-EFFECT DIAGRAM |

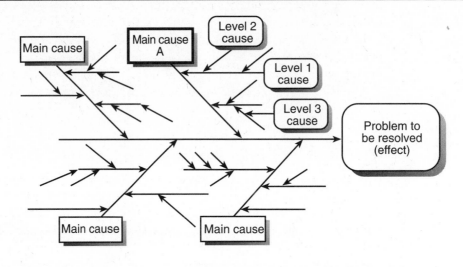

One of the most valuable attributes of this tool is that it provides an excellent means to facilitate a brainstorming session. It will focus the participants on the issue at hand and immediately allow them to sort ideas into useful categories, especially when the dispersion analysis or process classification methods are used.

DISPERSION ANALYSIS

Let's assume you are having difficulties with customer complaints. Let us further assume that you are able to pull together about seven individuals from various functions throughout the organization. Each of these individuals has sound knowledge of the overall business as well as an area of specific expertise. This team will provide a good example of the way to construct a cause-and-effect diagram using the dispersion analysis methods. There are three steps:

STEP 1.

It is quite simple to construct the diagram. First, determine the quality characteristic you wish to improve—perhaps customer satisfaction. You must be certain there is consensus when you write the problem statement. For example: "Customers are dissatisfied."

Write this brief statement of fact on a large sheet of paper, a white board, or similar area. Write it on the right side, center of the page, and draw a box around it with an arrow running to it. This problem statement constitutes the effect.

In a manufacturing process, you might use a specific characteristic of a product as the effect, such as a problem with paste thickness in a surface mount line, poor paint coverage, or welding errors. In an administrative or service area you might use customer complaints, decreased sales volume, or increased accounts receivable past due.

STEP 2.

Now the team must generate ideas as to what is causing the effect, contributing to customer dissatisfaction. The causes are written as branches flowing to the main branch. Figure 2 shows the main cause headings resulting from an actual session in a service/distribution business. In this case, the team determined five areas—product quality, service, order processing system, distribution system, and order fulfillment—as the main potential causes of dissatisfied customers. If there is difficulty in determining the main branches or causes, use generic headings—such as method, machine, people, materials, environment, or training—to help start the team.

STEP 3.

The next step is to brainstorm all the possible causes of problems in each of the major cause categories. These ideas are captured and applied to the chart

FIGURE 2   THE MAIN CAUSE HEADINGS

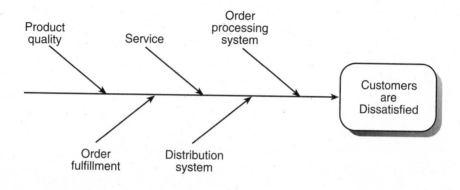

as sub-causes. It is important to continually define and relate causes to each other. It is acceptable to repeat sub-causes in several places if the team feels there is a direct, multiple relationship. This effort will ensure a complete diagram and a more enlightened team.

Returning to Figure 2, you can see that the team identified five main causes of customer dissatisfaction. Now the team members must ask themselves, "What could contribute to each of these five main causes?" Once several sub-causes have been identified, the team continues asking the same question until the lowest-level causes are discovered.

Figure 3 shows the completed portion of the diagram for one of the main causes: service. The team identified reliability issues, carrier issues (e.g., a trucking company), poor communications, and lack of, or poor, training.

The next level of causes is identified by asking the question "What could cause a problem in these areas?" In the case of the poor communications, the team focused on functions and jobs—sales people, field representatives, and managers—as potential causes. You can see that lack of knowledge of the customer can cause managers to communicate poorly. Subsequently you can see that inexperience and training can be two key contributors to a manager's lack of customer knowledge. Thus, there are six levels of causes in this example.

| **FIGURE 3** | **A DETAILED LOOK AT THE ONE MAIN COURSE** |

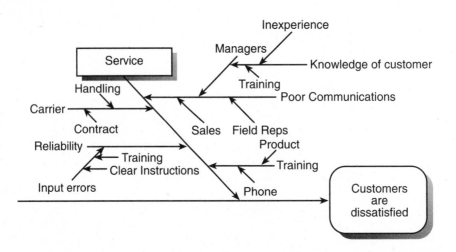

PROCESS CLASSIFICATION

Another type of diagram is known as the process classification diagram. I prefer to eliminate the word "production" from the chart title because it has a manufacturing ring to it. From my experience, this tool is as valuable in service-based businesses as it is in manufacturing companies. After all, every product or service is the result of a process.

Although the basic process for constructing this type of diagram is similar to the one used for dispersion analysis, there are some differences. These differences are driven by the application. For the process classification method, you identify the flow of the process you wish to improve and then list key quality-influencing characteristics at each of the steps.

STEP 1.

Identify the process and develop a flow diagram of the primary sequential steps. For example, in a generic selling process, the following steps might be identified: make initial customer contact, develop an understanding of customer needs, provide information to the customer follow up, close the sale, and follow up on the sale.

STEP 2.

Now add all the things that might influence the quality of each step. Use the method described in the previous section. Brainstorming with a team of knowledgeable people will make the finished diagram more like the actual process.

Figure 4 is an example of a completed process classification diagram. As you can see, the intent is to take the cause and effect to the lowest level to understand all the contributing factors to improve the process.

It is also advisable to consider the connecting steps from process step to process step. Everywhere there is a handoff from one step to the next, there are likely to be possible causes of dispersion. Many opportunities for improvement can be found in these areas.

CAUSE ENUMERATION

The cause enumeration method involves simply brainstorming all possible causes and listing them in the order they are offered. Once the brainstorm has exhausted itself, the team begins the process of grouping the causes as it did for the dispersion analysis diagram. The end result looks exactly the same.

| **FIGURE 4** | **A COMPLETED PROCESS CLASSIFICATION DIAGRAM** |

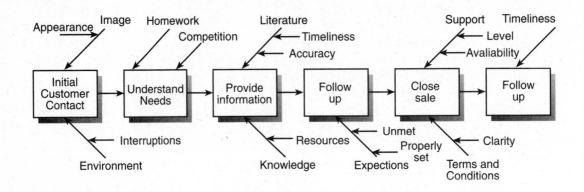

I have found this process can be enhanced dramatically using the affinity diagram process. It is a valuable method for gaining insight and organization of ideas. Basically, the brainstorm is conducted by capturing all ideas on cards or those handy little notepads with the gum on one end. Each card should contain only one idea. The cards are then arranged in groups and subgroups. Cards that have an affinity for one another are placed together. Once it is completed, the affinity diagram provides the basis for the cause-and-effect diagram.

FILLETING THE FISH

Understanding processes, using teams, and identifying areas of opportunity are excellent ways to move toward continuous improvement while solving some of today's tough issues. But they are only the beginning. To obtain the full value from the cause-and-effect diagram, it must be turned into action. It is therefore wise to quantify the problem and as many of the causes as possible. Once this has been done, the business can determine the priority areas to be addressed and can track improvements.

In the earlier example, the business was able to quantify the problem of customer dissatisfaction by measuring several key parameters, including number of calls about problems, number of requests to return material for specific reasons, and receivables aging.

In the areas where sub-causes were identified, various parts of the organization were surveyed to determine the primary areas of opportunity for addressing the causes identified by the cause-and-effect diagram. For example, one need was for training in simple statistical problem-solving methods. This need was quantified not only by the number of people needing training, but also by the results of the training applications.

As the team and business move to quantify the causes, other tools play key roles. Pareto analysis, histograms, control charts, scatter plots, and multivariate analysis might be particularly valuable.

HINTS AND CREATIVE USES

Here are some helpful hints for facilitating or participating in a cause-and-effect exercise.

1. CONSIDER THE BIG PICTURE.

When constructing a cause-and-effect diagram, think about the issue at hand in its broadest sense. Consider the environment, inside the business and externally; politics, including government policies if appropriate; employee issues; and external factors, such as the local or national economy. Granted, some of these areas are well beyond the control of the team. Nevertheless, there is a benefit to understanding the impact of such factors.

2. FACILITATION.

Facilitating a cause-and-effect session is very challenging. It is similar to facilitating any brainstorming session except that the thoughts must be written in a particular place as opposed to being listed. The facilitator must listen to the ideas of the participants, capture those thoughts in only one or two words, and write them in the appropriate position on the chart. This last step is the tricky part. My recommendation is to have the participants decide where the cause should be written. This approach helps ensure that the correct location is chosen and removes some of the burden from the facilitator.

3. REVIEW AND EMBELLISHMENT.

To ensure that the diagram is complete, have each member of the team review it the next day or have them show it to one or two additional people to obtain their opinion. Use your discretion in deciding whether to use second parties on very technical issues or problems unique to a particular job or area.

THE BENEFITS AND WEAKNESSES OF EACH CAUSE-AND-EFFECT DIAGRAM

- Diagram type: Dispersion analysis
  Key benefits:
  1. Helps organize and relate factors.
  2. Provides a structure for brainstorming.
  3. Involves everyone.
  4. It's fun.
  Potential drawbacks:
  1. Might be difficult to facilitate if developed in true brainstorming fashion.
  2. Might become very complex, requires dedication and patience.

- Diagram type: Process classification
  Key benefits:
  1. Provides a solid sequential view of the process and the factors that influence each step.
  2. Might help determine functional ownership for the work to be done in improvement.
  Potential drawback:
  1. It is sometimes difficult to identify or demonstrate interrelationships.

- Diagram type: Cause enumeration
  Key benefits:
  1. Easy to facilitate.
  2. Provides in-depth list of all possible causes.
  Potential drawbacks:
  1. The added step of creating an affinity diagram might add time to the process.
  2. The final diagram might be difficult to draw because of the random output of the brainstorming session.

4. BROAD-BASED PARTICIPATION.

If you want to add a creative flair to your development effort and, at the same time, encourage broad-based participation from your group or organization, try this. Hang a large white board or sheet of butcher paper in an accessible location. Ask the group or a manager to identify a problem that needs to be addressed. Write that problem statement in the ' head of the fish" and draw the arrow to it. Now invite the entire organization to participate in developing the diagram over a certain time frame—say two weeks. You will be amazed how many people will really get into working and understanding the process.

The obvious drawback to this approach is that you miss the brainstorming opportunity. However. reading what others have written in the diagram will generate ideas. The commitment that must be made is to take the input and act on it.

While this might sound a little out of the ordinary, I can tell you from first-hand experience that it works. I trained a vice president's staff in the use of cause-and-effect diagrams several years ago and suggested this approach. We hung a large white board outside his office and began writing a new issue on it every couple of weeks. Some of his people had been trained in the technique; many had not. The end result was that more than 100 people contributed to the first few diagrams and his staff was provided with invaluable information, insight. and suggestions for improving processes.

5. WORKING TOWARD THE DESIRED RESULT.

I have found it very useful to state the desired result—rather than a problem—in the head of the fish. For example, instead of writing 'Customers are dissatisfied,'- write "100% customer satisfaction." The exercise now focuses on finding means to achieve this goal rather than working the problem. Many of the findings will be the same but some unique approaches might find their way onto the chart.

The work could also be stated as "how to" arrive at some desired result. A few years ago, I trained a group of elementary teachers in the use of cause-and-effect diagrams. They needed to get students to perform as a team. Rather than trying to solve the problem of why students didn't perform as a team, we developed a cause-and-effect diagram using the statement "What makes an effective/winning team?"

Many of the teachers returned to their classes and used this exercise with students. The students wanted to be winners. Now they were asked to identify all the attributes of a winning team, and they were able to do so. They learned that it takes a lot of hard work and dedication.

The teachers then posted the completed diagram every day and, when the students did not demonstrate the behavior required to be a winner (in their own words), the diagram served as a reminder. This process has also worked for business issues such as how to improve competitiveness and how to ensure SPC applications will follow training.

UNDERSTANDING PROCESSES

In the past decade, quality has gained recognition as the competitive imperative for all businesses. The root of all quality improvement lies in understanding processes. Many existing tools assist managers, engineers, and others in this work. You need not always look for the newest tool, software, or management theory to construct a sound foundation on which to build improvements. If you are looking for a tool that fosters team work, educates users, identifies lowest-level issues on which to work, helps show a true picture of the process, guides discussion, can be used for virtually any issue your business might face, and is fun, look no further than this 46-year-old tool called the cause-and-effect diagram.

BIBLIOGRAPHY

Ishikawa, Kaoru, Guide to Quality Control (Tokyo: Asia Productivity Organization, 1986).

Wadsworth, Harrison M.. Kenneth S. Stephens, and A. Blanton Godfrey, Modern Methods for Quality Control and Improvement (New York: John Wiley & Sons, Inc., 1986).

Stephen Sarazen is president of EXL Group, a quality and business consulting company based in Bedford, NH. He is a senior member of ASQC.

Reading 6
The Tools of Quality:
Check Sheets

by The Juran Institute, Inc.

Quality improvement is an information-intensive activity. We need clear, useful information about problems and their causes to make improvements. In many cases, the absence of relevant information is the major reason why problems go unsolved for so long.

Most organizations have vast stores of data and facts about their operations. However, when quality improvement teams begin working on a project, they often find that the information they need does not exist. To resolve this apparent paradox, we need to understand some basic concepts about the difference between data and information:

- Data = facts.
- Information = answers to questions.
- Information includes data.
- Data does not necessarily include information.

Quality improvement teams are seeking the answers to questions: "How often does the problem occur?" or "What is causing the problem?" In other words, they are seeking information. But, while good information is always based on data (the facts), simply collecting data does not necessarily ensure that a team will have useful information. The data may not be relevant or specific enough to answer the question at hand.

The key issue, then, is not "How do we collect data?" but rather "How do we generate useful information?" Figure 1 presents a model for generating useful information.

Credit: The Juran Institute, Inc., "The Tools of Quality: Check Sheets," *Quality Progress* (October, 1990).

| **FIGURE 1** | GENERATING INFORMATION |

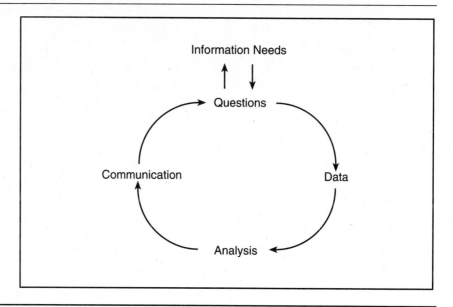

Information generation begins and ends with questions. To generate information, we need to:

- formulate precisely the question we are trying to answer.
- collect the data and facts relating to that question.
- analyze the data to determine the factual answer to the question.
- present the data in a way that clearly communicates the answer to the question.

Learning to ask the right questions is the key skill in effective data collection. Accurate, precise data collected through an elaborately designed statistical sampling plan are useless if they do not clearly address a question that someone cares about.

PLANNING TO COLLECT DATA

Planning for good data collection should proceed along the following lines:

- What question do we need to answer?
- How will we recognize and communicate the answers to the question?

- What data analysis tools (Pareto diagram, histogram, bar graph. etc.) do we envision using, and how will we communicate the results?
- What type of data do we need in order to construct this tool and answer the question?
- Where in the process can we get these data?
- Who in the process can give us these data?
- How can we collect these data from these people with minimum effort and chance of error?
- What additional information do we need to gather for future analysis, reference, and traceability?

Notice how this planning process essentially works backward through the model in Figure 1. We start by defining the question. Then, rather than diving into the details of data collection. We consider how we might communicate the answer to the question and what types of analysis we will need to perform. This helps us define our data needs and clarifies what characteristics are most important in the data. With this understanding as a foundation, we can deal more coherently with the where, who, how, and what else issues of data collection.

Of course, like most planning processes, some iteration might be required to complete the design of a good data collection system. For example, the discussion about where in the process to collect the data might require going back and restating the question more precisely.

We will look at the elements of this data-collection planning process in more detail later. First, we will look at some examples of when data collection is necessary and how it is used.

TYPES OF DATA COLLECTION

Three types of data collection forms are commonly used by quality improvement teams: check sheets, data sheets, and checklists. While these three types of forms are quite different, the similarity in their names often leads to confusion.

A check sheet is a simple data recording form that has been specially designed to readily interpret results from the form itself. Figure 2 shows an example of a simple check sheet for recording temperatures in a manufacturing process. Notice that the form was designed to allow the operator to enter the temperatures on a time vs. temperature grid. Because of this, the form does more than simply provide a record of the data—it allows the simultaneous analysis of trends in the data.

Data sheets are also used to gather data. They differ from check sheets, however, in that the data are recorded in a simple tabular or columnar format.

FIGURE 2   **A CHECK SHEET**

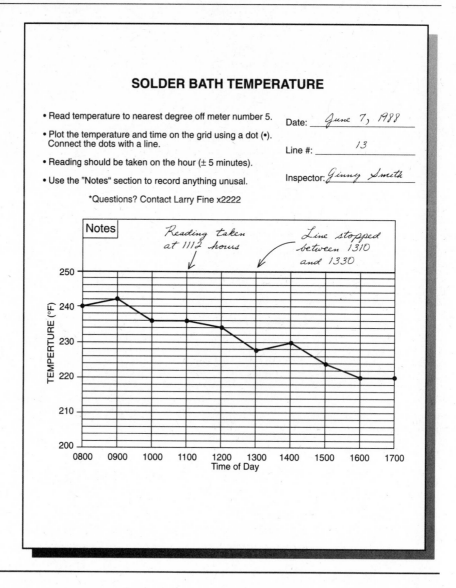

Specific bits of data—numbers, words, or marks (e.g., X)—are entered in spaces on the sheet. As a result, additional processing is typically required after the data are collected to construct the tool needed for analysis. Figure 3 shows an example of a data sheet for collecting temperatures.

A checklist contains items that are important or relevant to a specific issue or situation. Checklists are used under operational conditions to ensure that

FIGURE 3	A DATA SHEET

SOLDER BATH TEMPERATURE

- Read temperature to nearest degree off meter number 5.
- Record the temperature in the table below.
- Reading should be taken on the hour (± 5 minutes).
- Use the "Notes" section to record anything unusal.

*Questions? Contact Larry Fine x2222

Date: *June 7, 1988*

Line #: *13*

Inspector: *Ginny Smith*

Time of Day	Temperature (°F)	Time of Day	Temperature (°F)
0800	240	1300	227
0900	242	1400	230
1000	236	1500	224
1100	236	1600	220
1200	234	1700	220

Notes:

- 1100 hours reading taken at 1112

- The line was stopped between 1310 and 1330

all important steps or actions have been taken. Although completed checklists might be analyzed by a quality improvement team, their primary purpose is for guiding operations, not for collecting data. Checklists are therefore more commonly used in the remedial journey and holding-the-gains phases of problem solving; they are part of the solution. The preflight checklist that a commercial airline pilot must complete is a good example.

Much of the material in this article focuses on check sheets for two reasons: data sheets and checklists are straightforward and need little explanation; and check sheets are typically not used that often.

OBTAINING GOOD DATA

Collected data must be accurate. Inaccurate data might give the wrong answer to information questions. Most collected data are not perfect, but there are techniques that keep inaccuracies to a minimum. The most serious types of data inaccuracies are called biases.

Biases can come from many sources, including the design of the data collection instrument, the collection procedures, and the perceptions of the persons collecting the data. For some types of bias, it is helpful to conduct an audit of the data collection process while the data are being collected. As you study the following examples, notice how some of the teams considered and dealt with issues of bias.

REDUCING WARRANTY COSTS

A few years ago, a television manufacturer introduced a line of television sets that was a big commercial success. The style of the cabinet was attractive, the price was competitive, and the set offered a number of features that the public appreciated. As time went by, however, the company discovered that reliability was poor. A high percentage of television sets came back to be repaired within the 12-month warranty period.

A quality improvement project team was chartered to determine the causes of this problem, which was increasing warranty costs for the company to an unacceptable level. The team formulated the following information questions to guide the analysis of the symptoms:

- How many total components are replaced under warranty in each of the three existing models of the set (model numbers 1013, 1017, and 1019)?
- How many integrated circuits, capacitors, resistors, transformers, commands (i.e., switches), and CRTs are replaced under warranty in each of the three models?

These questions could be answered with a bar graph or Pareto diagram if the team had simple tallies of the number of each type of component replaced in each model during a typical week. The repair shop where all the sets came

HOW TO COLLECT DATA

Data collection is a type of production process itself and, like any process, needs to be understood and improved. Generally speaking, 10 points must be addressed when collecting data:

1. Formulate good questions that relate to the specific information needs of the project. It is much easier to get others to help collect data if they believe those in charge know precisely what they are looking for and that they are going to do something with the collected information.

2. Use the appropriate data analysis tools and be certain the necessary data are being collected. Whenever practical, collect continuous variable data. A few minutes of thought before gathering data can often prevent having to recollect data because they are incomplete or answer the wrong question.

3. Define comprehensive data collection points. The ideal is to set the collection point where the job flow suffers minimum interruption. An accurate flowchart of the work process can help immensely.

4. Select an unbiased collector. The collector should have the easiest and most immediate access to the relevant facts.

5. Understand data collectors and their environment. The training and experience of the collectors determine whether they can handle this additional assignment.

6. Design data collection forms that are simple; reduce opportunities for error; capture data for analysis, reference, and traceability; are self-explanatory; and look professional. The KISS (keep it simple, stupid) principle applies here.

7. Prepare the instructions for use. In some cases, a special training course might be necessary for data gatherers. In other cases, a simple sheet of instructions will suffice.

8. Test the forms and instructions. Try out the forms on a limited basis to make sure they are filled out properly. If they aren't, the forms or instructions might need revision.

9. Train the data collectors. Training should include the purpose of the study, what the data will be used for, a properly completed form, and a discussion about the importance of complete and unbiased information.

10. Audit the collection process and validate the results. Randomly check completed forms and observe data collection during the process. Look for missing or unusual data, and be wary of variations in the data that might result from biases in the data collection process.

for warranty repairs was the obvious data collection point. Since the repair technicians were the closest to the facts of each repair and had no reason to bias the data, they were selected as the data collectors. The team designed a check sheet, showed it to two of the technicians, made some modifications based on their comments, spent 15 minutes describing the study and the final form to the entire group, and then implemented the data collection system. Figure 4 is an example of the check sheet given to each workshop technician to record the components replaced during a one-week period.

It was immediately evident that there was a problem with capacitors. This problem was present in all three models. Model 1017 also had a specific problem associated with its command components. The on-off switch for that model failed much more often than did the switch in the other two models.

USING A LOCATION PLOT

When the data to be recorded refer to positions on the surface of an item, a variation of the check sheet called a location plot (or concentration diagram) is ideal in terms of ease of use and ability to transform data into information (Figure 5).

This check sheet was designed by a quality improvement project team to answer the question "Are certain areas on our household range more prone to chipped enamel damage during transportation?" It is clear from Figure 5 that the corners were the areas most prone to damage. This information was invaluable in indicating that certain corners of the appliances required more protection for safe transportation.

INTEGRATED CIRCUIT YIELD

The manufacture of integrated circuits begins with silicon slices that, after a sequence of complex operations will contain hundreds of thousands of chips on their surfaces. Each chip must be tested to establish whether it functions properly. During slice testing, some chips are found to be defective and are rejected. To reduce the number of rejects it is necessary to know not only the percentage but also the locations and the types of defects. There are normally two major types of defects: functional and parametric. A functional reject occurs when a chip does not perform one of its functions. A parametric reject occurs when the circuit functions properly, but a parameter of the chip, such as speed or power consumption is not correct.

Figure 6 is an example of a check sheet showing the location of rejected chips within the integrated circuit. Only those chips that had five or more defects during the testing of 1,000 circuits are colored in. The information shows that parametric rejects are mostly concentrated on the lower right of the slice, while functional rejects are distributed toward the edges.

FIGURE 4 CHECK SHEET FOR TV COMPONENT FAILURES

COMPONENTS REPLACED BY LAB
Enter a mark for each component replaced.
Mark like the following: / // /// //// ~~////~~
TIME PERIOD: 22 Feb to 27 Feb. 1994
REPAIR TECHNICIAN: Bob

TV SET MODEL 1013

Integrated circuits	~~////~~
Capacitors	~~////~~ ~~////~~ ~~////~~ ~~////~~ ~~////~~ //
Resistors	//
Transformers	////
Commands	
CRT	/

TV SET MODEL 1017

Integrated circuits	////
Capacitors	~~////~~ ~~////~~ ~~////~~ ~~////~~ ~~////~~ //
Resistors	/
Transformers	//
Commands	~~////~~ ~~////~~ ~~////~~ ///
CRT	/

TV SET MODEL 1019

Integrated circuits	/
Capacitors	~~////~~ ~~////~~ ~~////~~ ~~////~~ ///
Resistors	
Transformers	//
Commands	
CRT	/

This is an unusual check sheet because it takes advantage of the automated testing equipment. Chip failures are recorded by the test equipment for each circuit and displayed on the video screen attached to the test equipment. In addition, the results of each test are stored in the test computer and the results of hundreds or thousands of tests can be quickly summarized

| **FIGURE 5** | LOCATION PLOT OF CHIPPED ENAMEL ON RANGE |

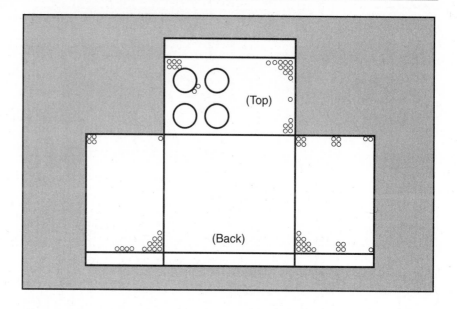

in the form shown in Figure 6. Such computerized applications, when available, should not be overlooked.

PROCESSING PURCHASE ORDERS

When a company wants to buy raw materials, piece parts, services, or other items from an outside supplier, a purchase requisition form must be filled out. After management approves the purchase, this request goes to the purchasing department. It will obtain offers from several different potential suppliers before one is selected and a purchase order is issued. At this point, with all the internal processing steps completed, the purchase order is sent to the selected supplier and a copy of it to the originator of the order.

A quality improvement project team was appointed to speed up this process. The team analyzed the time required to process purchase orders. The question of interest was "How many working days elapse from the date of the originator's signature to the date the purchase order is sent?" The team used a histogram to analyze the distribution of the total processing time in order to obtain insight into the structure of the process. The needed set of data was the elapsed time in days for 40 or more purchase orders.

FIGURE 6	LOCATION PLOT OF CHIP REJECTS

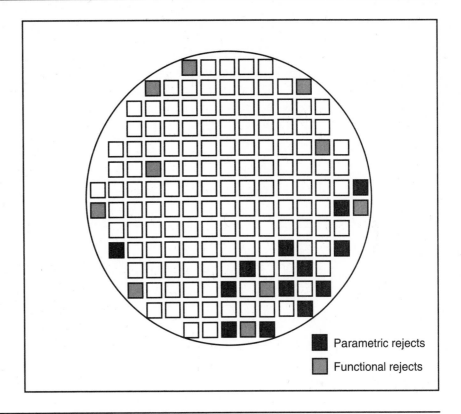

Asking purchasing clerks to record when they send out purchase orders is the obvious, ideal approach. However, it raises the issue of potential bias because the clerks might fear they would be blamed for delays. In this case, great care was taken to explain to the clerks that no blame was being placed. Furthermore, it was carefully explained that, unless they followed their normal routines during the study period, the data would be biased and things would never get better permanently. To make sure that this was understood, one of the clerks was enlisted to conduct casual interviews with her peers. These interviews confirmed that the study could be conducted using the clerks as collectors. The clerk was also relieved of some of her normal workload so that she could observe and audit the data collection process during the study period. A completed check sheet from the study is shown in Figure 7.

The design of the check sheet makes the distribution of times immediately obvious, and the distribution can be analyzed as discussed in the section on histograms without any additional processing. Note one nice feature of this check sheet: by providing boxes to mark in, the results will be easier to interpret. If the horizontal lines had not been provided, variations in the size and placement of the x's might make interpretation less exact.

While the use of a check sheet in this case was a good, quick way to obtain some initial insight, the team members realized that the check sheet had limitations when compared to a complete data sheet. For example, they would not be able to differentiate among the times required for different types of materials being purchased.

INTERPRETING DATA, VALIDATING RESULTS

Before starting to draw conclusions from collected data, the team should verify that the data are appropriate. It is helpful to review the questions that were originally asked. Does the data collected still appear to answer those questions?

Look at the results of any audits of the data collection phase. Is there any evidence of bias in the collection process? Is the number of observations collected the number specified? If not, why not?

FIGURE 7	CHECK SHEET FOR ELAPSED PROCESSING TIME

WORKING DAYS																								
1		3		5		7		9		11		13		15		17		19		21		23		25
										X	X	X												
										X	X	X												
									X	X	X	X	X											
								X	X	X	X	X	X											
								X	X	X	X	X	X	X										
							X	X	X	X	X	X	X	X										
							X	X	X	X	X	X	X	X	X									
						X	X	X	X	X	X	X	X	X	X									
		X				X	X	X	X	X	X	X	X	X	X	X	X				X		X	X

Enter an "X" in the lowest unoccupied box under the number of working days from the date of the originator's signature to the date the purchase order was sent out.

Are there any missing observations or responses? These can be a major source of error. Identify missing data for special treatment. In a survey of customers, for example, dissatisfied customers who are taking their business to your competitor might be the least likely to respond. But their views are vital. Never assume that missing data will, on average, look like the collected data. Generally, it will not.

Do some comparative tabulations of the data. For example, do the data gathered by each collector look, on average, about the same? If not, why not? Is the variability of the results from each data collector about the same? Excessively high or very low variability by one or two data collectors might indicate problems with the data collection process—or falsified data.

GREAT EXPECTATIONS

Do not expect too much from the data. The data should indicate the answer to the question asked during the design of the collection process. It might not be able to answer other unanticipated questions. Do not try to make inferences from the data that they will not support. Usually a check sheet, with its simple collection and analysis format, is intended for a quick answer to a single question. It will not usually support further analysis or stratification. A good complete data sheet, however, will often support many levels of analysis and stratification if they have been anticipated in the design.

For example, the team looking at enamel chips on kitchen ranges might later develop a theory that the location of the chips might also be, in part, related to the shipping method used—a particular railroad or truck line. The data in Figure 5 would not help test that theory.

INTERPRETATION PITFALLS

Most of the interpretation pitfalls relate to the application of specific tools to the data, but a few are generic to all collected data. The following biases might cause problems:

EXCLUSION BIAS.

The results will be biased if they are intended to represent the entire process and some part of the process being investigated has been left out. Data should be collected from all the places, times, and conditions under which the process operates.

INTERACTION BIAS.

The process of collecting the data itself might affect the process being studied. For example, a team was trying to improve the speed with which promotions were processed by a personnel office. Team members began to collect data on the process, but while they were collecting the data, the speed of processing increased by a factor of four.

PERCEPTION BIAS.

The attitudes and beliefs of the data collectors can sometimes color what they see and how they record it.

OPERATIONAL BIAS.

Failure to follow the established procedures is the most common operational bias. This bias usually arises because the instructions, training, and/or forms were not adequately prepared and tested in an operational environment. The transcribing and processing of the collected data can create additional errors.

NONRESPONSE BIAS.

Missing data can bias the results. As we noted above, it is not safe to assume that missing data, on average, look like the collected data. The fact that they are missing is a clue that they are different from the rest in some way.

ESTIMATION BIAS.

The formulas and methods used to calculate statistics form the collected data might give certain types of biases. These biases must be understood when using tools other than the simple ones described here.

KNOW THE QUESTION

Most quality improvement tools depend on reliable, accurate data. If such data are not available, they must be collected. The data collection process must be driven by the information from questions that we formulate based on our needs. In short, know what question is to be answered before collecting data.

READING 7
CONTROL CHARTS AND
PROCESS CAPABILITY

CONTROL CHARTS (PLURAL BECAUSE THERE ARE SEVERAL VARIATIONS ON THE CENTRAL IDEA) ARE THE LEAST SIMPLE OF THE SEVEN BASIC TOOLS. IN FACT, ENTIRE BOOKS HAVE BEEN DEVOTED TO THE SUBJECT. HOWEVER, THIS INTRODUCTORY READING REVIEWS ONLY THREE CONTROL CHARTS (P, $\overline{X}$, AND R) AND THE RELATED IDEA OF PROCESS CAPABILITY. THOSE SEEKING FULLER EXPLANATIONS SHOULD CONSULT GRANT AND LEAVENWORTH'S *STATISTICAL QUALITY CONTROL* OR AT & T'S *STATISTICAL QUALITY CONTROL HANDBOOK* (TO ORDER THE LATTER CALL 1-800-432-6600).

THE CONTROL CHART WAS DEVELOPED DURING THE 1920S BY WALTER SHEWHART OF AT & T. THIS WAS THE PRE-DIVESTITURE AT & T, WHEN THE BELL SYSTEM CONTROLLED MOST ASPECTS OF THE PHONE BUSINESS FOR MUCH OF THE UNITED STATES. IT WAS ALSO A TIME WHEN THIS "NEW TECHNOLOGY" WAS EXPANDING RAPIDLY. MOST BELL EQUIPMENT WAS MANUFACTURED IN A SINGLE PLANT IN CHICAGO AND THEN SHIPPED AROUND THE COUNTRY. THIS EQUIPMENT HAD TO BE INTERCHANGEABLE AND RELIABLE BECAUSE REWORK WAS COSTLY AND TIME-CONSUMING (CONSIDER THE TIME AND EXPENSE OF SHIPPING THE GEAR FROM CHICAGO TO, SAY, SEATTLE OR LOS ANGELES). IN THE EARLY '20S, BELL RELIED ON INSPECTION TO GUARANTEE QUALITY, BUT IT WAS AN EXPENSIVE METHOD. SHEWHART'S INVENTION MOVED THE FOCUS "UPSTREAM," AND BEGAN TO STUDY THE PROCESS ITSELF, NOT JUST ITS OUTPUT. WITH HIS INSIGHT, THE IDEAS OF MODERN QUALITY WERE FIRST INITIATED. AS W. EDWARDS DEMING NOTED IN *THE NEW ECONOMICS*, "TEXTBOOKS LEAD READERS TO SUPPOSE THAT THE PRINCIPLES CONTRIBUTED BY DR. SHEWHART ARE CONTROL CHARTS ON

THE SHOP FLOOR. ACTUALLY... THE MOST IMPORTANT APPLI-
CATION OF SHEWHART'S CONTRIBUTION IS IN THE MANAGE-
MENT OF PEOPLE...."

READING 7
CONTROL CHARTS AND PROCESS CAPABILITY

BY JOSEPH G. VAN MATRE

INTRODUCTION

The decade of the '80s saw the shift of the United States from the world's largest creditor nation to the world's largest debtor. How did this happen? Many observers would point to the trade deficit, and in particular the U.S. deficit with Japan, which in 1989 alone was unfavorable in the amount of some $50 billion. The Japanese captured an inordinate amount of world trade by the quality of both their products and their manufacturing processes. The success of Japan now, at last, has caused the quality movement philosophy to be imported here for American managers and corporations. There is much catching up to do.

For too long, U.S. managerial thinking about quality has suffered from three misconceptions. First, quality ideas/philosophy were thought to be applicable primarily in manufacturing, with little relevance to service industries. Perhaps this was because U.S. firms leading the quality transformation (e.g., Motorola, Xerox, Ford) were, indeed, manufacturers. Further, they were led to transformation by the challenge of their Japanese competitors. Generally, service industries were not similarly motivated by foreign competition and were thus slower to recognize the possibilities for their firms. Now, banks, insurers, and hospitals are adopting elements of the quality philosophy. In fact, the first U.S. firm to win the prestigious Japanese quality award (the Deming Prize) was an electric utility, Florida Power & Light, who won in 1989. (On a personal note, the one firm most in need of a quality transformation in my opinion is my former dry-cleaner.)

CREDIT: Joseph G. Van Matre, "Control Charts and Process Capability," chapter from forthcoming *Contemporary Business Statistics*, Dame Publications, Inc.

Second, quality has been largely viewed as a controlling activity that took place somewhere near the end of the production process. The primary emphasis was often on inspection, separating the good products from the bad. While inspection kept bad products from being shipped, it did little to keep bad products from being manufactured. Thus, the focus of quality activities was the product itself with little concern about the improvements in the *process* of product creation. Consider, for example, a Polo dress shirt that retails at Macy's for $60. That shirt had the *same* production costs as a damaged one sold as a factory "imperfect" or "second" for $15 at an outlet mall. While inspection has the desirable effect of insuring the Macy's customer of an unflawed product, it does nothing to address the problem of creating, at full costs, a shirt with noticeable shortcomings.

The third misconception, and related to the second, was the view that quality and productivity (and hence costs) were conflicting; one was improved only at the expense of the other. In contrast, the Deming chain reaction illustrated in Figure 1 holds that **improvements in the quality of the process leads to both lower costs and higher quality product.** Deming introduced this theory to the Japanese in 1950; they were to prove the theory over and over during the following 40 years.

American/Japanese quality differentials have been widely reported, but are too often anecdotal in nature. However, David Garvin's work provides us

---

FIGURE 1   THE DEMING CHAIN REACTION

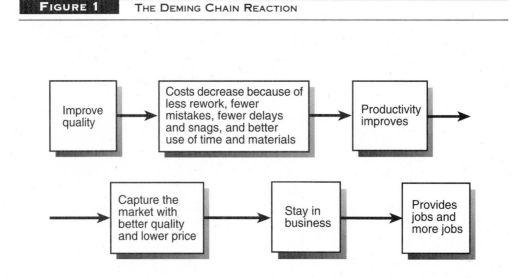

with a thorough and well-documented study. Garvin reported his results in several articles and a 1988 book, *Managing Quality*. In order to make comparisons between the two countries more valid, his study was confined to a single industry (room air conditioners); his findings were astounding:

> Japanese plants were superior across the board.... They averaged failure rates that were seventeen to sixty-seven times lower than their U.S. counterparts. Even more impressive, on all measures the poorest Japanese plant had a failure rate of less than half that of the best U.S. manufacturer.[1]

For example, he reports data concerning first year (warranty) service call rates per 100 air conditioners. See the dotplot below; the three values for each country are the minimum, median, and maximum values for that country's producers.

Note that Japan's *worst* producer had a 2.0 rate, while the *best* U.S. producer had a 5.3 rate. Thus, their worst is better than our best. Further, for the worst U.S. producer, about one of every four units required a service call (rate = 26.5). Garvin also discovered that the highest-quality producers had both the highest productivity (as measured by output per man-hour) and the lowest warranty costs. (For one U.S. manufacturer, warranty costs were 7% of sales; at the worst Japanese plant, the figure was 1%.) Of course, these results are perfectly consistent with Deming's chain reaction.

1ST YEAR SERVICE CALL RATE PER 100 UNITS

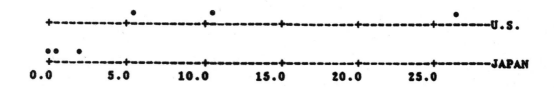

---

[1]David Garvin, *Managing Quality* (New York: Free Press, 1988), p. 200.

Garvin does, however, offer some cause for optimism. He notes that the perspective toward quality taken by top management at many organizations has shifted. CEO's have begun linking quality more closely with profitability, thereby causing quality to be viewed as an important competitive weapon. Consequently, some companies now include quality as an integral part of their strategic planning. Their goals often include an organization-wide commitment to quality, which then becomes integrated with other business objectives.

The quality movement has progressed into what is known as total quality management (TQM) company-wide quality control (CWQC), or continuous quality improvement (CQI). Whatever the name, the philosophy draws on elements from a variety of disciplines; e.g. psychology/organizational behavior, marketing research, and statistics. The latter is naturally what is emphasized here, and this chapter introduces one of the most important statistical tools: control charts.

VARIATION IN PRODUCTS AND SERVICES

Consider a process to be a set of related activities designed to accomplish some goal. Then, any product or service is the output or result of a process. (In fact, all work can be viewed as a process.) Unfortunately, for both managers and consumers, all processes exhibit variation. Kaoru Ishikawa, the Japanese quality expert, has noted:

> Even when the same person uses the same material, the same equipment, and the same method to produce something, effects will still vary. People may think that under a uniform process, uniform effects will occur, but they are wrong. As long as we have people who follow this pattern of thinking, we can never be free of false data from industries and workplaces.[2]

The developer of the control chart, Walter Shewhart, used a simple illustration to illustrate process variability: writing. I wrote the following letters very carefully:

$$9\ 9\ 9\ \ 9\ \ 9\ \ 9\ 9\ \ 9\ 9\ 9$$

---

[2]Ishikawa, *What is Total Quality Control?*, p. 68.

but, the variation is evident despite my care. We view such variation as routine, expected, and normal. Now, consider the next set of letters:

now you may notice something odd about the third letter. Perhaps my arm was bumped then, or perhaps someone else made the third letter? Actually, I made it, but with my right hand rather than my left. (I'm left handed.) In any event, the variation in the second set of "output from the process" is not routine or expected, and we wondered about the reason for the excessive variation.

Similarly, items produced in a machining or other manufacturing process are not all exactly alike. Each measurable dimension (e.g., length, diameter, weight) will vary to some extent, and quite often the measurements will follow a normal distribution. Because these variations are very small (perhaps as small as a few thousandths of an inch), the parts may appear to the naked eye to be identical. Precision gauges or test equipment, however, will reveal the differences. Since many of today's products are subject to very tight limits of variability, and excessive variability leads to rejects and waste, the control of variation is a major concern of those managing a process.

COMMON CAUSE VERSUS SPECIAL CAUSE VARIATION

Shewhart's writing examples help illustrate that process variation—i.e., the variability in the process' products—can be thought of as having two sources: common causes and special causes.

A **common cause** reflects routine variation inherent in any process.
A **special or assignable cause** reflects *additional* variation associated with a specific occurrence.
All processes exhibit common cause variation. *Some* processes have, in addition, special cause variation.

From the dictionary, the word "common" has meanings such as general, prevalent, ordinary, widespread, etc., and that is exactly the interpretation here. Common cause variation is general, routine variation that is "built-in";

it is a continuing characteristic of the process. Conversely, special cause variation occurs intermittently and is associated with a specific event, e.g., writing a letter with a different hand. **The ability to determine the presence (or absence) of special cause variation is crucial for effective management.** It is extremely important to make this determination because the two situations require very different actions for improvement of the process, e.g., more consistent, legible letters. As Deming points out, "Discovery of a special cause of variation, and its removal, are usually the responsibility of someone who is connected directly with some operation ..." He also recommends that "one should search at once for a special cause, once it is detected, before the trail goes cold." However, if only common cause variation is present, searching for a special cause will be, at best, futile and possibly make matters considerably worse. Common cause variation can be reduced only by changing the process, which is usually a managerial responsibility. Consider the following lists:

COMMON CAUSES
raw materials
machinery not suited to requirements
excessive dust
poor light
inadequate training
over-riding management emphasis on quantity
maintenance practices
poor design

SPECIAL CAUSES
poor eyesight
change in supplier (though both old and new met specs)
substance abuse
new employee
air-conditioning problems
measuring instrument malfunction
equipment failure
illness

Special causes can sometimes be addressed by individual workers, but common causes can be corrected only through management action. (If the raw materials are inadequate, can the worker change the requirements? If the equipment is ill-suited, can the worker authorize a capital expenditure?) In order to help determine the nature of variation, Shewhart developed the control chart. Since its appearance in the 1920s it has spread around the world and from line operations to executive offices.

A CONTROL CHART FOR PROPORTION DEFECTIVE: THE P CHART

The control chart is a simple yet powerful tool for determining the presence of special cause variation. The name "control" chart may be somewhat misleading as it does not control anything; rather, "control" reflects Shewhart's terminology when he introduced these ideas.

A process with only common cause variation is also said to be a **stable process** or **in control.**

A process that *also* demonstrates special cause variation is said to be an **unstable process** or **out of control.**

Thus, the chart is used to determine if the process is "in control" or "out of control." Several types of control charts have been developed; this section introduces the simplest one: a chart for proportion defective.

The most elementary form of inspection of a good or service classifies the outcome as either satisfactory or unsatisfactory (variations of this include good/defective, pass/fail, conforming/nonconforming, accept/reject, and go/no go). Examples illustrating this idea are:

GOOD/SERVICE	OUTCOMES
Bid/Proposal	Awarded/Not Awarded Contract
Lawn Mower	Crank/Not Crank on First Pull
Car Windshield	No/Some Visible Flaws
Plane Departure	On Time/Late
Invoice	Correct/Incorrect
Mechanical Assembly	Works/Does Not Work
Fast Food Order	Order Filled Correctly/Incorrectly

In any case, there are only two possible outcomes of the inspection of an item, and the results of an inspection of a sample of items are usually summarized by reporting **p, the proportion defective in the sample.**

When the sample size n is large, the sample proportion p is normally distributed with mean = π (the process proportion defective) and standard deviation = σ_p. Further, if the process is subject to only common cause variation, then variation in the proportion defective p from sample to sample is merely random variation. The question of whether a process is stable (only common cause variation) or unstable then becomes: Is the variation in p larger than what would ordinarily be observed from random variation? Figure 2 helps explain the situation.

The figure shows that almost all (99.7%) of the p's would have a value between $\pi + 3\sigma_p$ and $\pi - 3\sigma_p$ where

$$\sigma_p = \sqrt{\frac{\pi(1-\pi)}{n}}$$

A characteristic of a stable process is that the values of p occur randomly between the two limits.

Since a process is a continuing, dynamic phenomenon, its "status" could change from stable to unstable at any time. Hence, samples should be taken on a continuing regular basis, e.g. daily. Since the various samples are observed sequentially, one plot of the data could the run or sequence chart. In fact, the control chart is a run chart modified by the addition of a center line and two control limits. The center line represents the average of all the p's used to set up the chart (a *minimum of 20* samples is often suggested):

$$\bar{p} = \frac{\sum_{i=1}^{k} p_i}{k} = \frac{\sum p}{k} \tag{1}$$

where k = number of different samples with each being of the same size n. Then, the limits are obtained from:

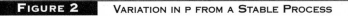

FIGURE 2	**VARIATION IN P FROM A STABLE PROCESS**

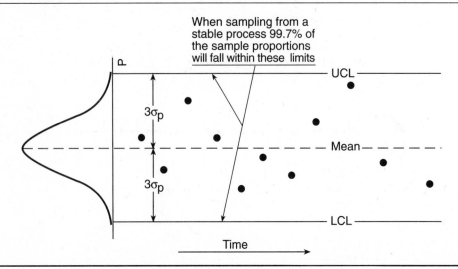

UCL $\quad$ = $\quad$ Upper control limit

$$= \quad \bar{p} + 3\hat{\sigma}_p \qquad\qquad (2)$$

LCL = Lower control limit

$$= \quad \bar{p} - 3\hat{\sigma}_p \qquad\qquad (3)$$

and, $\quad \hat{\sigma}_p = \quad \sqrt{\dfrac{\bar{p}(1 - \bar{p})}{n}} \qquad\qquad (4)$

An example to illustrate the computations and ideas is in order.

EXAMPLE: Doris Gordon is Claims Manager for HomeSure Inc., whose primary business is homeowners' insurance. She recently noticed that one of her assistants had a large stack of claims to be returned to local agents because of mistakes and/or omissions in the claim reports. Doris knows that returning a form for correction will delay payment to the homeowner (and thus decrease their satisfaction with HomeSure); further, this extra paperwork increases the cost of processing a claim and decreases HomeSure's profitability. She is tempted to go through the stack to see if she can determine which agent or agents has the most errors so corrective (disciplinary?) action can be initiated. (I.e., her initial reaction, like that of many managers, is to suspect a special cause is at work.) Instead, she decides to undertake an analysis of the problem. For the next four weeks (20 work days) Doris personally takes a random sample of 50 claims each day and examines them for errors before passing them on to her staff for processing. The results of her efforts are given below.

Day	Claims With Error	Proportion With Errors, p	Day	Claims With Error	Proportion With Errors, p
1	7	0.14	11	9	0.18
2	4	0.08	12	4	0.08
3	5	0.10	13	7	0.14
4	7	0.14	14	5	0.10
5	5	0.10	15	6	0.12
6	5	0.10	16	6	0.12
7	5	0.10	17	1	0.02
8	7	0.14	18	7	0.14
9	2	0.04	19	4	0.08
10	6	0.12	20	5	0.10

Then, $\bar{p}$ = $\quad \Sigma p/k = 2.14/20 = .1070$

$$\text{and, } \hat{\sigma}_p = \sqrt{\frac{\bar{p}(1-\bar{p})}{n}} = \sqrt{\frac{.107(.893)}{50}} = \sqrt{.00191} = \sqrt{0.437}$$

$$\begin{aligned}
\text{UCL} &= \bar{p} + 3\hat{\sigma}_p \\
&= .1070 + 3(.0437) = .1070 + .1311 = .2381
\end{aligned}$$

$$\text{LCL} = \bar{p} - 3\hat{\sigma}_p = .1070 - .1311 = -.0241$$

Note that the LCL is a negative number, but a proportion cannot be less than zero. **If the LCL for a p chart is negative, the LCL is undefined.**

Figure 3 is the p chart for Doris' claims data; the chart was prepared on a personal computer using Minitab.

When Doris studied the p chart, she found no evidence of special cause variation, and she concluded that this was a stable process. The variation in p (even though from .02 to .18) is consistent with random, sampling variation. Since the process is stable, i.e., in control, she could forecast the percentage error in tomorrow's claims: 10.7%! She also knows to decrease this

| **FIGURE 3** | **CHART FOR CLAIMS DATA** |

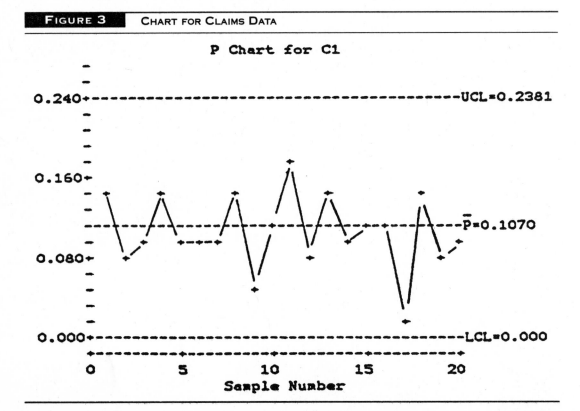

rate (and thus improve quality, productivity, and profitability), the *process* needs managerial attention, not certain districts or individual agents. Perhaps the claims form can be simplified, or perhaps agents were not instructed in this area during their training. She begins by calling a few agents and HomeSure's training director to get their views.

OTHER TESTS FOR SPECIAL CAUSE VARIATION

The previous discussion has mentioned only one indicator of special cause variation: a result outside of the control limits. However, other tests have been developed and are often recommended in the quality literature. These other tests' signals are based on looking for contradictions to the random behavior of a process in statistical control. (Harry Roberts' book, *Data Analysis for Managers,* has an excellent discussion of this matter in Chapter 1. Roberts reminds us that random behavior is "patternless.")

One example of a pattern would be the observation of nine points in a row on the same side of the center line $\bar{p}$. Since we have assumed large samples and thus a normal distribution for p, the probability that nine consecutive results would be less than the mean of the distribution is $(.5)^9 = .001953 \approx .002$, a very unusual occurrence that we will ascribe to the presence of special cause variation. Another pattern indicative of nonrandomness would be a run (six or more) of points steadily increasing or decreasing; this is called a **trend** in the data. These two additional signals will be considered a routine part of our search for special cause variation. Figure 4 summarizes this discussion.

There are other signals of special cause variation (see the Supplement at the end of the chapter), but no more will be elaborated on here. Remember, a point beyond the limits or an upward run may occur purely as a result of chance; if so, a false signal has been detected and a futile search for an assignable/special cause will take place. Using only the three tests above, the probability of getting a false signal is about one in a hundred. However, if a computer is used to create and analyze the control chart, more tests may easily be applied in the expectation of earlier detection of an unstable process. (For example, Minitab has eight tests available; the ones recommended above are Tests 1, 2, and 3.) Please remember no software detects all unusual patterns. For example, if every fifth point were below the center line, the software would *not* draw your attention to this occurrence; so don't blindly rely on the computer.

THE $\overline{X}$ AND R CHARTS

The p chart enjoys widespread use in business because inspections can often result in only a defective/nondefective outcome. For instance, when

FIGURE 4 ILLUSTRATION OF (PANEL A) ONLY COMMON VARIATION AND (PANELS B, C, AND D) THE ADDITION OF SPECIAL CAUSE VARIATION

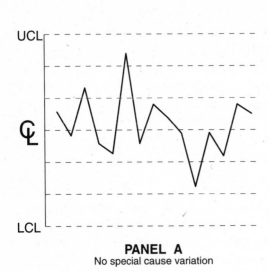

PANEL A

No special cause variation

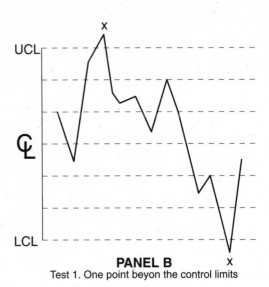

PANEL B

Test 1. One point beyon the control limits

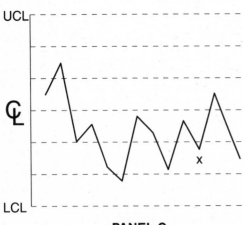

PANEL C

Test 2. Nine points in a row on one side or center line

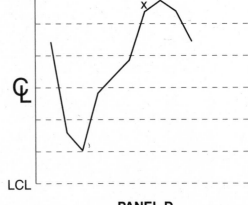

PANEL D

Test 3. Six points in a row, all increasing or all decreasing

inspections rely totally on human judgment to classify the product or service, there are no gauges, no measurements. The legibility of a fax copy or the finish on an office desk are judged by an observer, whether inspector or consumer. In these situations, the p chart is invaluable. However, in many other situations an actual measurement (e.g., length, weight, voltage, purity) can be made with an instrument, and the *quantitative* variable's values then recorded.

When defects are measured in parts per million (ppm), the use of quantitative variables becomes imperative in quality improvement efforts. (A 1992 *Wall Street Journal* article[3] reported companywide defects at Motorola of 30 ppm.) A defect rate of 30 ppm means a proportion defective of .00003, and even large samples of n = 1000 would then have *no* defects about 97% of the time. Thus, 97 samples out every 100 would show the same sample proportion: p = 0; not much of an opportunity here to study variation! However, we shall see that when quantitative variables are measured, samples of only three, four, or five items yield significant, useful information.

Control charts based on data for a quantitative variable are useful, even for small samples, because the data are "information rich." Now, each sample can be described in various ways by citing the mean, median, range, standard deviation, standard error, minimum, maximum etc. As usual though, we will focus on the two principal characteristics: central tendency (which we measure by the mean $\bar{x}$) and variability (which we measure first by the range R and later briefly discuss the standard deviation s). We shall see that a control chart can be developed for each of these statistics ($\bar{x}$, R, and s), but they will share several characteristics of the earlier p chart.

1. The values of the statistic are plotted on a run chart.
2. A centerline is added at the average value of the statistic.
3. Control limits are added at plus and minus three standard deviations from the centerline.
4. The resulting control chart is named according to the statistic being plotted, e.g. p chart or $\bar{x}$ chart.
5. Appropriate tests are made to determine if the process generating the data/statistics is in control or if special cause variation is present.

When only common cause variation is present, the process is stable or in-control, see Figure 5 A. Because the process is stable, each sample of size n = 3 can be viewed as having come from the same distribution. We know,

---

[3]G. Christian Hill, and Ken Yamada, "Motorola Illustrates How an Aged Giant Can Remain Vibrant," *The Wall Street Journal*, December 9, 1992: A1.

FIGURE 5	SAMPLING FROM (A) A STABLE PROCESS AND (B) AN UNSTABLE PROCESS

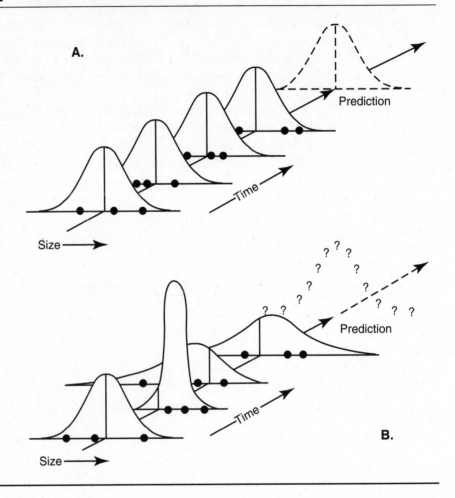

nevertheless, that the various samples over time consist of different values, and the descriptive statistics for the samples (say $\bar{x}$ and R) would also exhibit variation. But the variation would be routine, "normal" variation.

In Figure 5 B, special causes of variation are present, and the samples are not coming from the same distribution; the distributions are different because of a change in center/location, variability/spread, or both. When this is the case, the samples' statistics will exhibit abnormal (usually excessive) variation when the $\bar{x}$ and R charts are examined. For reasons to be explained, the R (or s) chart should be constructed first and studied for any out-of-control signals.

THE R CHART

When measures of variation are reviewed, the standard deviation is usually the preferred measure. However, in this chapter we emphasize the range. Why? For two reasons. First, the range is easily calculated and understood by anyone (no need for calculators or computers), and often control charts are constructed by a statistical layperson. Second, and more important, for small samples the range provides almost all of the information that would be provided by the sample standard deviation. The relative efficiency of the range to the standard deviation is:

Sample Size	Relative Efficiency
2	1.000
3	.992
4	.975
5	.955
6	.930

Control charts $\bar{x}$ and R almost always use small samples. For example, Ishikawa recommends a sample (or subgroup) size of n = 2 to 5. He also says "the subgroup size is sometimes taken as n = 6 to 10 in special cases, but it is better to split larger subgroups like these into smaller ones of size 5 or less." Note for these small samples ($n \le 5$), the range is very efficient (.955 or greater) vis-a-vis the more complex standard deviation. We suggest selecting the R chart over the s chart unless one has larger samples, say n > 10.

The centerline for the R chart will be at the mean of the R's:

$$\bar{R} = \frac{\Sigma R}{k} \tag{5}$$

where k is, as with the p chart, the number of samples of size n obtained from the process and recommended to be at least twenty. The control limits for the R charts are based on the usual relation: mean $\pm$ 3 standard deviations; however, the end result looks somewhat different:

$$UCL = D_4 \bar{R} \tag{6}$$

and

$$LCL = D_3 \bar{R} \tag{7}$$

D_3 and D_4 are coefficients whose values are determined by the sample/subgroup size, n. Values for these, and some others we shall need shortly, are given in Table 1. (For the development of Equations 6 and 7, see the footnote on the following page.)[4]

| TABLE 1 | COEFFICIENTS FOR $N \leq 10$ | | | |

| Sample size | | | | |
n	D3	D4	d2	A2
2	*	3.267	1.128	1.880
3	*	2.574	1.693	1.023
4	*	2.282	2.059	0.729
5	*	2.114	2.326	0.577
6	*	2.004	2.534	0.483
7	0.076	1.924	2.704	0.419
8	0.136	1.864	2.847	0.373
9	0.184	1.816	2.970	0.337
10	0.223	1.777	3.078	0.308

[4]If the process variable being studied (i.e., the X values) has a normal distribution and if the process is stable, statistical theory tells us that the distribution's standard deviation can be estimated by:

$$\hat{\sigma}_x = \frac{\overline{R}}{d_2},$$

where d_2 is a constant determined by the samples' size. We also know that the standard deviation of R, σ_R, can be estimated by

$$\hat{\sigma}_R = d_3 \, \hat{\sigma}_x.$$

Putting these two results together

$$\hat{\sigma}_R = d_3 \, \hat{\sigma}_x = d_3 \, \frac{\overline{R}}{d_2} = \frac{d_3}{d_2} \overline{R}$$

Values of d2 are given in Table 1; select values of d_3 are given below.

n:	2	3	4	5
d_3:	.853	.888	.880	.864

The control limits for R are given by:

$$\overline{R} \pm 3\hat{\sigma}_R.$$

For the upper limit,

$$\text{UCL} = \overline{R} + 3\hat{\sigma}_R = \overline{R} + 3\frac{d_3}{d_2} \overline{R}$$
$$= \left(1 + 3\frac{d_3}{d_2}\right) \overline{R} = D_4 \, \overline{R}.$$

Values of D_4 are given in Table 1 for example, when n = 4,

$$D_4 = 1 + 3\frac{d_3}{d_2} = 1 + 3\left(\frac{.880}{2.059}\right) = 1 + 1.282 = 2.282.$$

Similarly,

$$\text{LCL} = \overline{R} - 3\hat{\sigma}_R = \overline{R} - 3\frac{d_3}{d_2} \overline{R}$$
$$= \left(1 - 3\frac{d_3}{d_2}\right) \overline{R} = D_3 \, \overline{R}.$$

If, as when n = 4, D_3 results in a negative value, D_3 is set to undefined. The range, by definition R = MAX − MIN, cannot be negative.

Note that the table has missing values (i.e., '*') for D_3 when n is less than or equal to six. This means **there is NO lower control limit for R if $n \leq 6$.** Some texts record zero for $D_3 = 0$ when $n \leq 6$; instead, remember the LCL in this case is said to be missing or not defined.

When the R chart is completed, it is examined for any of the three out-of-control signals discussed earlier. If one of the signals is detected, a search begins for a special or assignable cause. Remember that the R chart reflects variation or inconsistency within samples; thus, the AT&T *Quality Control Handbook* recommends looking for "poor repair or poor maintenance if this is a machine-controlled process ... for new operators or something disturbing the operators if this is an operator-controlled process" (p. 30). Special causes affecting the R chart could then include worker fatigue, worn tools, etc. In any event, the hunt for the special cause should begin as soon as possible while "the trail is warm" and memories are fresh. **If the special cause can be ascertained for a particular sample, that sample should be dropped from the data, and the centerline and control limits recomputed.**

EXAMPLE: Thirty samples each of size five were obtained from a process in order to set up the R and $\bar{x}$ charts. For the R chart, the range was determined for each sample and summed to yield 184.50. The centerline was determined using Equation 5:

$$\bar{R} = \frac{\Sigma R}{K} = \frac{184.50}{30} = 6.15$$

The control limits were determined using Equations 6 and 7 and coefficients D_3 and D_4 obtained from Table 1.

LCL $= D_3 \bar{R} = $ * since $n \leq 6,$
UCL $= D_4 \bar{R} = 2.114\,(6.15) = 13.00$

The R chart was set up with the values above and then examined for signs of special cause variation. The entire procedure will be illustrated in detail after the following introduction of the $\bar{x}$ chart.

THE $\bar{x}$ CHART

The R chart shows the variation of the values within the k samples of size n being studied. When the R chart shows control—i.e., no evidence of the presence of special causes—the $\bar{x}$ chart can then be prepared. The reason for doing the R chart first is that the process standard deviation (σ) and thus the standard error of the mean ($\sigma_{\bar{x}} = \sigma/\sqrt{n}$) are estimated from the R chart. If the R chart is out of control, there is no *single* process standard deviation; rather, the samples are drawn from distributions having *different* standard deviations instead of a common, constant one. (Refer back to Figure 5.) Assuming the R chart is in control, we can estimate the process standard deviation from

$$\hat{\sigma} = \frac{\bar{R}}{d_2} \tag{8}$$

where d_2 is a constant based on the sample size n; values for d_2 are given in Table 1.

The control chart for $\bar{x}$ has a centerline given by:

$$\bar{\bar{x}} = \frac{\Sigma\bar{x}}{k} \tag{9}$$

where $\bar{\bar{x}}$ is simply the mean of the k sample means. The control limits for the $\bar{x}$ chart are based on the usual relation: mean ± 3 standard deviations, where here the "standard deviation" is the standard deviation of the sample mean, i.e. the standard error of the mean. Since Equation 8 yields an estimate of the process standard deviation, then the standard error of the mean is estimated by:

$$\hat{\sigma}_{\bar{x}} = \frac{\hat{\sigma}}{\sqrt{n}} = \frac{1}{\sqrt{n}} \cdot \frac{\bar{R}}{d_2}$$

The control limits are given by:

$$\bar{\bar{x}} \pm 3\hat{\sigma}_{\bar{x}}$$

$$= \bar{\bar{x}} \pm 3\frac{1}{\sqrt{n}} \cdot \frac{\bar{R}}{d_2}$$

$$= \bar{\bar{x}} \pm \frac{3}{d_2\sqrt{n}} \cdot \bar{R}$$

Then, letting $A_2 = \dfrac{3}{d_2\sqrt{n}}$

$$UCL = \bar{\bar{x}} + A_2\bar{R} \tag{10}$$

and

$$LCL = \bar{\bar{x}} - A_2\bar{R} \tag{11}$$

Values for A_2 are given in Table 1.

EXAMPLE: To verify a value of A_2, let $n = 4$; from Table 1, $d_2 = 2.059$. Then,

$$\frac{3}{d_2\sqrt{n}} = \frac{3}{2.059\sqrt{4}} = \frac{3}{(2.059)2} = \frac{3}{4.118} = .729,$$

which is the value reported for A_2 in the table.

When the $\bar{x}$ chart is completed, it is examined for any of the three out-of-control signals previously discussed. If the chart is not in-control, samples which indicate an abnormality should be investigated for special causes. If/when the special causes can be found and rectified, the affected samples should be dropped from the data, and the centerline and control limits recalculated. Should new samples then exhibit special cause variation, they too are investigated and subsequently dropped if the cause can be ascertained.

The search for special causes will be more effective if we follow the suggestions of the AT&T *Quality Control Handbook*. (By the way, two units of AT&T each won a Malcolm Baldrige National Quality Award in 1992.) The handbook defines **direct or "true"** $\bar{x}$ **causes** as "causes capable of affecting an $\bar{x}$ chart directly... when they [direct causes] enter the process they are capable of affecting all the product at once or in the same general way... **This type of cause is able to shift the *center* of a distribution without affecting its spread.** It is the most common type of cause which shows up on the $\bar{x}$ chart" (p. 152). For example, if a manufacturer changes to a new type or grade of raw material, all subsequent output using this material could be changed in a significant fashion. Changes in operators, suppliers, procedures, machinery, or the environment (e.g., install air-conditioning) could also be a direct $\bar{x}$ cause. The handbook also defines **indirect or "false"** $\bar{x}$ **causes as causes that show up on *both* the $\bar{x}$ and R charts, but are in reality "R-type causes."** For example, if an unusually large value appeared in a sample, the mean would be heavily influenced by the outlier , and that sample's $\bar{x}$ might fall above the UCL. But, the "true source" is the *variation* in the values. Hence, the *Quality Control Handbook* advises:

> **Do not attempt to interpret an x̄ chart while the R chart is out of control. Eliminate the R causes first and the chances are that the x̄ causes will disappear along with them.**

EXAMPLE: Twenty-five samples, each of size three, were obtained to set up R and x̄ charts. The R chart had been prepared and studied, and appeared to be in control with $\overline{R} = 9.20$. The sum of the sample means had been calculated and was equal to 827.50. For the x̄ chart, the centerline was determined with Equation 9:

$$\overline{\overline{x}} = \frac{\Sigma \overline{x}}{k} = \frac{827.50}{25} = 33.10$$

The control limits are given by:

$$\begin{aligned} UCL &= \overline{\overline{x}} + A_2\overline{R} \\ &= 33.10 + (1.023)9.20 \\ &= 33.10 + 9.41 \\ &= 42.51 \end{aligned}$$

Similarly, $LCL = \overline{\overline{x}} - A_2\overline{R} = 33.10 - 9.41 = 23.69$. Now for a more detailed illustration.

EXAMPLE: Customer satisfaction is a fundamental goal of Total Quality Management (TQM). When Park Nicollet Medical Center (PNMC) in Minneapolis began its TQM program, a patient satisfaction survey was undertaken to help direct PNMC's efforts. They found that telephone access was clearly the leading cause of patient dissatisfaction. Although there are many dimensions to telephone access (e.g., access to whom: receptionist, nurse, or physician?), PNMC's major focus was on time to answer (TIME, measured in seconds) for the medical information nurse; this time occasionally ran as long as 600 seconds = 10 minutes! (Although the following data are not real, the example illustrates a part of PNMC's successful analysis. A more detailed report of this and other quality improvement projects is available in *Curing Health Care* cited in the References.)

Patients phone their health care provider for a variety of reasons: to learn test results, have a prescription drug ordered, etc. Delays are frustrating as evidenced by the patient survey. The family practice department gathered data for twenty days between 9:00 and 10:00 a.m., one of the busiest times of the day. Four calls to the medical information (MI) nurse were sampled each period, and the nurse's time to answer, TIME, was recorded for each call. The data and each sample's mean ($\bar{x}$) and range (R) are reported on the following range chart.

The range chart was constructed and analyzed first, for reasons mentioned earlier. The mean range was calculated:

$$\bar{R} = \frac{\Sigma R}{k} = \frac{3986.0}{20} = 199.3$$

For subgroups or sample of size n = 4, the values of D_3 and D_4 from TABLE 1 are undefined and 2.282 respectively; therefore there will be no LCL for R. The UCL is given by:

$$\begin{aligned} \text{UCL} &= D_4\,\bar{R} \\ &= 2.282(199.3) \\ &= 454.80 \end{aligned}$$

Now with the centerline and control limits, the R chart can be constructed; see Figure 6. (Note: the lines connecting successive values of R were added "by hand" with a straight edge.)

A quick look at the R chart shows an out-of-control point for the fourth sample (i.e., day 4); its R = 522. The data show that two of the four sampled calls for day 4 had very large values of time: 580 and 453 seconds (these are the two largest values of the entire dataset; the next largest is 387). The

ROW	1ST CALL	2ND CALL	3RD CALL	4TH CALL	MEAN	RANGE
1	102	282	71	143	149.50	211
2	245	106	387	312	262.50	281
3	319	104	230	168	205.25	215
4	169	580	58	453	315.00	522
5	132	159	289	334	228.50	202
6	380	191	163	351	271.25	217
7	165	64	194	247	167.50	183
8	183	347	22	218	192.50	325
9	261	293	261	288	275.75	32
10	181	179	352	215	231.75	173
11	187	366	218	327	274.50	179
12	243	166	242	5	164.00	238
13	226	96	370	84	194.00	286
14	153	169	292	186	200.00	139
15	165	304	187	155	202.75	149
16	333	106	276	330	261.25	227
17	180	167	249	233	207.25	82
18	207	141	205	195	187.00	66
19	290	128	228	166	203.00	162
20	117	131	214	171	158.25	97

team analyzing the data undertook a search for a special or assignable cause. They learned that on this particular day, the MI nurse had experienced a 24 hour intestinal flu virus that caused her to be away from her desk off and on throughout the morning. Having ascertained the special cause, the team dropped day 4 from the data (now k = 19) and developed a revised range chart for TIME with

$$\overline{R} = \frac{\Sigma R}{k} = \frac{3464}{19} = 182.32$$

and

$$\begin{aligned} UCL &= D_4\,\overline{R} \\ &= 2.282\,(182.3) \\ &= 416.1 \end{aligned}$$

FIGURE 6 $\overline{R}$ CHART FOR TIME

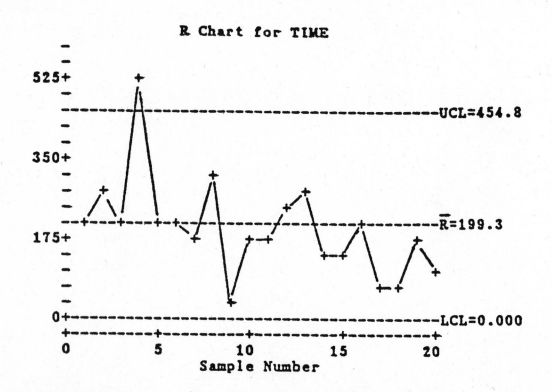

R Chart for TIME

This new R chart is shown in Figure 7. (Note: With Minitab's high resolution graphics command GRCHART, the software connects successive observations.)

A study of Figure 7 reveals no out-of-control signals; there are

1. no points beyond the control limits
2. no long runs on one side of the center line
3. no long runs up or down, i.e. no trending as discussed earlier.

Since the R chart was in control, the $\bar{x}$ chart was then constructed with the values for day 4 omitted.

$$\bar{\bar{x}} = \frac{\Sigma \bar{x}}{k} = \frac{4036.5}{19} = 212.4$$

FIGURE 7   REVISED $\bar{R}$ CHART FOR TIME

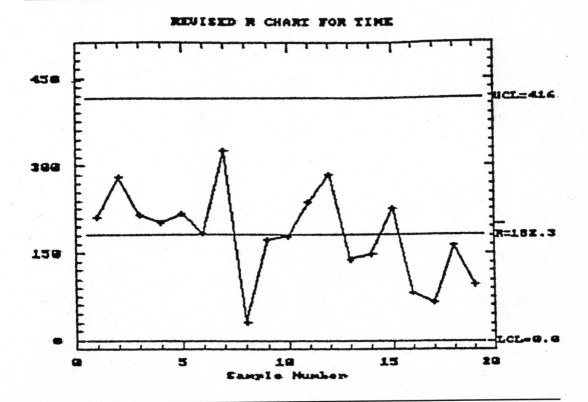

and,

$$LCL = \bar{\bar{x}} - A_2\bar{R}$$
$$= 212.4 - (.729)(182.3)$$
$$= 212.4 - 132.9 = 79.5$$
$$UCL = \bar{\bar{x}} + A_2\bar{R}$$
$$= 212.4 + 132.9 = 345.3.$$

The $\bar{x}$ chart is shown in Figure 8.

An examination of Figure 8 shows no problems with any of our three tests for special cause variation; there is only common cause variation. Of course, in conjunction with the stable R chart, this is indicative of a stable, predictable process. Thus, we predict that in the future, patients will have to hold an average of 212 seconds or about *three-and-a half minutes* to get to the MI nurse.

FIGURE 8   REVISED X-BAR CHART FOR TIME

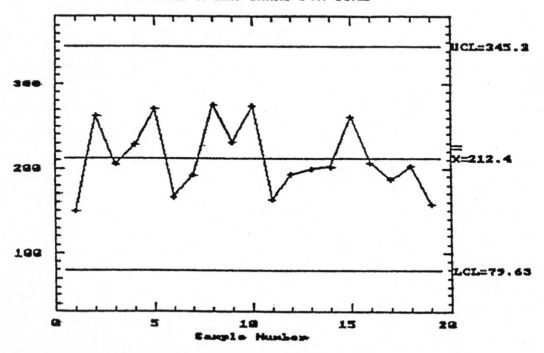

(To see how long this is, just pick up your phone and hold it for three or four minutes.) This prediction or expectation can be changed only through changing/improving the process. In fact, that's exactly what happened at Park Nicollet Medical Center. PNMC initiated a number of changes including having the MI nurse's schedule moved to a slightly earlier time of the day and by staffing one additional person during the busiest hours. The changes made at PNMC cut the average value of TIME by about one-half and thus improved patient satisfaction.

THE S CHART

The s chart is also used to measure the variation within samples, and can be used as an alternative to the R chart. When using the latter, the standard deviation, s, of each of the k samples is calculated, and these are the values to be plotted. The centerline of the s chart is given by:

$$\bar{s} = \frac{\Sigma s}{k} \tag{12}$$

and the control limits are at $\bar{s} \pm 3\hat{\sigma}_s$. Equations for these limits are usually calculated by:

$$UCL = B_4 \, \bar{s} \tag{13}$$

$$LCL = B_3 \, \bar{s} \tag{14}$$

The $\bar{x}$ chart could then be determined using $\bar{s}$; its centerline would be at $\bar{\bar{x}}$ and limits at $\bar{\bar{x}} \pm A_3 \, \bar{s}$. The coefficients, B_4, B_3, and A_3, are not reported herein, but are available in many books on quality and/or statistical process control (SPC). These are not included here because the range chart is usually preferred over the s chart for the reasons discussed earlier. *If* you can prepare your charts on a computer using statistical software similar to Minitab and *particularly if* your samples are large (n > 10), then, by all means, use the s and $\bar{x}$ charts; however, such conditions should be encountered rather rarely.

PROCESS CAPABILITY

Suppliers of goods and services strive to furnish their customers with products that meet or exceed the customers expectations; otherwise, the customer may select a new supplier in the future. The customer's needs are expressed in such statements as "I need this package delivered by tomorrow at noon," or "The length of the part shall be 5.125 inches ± .005 inches." These statements specify characteristics the "product" (good or service) must possess to be acceptable, and are referred to as specifications or specs. As concerns manufactured goods, the specs $5.125 ± .005$ inches is a compact summary of three standards:

1. the **target (or nominal) value T** = 5.125 *desired value*
2. the **upper spec limit USL** = 5.130
3. the **lower spec limit LSL** = 5.120.

The specs are thus the customer's definition of allowable or tolerable variation in the product, and this allowable variation = USL − LSL is sometimes referred to as the **tolerance.**

This chapter earlier discussed the idea of a stable process: a process free from special cause variation, a process that is predictable, one that has *a* mean and *a* standard deviation. The process mean and process standard deviation, estimated by $\bar{x}$ and $\overline{R}/d_2$ respectively, are determined from and by the process without reference to any external standards, e.g., customer specifications. When customer needs become known (new customer) or change (old customer), both the producer/supplier and customer want to "know about the process" in reference to product specs. In other words, they both want information about the process's ability to produce products that satisfy customer specs. Measures of process capability attempt to provide such information in quantitative form, and this section discusses two of them.

FIGURE 9   PROCESS DISTRIBUTION AND SPECIFICATION LIMITS

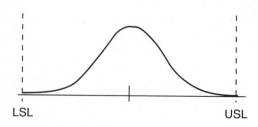
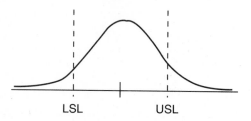

LSL   USL   LSL   USL

C_p: THE PROCESS POTENTIAL INDEX

Process capability can be defined in several ways and, thus, several alternative measures have been developed. The first measure we discuss, C_p, focuses on allowable variation versus the natural variation of the process. C_p, like all the process capability measures discussed here, assumes (1) the process is stable/in-control and (2) the process output is normally distributed. Figure 9 shows two possible situations.

The left figure shows a stable process where all output appears to be comfortably within specs, and the process is said to be capable. The right figure shows a stable process with considerable output that will fail to meet specs, and such a process is said to be not capable. (The second figure also serves to remind us that even though a process is stable, it may be quite unsatisfactory and in need of improvement.) C_p measures process capability by expressing the ratio of allowable variation from the specs to "natural" variation of the process:

$$C_p = \frac{\text{allowable variation (or specification width)}}{\text{"natural" variation in process}} \qquad (15)$$

$$= \frac{USL - LSL}{6\,\hat{\sigma}}$$

where $\hat{\sigma}$ is the estimated process standard deviation and is obtained by $\hat{\sigma} = \overline{R}/d_2$. Note that neither the estimated process mean $\overline{\overline{x}}$ nor the target value T appear in Equation 15; this is because C_p assumes they are equal. **A process is said to be centered if $\overline{\overline{x}} = T$.**

EXAMPLE: Specifications on a dimension of a part are 220.00 ± 10 mm. The production process for this part is stable with $\overline{R} = 11.63$ (with $n = 5$). Determine the value of C_p. First, from the specs,

$$USL = 220 + 10 = 230$$
$$LSL = 220 - 10 = 210.$$

Then, the estimated process standard deviation is given by:

$$\hat{\sigma} = \frac{\overline{R}}{d_2} = \frac{11.63}{2.326} = 5.00.$$

Using Equation (15),

$$C_p = \frac{USL - LSL}{6\,\hat{\sigma}}$$

$$= \frac{230 - 210}{6(5)} = \frac{20}{30} = .67.$$

Traditionally, a process with a $C_p < 1.00$ is termed not capable. (More recently, however, the minimum required value for capability has been rising, more on this later.) What exactly does this $C_p = .67$ mean? Under the assumptions of a centered, stable process with a normally distributed output, the proportion of out-of-spec product is obtained using the Z transformation and a table of the standard normal distribution.

$$Z = \frac{X - \mu}{\sigma}$$

$$= \frac{230 - 220}{5} = \frac{10}{5} = 2.00$$

Then, from a table of standard normal distribution,

$$\begin{aligned}
P(X > 230) &= P(Z > 2.00) \\
&= 1 - P(Z \le 2.00) \\
&= 1 - .97725 = .02275
\end{aligned}$$

Because of symmetry,

$$P(Z < 210) \text{ is also } .02275 \text{ so that}$$

$$P(\text{out-of-specs}) = .02275 + .02275 = .0455$$

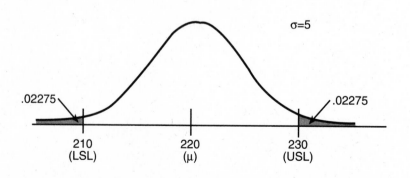

Thus, about 4.5% of the output will fail to meet customer specs. Expressed on a parts per million (ppm) basis, defective ppm = 45,500! Table 2 below relates defective ppm to various values of C_p.

C_{PK}: THE PROCESS PERFORMANCE INDEX

Another measure of process capability is C_{PK}, the process performance index. Like C_p, C_{PK} assumes the process is stable and that output is normally distributed. Unlike C_p, this measure uses both the process standard deviation *and* the process mean in assessing capability; in particular, C_{PK} does *not* assume the process is centered. Furthermore, C_{PK} is also defined for unilateral specifications which occur when only **one** limit is specified (either USL or LSL) and the other limit is open-ended. For example, the tensile strength of wire might be specified with only the LSL, the customer defined minimum acceptable breaking strength. Or, a utility with a coal-fired generator might specify that suppliers' coal have a maximum % ash content, hence only an USL. (The higher the ash content, the fewer btu's *and* the greater pollution problem.)

The following measures consider centering (i.e., where is the process mean located/what is its value?) in estimating process capability. For a unilateral specification, calculate either:

$$C_{PU} = \frac{USL - \bar{\bar{x}}}{3\hat{\sigma}} \text{ (if only USL is specified)} \tag{16}$$

or

$$C_{PL} = \frac{\bar{\bar{x}} - LSL}{3\hat{\sigma}} \text{ (if only LSL is specified)} \tag{17}$$

TABLE 2	EXPECTED NUMBER OF DEFECTIVE PARTS PER MILLION (PPM) FOR A STABLE PROCESS AT VARIOUS VALUES OF C_p (ASSUMES PROCESS IS CENTERED AND NORMALLY DISTRIBUTED)

PROCESS CAPABILITY, C_p	DEFECTIVE PARTS PER MILLION
.50	133,620
.67	45,500
1.00	2,700
1.33	60
1.50	7
1.67	.57
2.00	.0018

For a bilateral specification, use

$$C_{PK} = \min (C_{PU}, C_{PL}) \tag{18}$$

These calculations all assume that the process is stable with normally distributed output, and that $\bar{\bar{x}}$ is the estimate of the process mean and $\hat{\sigma} = \bar{R}/d_2$ the estimate of the process standard deviation. For both C_{PU} and C_{PL} we further assume the respective numerator is positive—i.e., that $\bar{\bar{x}}$ is not on the "wrong" side of the spec limit; consequently, C_{PU} and C_{PL} are never negative. For bilateral (two-sided) specs, it is useful to contrast C_P and C_{PK}. C_P reflects only process variability, not where the distribution is located; in fact C_P makes the (optimistic) assumption that the process is centered. For this reason, C_P is referred to as a process *potential* index, indicative of the process' potential or capability *if or when* the process is centered. C_{PK} goes farther and also takes into account where the process is currently located (as measured by $\bar{\bar{x}}$ and thus measures current process *performance*. Assuming that, as is the usual case, $T =$ the target or nominal value is halfway between USL and LSL,

$$C_{PK} \leq C_P.$$

The two will be equal only if the process is centered. The size of the difference between C_P and C_{PK} depends on the degree the process is off center. In fact, another equation for computing C_{PK} is:

$$C_{PK} = C_P(1 - k) \tag{19}$$

where

$$k = \frac{2 \, | \, T - \bar{\bar{x}} \, |}{USL - LSL} \tag{20}$$

and k clearly reflects how far the target value is from the estimated process mean.

   EXAMPLE: Suppose USL = 180 and LSL = 170, and the control chart for the process shows stability with $\bar{\bar{x}} = 174$ and $\hat{\sigma} = 1.5$. Calculate C_P and C_{PK} and estimate defective ppm for each scenario.

First, $C_P = \dfrac{USL - LSL}{6\hat{\sigma}}$

$$= \frac{180 - 170}{6(1.5)} = 1.11.$$

Then, $C_{PU} = \dfrac{USL - \bar{\bar{x}}}{3\hat{\sigma}}$

$$= \frac{180 - 174}{3(1.5)} = \frac{6}{4.5} = 1.33$$

$$C_{PL} = \frac{\bar{\bar{x}} - LSL}{3\hat{\sigma}}$$

$$= \frac{174 - 170}{3(1.5)} = \frac{4}{4.5} = .888$$

and

$$C_{PK} = \min(C_{PU}, C_{PL}) = .888.$$

Or, using equations (19) and (20) with $T = (USL + LSL)/2$,

$$K = \frac{2|T - \bar{\bar{x}}|}{USL - LSL}$$

$$= \frac{2|175 - 174|}{(180 - 170)} = \frac{2}{10} = .2,$$

and,

$$C_{PK} = C_P(1 - k)$$

$$= 1.11(1 - .2) = .888.$$

Note that $C_{PK} < C_P$ because the process is not centered, i.e., $T \ne \bar{\bar{x}}$; the process's actual performance is not reaching its potential.
For C_P (see Figure 10A),

$$Z = \frac{(x - \mu)}{\sigma}$$

$$= \frac{(180 - 175)}{1.5} = 3.33$$

Then, $P(x > 180) = P(Z > 3.33) = .00043$, and $P(x < 170)$ is also .00043, so $P(\text{not meeting specs}) = .00086$, or expected defectives equals 860 ppm. (Note the agreement with Table 15.9 where for $1.00 \le C_P \le 1.33$], defective ppm is between 2700 and 60.)

For C_{PK} (see Figure 10 B),

$$Z = \frac{(x - \mu)}{\sigma} = \frac{(180 - 174)}{1.5} = \frac{6}{1.5} = 4.0$$

and,

$$Z = \frac{(x - \mu)}{\sigma} = \frac{(170 - 174)}{1.5} = \frac{-4}{1.5} = -2.67$$

Then, using a table for the standard normal distribution,

$$
\begin{aligned}
P(\text{not meeting specs}) &= P(Z > 4.0) + P(Z < -2.67) \\
&= (1 - .99997) + (1 - .99621) \\
&= .00382,
\end{aligned}
$$

and expected defects are 3820 ppm. Thus, as indicated by $C_{PK} < C_P$, the process is not operating at its potential and could be improved by centering.

Three final comments: 1) When discussing process stability and process capability be sure to distinguish between the two. Process capability measures should only be calculated and interpreted for a stable process, but a stable process could be producing very many *or* very few out-of-spec product. Merely because a process is stable does not provide information about its ability to meet customer specs. 2) Do not confuse spec limits and control limits; the former are externally derived (from the customer) and applied to individual units. The latter are obtained "internally" from process data and applied to the *sample* statistics (say mean for n = 5) rather than to single

| **FIGURE 10** | LOCATION OF DISTRIBUTION AND SPEC LIMITS FOR (A) $\bar{\bar{x}}$ = T = 175 AND (B) $\bar{\bar{x}}$ = 174 |

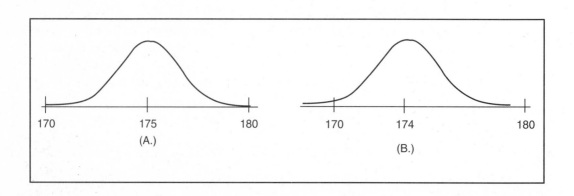

items. 3) Until recently, a process was termed "capable" if its $C_p = 1.0$; meaning, if centered, the process defective rate was "only" 2700 ppm. With demand from consumers for every-increasing quality levels, this standard is, for many industries, too low. For example:

> Motorola stresses to all suppliers ... that their defective units are measured in parts per million. Moreover, Motorola's goal is to reduce the number of its suppliers by an average of about 50% each year; only those suppliers that meet its expectations for superior quality will be retained or added to its supplier base. Motorola has substantially improved as its suppliers have continually improved their quality. Each supplier must indicate its C_{PK} performance (process capability index, which accounts for non-centered process averages). Suppliers should have an acceptable C_{PK} and a program to achieve a C_{PK} of 2.[5]

The supplier certification programs of companies like Ford, Motorola, and Xerox have done much to increase quality awareness among large numbers of suppliers' firms.

SUMMARY

Total quality management (TQM) is the capstone of the quality movement that began at AT&T in the early 1920s when Walter Shewhart invented the control chart. Although initiated by Americans such as Shewhart, W. Edwards Deming, and Joseph Juran, it is the Japanese who brought the quality movement to international attention. Their widespread success in the global marketplace led their competitors to adopt similar strategies. In the United States, firms leading the way in the 1980s were primarily manufacturers such as Motorola, Ford, and Xerox. Their experiences coupled with the success of "Japanese management" with American labor in Ohio (Honda), Kentucky (Toyota), Tennessee (Nissan), and California (Sony), further increased the credibility of TQM as a major managerial development. Now many firms, service as well as manufacturing, are implementing with the new philosophy.

The TQM organization uses various tools to facilitate the continuous improvement of processes and products; this chapter reviewed two of the most widely used tools: control charts and process capability measures. The former are used to learn when/if special cause variation is present in a process; this knowledge is useful in guiding process improvement. When a process is subject to only common cause variation, it is said to be stable, i.e. predictable. For stable processes we can further study the capability of the process to meet customer requirements. Process capability measures like C_{PK} are widely used by quality leaders in assessing their suppliers' abilities.

---

[5]Ed Peña, "Motorola's Secret To Total Quality Control," *Quality Progress,* October 1990: 43.

The price of quality lapses can be enormous. Sears received immense negative publicity in 1992 when charged with defrauding auto-repair customers. A jury awarded a $100 million claim against General Motors in 1993 in a suit involving the fuel tank on its pickup truck. But the rewards of quality leadership are equally great as Xerox and Motorola can attest. Hopefully, your future employer has the vision to adopt the TQM model.

REFERENCES

Berwick, Donald M., A. Blanton Godfrey, and Jane Roessner. *Curing Health Care*. San Francisco: Jossey-Bass, Inc., 1990.

Deming, W. Edwards. *Out of the Crisis*. Cambridge, MA: Massachusetts Institute of Technology, 1986.

Dumaine, Brian. "Who Needs a Boss?" *Fortune*, May 7, 1990: 52-60.

Duncan, W. Jack, and Joseph G. Van Matre. "The Gospel According to Deming: Is It Really New?" *Business Horizons*, July-August 1990: 3-9.

Garvin, David A. *Managing Quality*. New York: Free Press, 1988.

————— "Quality on the Line." *Harvard Business Review*, September-October 1983: 64-75.

Hill, G. Christian, and Ken Yamada. "Motorola Illustrates How an Aged Giant Can Remain Vibrant." *The Wall Street Journal*, December 9, 1992: A1.

Ishikawa, Kaoru. *Guide to Quality Control*. Tokyo, Japan: Asian Productivity Organization, 1982.

Kane, Victor E. *Defect Prevention*. New York: Marcel Dekker, Inc., 1989.

Peña, Ed. "Motorola's Secret to Total Quality Control." *Quality Progress*, October 1990: 43-45.

Phillips, Stephen, et.al. "King Customer." *Business Week*, March 12, 1990: 88-94.

Van Matre, Joseph G. "The D*A*T Approach to Total Quality Managment." *Journal of the American Health Information Management Association*, November 1992: 38-44.

Western Electric. *AT&T Statistical Quality Control Handbook*. Indianapolis, IN: AT&T Customer Information Center, 1958.

SUPPLEMENT   Test for Special Causes

The following is an excellent summary of eight tests for special cause variation. You may recognize tests 1-3 as they were earlier discussed. We restricted our discussion for simplicity and because there is not complete unanimity among experts as concerns "the" set of tests. However, we wanted to share this larger set and note that these are all built into Minitab.

FIGURE 1	ILLUSTRATIONS OF TESTS FOR SPECIAL CAUSES APPLIED TO SHEWHART CONTROL CHARTS

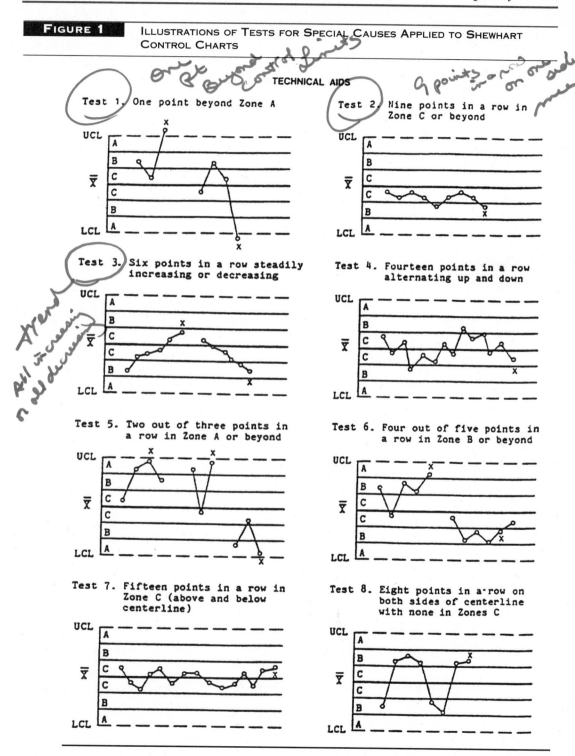

TECHNICAL AIDS

One Pt Beyond Control Limits

9 points in a row on one side of mean

Test 1. One point beyond Zone A

Test 2. Nine points in a row in Zone C or beyond

Test 3. Six points in a row steadily increasing or decreasing

Trend increasing n ol decreasing

Test 4. Fourteen points in a row alternating up and down

Test 5. Two out of three points in a row in Zone A or beyond

Test 6. Four out of five points in a row in Zone B or beyond

Test 7. Fifteen points in a row in Zone C (above and below centerline)

Test 8. Eight points in a row on both sides of centerline with none in Zones C

The author of the summary is Lloyd S. Nelson, Director of Statistical Methods for the Nashua Corp., one of the early American firms to adopt the Deming philosophy. Mr. Nelson is an active member of the American Society for Quality Control (ASQC) and a frequent contributor to its publications. The following originally appeared in the *Journal of Quality Technology* (October 1984), and we appreciate the Society's permission to reproduce this material.

FIGURE 2   COMMENTS ON TESTS FOR SPECIAL CAUSES

SHEWHART CONTROL CHARTS: NOTES ON TESTS FOR SPECIAL CAUSES

1. These tests are applicable to $\bar{x}$ charts and to individuals (X) charts. A normal distribution is assumed. Tests 1, 2, 5, and 6 are to be applied to the upper and lower halves of the chart separately. Tests 3, 4, 7 and 8 are to be applied to the whole chart.

2. The upper control limit and the lower control limit are set at three sigma above the centerline and three sigma below the centerline. For the purpose of applying the tests, the control chart is equally divided into six zones, each zone being one sigma wide. The upper half of the chart is referred to as A (outer third), B (middle third) and C (inner third). The lower half is taken as the mirror image.

3. When a process is in a state of statistical control, the chance of (incorrectly) getting a signal for the presence of a special cause is less than five in a thousand for each of these tests.

4. It is suggested that Tests 1, 2, 3 and 4 be applied routinely by the person plotting the chart. The overall probability of getting a false signal from one or more of these is about one in a hundred.

5. It is suggested that the first four tests be augmented by Tests 5 and 6 when it becomes economically desirable to have earlier warning. This will raise the probability of a false signal to about two in a hundred.

6. Tests 7 and 8 are diagnostic tests for stratification. They are very useful in setting up a control chart. These tests show when the observations in a subgroup have been taken from two (or more) sources with different means. Test 7 reacts when the observations in the subgroup always come from both sources. Test 8 reacts when the subgroups are taken from one source at a time.

7. Whenever the existence of a special cause is signaled by a test, this should be indicated by placing a cross just above the last point if that point lies above the centerline, or just below it if it lies below the centerline.

8. Points can contribute to more than one test. However, no point is ever marked with more than one cross.

9. The presence of a cross indicates that the process is not in statistical control. It means that the point is the last one of a sequence of points (a single point in Test 1) that is very unlikely to occur if the process is in statistical control.

10. Although this can be taken as a basic set of tests, analysts should be alert to any patterns of points that might indicate the influences of special causes in their process.

PART FOUR

CONTINUOUS
IMPROVEMENT

READING 8
ACCELERATING IMPROVEMENT

THIS IS THE FIRST OF TWO ARTICLES DEALING WITH THE PRO-
CESS OF CONTINUOUS IMPROVEMENT/PROBLEM-SOLVING.
THE THREE PREVIOUS READINGS WERE CONCERNED WITH
THE TOOLS OF QUALITY IMPROVEMENT, BUT THE TOOLS WERE
REVIEWED IN A RATHER ISOLATED FASHION. WE NOW TURN
OUR ATTENTION FROM THE TREES TO THE FOREST; WE NOW
WANT TO SEE THE PROBLEM-SOLVING PROCESS "AS A PIECE"
RATHER THAN AS AN ASSORTMENT OF DESCRIPTIVE AND ANA-
LYTICAL DEVICES.

WHETHER CALLED THE PROBLEM-SOLVING PROCESS
(XEROX), THE QUALITY IMPROVEMENT CYCLE (AT&T), OR THE
QUALITY-IMPROVEMENT STORY (FLORIDA POWER & LIGHT),
THESE PROCEDURES ARE BASICALLY VARIATIONS OF THE SCI-
ENTIFIC METHOD AND THE PLAN-DO-CHECK-ACT (PDCA)
CYCLE. THEY OFFER A SYSTEMATIC APPROACH, A STANDARD-
IZATION TO THE PROBLEM-SOLVING PROCESS. THIS ARTICLE
INTRODUCES THE SEVEN STEP METHOD, A STRUCTURED
APPROACH TO PROBLEM SOLVING AND PROCESS IMPROVE-
MENT. "IT LEADS A TEAM THROUGH A LOGICAL SEQUENCE OF
STEPS THAT FORCE A THOROUGH ANALYSIS OF THE PROBLEM,
ITS POTENTIAL CAUSES, AND POSSIBLE SOLUTIONS. THE
STRUCTURE IMPOSED BY THE SEVEN STEP METHOD HELPS A
TEAM FOCUS ON THE CORRECT ISSUES...." THE AUTHORS
ATTRIBUTE THE MODEL TO JOINER ASSOCIATES INC., A LEAD-
ING QUALITY CONSULTING FIRM WITH HEADQUARTERS IN
MADISON, WISCONSIN.

READING 8
ACCELERATING IMPROVEMENT

BY MARIE GAUDARD, ROLAND COATES, AND LIZ FREEMAN

"Catch up? People inquire how long it will take America to catch up with the Japanese.... Does anyone suppose that the Japanese are going to sit still and wait for someone to catch up? How can you catch up with someone that is all the time gaining speed?"—W. Edwards Deming, *Out of the Crisis*

The need to improve quality has captured the attention of American industry. The need to accelerate the improvement process, however, is just now being realized, and ways to accelerate it are just beginning to be explored. The Seven Step Method and the Project Team Review Process are related techniques that, in the proper management setting, can accelerate process improvement.

The Seven Step Method is a structured approach to problem solving and process improvement. It leads a team through a logical sequence of steps that force a thorough analysis of the problem, its potential causes, and possible solutions. The structure imposed by the Seven Step Method helps a team focus on the correct issues rather than diffuse its energy on tangential or even counterproductive undertakings. The Seven Step Method has been used successfully by U.S. and Japanese companies for several years.

The Seven Step Method is most successful when accompanied by regular project reviews performed by managers with a vested interest in the project's outcome. In many organizations, project teams are not reviewed until a solution or recommendation is to be presented—the notion of a status review is foreign. However, there is a formal review process in which peers and superiors guide, support, and monitor project teams while they are working on problems. This Project Team Review Process structures a session so that it becomes a productive meeting with positive consequences, thereby providing teams with support and focus.

CREDIT: Marie Gaudard, Roland Coates, and Liz Freeman, "Accelerating Improvement," *Quality Progress* (October 1991).

The Seven Step Method and Project Team Review Process were part of a program designed to help a small printing company, which will be called Sprinters, with its organizational change. When designing this program, we drew from our own experience working with companies and from the Seven Step and Project Team Review models developed by Joiner Associates Inc.[1] These models emphasize interaction between the project team and a guidance team.

Sprinters employs about 150 people, and its management group consists of 13 people. In December 1989, we helped form the management group into three project teams, each with a loosely defined problem to solve. Each team was supplemented, as appropriate, by employees who were not part of the management group. The result was three teams, one of five members, one of six, and the third of seven members. Over the next eight months, these teams were trained in and practiced using basic group process skills, the Seven Step Method, and the Project Team Review Process.

THE SEVEN STEP METHOD

The value of the Seven Step Method lies in the discipline and logic that it imposes. The seven steps are briefly described in Table 1. Here is a simple case study that generally illustrates the use of the method:

A restaurant caters to business travelers and has a self-service breakfast buffet. Interested in customer satisfaction, the manager constructs a survey, distributes it to customers over a three-month period, and summarizes the results in a Pareto chart (Figure 1). The Pareto chart indicates that the restaurant's major problem is that customers have to wait too long to be seated. A team of employees is formed to work on this problem.

STEP ONE: DEFINE THE PROJECT.

With the survey as the background, the team undertakes the first step. The problem is that customers wait too long to be seated. They should not have to wait at all. The problem is important because customers have complained, and this is supported by the Pareto chart constructed from the survey data. Most of the customers are business travelers who want either a speedy breakfast or a chance to conduct business during breakfast. Decreasing the wait to be seated will increase the restaurant's ability to respond to these key quality characteristics. Progress can be measured by the percent of customers each day who have to wait in excess of, say, one minute to be seated. The team develops an operational definition of "waiting to be seated" to answer such questions as: When does the wait start? When does it end? How is it measured?

TABLE 1	THE SEVEN STEP METHOD

Step 1 Define the Project

1. Define the problem in terms of a gap between what is and what should be. (For example, "Customers report an excessive number of errors. The team's objective is to reduce the number of errors.")

2. Document why it is important to be working on this particular problem:
   - Explain how you know it is a problem, providing any data you might have that supports this.
   - List the customer's key quality characteristics. State how closing the gap will benefit the customer in terms of these characteristics.

3. Determine what data you will use to measure progress:
   - Decide what data you will use to provide a baseline against which improvement can be measured.
   - Develop any operational definitions you will need to collect the data.

Step 2 Study the Current Situation

1. Collect the baseline data and plot them. (Sometimes historical data can be used for this purpose.) A run chart or control chart is usually used to exhibit baseline data. Decide how you will exhibit these data on the run chart. Decide how you will label your axes.

2. Develop flowcharts of the processes.

3. Provide any helpful sketches or visual aids.

4. Identify any variables that might have a bearing on the problem. Consider the variables of what, where, to what extent, and who. Data will be gathered on these variables to localize the problem.

5. Design data collection instruments.

6. Collect the data and summarize what you have learned about the variables' effects on the problem.

7. Determine what additional information would be helpful at this time. Repeat substeps two through seven until there is no additional information that would be helpful at this time.

Step 3 Analyze the Potential Causes

1. Determine potential causes of the current conditions:
   - Use the data collected in step two and the experience of the people who work in the process to identify conditions that might lead to the problem.
   - Construct cause-and-effect diagrams for these conditions of interest.
   - Decide on most likely causes by checking against the data from step two and the experience of the people working in the process.

2. Determine whether more data are needed. If so, repeat substeps two through seven of step two.

3. If possible, verify the causes through observation or by directly controlling variables.

Step 4 Implement a Solution

1. Develop a list of solutions to be considered. Be creative.

2. Decide which solutions should be tried:
   - Carefully assess the feasibility of each solution, the likelihood of success, and potential adverse consequences.
   - Clearly indicate why you are choosing a particular solution.

3. Determine how the preferred solution will be implemented. Will there be a pilot project? Who will be responsible for the implementation? Who will train those involved?

4. Implement the preferred solution.

Step 5 Check the Results

1. Determine whether the actions in step four were effective:
   - Collect more data on the baseline measure from step one.
   - Collect any other data related to the conditions at the start that might be relevant.
   - Analyze the results. Determine whether the solution tested was effective. Repeat prior steps as necessary.

2. Describe any deviations from the plan and what was learned.

Step 6 Standardize the Improvement

1. Institutionalize the improvement:
   - Develop a strategy for institutionalizing the improvement and assign responsibilities.
   - Implement the strategy and check to see that it has been successful.

2. Determine whether the improvement should be applied elsewhere and plan for its implementation.

Step 7 Establish Future Plans

1. Determine your plans for the future:
   - Decide whether the gap should be narrowed further and, if so, how another project should be approached and who should be involved.
   - Identify related problems that should be addressed.

2. Summarize what you learned about the project team experience and make recommendations for future project teams.

| FIGURE 1 | PARETO CHART OF COMPLAINTS |

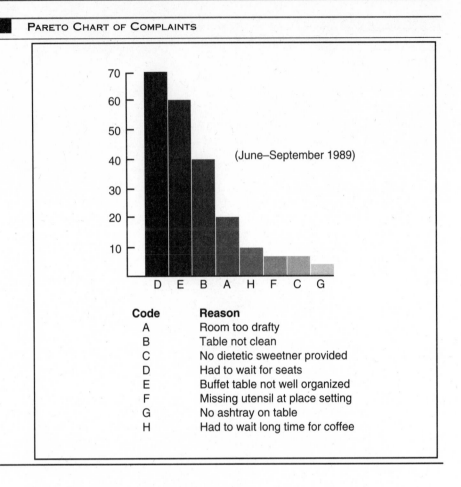

(June–September 1989)

D E B A H F C G

Code	Reason
A	Room too drafty
B	Table not clean
C	No dietetic sweetner provided
D	Had to wait for seats
E	Buffet table not well organized
F	Missing utensil at place setting
G	No ashtray on table
H	Had to wait long time for coffee

STEP TWO: STUDY THE CURRENT SITUATION.

The team collects base-line data and plots them (Figure 2). At the same time, it develops a flowchart of seating a party. The team members feel that a floor diagram might be helpful, so they produce one (Figure 3). The variables they identify as potentially affecting the problem are: day of the week, size of the party, reason for waiting, and time of the morning. Data relating to these variables are collected.

From the baseline data, the team learns that the percent of people served who have to wait is higher early in the week and decreases during the week, with only a small percent waiting on weekends. This is reasonable, since the restaurant's clientele primarily consists of business travelers. The size of the party does not appear to be a factor, because parties of all sizes wait in approximately the same proportions. A histogram of the number of people waiting by the time of the morning reveals nothing surprising: more people wait during

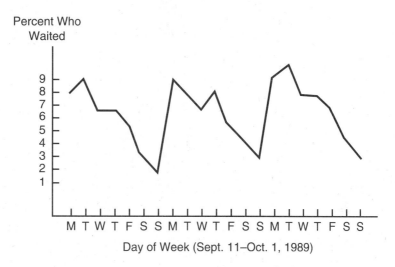

Percent Who Waited

Day of Week (Sept. 11–Oct. 1, 1989)

the busy hours than during the slow hours (Figure 4). The reason for waiting, however, is interesting. Most people wait because a table is not available or because they have a seating preference (as opposed to the hostess not being around to seat customers or customers waiting for friends to join them).

At this point, it would be easy for the team to jump to the solution of putting more staff on early in the week and during busy hours in the morning—but analyzing causes is not done until the next step.

The team decides additional information is needed on why tables are not available and how seating preferences affect waiting. After data are collected, it learns that tables are generally unavailable because they are not cleared (as opposed to being occupied) and that most of the people who have a seating preference wait for a table in the nonsmoking area.

STEP THREE: ANALYZE THE POTENTIAL CAUSES.

A cause-and-effect diagram is constructed for "Why tables are not cleared quickly," with particular emphasis on identifying root causes (Figure 5). This diagram, together with the rest of the data the team has gathered, leads the team to conclude that the most likely cause is the distance from the tables to the kitchen, particularly in the nonsmoking area.

FIGURE 3   RESTAURANT FLOOR PLAN

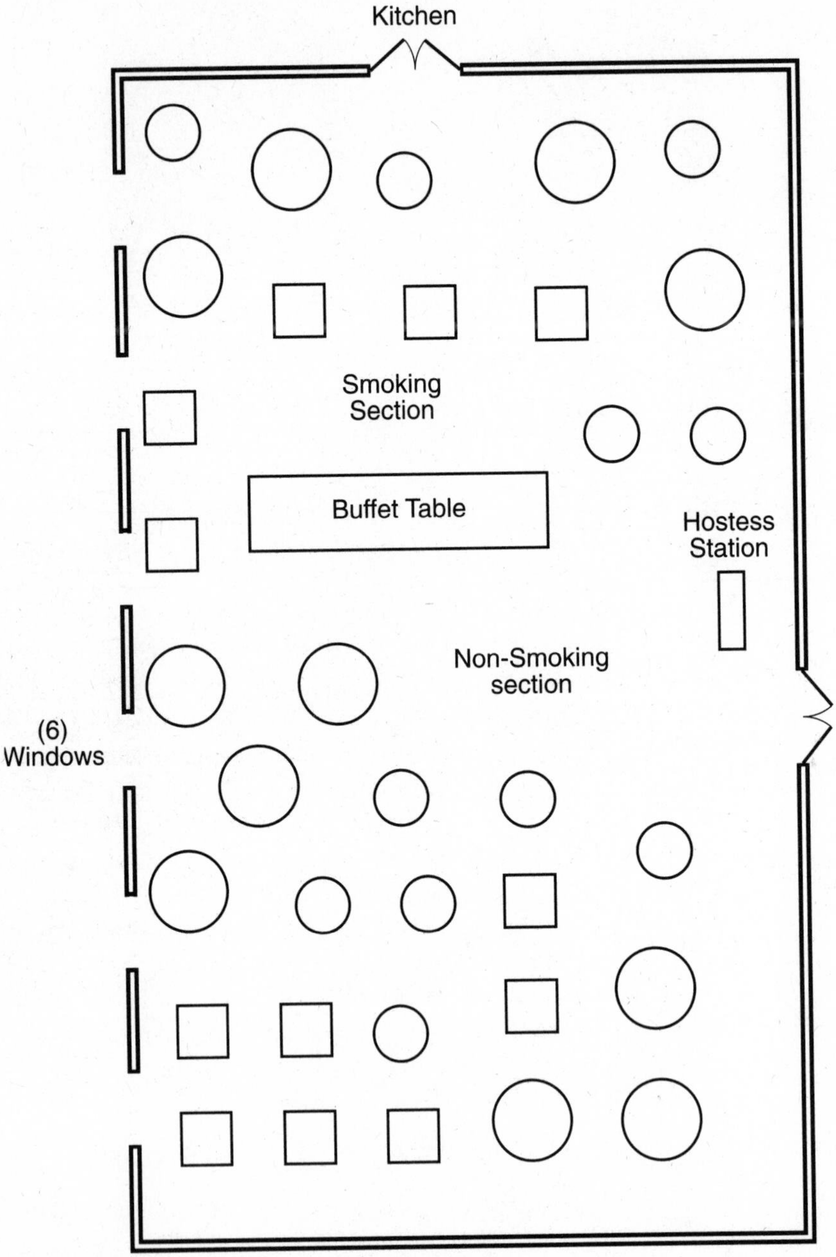

Kitchen

Smoking
Section

Buffet Table

Hostess
Station

Non-Smoking
section

(6)
Windows

FIGURE 4	HISTOGRAM OF THE NUMBER OF CUSTOMERS WAITING IN EXCESS OF ONE MINUTE BY THE TIME OF MORNING

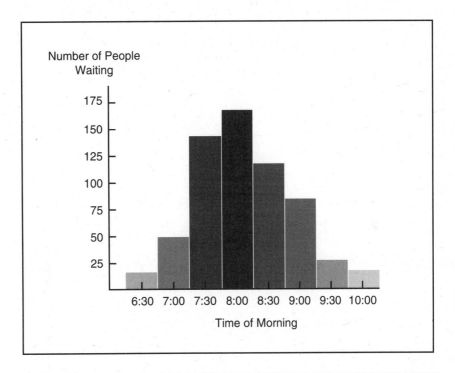

STEP FOUR: IMPLEMENT A SOLUTION.

The team develops a list of possible solutions. Since the team has not been able to verify the cause by controlling the variables, it chooses a solution that can be easily tested: set up temporary workstations in the nonsmoking area. No other changes are made. The team continues to collect data on the percent of people waiting longer than one minute to be seated.

STEP FIVE: CHECK THE RESULTS.

After a month, the team analyzes the data collected in step four. As Figure 6 shows, the improvement is dramatic.

STEP SIX: STANDARDIZE THE IMPROVEMENT.

The temporary workstations are replaced with permanent ones.

| FIGURE 5 | CAUSE-AND-EFFECT DIAGRAM FOR "WHY TABLES ARE NOT CLEARED QUICKLY" |

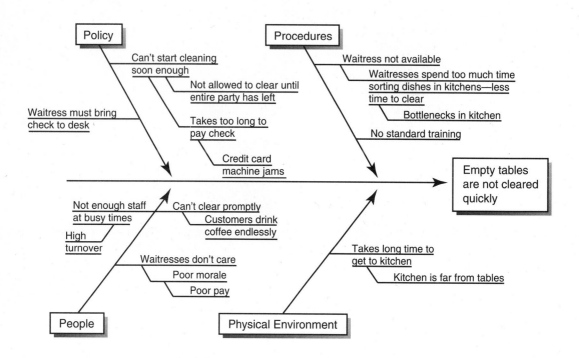

STEP SEVEN: ESTABLISH FUTURE PLANS.

The team decides that the next highest bar in the Pareto chart of customer complaints—buffet table not well organized—should be addressed.

THE PURPOSE OF THE SEVEN STEPS

The overall purpose of the Seven Step Method is to facilitate process improvement. Each step has a specific purpose, and these are given in Table 2.

Since the plan-do-check-act (PDCA) cycle also has process improvement as its goal, it seems natural to ask how it and the Seven Step Method are related. W. Edwards Deming's thoughts on the PDCA cycle are presented in *The Team Handbook*.[2] The "plan" step consists of planning a change or test aimed at improvement; the "do" step consists of carrying out the change or

FIGURE 6	RUN CHART OF PERCENT OF CUSTOMERS WAITING IN EXCESS OF ONE MINUTE TO BE SEATED

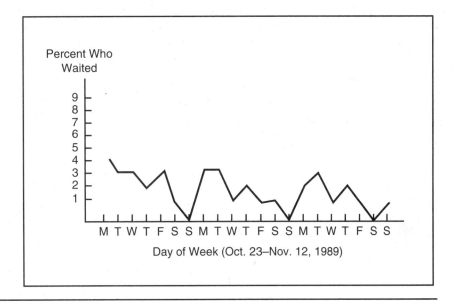

test, preferably on a small scale: the "check" step involves studying the results to understand what has been learned: and the "act" step consists of adopting the change, abandoning it, or repeating the cycle.

It seems clear that much of the PDCA thinking is imbued in the Seven Step Method. The PDCA cycle, however, is a broad paradigm for process improvement that applies in situations where the Seven Step Method does not. The Seven Step Method is appropriate when a deep understanding of the problem is needed to determine and plan an effective solution. A team acquires this understanding through the data-based localization and cause analysis in steps two and three. In these steps, the team is continually restrained from jumping to solutions. Only in step four does the team formulate and implement a solution. This step is similar to the "plan" and "do" steps in the PDCA cycle. In step five, which is comparable to the PDCA cycle's "check" step, the team checks its results. After checking, the team either standardizes its findings (step six) or returns to a prior step to obtain an even deeper understanding of the problem or possible solutions—a process much like the "act" step of the PDCA cycle. In addition to reflecting on its experience in terms of tasks, group processes, and organizational issues, in step seven the team identifies future needs. Identification of these needs continues the PDCA cycle, and if appropriate, those needs are addressed using the Seven Step Method.

TABLE 2	THE PURPOSE OF THE SEVEN STEPS

Step 1 Define the Project

To show the importance of the project and to indicate why energy should be spent here (instead of elsewhere) in order to use resources efficiently, obtain the support of management, and motivate the team.

To reach an agreement on how success will be measured.

Step 2 Study the Current Situation

To use data (rather than opinion) to narrow the focus and to refrain from jumping to possibly incorrect solutions or causes.

To develop baseline data to be used to verify solutions.

Step 3 Analyze the Potential Causes

To find root causes (rather than symptoms) of the problem.

To narrow the focus in order to change the most fundamental causes that can be changed.

Step 4 Implement a Solution

To find the best possible solution, plan its implementation, and implement it (preferably on a small scale).

Step 5 Check the Results

To determine whether the preferred solution is effective.

To decide whether to standardize the solution or return to an earlier step.

Step 6 Standardize the Improvement

To ensure that the problem stays fixed.

Step 7 Establish Future Plans

To determine whether more work needs to be done on this particular problem.

To promote the practice of continuous improvement in terms of organizational and team effectiveness.

The Seven Step Method is directed at analytic rather than enumerative studies. In an enumerative study, an existing population is studied; an analytic study focuses on prediction.[3] In analytic situations, the key is to learn about the cause systems that underlie the processes of interest to understand the effects of various conditions. Since organizations are usually interested in learning about the future, almost all problems in industry—and certainly the most important ones—are of an analytic nature. The Seven Step Method helps solve analytic problems efficiently because it focuses on understanding causal relationships, as evidenced in steps two through five.

THE METHOD'S VALUE

After the management group at Sprinters had been using the Seven Step Method in their project teams for about three months, we asked them, at a training session, to brainstorm what they had learned as a result of the method. The managers overwhelmingly found the method's focus and restraint to be difficult but valuable. They also valued the way the method provides organization, logic, and thoroughness. They were impressed by the use of data instead of opinions. A number of people commented on how they were listening to each other more carefully and respecting each other's ideas more and on how, perhaps because of the focus on data, there had been a lowering of territorial fences and a promotion of cooperation and trust. The managers' perceptions concerning the method were also shaped by the group process skills they had been practicing and the project reviews they had undertaken.

As consultants, we viewed the benefits to the project team members in the same light and were impressed by what seemed to be a significant cultural change. In addition, we felt that the team members learned a great deal about each other and about the organization during their struggles with various tasks and issues.

DIFFICULT ISSUES

The three project teams found several concepts in the first two steps extremely difficult. The first was arriving at a problem statement. The initial tendency was to frame a solution as a problem. The analog of this in the restaurant case study would be to state the problem as "There aren't enough tables" or "The waitresses and waiters need to work harder" instead of "The customers wait too long." Once this hurdle was crossed, there were others. One team needed to agree on several operational definitions before it could even begin to formulate a problem statement. Another team kept revisiting its problem statement during the first four months before settling on one that was consistent with what the team was doing. The third team arrived at a problem statement relatively easily by comparison, but even they struggled.

Localization—the process of focusing on smaller and smaller vital pieces of the problem—is another task that the teams found difficult. Localization is usually achieved by stratifying data using Pareto charts with categorical data and run charts with continuous data. Localization is what makes a problem tractable. Although team members could see the value of localization in solving sample problems, they found it hard to internalize this in solving their own problems. Realizing that their own problems were not overwhelming but instead tractable through localization was an important achievement for the project teams.

There were other issues that proved difficult. It was much easier for the teams to justify the importance of the problem in terms of internal considerations rather than in terms of the customer's key quality characteristics. We sensed that this occurred because the team members had not yet internalized the idea that improvement should be driven by customer requirements, not internal indicators. Some team members could not see the benefits of collecting data accurately and consistently, so they resisted devising ways to accomplish this. The teams had trouble understanding how baseline data would be used to validate a solution. Causes of the problem often crept into discussions where they did not belong. The teams had difficulty keeping an open mind about potential causes. For example, they resisted investigating the effects of variables that they felt were not causes. The teams needed a significant amount of coaching in how to obtain information in a nonthreatening way (through interviews or surveys) from the people who work in the system. The teams also faced several organizational challenges, such as finding the time to work on their projects, arranging meetings to accommodate second- and third-shift employees, and getting support from line workers who were to collect the data.

PROJECT TEAM REVIEW PROCESS

The Project Team Review Process was introduced to the teams when they had been working on their projects for only a month. We felt it best to introduce this process early to emphasize the value of communication among teams, to keep the teams apprised of each other's progress, and to promote a supporting environment. Reviews were then conducted about every two months. An outline of the review process appears in Table 3.

The review—consisting of positive feedback, clarifying questions, and "one more thing" suggestions—was designed by Joiner Associates. For our purposes, we made three innovations: using it in a context where project teams reviewed each other, teaching it after the teams had held only one or two meetings, and compressing the time for the review.

The three Sprinters teams were reviewed during a four-hour meeting. Each team was asked to make a 10-minute presentation of its progress. After this presentation, the other two teams and a team of three consultants brainstormed independently to come up with:

- positive comments about the presenting team's efforts, choosing two to share with the team.
- clarifying questions about the presenting team's logic and data, choosing two to share.
- suggestions in the form of "If there were one more thing we could ask you to do, it would be..." choosing one to share.

Each reviewing team was given 15 minutes to select an individual to present that team's review and to prepare for it. Meanwhile, the presenting team

TABLE 3	THE REVIEW PROCESS

1. Team Presentation
2. Preparation for Review
    *   Brainstorm positive comments, and agree on two.
    *   Brainstorm questions about the logic and data, and agree on two.
    *   Brainstorm ideas on the premise "If I could ask the team to do one more thing, it would be to...," and agree on one. While the reviewers are preparing, the presenting team reflects on its presentation.
3. Review of Team
    *   Each reviewer gives two positive comments.
    *   Each reviewer asks two questions about logic and data.
    *   Each reviewer asks the team to do "one more thing."
4. Presenting Team Reflects on Review
    *   What were the main messages the team heard?
    *   How did it feel to be reviewed?

Figure 1. Pareto Chart of Complaints

Figure 2. Run Chart of Percent of Customers Waiting in Excess of One Minute to be Seated

Figure 3. Restaurant Floor Plan

Figure 4. Histogram of the Number of Customers Waiting in Excess of One Minute by the Time of Morning

Figure 5. Cause-and-Effect Diagram for "Why Tables Are Not Cleared Quickly"

Figure 6. Run Chart of Percent of Customers Waiting in Excess of One Minute to be Seated

was asked to reflect on its presentation. Seven minutes were allotted for each review, during which the reviewer shared the two positive comments, two clarifying questions (to which the presenting team responded), and the "If I could ask you to do one more thing" suggestion.

After the three teams had conducted their reviews, the presenting team members spent 15 minutes debriefing. In the debriefing, they brainstormed the main messages they had heard and discussed how it felt to be reviewed.

THE PURPOSE OF THE REVIEW PROCESS

Because most organizations conduct reviews after a solution is found, the term "review" has a negative connotation. Consequently, such organizations find it difficult to accept that team reviews are conducted to stimulate communication, promote a supporting environment, and keep teams focused and on track. Since the individuals on the Sprinters management team would eventually be directing teams of their subordinates, we felt it critical that they should experience the value of team reviews and learn to perform productive reviews. In addition, we felt that if they experienced reviewing and being reviewed, they would be more sensitive to the needs of their employees when reviewing them in the future.

The approach we used is very structured both in terms of time and content. The rationale for limiting the time was to make the point that, with discipline, a team review need not be a lengthy undertaking. Thus managers would view reviews as tractable and be willing to review projects frequently. The rationale for the structure was to give the managers exposure to a good process, one they could use as a model when conducting their own reviews. The rationale for limiting a reviewing team to only two positive comments, two clarifying questions, and one suggestion was that it forced the team members to focus on the most vital issues.

By beginning the review with positive comments, both the reviewers and the presenting team must acknowledge the good aspects of what the team has accomplished; thus, the review builds on the team's strengths. The clarifying questions help both the reviewers and the team being reviewed understand and clear up any ambiguities, misunderstandings, or misconceptions. The final suggestion allows the reviewers to direct the presenting team while acknowledging the considerable effort the team has already expended.

THE REVIEW'S VALUE

The teams' reactions to the review process have been and continue to be very positive. Although beginning the review with positive comments might be perceived by some onlookers as artificial, the teams do not view it as such. Team members are interested in the particular aspects of their work that the reviewers single out as worthy of praise. These positive comments generate a system of values within the organization. For example, if reviewers often praise teams for resisting jumping to solutions, it is perceived as desirable behavior and thus an organizational value. When the teams felt frustrated with their tasks, the reviews gave them support and renewed their enthusiasm. This was partially due to the reviewers' understanding, born out of experiences on their own project teams, that they shared with the team being reviewed. Part of it was also due to the direction and guidance the reviews provided.

Like any learning tool, the review process surfaced difficulties from which the teams learned. The reflection sessions were of great value in teaching managers what does and doesn't work well in a review and in helping them be more sensitive during a review. For example, during an early review, a presenting team perceived one clarifying question—"Aren't you jumping to conclusions by doing...?"—as accusatory. In their reflection period, the presenting team members revealed that this question dampened their enthusiasm for the rest of the review. The teams then discussed the question and concluded that it is important to frame questions, especially sensitive ones, in a positive and open context. A better strategy would have been to refocus the presenting team's attention using a statement such as "Please explain again the logic of how you got from your data to your conclusion."

Perhaps the greatest benefit of the review process to the three management-based teams at Sprinters was its influence in forming the managers into a team. When the company began its quality improvement effort, the managers were territorial and defensive. The review process was quite successful in promoting and communicating support among the three management-based teams. In fact, after one of the early review sessions, an influential manager said, "It sounds to me as if we [the people on the three project teams] have become a team!" Although overstated, this comment indicated a breakthrough in the managers' ability to envision themselves working as a team. The managers continue to struggle toward that goal, consistently growing in their shared values and support for each other.

INSTRUCTIONAL CONSIDERATIONS

Our philosophy of training is that it should be given on a just-in-time basis, because people learn methods and techniques better when they have an immediate application for them. Thus, we covered only the methods and techniques the teams needed when they needed to use them.

Our work with the teams began with a one-day introduction to the Deming management philosophy. This orientation stressed the value of process management vs. hierarchical management; discussed the notion of operational definitions and the customer's key quality characteristics; introduced the concept of process variability, process stability, and control charts; and demonstrated the consequences of tampering with the process.

In another one-day program, the teams were introduced to a process for brainstorming and consensus decision making. The work on the projects was launched with a half-day introduction to the Seven Step Method during which the teams worked through steps one to three in the restaurant case study. Half-day training sessions were then held at one-month intervals, and the topics included meeting skills, run charts, special and common causes, process stability, classical flowcharts, top-down flowcharts, deployment flowcharts, Pareto charts, localization, check sheets, collecting data, involving people who work in the process as resources, interviews, surveys, stem-and-leaf plots, histograms, stratification, and scatter plots.

PEDAGOGICAL APPROACH

The pedagogical approach we used is based on the constructivist perspective, which assumes that learning occurs when an individual interacts with the environment to construct his or her own knowledge.[4] In such a model, the individual or team builds on existing concepts. Because learning results from resolving conflicts or fulfilling needs, the individual or team is the primary decision maker and is in charge of the progress. The instructor is a facilitator who guides participants as they set their own pace.

As mentioned earlier, the teams were trained on a just-in-time basis, an approach that is consistent with the constructivist perspective. At half-day monthly meetings, we addressed the needs common to all the teams. We also regularly met with the teams individually to monitor their progress, to learn of any training needs (sometimes providing the training to meet a particular need), and to give guidance. These meetings also provided the teams with observations on their use of group process skills.

Whenever appropriate, we modeled the behavior we were teaching. For example, when teaching the teams how to review each other, we became a reviewing team ourselves and participated in the review process alongside the other teams. While attending team meetings, we often behaved as team members, participating in the group process, asking questions, and making observations relevant to the task.

In formal teaching sessions that introduced new techniques, almost all the examples were from the printing industry and Sprinters' data were used whenever possible. In fact, data that the teams had gathered for their projects were used whenever appropriate. This was especially valuable because the teams could relate to the revealed peculiarities of the data-gathering process. Most of the examples were followed with exercises requiring the teams to apply the technique being learned to their own problems.

SPEEDING THE TRANSITION

The goal in introducing the Seven Step Method and the Project Team Review Process at Sprinters was to speed the transition to a management culture that enabled employees to implement Deming's principles, thereby accelerating improvement. The necessary infrastructure involved strong management commitment, including top managers' willingness to form the first project teams and receive training and coaching in group process and meeting skills. Our primary objective was to provide them with a learning experience in team and problem-solving processes. From what we have seen, these managers have developed a sound appreciation of the factors involved and will be able to make the transition to guiding project teams composed of their own subordinates with relative ease and success.

The synergistic effect of the Seven Step Method and the Project Team Review Process has contributed value to both the project teams at Sprinters and to the educational goals we set for the company's top managers. The three management based teams are steadily making progress in solving their problems, and the managers are applying what they have learned to other areas of their management responsibilities. We feel strongly that the progress of the teams and of the organizational change effort has been accelerated by the Seven Step Method, which provides a road map for solving difficult problems, and by the Project Team Review Process, which bolsters commitment and elicits support and guidance.

REFERENCES

[1]We were first exposed to the Seven Step Method and the review process through Joiner Associates, a consulting firm in Madison, WI. Joiner Associates is actively developing and promoting these powerful tools.

[2]A seven-step model that resembles the one developed by Joiner Associates is given in Hitoshi Kume. *Statistical Methods for Quality Improvement* (Tokyo: Association for Overseas Technical Scholarship, 1985).

[3]Peter R. Scholtes and other contributors, *The Team Handbook* (Madison, WI: Joiner Associates, 1988) 5-31.

[4]W. Edwards Deming, *Out of the Crisis* (Cambridge, MA: MIT Center for Advanced Engineering Study, 1982).

[5]E. Von Glasersfeld. "Learning as a Constructive Activity," in J.C. Gergeron and N. Herscovics. eds. *Proceedings of the Fifth Annual Meeting of the North American Chapter of the International Group for the Psychology of Mathematics Education*, 1983. Vol. 1: 41-69.

[6]Joan Ferrini-Mundy, Marie Gaudard, Samuel D. Shore, and Donovan Van Osdol. "How Quality Is Taught Can Be as Important as What Is Taught," *Quality Progress*, January 1990, 56-59.

Marie Gaudard is an associate professor in the Department of Mathematics at the University of New Hampshire in Durham. She received a doctorate in statistics from the University of Massachusettes in Amherst. Gaudard is a member of ASQC.

Roland Coates is the president of Coates Freeman Associates in New Ipswich, NH. He received a bachelor's degree in psychology from Middlebury College in Middlebury, VT. Coates is an ASQC member.

Liz Freeman is the vice president of Coates Freeman Associates in New Ipswich, NH. She received a master's degree in adult learning from Boston University in Boston, MA.

READING 9
DOING MORE WITH LESS
IN THE PUBLIC SECTOR:
A PROGRESS REPORT FROM
MADISON, WISCONSIN

THIS ARTICLE REPORTS THE EXPERIENCES OF TWO QUALITY-IMPROVEMENT PROJECTS IN THE PUBLIC SECTOR. THE FIRST DEALS WITH THE CITY OF MADISON'S MUNICIPAL GARAGE, AND THE SECOND THE STATE OF WISCONSIN'S DEPARTMENT OF REVENUE WORD PROCESSING POOL. THE AUTHORS DESCRIBE THE "SUCCESSES AND STRUGGLES" OF THE TEAMS AND "ILLUSTRATE THE BASIC ELEMENTS OTHER MANAGERS NEED TO CONSIDER—HOW TO GET EMPLOYEES WORKING TOGETHER, HOW TO GATHER AND USE DATA, AND HOW TO AVOID CERTAIN PITFALLS." ONE MAY BE REMINDED OF READING 3 AND THE D*A*T MODEL WHEN THE ARTICLE SAYS "ONLY WHEN COMBINED WITH OPEN COMMUNICATION AND AN OBSESSION WITH MEETING CUSTOMER NEEDS CAN TOOLS BE USED EFFECTIVELY. DATA CANNOT BE GATHERED WITHOUT WIDESPREAD COOPERATION AND TEAMWORK."

A NUMBER OF INDIVIDUALS MENTIONED IN THE ARTICLE ARE KNOWN TO THOSE IN QUALITY MANAGEMENT. FIRST, OF COURSE, IS W. EDWARDS DEMING; DAVID MILLER, A MAYORAL AIDE, AND THEN MAYOR F. JOSEPH SENSEBRENNER ATTENDED A DEMING SEMINAR. SENSEBRENNER IS NOW A TQM CONSULTANT AND AUTHOR OF "QUALITY COMES TO CITY HALL" IN THE MARCH–APRIL 1991 ISSUE OF THE *HARVARD BUSINESS REVIEW*. THE LATE WILLIAM HUNTER WAS A CO-AUTHOR OF *STATISTICS FOR EXPERIMENTERS* AND CO-FOUNDER (ALONG WITH GEORGE BOX) OF THE CENTER FOR QUALITY AND PRODUCTIVITY IMPROVEMENT AT THE UNIVERSITY OF WISCONSIN-MADISON. JAN O'NEILL IS NOW WITH

JOINER ASSOCIATES, A LEADING QUALITY MANAGEMENT CONSULTING FIRM WITH HEADQUARTERS IN MADISON. PETER SCHOLTES, A CITY EMPLOYEE AND TEAM FACILITATOR DURING THE MUNICIPAL GARAGE PROJECT, IS ALSO NOW WITH JOINER ASSOCIATES AND WAS LEAD AUTHOR ON THE VERY POPULAR *THE TEAM HANDBOOK: HOW TO USE TEAMS TO IMPROVE QUALITY.*

READING 9
DOING MORE WITH LESS IN THE PUBLIC SECTOR: A PROGRESS REPORT FROM MADISON, WISCONSIN (REPORT NO. 13)

WILLIAM HUNTER, JAN O'NEILL, AND CAROL WALLEN

INTRODUCTION

In the past decade, the City of Madison's Motor Equipment Division lost six staff positions (down from 35 to 29), while the number of vehicles it serviced grew from 546 to 725. Just this year, state agencies in Wisconsin were directed to slash 7.7 percent from their operating costs because a slower-than-expected economy had led to a projected $350 million revenue shortfall. Across the country, belt-tightening is now the rule in the public sector as the growth rate of tax revenues drop and services are shifted from the federal government to state and local levels. Whatever the reason, public administrators are being asked to "do more with less"—to maintain, or even *increase* productivity in the face of budget and staff cuts.

How can the public sector begin to cope with this pressure?

In this article, we examine projects in Madison's city government and in the state's Department of Revenue to show how the employees in these organizations learned to improve productivity by focusing on quality. Managers started these efforts approximately two years ago. Their successes and struggles illustrate the basic elements other managers need to consider—how to get employees working together, how to gather and use data, and how to

CREDIT: William Hunter, Jan O'Neill, and Carol Wallen. "Doing More With Less in the Public Sector: A Progress Report from Madison, Wisconsin," Center for Quality and Productivity Improvement (Report No. 13), University of Wisconsin (June, 1986). (c) 1987 American Society for Quality Control.

avoid certain pitfalls. After describing a project that decreased downtime in a municipal garage and one that eased the backlog of typing requests in a state word-processing office, we will offer our reflections and some guidelines for doing more with less.

The key idea is to compensate for dwindling financial resources by getting the most out of *human* resources (see Figure 1). Some state and municipal leaders have boldly allocated portions of their dwindling budgets to educate themselves and their employees in the basics of quality improvement methods advocated by W. Edwards Deming, Kaoru Ishikawa, Joseph M. Juran, and others. People in their organizations are learning how to work *smarter*—not harder.

Quality improvement, whether in public or private sectors, demands three major changes: First, it calls for a *total transformation of management philosophy* in order that all employees can focus on the never-ending improvement of quality. Second, quality improvement means making *decisions based on data,* not just on hunches and guesses. All employees must scrutinize all key

FIGURE 1 COMPENSATING FOR DECREASES IN FLOW OF FINANCIAL RESOURCES BY INCREASING FLOW OF HUMAN RESOURCES

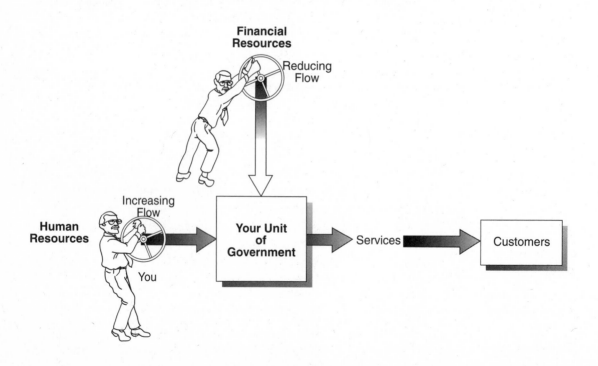

processes in the organization to determine where and how they break down, and how they can be improved. Third, improving quality requires an almost *fanatical devotion to customers*. The goal is to meet—and preferably exceed—customers' needs and expectations.

Traditional American management philosophies have become obsolete. Most managers in this country have been taught how to control rather than lead (Joiner and Scholtes, 1986). They give the direction and establish the controls that everyone else follows. This entrenched management style, developed in the mid-1800s, is—surprisingly—the last real innovation in American management. Well over a century later we're still using methods developed with the help of the military by railroad barons, the first managers of large, complex business organizations in the country (Chandler, 1977; Joiner and Scholtes, 1986).

The most destructive feature of management by control, with its militaristic overtones, is the fear it engenders and on which it depends. Commands and information flow one way—from the top down—inhibiting employees lower on the ladder and discouraging them from contributing their ideas and talents. After all, how often does a general listen to a private? It is essential that fear be removed from the workplace. Then employees can begin to feel comfortable in using their creativity and talents to solve problems.

Fear, however, is just one of the problems caused by traditional management practices. Managers typically focus on the *final* product or service. In the public sector this focus translates into a reliance on audits, reviews, and hearings: attention that comes too late, allowing resources to be wasted on error-inspection rather than error-prevention. (For example, McDonnell Douglas was subject to 6000 separate government audits in 1985—meaning three new audits started every hour of each working day that year!)

Plans to increase productivity also go awry. Then quality is only a secondary focus, managers typically try to get more for their dollars by either cutting costs or increasing quotas and exhorting their employees to work harder. The end result is the exact opposite of the goal: slashing funds or raising quotas almost always causes a drop in quality, which in turn means more rework and discouragement for the front-line workers. Productivity begins to fall, and managers get trapped in the blame game—"Who's at fault? Can't you work harder?" Since employees have no control over this situation, they tend to disassociate themselves from their work, no longer taking pride in the quality of what they do.

One requirement for changing these damaging management practices is to permit employees to take *pride in their work*. They need to become involved in making decisions, and their contributions need to be acknowledged. Managers and workers need to become *team* members who are all pulling in the same direction.

But employee involvement alone is not enough. A second requirement for all employees and managers is to use a *scientific approach* for improving processes and solving problems. Data can be collected and analyzed by teams of managers and employees working together to reduce—and ultimately prevent—problems. To learn how to do this work requires considerable training.

Even teamwork and a scientific approach are insufficient to transform old-style management practices. The final key requirement is to *build quality into every step of every process,* from design to execution.

Nothing is perfect; processes can always be improved. Quality therefore demands continuous, never-ending attention. Closer attention must be given to *internal customers,* the people within the organization who are the *recipients* of products produced by co-workers, and to *external customers,* the ultimate beneficiaries of the work being done. Who are they? What do they want? The answers to these questions will point the way to quality improvement.

What happens when the primary focus is on quality? As quality improves, the amount of rework and repair drops, and employees are able to use their time more effectively. This approach leads to an increase in productivity and a drop in costs. To show how this focus on quality has worked in the public sector, we next summarize two examples.

QUALITY IMPROVEMENT IN ACTION

FIRST STREET GARAGE (MUNICIPAL SERVICE)

In November 1983, a Madison city audit highlighted poor productivity, labor-management relations, and inter-departmental communications in the Motor Equipment Division of the city's Department of Public Works. Efforts to improve the situation had repeatedly failed in the past. The auditors recommended they use some quality improvement techniques in the division.

A few months earlier, David E. Miller, an aide to Mayor F. Joseph Sensenbrenner, had attended a seminar organized by the University of Wisconsin–Madison and presented by W. Edwards Deming. Recognizing that Deming's mandate for quality improvement was as true for governmental agencies as it was for industries, he convinced the mayor and city council to appropriate a portion of the 1984 budget for instruction in and trials of Deming's approach.

Peter Scholtes, a city employee who was a specialist in organizational development, learning of the audit's recommendation and of Miller's budget proposal, combined the two and began a push for getting this new management approach used at the First Street Garage (the primary facility of the

Motor Equipment Division). With additional support from Miller and Mayor Sensenbrenner, the program was up and rolling by March of 1984.

Initially, four employees from the Motor equipment Division met with Scholtes, and later also with Bill Hunter, a professor from the University of Wisconsin–Madison. The team spent the first meetings learning the fundamentals of quality improvement. They initially proposed "morale" as a problem that desperately needed attention, but Scholtes suggested that if they stuck with more concrete targets, morale would probably take care of itself. Heeding this advice, the team chose to focus on two areas: customer research and causes of vehicle downtime. After adding several other employees, they then split into two separate groups.

The customer research team interviewed supervisors in five "user" agencies and surveyed other agency employees and managers by mail using a random sample. Through another survey of the above groups, the city's common council, and the Board of Public Works, the customer research team was able to rank repair priorities.

Since the customer research team was convinced the surveys would be an open invitation to criticize the division unmercifully, they approached their tasks with some trepidation. The customers rated the overall quality of Motor Equipment's service above the employees' expectations, which resulted in a boost to the employees' morale. Another surprise for the employees was that "safety" appeared at the top of every customer's priorities, not "repair costs" as had been assumed (repair cost ranked sixth out of seven possible answers). Employees at the First Street Garage were glad to learn of this result because they had long felt dissatisfied when they were forced by the "hurry-up" atmosphere to put vehicles back into service that they judged to be unsafe. As expected, customers identified the division's biggest problem as "duration of downtime."

Even before these surveys were finished, the downtime group had begun its task. What in their process caused long repair delays? The team flow charted the entire process, defining fifteen steps from the time a vehicle was brought in until it was put back in use (see Figure 2). These steps were then listed on checksheets which were subsequently used by the division to track equipment passing through the garage over a one-month period. The checksheets helped the team to see how long each step took by type of vehicle, customer, and repair priority.

The team then examined these checksheets. They discovered that 28 percent of a low-priority vehicle's time was spent in the lot waiting for repairs to begin. Further, about 15 percent of all vehicles' time in the garage was spent waiting for parts to be delivered. Some of this latter delay was caused by problems in Motor Equipment's "parts" room, but since the system was being computerized, the group was convinced they should wait until the conversion was complete before tackling the parts problem.

FIGURE 2   CITY OF MADISON MOTOR EQUIPMENT DIVISION DOWNTIME FLOW DIAGRAM
FOR REPAIR OF VEHICLES

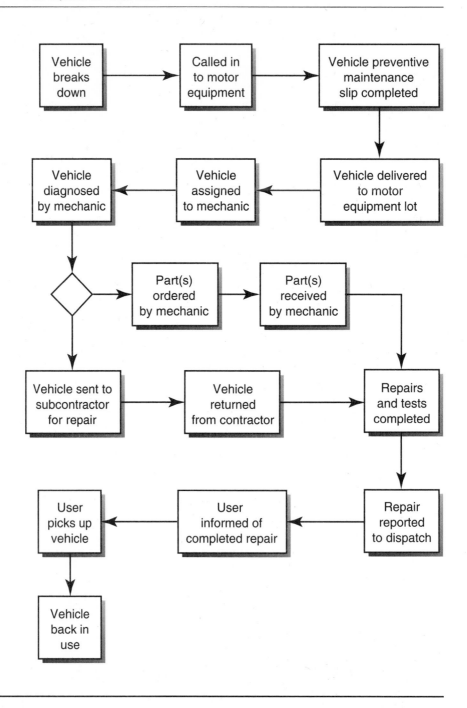

At this point many teams would have moved immediately to start looking for solutions. (Tempting as it may be, such an approach is often inefficient in the long run.) The Motor Equipment team, however, guided by Scholtes and Hunter, decided to dig for underlying causes of excessive vehicle downtime. They found that: 1) vehicles were being replaced on the average less frequently than a decade ago (every 21 years for non-police vehicles now vs. every 10 years before), and thus the fleet was aging rapidly—based on the fact that, for example, approximately 5 percent of the fleet was currently being replaced each year; 2) the division had lost six staff positions during a period when the fleet had grown enormously; and 3) other agencies, also suffering staff cuts, had been buying "high-tech" equipment that required fewer operators but was more expensive to repair and maintain. To make matters worse, for the past two decades the division had operated under an "if it ain't broke, don't fix it" policy handed down from the early 1960s. Minor problems, therefore, had to become major before they could be handled.

With these and other carefully documented facts to support their case, the mechanics personally persuaded the City Council and the mayor to reinstate a preventive maintenance program deleted from the City budget 20 years before. The mechanics predict savings will grow and downtime will decrease as small problems are caught early.

The downtime team recommended other steps that helped reduce downtime. They had their customers develop a "repair priority" list (which repair jobs take precedence?), they established agency contacts to facilitate communications, and they streamlined repair procedures.

However, it is painting too rosy a picture to imply every employee is now "on board," and every customer satisfied. Some employees not on the project teams were unhappy about being excluded and having to pick up their colleagues' work when those team members met. (To alleviate this problem, more people have been either added to project teams or encouraged to join future teams.) The division has also had to deal with resentment from customer agencies whose vehicles are now designated as low priority. Making decisions about priorities—and sticking by them—has often put Motor Equipment personnel in tough spots.

WORD PROCESSING POOL (STATE SERVICE)

Imagine sending a one-page letter to a word-processing pool and getting it back two or even three weeks later—with errors. Now imagine coming to work each day and having to face an entire wall of floor-to-ceiling shelves packed with a backlog of typing requests. Such was the dismal reality faced by customers and operators of the Compliance Bureau of the Wisconsin State Department of Revenue. They tried countless adjustments, but the turnaround time stubbornly remained at unacceptably high levels. Communication and trust kept deteriorating and employee turnover rates continued to rise.

In June 1985, the Department of Revenue began its first wave of quality improvement projects, and the word processing problem was a main target. Nine people participated on a quality-improvement team: the Bureau Director (now Division Administrator), three section chiefs (representing the "customers"), the word processing supervisor, three operators, and a systems analyst. The team met weekly for three months.

The first meeting broke new ground for all team members. It was the first time operators had sat down with managers to analyze word processing tasks and to identify all their customers and suppliers. To maximize individual input, the team completed a nominal group exercise (Delbecq, Van de Ven, and Gustafson, 1975): brainstorming problems, then listing, discussing and clarifying ideas, and eventually ranking problems in order of importance (see Figure 3). Since all team members ranked "low quality" as the number one problem, the team mapped the possible *causes* of poor quality on a cause-and-effect diagram, as shown in Figure 4 (Ishikawa, 1982). The primary problems in their jobs were illegibility, missing information, spelling, punctuation, grammar, missing signature, and repeated use of a single form for different typing requests. This request form was the crucial link between customers and operators, and when the forms were improperly filled out, operators had difficulty ascertaining what the customers really wanted. The result was product of poor quality.

To pinpoint where problems were occurring, the team broke into two groups (customers and operators evenly distributed in each group). Each drew a flow chart for the entire process. These two were merged into a single flow chart, which proved to be an excellent vehicle for communication. The team used the chart to focus discussion on specific points. From these discussions, the team decided to collect two types of data. The section chiefs conducted a customer survey to find out what the users wanted and expected; the operators developed and used a checksheet to track each work order as it passed through the word processing unit so they could locate where different kinds of errors occurred.

The results of the customer survey indicated that collectively the users estimated that they submitted about 2900 documents *per week* to the pool and that about 18 percent of the documents contained errors when first returned. These customers ranked the pool "adequate" on overall quality (see Figures 5 and 6), and further indicated quick turnaround time, accuracy, completeness, and correct format were highly important "quality" characteristics.

Using checksheets, the operators gathered data for *two weeks*. They noted times in and out for all documents, sources of requests, and problems

PARETO DIAGRAM FOR NOMINAL GROUP RESULTS OF WISCONSIN STATE DEPARTMENT OF REVENUE WORD PROCESSING TEAM.

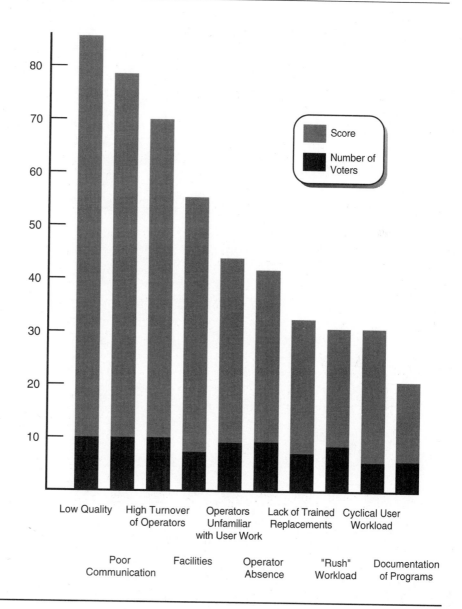

encountered. Over these two weeks the actual workload was about 7900 documents (from over 1900 requests)—or over *35 percent more* documents per week than the customers had estimated. Moreover, the time covered was a

FIGURE 4–A   WISCONSIN STATE DEPARTMENT OF REVENUE WORD PROCESSING TEAM CAUSE-AND-EFFECT DIAGRAM SHOWING OPERATOR ABSENCE, LACK OF TRAINING, AND WORKLOAD AS THE MAJOR CAUSES OF POOR QUALITY

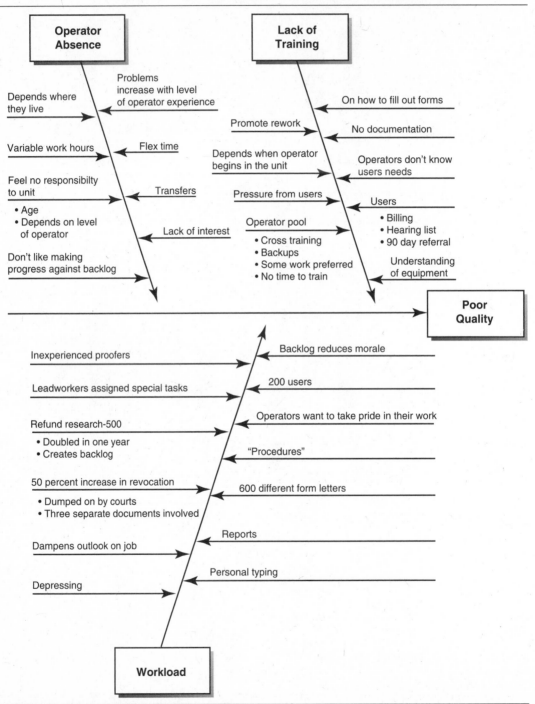

FIGURE 4–B | WISCONSIN STATE DEPARTMENT OF REVENUE WORD PROCESSING TEAM CAUSE-AND-EFFECT DIAGRAM SHOWING HOW COMMUNICATION, OPERATORS, AND USERS AFFECT POOR QUALITY

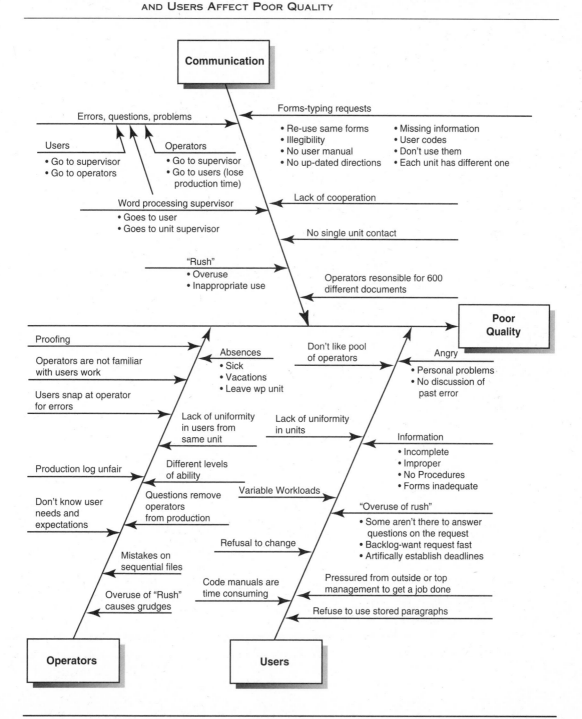

| **FIGURE 5** | WISCONSIN STATE DEPARTMENT OF REVENUE WORD PROCESSING CUSTOMER SURVEY (N = NUMBER OF RESPONSES AND X̄ = AVERAGE RATING): GENERAL TURNAROUND TIME AND CORRECTIONS TURNAROUND |

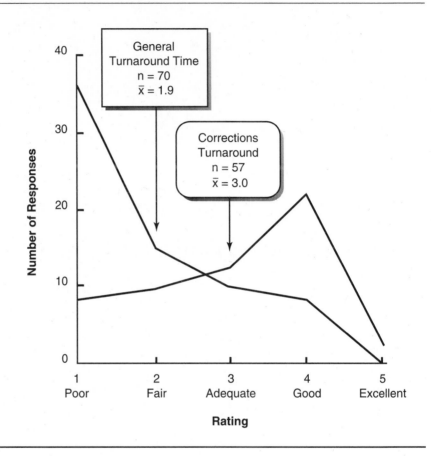

slow work period! Of the 1900 typing requests, 27 percent had errors caused by the customers. (For a breakdown of errors see Figure 7.)

In subsequent weeks, the team segregated typing requests into REGU-LAR and RUSH piles and examined the flow of work by customer unit. They found that 49 percent of all typing requests were designated RUSH when submitted, with one unit alone accounting for more than half of that total. This unit's employees, fearful they would miss a legally mandated 15-day turnaround for correspondence, marked all requests RUSH. These requests clogged the normal channels, and were in fact one of the primary causes of the two to three week turnaround time.

With data in hand, the section chiefs enacted a requirement that the RUSH designation be used only for documents needed within two days.

| **FIGURE 6** | WISCONSIN STATE DEPARTMENT OF REVENUE WORD PROCESSING CUSTOMER SURVEY (N = NUMBER OF RESPONSES AND X̄ = AVERAGE RATING): OVERALL QUALITY OF WORD PROCESSING |

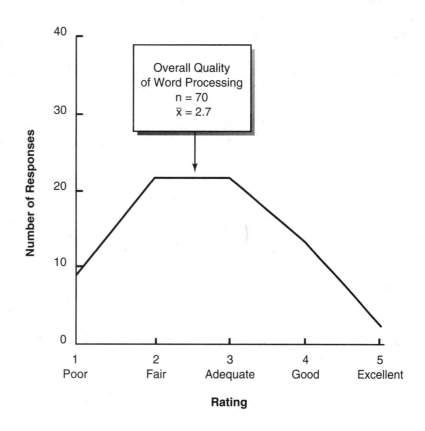

They also monitored the RUSH baskets to prevent customers from under-cutting this new policy. At the same time, word-processing operators were given the authority to reject illegible or incomplete requests. Another essential step was allowing the operators to work overtime on two Saturdays to eliminate the backlog. The team was further able to reduce the workload after an inventory they took of typing requests showed the pool was handling requests that should have gone to other units. This inventory also helped customers and operators anticipate peak workload periods.

Following these changes, the turnaround time quickly decreased to two days, reaching (and staying) at eight hours soon thereafter. (Recall that the original turnaround time was two to three weeks.) The customers and operators continue to meet voluntarily once a week to continue the improvement process.

FIGURE 7   WISCONSIN STATE DEPARTMENT OF REVENUE WORD PROCESSING TEAM DATA ON TYPES OF ERRORS

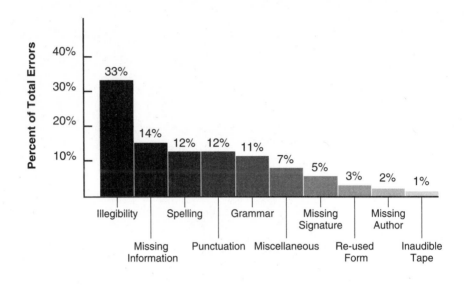

REFLECTIONS: PATTERNS SEEN, LESSONS LEARNED

The initial successes in the Motor Equipment Division and Department of Revenue have inspired many other municipal and state agencies in Madison to give quality improvement techniques a try. In the City of Madison and the Department of Revenue themselves, much additional activity has taken place. Most, but not all, projects have been successful. We've learned valuable lessons by comparing the more successful projects and project teams with those that were less successful.

More progress has been made by teams with some or all of the following ingredients.

Selected projects—

- were clearly linked to customer needs
- were important to the employees
- were manageable, neither too large nor too small
- concerned processes responsive to changes
- focused on statistically measurable processes rather than on policies or attitudes

Selected teams—

- included line-workers who had hands-on experience with the studied processes
- had supervisors and managers committed to quality improvement
- included union representatives when appropriate
- became enthusiastic about their participation, and communicated this enthusiasm to employees not on the team
- were guided and coached by neutral third-party "facilitators" who were able to keep teams focused on the data and underlying *causes* of problems

Let's take a closer look at each of these ingredients.

Madison's Motor Equipment Division and the State Department of Revenue's Word Processing Unit knew their customers and employees were unhappy, and that line supervisors were caught in the middle. Motor Equipment's customers complained about having to wait weeks or months for repairs. In the word processing unit, the operators and supervisors had endured years of complaints from all of their customers. The supervisor was involved in daily "fire-fighting" as she sought to smooth out problems created by long turnaround times.

Both of these project teams selected manageable projects. Neither team attempted to tackle diffuse or broad problems. They correctly viewed projects such as "communication" or "worker morale" as too complex and abstract, and as *symptoms* of other, more direct causes. They avoided taking aim at only small pieces of the larger problems, such as equipment shortages or grammatical errors.

Furthermore, both downtime and turnaround time are easily measured processes that are responsive to change. The records kept by the Motor Equipment mechanics and the operators in the Department of Revenue helped these employees to isolate problems by comparing lapsed time for the steps in their processes. Their data also allowed them to strike at the *real* causes of problems. Having eliminated the causes, they could take steps to *prevent* future problems, thereby improving the process as a whole.

The composition of these teams also contributed to their success. Terry Holmes, the president of the local labor union, was crucial in motivating the Motor Equipment mechanics, assuaging their fears, anticipating potentially troublesome situations, and taking steps to resolve them ahead of time. The word processing team was a mix of line workers and supervisors daily involved in the process being studied, and of customers, resulting in a rich flow of useful information the Bureau had never before had available.

Another factor was the knowledge, commitment, and involvement of these agencies' top managements. Revenue's Secretary Michael Ley, Deputy Secretary Eileen Mershart, and Madison's Mayor, F. Joseph Sensenbrenner, have all made extensive efforts to educate themselves and others in the new philosophy and its tools and techniques. They have communicated their commitment in word and action, and are seeking to create an organizational atmosphere free of the fear of failure. Once the Department of Revenue's projects had been completed, Secretary Ley held an all-day senior management retreat in order to begin developing a collective vision of what the department should look like in the future. Mayor Sensenbrenner also met with his managers to review a quality improvement implementation plan in December 1985.

These top managers' commitment has encouraged other managers naturally inclined toward this approach to emerge. Lee Cheaney, Revenue's Bureau Director of Inheritance and Excise Taxes, is now leading his bureau using the quality improvement style and methodology. Other departments are beginning to contact Cheaney for help in getting teams started. Madison Police Chief David Couper has always felt comfortable with participative management, and he now has a viable framework within which management and project teams can more scientifically do their work. Other departments throughout the city and state are now seeking information and hoping to get involved.

The final important ingredient is guidance by neutral third parties. Skilled at team-building, unencumbered by group power dynamics, the outside facilitators on the Motor Equipment and Department of Revenue teams were also well-versed in quality improvement philosophy, goals, and methodology. Through their guidance, teams stayed focused on customers' needs and the causes of problems, teams let the data do the talking, and they gained valuable education and skills in the process.

What of other, less-successful projects? What went wrong? Again, some common patterns emerge. If team members were either unwilling to speak up or inclined to dominate, communication and information flow halted. If customers and other co-workers were neither surveyed nor interviewed, teams found themselves running in circles, unable to focus on root causes and concrete problems because they didn't know what their customers wanted. When teams chose a "fuzzy" issue or abstract process to study, the sheer complexity caused months of wheel spinning. On the other hand, if teams tackled relatively insignificant projects, they sometimes felt deflated after solving the problem: "You mean it was that simple?" For these teams to reap any benefits, it was important for them to step back periodically and ask, "What do we know now that we didn't know before?" Otherwise frustration, conflict, and boredom could set in.

BASIC GUIDELINES

How do the examples described above fit within the larger context of quality improvement strategies?

The processes studied and improved involved front-line workers. Higher-level processes such as preparing budgets and making policy can also be studied and improved. Teams in such instances will be composed of senior managers.

A key step toward quality and productivity improvement is to open all lines of communication: between managers and employees, between an agency and the people who use its services and whose services it uses, between the various units in an agency. The result will be a flow of ideas and creativity—tapping into human resources—that will allow agencies to improve services without having to increase the flow of financial resources.

"Looks good on paper," one might be thinking, "but I can't just open up those floodgates. How could I handle all those ideas?"

The traditional structure of organizations leaves people ill-equipped to deal with this creativity. As seen in the above examples, employees had to be given new tools and a new framework in which to act. The most powerful tools are scientific methods, the most effective of which are easy to learn. Statistical methods, for example, allow people to learn from data: how to *collect* data most efficiently and how to *extract* useful information from data once they have been collected.

Yet statistics and other scientific tools are no panacea. Their power can remain unrealized in cramped environments. Only when combined with open communication and an obsession with meeting customer needs can these tools be used effectively. Data cannot be gathered without widespread cooperation and teamwork.

Top management must take the lead here by creating an open, collaborative climate. Otherwise employees may be hesitant to collect data on work they are doing because of the fear that such information will be used against them or their co-workers. They may worry that, if gains in productivity are realized as a result of such activity, some of them may lose their jobs. Consequently, management methods in most organizations must be drastically overhauled to change the atmosphere from one of fear to one of trust. The idea of collecting data is not to blame and criticize individuals but rather to improve all processes and systems within the organization.

When top management removes barriers, employees at all levels will be encouraged to learn techniques for effective use of technical and human resources. This re-education process—developing a united team, a scientific approach to problem-solving, and unrelenting focus on customer and quality—is hard work.

As Madison's leaders are discovering, a large portion of the learning comes by doing. Their projects can serve as models for projects elsewhere. To help other public administrators got started, we offer the following guidelines in nine stops that represent the best features of the projects we've observed (see Figure 8). This nine-step sequence need not be followed in a lock-step fashion. Depending on circumstances, some modifications may be desirable.

STEP 1: Conduct a Nominal Group Technique exercise.
These sessions are structured meetings that are extremely useful at the outset of a quality improvement project. The format allows teams to identify, through a voting process, a *vital few* problems needing attention.

STEP 2: Outline the process step by step and draw flow chart.
Flow charts are one of the simplest and most effective techniques to use because they allow teams to understand the process on which they are working and to pinpoint *where* problems are occurring.

STEP 3: Draw a cause-and-effect diagram for selected problem.
Like flow charts, cause-and-effect diagrams are powerful yet simple tools. They enable teams to focus on possible *causes* of problems. (Once a problem is isolated through the flow chart, a cause-and-effect diagram helps identify the exact kind of information that needs to be collected.)

STEP 4: Collect data.
If the team has followed the above steps, it should have some idea of *where* problems are occurring and what kinds of data are needed to find the actual causes of problems.

STEP 5: Analyze the data.
Analyzing data also varies according to specific situations. Most often, however, simple techniques can reveal patterns in the data and point the way towards solutions. Pareto charts, bar charts, dot diagrams, and trend plots are particularly useful.

STEP 6: Plan the changes.
What skills or resources are needed to make the changes indicated as necessary by the data? Who will do the training? By what steps will the changes be introduced into the old system?

STEP 7: Make changes, collect data.
Carry through with planned changes *while continuing to collect data*. This way the team will be able to assess the effectiveness of the changes.

STEP 8: Analyze the additional data.

Analyze the data on the altered process. Did the changes help? If the changes did not help, try to find out why. Go back to flow chart and cause-and-effect diagrams. Was the process assessed correctly in the first place? Are there factors left out of initial considerations? Decide on a course of action and begin again at an earlier step.

STEP 9: Monitor changes.

Did further changes the team make have desired effects? Did problems arise on a broader scale when changes were implemented? Did other aspects of the problem surface? This analysis should point out how the process can be improved further. Since quality improvement is a never-ending process, the team will probably pick up the loop again at an earlier stage. How far back it goes will depend on how different subsequent problems are from the original one. The team may need to draw up new flow charts and cause-and-effect diagrams.

| **FIGURE 8** | GUIDELINE FOR GETTING STARTED: A SUGGESTED SEQUENCE OF NINE STEPS |

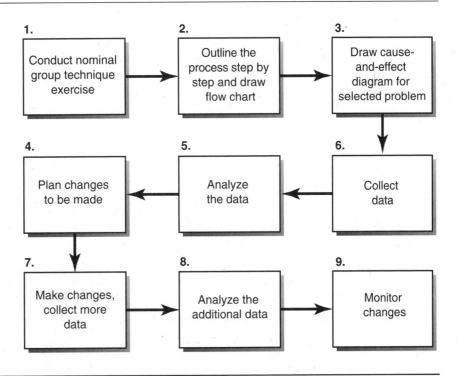

Keep in mind the philosophy behind the entire process of quality improvement. Concentrate on these principles:

- The purpose of quality improvement is to meet, and if possible exceed, the needs and expectations of customers.
- A focus on quality as defined by the customers will result in increasing productivity and decreasing costs.
- Keep the communication lines open in all directions—customers, suppliers, and employees are all valuable sources of ideas and suggestions.
- At most, 15 percent of the problems in any process are within a worker's control. The other 85 percent or more are *system* problems, which only management has the power to correct.
- A long-range collective *vision* for where an organization is going is vital to the success of any quality improvement effort. Develop this vision with the help of managers at all levels. Begin working in management *teams* to articulate this vision.
- Think of quality improvement as a *never-ending continuous process*. Be forever obsessed with quality in order to keep improving.
- Learn gradually by doing; build your confidence.

Finally, remember that the core of quality improvement is utilizing *human* resources. American managers have tended to ignore them for too long, and they may not know where to begin. Our suggestion is to add the following four sentences to *all* job descriptions:

- Always be asking: "How can we make things better around here?"
- Ask: "How can we serve our customers better?"
- Ask: "What hassles, frustrations, and inefficiencies prevent me from doing my job as well as I would like?"
- Share the answers with colleagues, managers, suppliers, and as appropriate, customers.

The public administrators who are attempting to implement this new management philosophy in Madison are pioneers. Although this management style is firmly entrenched in many Japanese businesses, it has rarely been used in any Japanese public sector organizations. As far as we know, no other American government organizations are attempting to implement this approach in its entirety (although we'd be glad to be corrected on this point). Learning by doing takes time, patience, and courage—especially when there are few models to emulate.

Unfortunately, there are special problems inherent in the public sector. Long-term planning is extremely difficult to do. With one eye on re-election or appointment every two to four years, top management is faced with transforming an entire organization in an impossibly short time. The public may be quick to criticize when changes are slow, and public officials are often hesitant to take the necessary risks. Civil servants who enjoy long-term employment, however, may be able to keep quality improvement alive. There is the potential in this group for building what W. Edwards Deming calls "constancy of purpose" (Deming, 1986).

It takes courage for public leaders to commit themselves and their organizations to this approach. As one Japanese executive remarked, however, "You cannot afford to be faint-hearted about improving quality."

A PARABLE

Once upon a time in a tropical country, several people lounged under a bright, hot sun. Some swam in a nearby pool. A young man who happened by was entranced by what he saw. He had never been swimming, but it looked enticingly refreshing. After a few captivating minutes, the young man resolved to give this thing a try. He must have thought it looked so easy. After all, these people just moved their arms and legs about in simple patterns.

Confident he knew what to do, the young man ran straight to the pool, jumped in ... and sank ten feet to the bottom. Fortunately, a woman had seen what happened. She dove in and hauled him out of the pool, where he was revived.

Like this young man, many of us hear about innovative management practices and think to ourselves, "How easy it all looks." We jump in without proper guidance and wonder where we went wrong as we sink to the bottom of the deep end.

There is much more to both swimming and quality improvement than meets the eye. The "visible pieces" are only part of the story. Some people reading about Madison's quality improvement projects may say, "It's really nothing new." They will look at their own practices or employee participation programs and think they have all the tools and methods they need; they've just never combined elements in the ways we've discussed. They're ready to imitate the success of others, envisioning quick and glorious results.

Unfortunately, they are as mistaken as the young man at the swimming pool. Quality improvement, like staying afloat, can become second nature, but it also takes education, patience, and practice before you can do it on your own. For quality improvement, a sweeping overhaul of attitudes and approaches is needed. Also required are commitment, energy, perseverance, and creativity. In mastering this transformation, America may again be able to proclaim advances in management. Public administrators who, to an even greater degree than their private sector counterparts, are frustrated by having to do more with less, *can* take the lead.

The references at the end of this article provide further details for readers who want to learn more. We would enjoy hearing from anyone about their successes and failures in shifting to this new style of management.

As a final note, what do the managers and workers have to say about the time and energy they have invested in these efforts? In Madison, one supervisor said about labor-management relations in his division: "It used to be us against them. Now it's just us." In turn, Joe Turner, a division foreman, observed, "Now there's less cussin' and more discussin'." Quality improvement can work in the public sector.

ACKNOWLEDGEMENTS

We are grateful for financial support that was provided for this work by the First Wisconsin National Bank, Wisconsin Power & Light Company, City of Madison Economic Development Commission, Mayor's Civic Improvement Fund, and the National Science Foundation through Grant Number DMS-8420968. Assistance provided by the University–Industry Research Program of the University of Wisconsin–Madison is also gratefully acknowledged.

We would like to thank the City of Madison's and the State Department of Revenue's managers and employees who had the courage to risk, get involved and stay committed to continuous never-ending improvement of their services. Specifically, we are grateful to Mayor F. Joseph Sensenbrenner, Secretary Michael Ley, Deputy Secretary Eileen Mershart, Lee Cheaney, Jerry Pionkowzki, Jerry Franklin, Terry Holmes, and Joe Turner. In addition, we would like to thank Peter Scholtes and David Miller, without whose energy, enthusiasm, and insight these efforts in the public sector would not have begun. Finally, our eternal gratitude to Sue Reynard, editor and advisor extraordinaire.

NUTS AND BOLTS REFERENCES

Box, George E.P., William G. Hunter, and J. Stuart Hunter. *Statistics for Experimenters.* New York: John Wiley & Sons, 1978.

Delbecq, A., A. Van de Ven, and D. Gustafson. *Group Techniques for Program Planning—A Guide to Nominal Group and Delphi Processes.* Chicago: Scott Foresman, 1975.

Fuller, F. Timothy. "Eliminating Complexity from Work: Improving Productivity by Enhancing Quality." *National Productivity Review* (Autumn 1985): 327–344.

Grant, Eugene L. *Statistical Quality Control.* New York: McGraw-Hill, 1972.

Ishikawa, Kaoru. trans. Asian Productivity Organization. *Guide to Quality Control,* 2nd ed. Hong Kong: Nordica International Limited, 1982.

Juran, Joseph M., ed. *Quality Control Handbook,* 3rd ed. New York: McGraw-Hill, Inc., 1951.

Ryan, Barbara F., Brian L. Joiner, and Thomas A. Ryan, Jr. *Minitab Handbook,* 2nd ed. Boston: Duxbury Press, 1985.

Western Electric. *Statistical Quality Control Handbook.* Easton, PA: Mack Printing Company, 1956.

MANAGEMENT REFERENCES

Chandler, Alfred D., Jr. *The Visible Hand: The Managerial Revolution in American Business.* Cambridge, MA: Belknap Press of the Harvard University Press, 1977.

Deming, W. Edwards. *Out of the Crisis.* Cambridge, MA: MIT Press, 1986.

Hunter, William G. "Managing Our Way to Economic Success: Two Untapped Resources." Report Number 4, Center for Quality and Productivity Improvement, University of Wisconsin–Madison, 1986.

Ishikawa, Kaoru. trans. by David J. Lu. *What is Total Quality Control?: The Japanese Way.* Englewood Cliffs, NJ: Prentice-Hall, 1985.

Joiner, Brian L., and Peter Scholtes, "Total Quality Leadership vs. Management by Control." Report Number 6, Center for Quality and Productivity Improvement, University of Wisconsin–Madison, 1986.

Juran, Joseph M. *Managerial Breakthrough.* New York: McGraw-Hill, 1964.

Sheehy, Barry, "A Near-Run Thing: An Inside Look at a Public-Sector Productivity Program." *National Productivity Review* (Spring, 1985): 139–145.

PART FIVE

THE BALDRIGE AWARD

READING 10
HISTORY OF THE
MALCOLM BALDRIGE
NATIONAL QUALITY AWARD

THE BALDRIGE AWARD (MBNQA) WAS CREATED THROUGH LEGISLATION APPROVED BY CONGRESS IN 1987; THE FIRST AWARDS WERE PRESENTED IN 1988 TO MOTOROLA, THE COMMERCIAL NUCLEAR FUEL DIVISION OF WESTINGHOUSE, AND, IN THE SMALL BUSINESS CATEGORY, GLOBE METAL-LURGICAL. READINGS 21 AND 22 FOCUS ON TWO LATER BALDRIGE WINNERS: THE RITZ-CARLTON HOTEL CO. (1992) AND XEROX (1989). DAVID GARVIN, HARVARD PROFESSOR AND AUTHOR OF READING 1, SAYS THE BALDRIGE AWARD "HAS BECOME THE MOST IMPORTANT CATALYST FOR TRANS-FORMING AMERICAN BUSINESS. MORE THAN ANY OTHER INI-TIATIVE, PUBLIC OR PRIVATE, IT HAS RESHAPED MANAGERS' THINKING AND BEHAVIOR."

THE BALDRIGE AWARD'S SUCCESS AS A STIMULUS FOR CHANGE IS DUE TO THE GREAT PUBLICITY IT GENERATES (PRESENTATIONS ARE MADE IN WASHINGTON, D.C. BY THE PRESIDENT) AND, MORE IMPORTANTLY, THE AWARD CRITE-RIA. THE LATTER DEFINE THE ESSENTIAL CHARACTERISTICS OF TOTAL QUALITY MANAGEMENT AND PROVIDE MBNQA JUDGES WITH A FRAMEWORK FOR CONDUCTING ORGANIZA-TIONAL ASSESSMENT. MANY FIRMS, IN TURN, USE THE CRI-TERIA TO CONDUCT A SELF-ASSESSMENT; THROUGH FALL 1993, OVER 900,000 COPIES OF THE AWARD CRITERIA HAD BEEN DISTRIBUTED. (FOR A FREE COPY OF THE COMPLETE AWARD CRITERIA, CALL THE NATIONAL INSTITUTE OF STAN-DARDS AND TECHNOLOGY IN MARYLAND AT 301-975-2036.) READING 13 REVIEWS THAT PORTION OF THE CRITERIA DEALING WITH CUSTOMER FOCUS AND SATISFACTION.

READING 10
HISTORY OF THE
MALCOLM BALDRIGE
NATIONAL QUALITY AWARD

BY NEIL J. DECARLO AND W. KENT STERETT

The Malcolm Baldrige National Quality Improvement Act was signed by President Ronald Reagan on August 20, 1987. The Act is part of a national campaign to improve the quality of goods and services in the United States. It demonstrates the growing cooperation of business and government to achieve this goal.

Named after the late secretary of commerce, the National Quality Award represents the highest level of recognition for quality that an American company can receive. The award program, however, did not simply appear overnight: it was the culmination of years of effort by a diverse coalition. The roots of the effort go back to the beginning of the 1980s.

INITIAL SUPPORT

By the early 1980s, government and industry leaders in the United States had become concerned about the nation's ability to increase productivity and compete for world markets. With the intention of encouraging greater productivity and competitiveness, President Reagan signed legislation mandating a national study/conference on productivity in October 1982.

The law stated that American productivity was declining. As a result, American goods were becoming more costly—and less competitive—in the international market and jobs were being lost. The bill also pointed to a possible solution to the problem of declining productivity: "Productivity

CREDIT: Neil J. DeCarlo and W. Kent Sterett, "History of the Malcolm Baldrige National Quality Award," *Quality Progress* (March 1990) pp. 21-27. Reprinted with permission of the authors.

improvement can be restored in the United States through the application of policies and management techniques which have brought substantial productivity gains on a broad scale in other countries and in some businesses within the United States."

At the time of this legislation, an effort was already under way to advise labor, management, and government on ways to develop national quality awareness through a mutual spirit of commitment, consensus seeking, and cooperation. The effort began in late 1981 under the leadership of the American Society for Quality Control and Alvin O. Gunneson, then corporate vice president of quality for Revlon. The effort led to the formation in February 1982 of the National Advisory Council for Quality (NACQ), a broad-based group of private- and public-sector executives committed to quality.

The goal of NACQ was to become the recognized center for training, publications, conferences, and research in the quality disciplines.

Parallel efforts were being driven by the American Productivity and Quality Center (APQC)—formerly the American Productivity Center—a nonprofit organization committed to improving productivity, quality, and competitiveness. In preparation for the upcoming White House Conference on Productivity, APQC sponsored seven computer networking conferences from April to September 1983. The organization raised $1 million to pay for the conferences, which received and coordinated input from about 175 corporate executives, business leaders, and academicians. The need for a national quality and productivity award was an idea that surfaced repeatedly during the computer networking sessions.

The final report on the computer conferences recommended that "a National Quality Award, similar to the Deming Prize in Japan, [should] be awarded annually to those firms that successfully challenge and meet the award requirements. These requirements and the accompanying examination process should be very similar to the Deming Prize system to be effective." A special task force, comprised of members of the computer conferences, had already begun examining ways to set up the award.

The report also recommended the creation of a national quality association to promote quality in American products and services, similar to the Union of Japanese Scientists and Engineers (JUSE). Association membership would consist of senior managers and CEOs drawn from a broad spectrum of industries, representatives from labor and academia, and senior government officials.

In the same month that the final report was issued—September 1983—the White House Conference on Productivity was conducted. Keynote speakers were President Reagan, Vice President George Bush, Treasury Secretary Donald Regan, counselor to the president Edwin Meese III, and Commerce Secretary Malcolm Baldrige.

In December 1983, the National Productivity Advisory Committee (NPAC)—a group of corporate executives, academicians, labor leaders, and government officials appointed by the president—recommended the creation of a national medal for productivity achievement. The recommendation, however, was tabled by the Cabinet Council on Economic Affairs because the committee was unable to offer viable direction for funding, guidelines, criteria, and other details of award administration.

A report on the White House Conference on Productivity was published in April 1984. The opening paragraph of the executive summary put the matter bluntly: "America is the most productive nation in the world, but its growth in productivity has faltered. Some of the factors contributing to slower productivity growth are within our control and some are not, but it is important that we respond to this challenge." Further on, the executive summary struck an optimistic note: "Leaders from business, labor, academia, and government assembled for the White House Conference concluded that we can attain a higher rate of productivity growth if management and labor, and business and government, will work together to do it."

The report called for a national medal for productivity achievement to be awarded annually by the president in recognition of high levels of productivity achievement by organizations. Also recommended was a quality awareness campaign at the national level in both the public and private sectors to demonstrate The importance of improving quality, productivity, and international competitiveness.

ONGOING EFFORTS

By the mid-1980s, business and government leaders had drawn considerable attention to concerns about productivity and quality. Groups in both the public and private sector made hundreds of recommendations to improve quality and productivity growth in America. Many of these recommendations called for a national award.

About this time Jackson Grayson, APQC's chairman of the board, contacted Roger Porter, deputy assistant to President Reagan, to solicit presidential involvement in the award program. Grayson proposed that the award be presented by the president to ensure its impact, visibility, and prestige. He was careful to point out, however, that winners should be selected by the private sector to avoid political influence.

Substantive work on the award was begun in September 1985 with the formation of the Committee to Establish a National Quality Award, an entirely private-sector group of academicians and corporate quality business leaders from ASQC, APQC, NASA, Ford Motor Co., AVCO, McDonnell Douglas Corp., and other organizations.

The first matter that had to be settled was the name of the award. The committee—chaired by Frank Collins, rear admiral and executive of quality assurance for the Defense Logistics Agency—spent the first day of a meeting in Washington, D.C., discussing that issue. The group was split among three choices: the National Quality-Productivity Award, the National Productivity-Quality Award, and the National Quality Award. The third option won out.

The effort had begun to gather momentum. In the ensuing months, basic structures for award administration, funding, and criteria began to take shape. Sanford McDonnell of McDonnell Douglas made a preliminary funding commitment and agreed to line up other corporate support. A representative of Florida Power & Light (FPL)—which was already active in the concurrent effort to enact federal legislation for a national quality award—joined the committee's efforts in May 1986.

By the fall of that year, draft criteria had been developed by the National Organization for the United States Quality Award, as the committee was now called. Meanwhile, White House officials had indicated support for the award, though no commitment was made for the president to present the award. By March 1987 the committee received indications that Vice President Bush might present the award.

The importance of these early efforts by ASQC, NACQ, APQC, and the award organization cannot be underestimated Their work created the private sector mechanisms and laid the groundwork for a national quality award. But it was the legislation—the Malcolm Baldrige National Quality Improvement Act of 1987—that lifted the national quality award from idea to reality.

LEGISLATION FOR A NATIONAL QUALITY AWARD

The effort to legislate a national quality award began on Jan. 20, 1985. FPL's chairman and CEO, John J. Hudiburg, and FPL Group's chairman, Marshall McDonald, met with Congressman Don Fuqua (D-FL), then chairman of the House Committee on Science and Technology, and members of his staff. After hearing about the national revival in quality and the need for a national quality award, Fuqua asked FPL to work with his staff to draft legislation for the award. Subsequently, Hudiburg helped arrange for Fuqua and committee staff to visit Japan for the fourth meeting of the United States-Japan Parliamentary Committee on Science and Technology. There, Hudiburg explained the quality improvement program at FPL, while Kaoru Ishikawa explained the history and activities of JUSE.

In March 1986, Fuqua sent staff members of the House Science, Research, and Technology Subcommittee to learn more about FPL's quality improvement program. The two-day visit with FPL's quality director, W. Kent Sterett, convinced the subcommittee staff members that quality was worth their attention. The following six months were spent drafting legislation for a national quality award.

On June 25, 1986, Hudiburg, Joseph M. Juran, and John Hansel, ASQC's chairman of the board, testified before the subcommittee on "Strategies for Exploiting American Inventiveness in the World Marketplace" It was the first time a national quality award was discussed in a formal legislative meeting.

By this time legislation for a national quality award was written, and in August 1986 Fuqua introduced House Bill 5321 "to establish a National Quality Improvement Award, with the objective of encouraging American business and industrial enterprises to practice effective quality control in the provision of their goods and services." Among the findings and purposes of the National Quality Improvement Act were that:

1. "the leadership of the United States in product and process quality has been challenged strongly (and sometimes successfully) by foreign competition;
2. "our Nation's productivity growth has decreased in relation to our competitors over the last two decades as American business has grown more concerned about short-term profitability;
3. "failure to alter this trend will lead to a lower standard of living and less opportunity for all Americans;
4. "although several other factors may have contributed, the year 1985 saw Japan becoming the world's top creditor nation while the United States became a net debtor nation for the first time;
5. "in Japan, the Union of Japanese Scientists and Engineers sponsors a national quality award-the Deming Prize-which provides a powerful incentive to Japanese companies to promote quality improvement;
6. "American business and industry are beginning to understand that improved quality of goods and services goes hand in hand with improved productivity, lower costs, and increased profitability."

The bill also stated that the award program would help improve quality and productivity by:

- "helping to stimulate American companies to improve quality and productivity for the pride of recognition while obtaining a competitive edge through increased profits.
- "recognizing the achievements of those companies that improve the quality of their goods and services and providing an example to others.

- "establishing guidelines and criteria that can be used by business, industrial, governmental, and other enterprises in evaluating their own quality improvement efforts.
- "providing specific guidance for other American enterprises that wish to learn how to manage for high quality by making available detailed information on how winning enterprises were able to change their cultures and achieve eminence."

The bill called on the president or the secretary of commerce to present the award.

Although congress took no further action on this bill and Fuqua left the House of Representatives, efforts continued to gain momentum. Congressman Doug Walgren (D-PA)—who had chaired the June 1986 hearings on exploiting American inventiveness in the world marketplace—maintained the momentum by introducing House Bill 812, "National Quality Improvement Act of 1987." The bill was essentially the same as Fuqua's. Meanwhile, John Hudiburg tried to generate Senate support of the bill by contacting Senator Bob Graham (D-FL), former governor of Florida. This resulted in activity by Graham's staff that would later produce Senate Bill 1251, sponsored by Graham.

In March 1987, the House Subcommittee on Science, Research, and Technology held hearings on Walgren's bill. Testifying were Hudiburg, Frank Gryna of the Juran Institute, and William W. Eggleston, then IBM's corporate vice president for quality.

On June 8, the measure passed the House and was sent to the Senate Committee on Commerce, Science, and Transportation. Before the Senate could act, a tragic accident occurred Commerce Secretary Malcolm Baldrige was killed in a rodeo accident. Three days after Baldrige's death, the Senate committee renamed the legislation in his honor.

The bill was sent to the Senate floor and passed. The House unanimously agreed to the amendment, and on August 20, 1987, President Reagan signed the Malcolm Baldrige National Quality Improvement Act of 1987 into law.

AWARD ORGANIZATION AND FUNDING

The National Institute of Standards and Technology (NIST), formerly the National Bureau of Standards, was chosen to direct and manage the award program. A well-respected organization, NIST was selected because of its reputation for impartiality.

The Baldrige legislation called for a Board of Overseers, consisting of at least five persons selected for their preeminence in the field of quality management. The board, which was appointed by the secretary of commerce in consultation with the director of NIST, provides broad direction to the program. It meets annually to review award activities and make recommendations for improvement.

Commerce Secretary C. William Verity asked John Hudiburg and Sanford N. McDonnell to raise money for the award program. The Foundation for the Malcolm Baldrige National Quality Award was created in February 1988, with FPL and McDonnell Douglas as its co-founders. The foundation now has a 42-member Board of Trustees, a select group of CEOs and presidents of major U.S. companies that strongly support total quality improvement.

The foundation and NIST have a mutual interest in soliciting gifts to support the program. However, every attempt is made to diminish the possibility of foundation contributors influencing the selection of winners. Information about contributors with respect to a particular award cycle is not furnished to NIST until all awards for that cycle have been granted. Moreover, information pertaining to contributions cannot be disclosed to a government employee or an individual serving on the Board of Examiners.

The foundation raised money by asking a broad cross-section of companies to make donations ranging from $25,000 to $150,000, payable in thirds over three years. Current pledges equal $10.4 million. Interest on that endowment, plus application fees, fund the program.

Day-to-day operations and administration of the award program are carried out by the Malcolm Baldrige National Quality Award Consortium—consisting of the American Society for Quality Control and the American Productivity and Quality Center—under contract with NIST. The consortium also designs and prepares instructional materials for use in the information transfer program and assists with award publicity.

The Board of Examiners is a three-tiered structure consisting of nine judges, 28 senior examiners, and about 100 examiners. Selected on the basis of expertise, experience, and peer recognition by the director of NIST in cooperation with the consortium, judges and examiners are quality experts. They come primarily from the private sector, but there is some representation from academia and government.

The judges were chosen by the director of NIST, Ernest Ambler, in consultation with consortium members; as government appointees, the judges underwent a White House clearance process. A slate of examiner nominees was developed by NIST with the aid of affiliated professional societies and miscellaneous recommendations.

The judges, in conjunction with NIST and consortium members, selected the senior examiners and the examiners. Attention was paid, particularly at the judge and senior examiner level, to obtaining representation from different industries.

Affiliated organizations—such as professional societies, trade associations, and area councils—make award findings available for use in education and training throughout the United States.

CRITERIA DEVELOPMENT

The development of criteria for the 1988 award cycle was spearheaded by Curt Reimann of NIST, the award program director. Although Reimann reviewed the criteria developed by the National Organization for a United States Quality award, as well as Deming Prize and NASA criteria, the final set of criteria represented a break from any previous versions.

Reimann spoke with about 75 quality leaders in the United States to extract the main ideas for the examination categories. The result was a basic structure of seven examination categories intended to unite the quality community. Although much of the award program is expected to evolve through annual improvements, the seven examination categories are intended to remain static. giving the program a foundation and continuity.

The relative weights and relationships of these seven basic categories are shown in Figure 1.

FIGURE 1   RELATIONSHIP OF NATIONAL QUALITY AWARD EXAMINATION CATEGORIES 1988

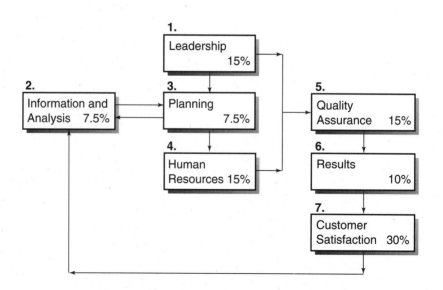

Within the seven basic categories were 44 subcategories, within which were a total of 62 examination items. Within the 62 examination items were 278 scoring criteria, or areas to address, for 1988—the factors that the Board of Examiners considers in scoring the written responses to the examination items.

An outline of the 1988 examination categories and subcategories and scoring weights is shown in Figure 2.

IMPROVEMENT PROCESS

With NIST in the middle listening to all sides, the award program's improvement cycle can turn without conflict and without major changes to the award's basic value system. The intention is to broaden the base of inputs each year to establish representation from more quality communities.

Feedback on virtually every aspect of the award program—criteria, application, examination, and examiner training—was collected throughout 1988. The feedback came from multiple sources. From February through May, after award criteria were made public, comments were collected from examiners just being selected and from companies in the application process. During the examiner training courses and the application review period, from May through September, comments were collected again from the examiners. Finally, after the application review process was over, comments were collected from examiners, companies that had applied for the award, and companies that had not applied but had been exposed to the program.

Based on these inputs, a draft of improved award criteria was prepared and reviewed in December at NIST. This version was sent out to about 200 people for review and comments, which were then incorporated in early 1989. After this, improvements to award criteria were made at the level of the examination item.

The relative weights and relationships of examination categories and an outline of examination categories, subcategories, and scoring weights for 1989 are shown in Figures 3 and 4, respectively.

The process of synthesizing improvement comments and recommendations for the 1989 award cycle took three months. The 1988-89 improvement process resulted not only in improved criteria, but also in:

- sharpened boundaries between categories.
- a more streamlined application review process.
- a more reliable scoring and reporting system.
- a tighter site visit system with more documentation of the on-site examination and better examiner consensus, enabling examiners to work together better.

FIGURE 2	1988 EXAMINATION CATEGORIES/SUBCATEGORIES	

EXAMINATION CATEGORIES/ITEMS	MAXIMUM POINTS
Leadership	150
1 Senior corporate leadership	50
2 Policy	30
3 Management system and quality improvement process	30
4 Resource allocation and utilization	20
5 Public responsibility	10
6 Unique and innovative leadership techniques	10
Information and Analysis	75
1 Use of analytical techniques or systems	15
2 Use of product or service quality data	10
3 Customer data and analysis	20
4 Supplier quality and data analysis	10
5 Distributor and/or dealer quality and data analysis	10
6 Employee-related data and analysis	5
7 Unique and innovative information analysis	5
Strategic Quality Planning	75
1 Operation and strategic goals	20
2 Planning function	20
3 Planning for quality improvement	30
4 Unique and innovative planning	5
Human Resource Utilization	150
1 Management and operations	30
2 Employee quality awareness and involvement	50
3 Quality training and education	30
4 Evaluation, incentive and recognition systems	30
5 Unique and innovative approaches	10
Quality Assurance of Products and Services	150
1 Customer input to products and services	20
2 Planning for new or improved products and services	20
3 Design of new or improved products and services	30
4 Measurements, standards, and data system	10
5 Technology	10
6 Audit	15
7 Documentation	10
8 Safety, health, and environment	10
9 Assurance/validation	15
10 Unique or innovative indicators of quality improvements or economic gains	10
Results from Quality Assurance of Products and Services	100
1 Reliability and performance of products or services	25
2 Reductions in scrap, rework, and rejected products or services	20
3 Reductions in claims, litigation, and complaints related to quality	25
4 Reductions in warranty or field support	20
5 Unique or innovative indicators of quality improvements or economic gains	10

FIGURE 2	1988 EXAMINATION CATEGORIES/SUBCATEGORIES (CONT.)

EXAMINATION CATEGORIES/ITEMS	MAXIMUM POINTS
Customer Satisfaction	300
1 Customer views of quality of products or services	100
2 Competitive comparison of products or services	50
3 Customer service and complaint handling	75
4 Customer views of guarantees/warranties	50
5 Unique or innovative approaches assessing customer satisfaction	25
Total Points	1,000

FIGURE 3	RELATIONSHIP OF NATIONAL QUALITY AWARD EXAMINATION CATEGORIES 1989

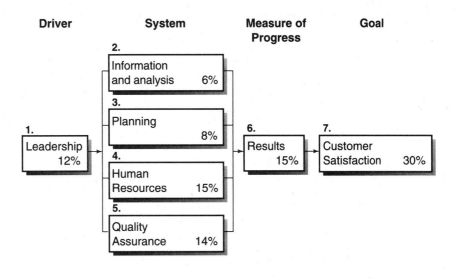

All improvements were factored into the examiners' training program for 1989. Training materials from six cases were used to train the examiners in 1989, compared with materials from one case in 1988.

1989-90 IMPROVEMENT CYCLE

The 1989-90 improvement cycle went much as it had in 1988-89. Comments from examiners and award applicants were collected and synthesized

FIGURE 4	1989 EXAMINATION CATEGORIES/SUBCATEGORIES	
EXAMINATION CATEGORIES/ITEMS		**MAXIMUM POINTS**
Leadership		120
1 Senior management	30	
2 Quality values	20	
3 Management system	50	
4 Public responsibility	20	
Information and analysis		60
1 Scope of data and information	25	
2 Data management	15	
3 Analysis and use of data for decision making	20	
Planning for Quality		80
1 Planning process	30	
2 Plans for quality leadership	50	
Human Resource Utilization		150
1 Management	25	
2 Employee involvement	40	
3 Quality education and training	30	
4 Employee recognition	20	
5 Quality of worklife	35	
Quality Assurance of Products and Services		140
1 Design and introduction of products and services	25	
2 Operation of processes	20	
3 Measurements and standards	15	
4 Audit	20	
5 Documentation	10	
6 Quality assurance of operations business processes	25	
7 Quality assurance of external providers of goods and services	25	
Quality Results		150
1 Quality of products and services	70	
2 Operational and business process quality improvement	60	
3 Quality improvement applications	20	
Customer Satisfaction		300
1 Knowledge of customer requirements and expectations	40	
2 Customer relationship management	125	
3 Customer satisfaction methods, measurements, and results	135	
Total Points:		1,000

for inclusion in the 1990 award program guidelines. Award criteria were tightened by eliminating the award subcategories and reducing the number of examination items from 44 to 33. The areas to address were revised to provide clearer guidance for applicants. The relative weights and relationships of examination categories and an outline of examination categories, examination items, and scoring weights for 1990 are shown in Figures 5 and 6, respectively.

As a result of the improvement process, the 1990 award guidelines will have clearer instructions, more clarifying notes, and more information on the evaluation process for service companies and small businesses.

THE AWARD AS IMPETUS

The Malcolm Baldrige National Quality Award Program is the result of cooperative efforts by business and government leaders concerned about the quality and competitiveness of American products and services. In its first two years the award program exceeded the expectations of those who worked to establish and implement it. The task now is to maintain the gains and continue to enhance the award's prestige and value.

The award program is intended to spark interest and involvement in quality programs, drive American products and services to higher levels of quality, and better equip companies to meet the challenges of world markets.

The Malcolm Baldrige National Quality Award is more than an annual presentation by the president. It is the driving force of a national movement, the hub around which the wheel of quality improvement in America turns.

FIGURE 5   RELATIONSHIP OF NATIONAL QUALITY AWARD EXAMINATION CATEGORIES 1990

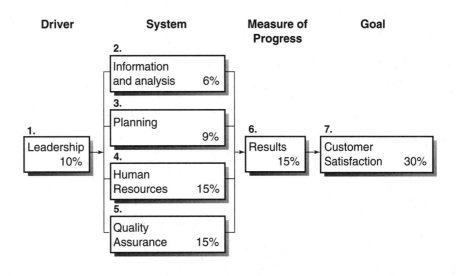

FIGURE 6	1990 EXAMINATION CATEGORIES, ITEMS, AND POINT VALUES

EXAMINATION CATEGORIES/ITEMS		MAXIMUM POINTS
Leadership		100
1 Senior executive leadership	30	
2 Quality values	20	
3 Management for quality	30	
4 Public responsibility	20	
Information and Analysis		60
1 Scope and management of quality data and information	35	
2 Analysis of quality data and information	25	
Strategic Quality Planning		90
1 Strategic quality planning process	40	
2 Quality leadership indicators in planning	25	
3 Quality priorities	25	
Human Resource Utilization		150
1 Human resource management	30	
2 Employee involvement	40	
3 Quality education and training	40	
4 Employee recognition	20	
5 Employee well-being and morale	20	
Quality Assurance of Products and Services		150
1 Design and introduction of quality products and services	30	
2 Process and quality control	25	
3 Continuous improvement of processes, products, and services	25	
4 Quality assessment	15	
5 Documentation	10	
6 Quality assurance, quality assessment, and quality improvement of support services and business processes	25	
7 Quality assurance, quality assessment, and quality improvement of suppliers	20	
Quality Results		150
1 Quality of products and services	50	
2 Comparison of quality results	35	
3 Business process, operational, and support service quality improvement	35	
4 Supplier quality improvement	30	
Customer Satisfaction		300
1 Knowledge of customer requirements and expectations	50	
2 Customer relationship management	30	
3 Customer service standards	20	
4 Commitments to customers	20	
5 Complaint resolution for quality improvement	30	
6 Customer satisfaction determination	50	
7 Customer satisfaction results	50	
8 Customer satisfaction comparison	50	
Total Points:		1,000

Neil J. Decarlo is a communications specialist working in the quality improvement department at Florida Power & Light Company, Juno Beach, FL. He holds a BA in psychology from Harding University in Searcy, AK. He is pursuing an MA in communications from Florida Atlantic University in Boca Raton, FL.

Kent Sterett is assistant vice president of quality at Union Pacific Railroad in Omaha, NE. Sterett joined Union Pacific after 18 years of management experience at Florida Power & Light, where he was responsible for the creation of FPL's quality initiative, which recently won Japan's Deming Prize. He has been active in the development of the Malcolm Baldrige National Quality Award and has served as a judge since its inception.

READING 11
THE 1993 STATE OF U.S. TOTAL QUALITY MANAGEMENT: A BALDRIGE EXAMINER'S PERSPECTIVE

GEORGE EASTON, OF THE UNIVERSITY OF CHICAGO GRADU-
ATE SCHOOL OF BUSINESS, HAS BEEN A BALDRIGE AWARD
EXAMINER AND, MORE RECENTLY, A SENIOR EXAMINER. IN
HIS FOUR YEARS OF BALDRIGE SERVICE, HE HAS PARTICI-
PATED IN THE SCORING AND/OR FEEDBACK PROCESS FOR
TWENTY-TWO COMPANIES, AND THIS ARTICLE IS BASED ON
THOSE EXPERIENCES. THE MAJOR PORTION OF THE ARTICLE
IS HIS ASSESSMENT (VIA REPORTING BOTH STRENGTHS AND
AREAS FOR IMPROVEMENT) OF THE STATE OF QUALITY MAN-
AGEMENT FOR EACH OF THE SEVEN CATEGORIES OF THE
BALDRIGE AWARD CRITERIA. NOTE, THAT HIS ASSESSMENT
IS APPLICABLE ONLY TO THE POPULATION OF COMPANIES
THAT APPLY FOR THE AWARD. THIS POPULATION, AS HE
NOTES, IS "GENERALLY FAR SUPERIOR TO TYPICAL COMPA-
NIES." HE ALSO REPORTS SOME "CROSS-CUTTING THEMES
WHICH APPEAR TO BE LIMITING REALIZATION OF TQM'S
FULL POTENTIAL IN THE UNITED STATES." HIS COMMENTS
CAN HELP ORGANIZATIONS IDENTIFY LIKELY IMPLEMENTA-
TION/IMPROVEMENT PROBLEMS.

THE *CALIFORNIA MANAGEMENT REVIEW* IS PUBLISHED BY
THE WALTER A. HASS SCHOOL OF BUSINESS, UNIVERSITY
OF CALIFORNIA, BERKELEY. THIS IS THE FIRST OF TWO ARTI-
CLES (ALSO SEE READING 15) TAKEN FROM THE SPRING
1993 SPECIAL ISSUE, WHICH DEALT EXCLUSIVELY WITH
MATTERS CONCERNING TOTAL QUALITY MANAGEMENT.

READING 11
THE 1993 STATE OF U.S. TOTAL QUALITY MANAGEMENT: A BALDRIGE EXAMINER'S PERSPECTIVE

BY GEORGE S. EASTON

Quality began to emerge as a key management focus in the U.S. around 1980. This emergence was primarily in manufacturing companies that were suffering severe foreign competitive pressure, most notably from Japan. Since that time, "quality management" has coalesced into a major management movement which has influenced nearly every industry. "Quality management," in this context, means the recognition by senior management that quality is a key strategic issue and therefore an important focus for *all* levels of the organization. Creation of the Malcolm Baldrige National Quality Award by Congress in 1987 contributed to the national visibility of quality management and thus to the momentum of the U.S. quality management movement.

Much of the U.S. quality movement is based on tools and techniques which have been key features in the development of Japanese quality management over the last 40 years. Many of these techniques, such as statistical process control, were originally developed in the U.S. Japanese management approaches, such as widespread employee involvement in quality improvement teams, have also been adopted by many U.S. companies. These approaches have often required complete re-development as substantial changes in both methods and emphasis are necessary for successful implementation in U.S. organizations. There have also been many genuine U.S. quality management innovations. In particular, prevailing traditional U.S.

CREDIT: George S. Easton, "The 1993 State of U.S. Total Quality Management; A Baldrige Examiner's Perspective," pp. 32-54. Copyright 1993 by The Regents of California, Reprinted from the *California Management Review*, Vol. 35, No. 3. By permission of The Regents..

management approaches have been successfully re-focused to address quality management issues.

The most critical challenge facing the U.S. quality movement is the development and implementation of quality-focused corporate management systems that achieve the coherence, integration, and comprehensiveness of quality management in Japan. Such comprehensive quality-driven approaches to corporate management are becoming known in the U.S. as Total Quality Management (TQM). Much consensus exists about some of the key components of TQM systems, including the necessity of a customer focus, the critical role played by leadership, and the importance of widespread employee involvement. Major differences in opinion remain, however, about both the appropriate components of TQM and the appropriate emphasis among the various components. There is also much disagreement concerning the details of implementation, even in the areas of general consensus.

One of the factors contributing to the difficulty of developing in the U.S. the same level of unification and integration achieved by Japanese quality management systems is that few U.S. managers understand the philosophical orientation underlying Japanese management. These more subtle aspects of Japanese quality management, however, may be critically important to the success of quality management in any culture. These nuances are difficult for U.S. managers to fully understand because mastering them requires changing unstated assumptions that are intrinsic in U.S. management thought. These misunderstandings contribute greatly to many managers' tendency to trivialize the intellectual content of TQM and to believe they have complete understanding based on superficial experience with a few quality techniques.

As a result of both the consensus and disagreement discussed above, many questions remain concerning both what U.S. TQM currently is and what it ought to be. In this article, I attempt to contribute to the discussion of these questions by providing a critical assessment of the current state of TQM in the U.S. This assessment is primarily based on my experience evaluating companies as a member of the Board of Examiners of the Malcolm Baldrige National Quality Award over the last four years.

The assessment of TQM described in this article is unusual in that it does not focus just on describing the characteristics of winning companies. The focus here is not only on the small number of winners, but on the larger group of very good companies which receive high scores in the evaluation process. Further, the article presents a critical evaluation of the overall state of development of the TQM systems of these companies as a group. Examination of this larger group of companies aids in discerning patterns in the approaches taken and more accurately reflects the overall state of TQM in the U.S. The sample of companies which are the basis for this assessment, and the target group of companies the assessment attempts to characterize, are described in more detail in the next two sections.

The assessment is reported in a format similar to the Feedback Reports that all Baldrige Award applicants receive. For each of the seven major Categories of the Award, strengths and areas of improvement are described. The strengths identify common successful approaches high-scoring companies are taking in their development and implementation of TQM. In most cases, these approaches are quite similar to those taken by companies that actually win. The areas for improvement identify common difficulties, errors in approach, failures, and confusions that limit the potential of these companies' TQM programs. As with the strengths, many of these areas for improvement are also often found in winning companies. It is my hope that specific discussion of the common weakness in approaches will shed some light on, or at least create some discussion of, the factors limiting the continued successful evolution of TQM in the U.S.

Any critical evaluation of the state of U.S. TQM requires comparison to some conceptualization of what TQM should be. The Baldrige Award Criteria attempt to provide such a conceptualization at the level of the issues that must be effectively addressed by a TQM system. The Award Criteria, however, deliberately avoid prescribing specific approaches and allow a great deal of latitude in interpretation. Thus, they give little specific guidance.[1] As a result, the strengths and areas for improvement described in this article inevitably heavily reflect my own conceptualization of TQM.[2] A brief introduction to the Baldrige Award and the Award's scoring process is given in the Appendix.

THE SAMPLE

The assessment described in this article is based on my experience as an Examiner and Senior Examiner with the Baldrige Award over the last four years. During this time, I have been involved in the scoring and/or feedback process for 22 companies that have applied for the Award. For three of these companies, I have participated in Site Visits. The 22 companies have been in all categories of applicants for the Award: large manufacturing, large service, and small business (both manufacturing and service). Table 1 shows the

---

[1]This article does not discuss the merits of the Baldrige Award. For such a discussion see D.A. Garvin, "How the Baldrige Award Really Works," *Harvard Business Review* (November/December 1991).

[2]The discussion in this article should be interpreted as one person's opinion and in no way as official doctrine of the Baldrige Award.

TABLE 1	TYPES OF COMPANIES IN THE SAMPLE	
SIZE	MANUFACTURING	SERVICE
Large	5	10
Small	5	2

number of companies of each type. These 22 companies form the "sample" on which this assessment is based.

This "sample" is clearly not random. It is, however, of sufficient scope to develop a very good idea of the characteristics of the population of companies that apply for the Award. It should also be emphasized that the population of companies that apply for the Award is not a representative cross section of U.S. businesses or even of companies that are trying to implement quality management systems. Because of self-selection, companies that do apply are generally far superior to typical companies. Many more companies use the Baldrige Award Criteria for diagnostic purposes than apply or ever intend to apply for the Award.

Finally, my analysis of this population of companies is largely subjective. Systematic analysis would be difficult because the Award's confidentiality requirements prohibit disclosure of information concerning any applicant. In addition, the applicant's materials can only be used by the Examiner during the actual scoring process. Thus, my "analysis" is based on observation and subjective assessment of common approaches and characteristics—in short, on my experience.

THE TARGET

The assessment which begins in the next section attempts to capture the state of TQM in very good U.S. companies that are committed to quality management and have achieved considerable success. The focus is not only on exceptional companies, such as those that have won the Baldrige Award, but also on the next level of companies which score about 600 or higher out of 1,000 in the Award process. While understanding the approaches that winners have used successfully can clearly be beneficial, winning companies are often quite unique in both the approaches they take as well as in their success in deploying TQM and obtaining results. To assess the overall state of the TQM movement and its potential for widespread influence on U.S. management practice requires focusing on the larger number of very good companies that are committed to TQM rather than only on the occasional unique and exceptional company. It is the dissemination of quality management approaches into this larger group that will ultimately determine the success or failure of TQM as a management revolution in the United States. The reason is that these companies are both leaders in management thought and sufficient in number to have widespread influence. In addition, the fact that there are a larger number of companies in this group allows common patterns to be discerned. Baldrige winners are so few in number that even subjective inference is difficult.

While the group of companies targeted by this assessment is broader than just winners of the Award, the strengths and areas for improvement identified are also typical in winning companies. Winning the Baldrige Award is often interpreted as a blanket endorsement of all aspects of the winner's quality management systems. This, however, is not the case. Winning companies are selected to be role models. What role model means in this context is that winning companies do some things exceptionally well and with exceptional results, do most things well, and do not have major flaws or omissions that veto their role-model status. Thus, winning companies generally score above the 600 level in all *key* areas, indicating overall high levels of deployment of their basic approaches. But as the assessment which follows indicates, there are many important areas for improvement in 600-level companies as well as many strengths. These areas for improvement are also often found in winning companies.

ASSESSMENT BY CATEGORY

In this section, the strengths and areas for improvement that are common among very good TQM companies are described. The assessment is given for each of the seven Categories of the Baldrige Award Criteria. Some important differences between manufacturing and service companies are noted.

CATEGORY 1: LEADERSHIP

STRENGTHS

- Senior management is committed to quality. Senior managers are actively involved in promoting the importance of quality and customer satisfaction and they devote a substantial fraction of their time to quality-related issues (10 percent or more). Their involvement includes activities such as speeches, meeting with employees, meeting with customers, giving formal and informal recognition, receiving training, and training others (e.g., new employee orientation).

- Senior management has developed and communicated a set of company quality values. The key values of TQM are emphasized such as the importance of the customer, process orientation, continuous improvement, teamwork, management-by-fact, mutual respect and dignity, and value of individual employees and their contributions.
- The entire organization understands the importance of the external customer. The concept and importance of internal customers is also understood, and most employees feel some connection between what they do and the company's ability to respond to and satisfy the external customers.
- Elements of a quality management structure are in place, such as a senior management TQM council or division and department councils. These councils are involved in the management of the quality improvement teams, suggestion system, and recognition systems.

AREAS FOR IMPROVEMENT

- Senior management's *primary* focus is still on "strategy" and strategic business units (SBUs). Management still views the company almost exclusively in terms of financial, not operational, measures. There is only limited awareness of direct quality measures, especially on a month-to-month or day-to-day basis.
- Senior management does not systematically develop or carefully plan its leadership activities. Senior managers do not apply the concept of processes to their own functions. In addition, there is little real management-by-fact. Instead, senior management primarily relies on experience together with financial and cost measures. The measures often have limited effectiveness in guiding management decisions.
- Overall, senior management's understanding of TQM is quite superficial. While senior management supports TQM in principle, they feel that, other than to promote its importance, it is not a primary activity in their realm. As a result, the scope of senior management's involvement is limited. In addition, senior management does not have a clear conceptualization of the specific roles of lower levels of management in TQM.
- Management still has, almost exclusively, a results, not process, orientation.
- In many cases, senior managers have very little specific knowledge and understanding of the company's processes or of direct customer, operational, employee-related, and supplier data. They do not routinely apply the Pareto principle, either formally or subjectively, and as a result they cannot identify the key problem areas or underlying causes. For

RESULTS VS. PROCESS ORIENTATION

In a results-oriented approach, management is still primarily based on setting objectives, feedback, and creating incentives. Behind this orientation is an unspoken belief that the results belong to the individuals, and that management's role is to hire the best people and to create incentives for obtaining the desired results. This presumes that the individuals will be able to figure out how to achieve the goals if left to their own devices.

In a process-oriented approach, the belief is that the results belong to the processes, and the processes belong to the organization. The role of the individuals is process operation and development including improvement of existing processes and development of new ones. The role of results is to guide process development and improvement. Thus, in TQM the emphasis is on developing methods and strategies, and approaches for implementing them, that will generate the best possible results.

At management levels, the development of methods and strategies may be directly tied to achieving particular important goals, but in addition it is focused on providing methods which will enable lower levels of the organization to develop strategies and methods for achieving their goals. The Plan-Do-Check-Act cycle, together with the associated quality tools, is an example. It is not a method for achieving a particular objective, but rather a method for enabling quality-improvement teams to solve problems and generate improvement.

example, they are unaware of the key types and causes of customer complaints or the key types and causes of employee injuries. They are also often unaware of adverse trends and have difficulty interpreting the levels and trends in the context of the variation that is generally present in the data.

- While some quality management structure is in place, for the most part the roles of managers and supervision in TQM have not been developed. As a result, most managers are not clear about what they should do other than promote quality in general terms. They believe that TQM is primarily about attitude and motivation.

- Management often does not fully appreciate the scope of their business as viewed by the customer, focusing instead on what management perceives the product to be. As a result, the scope of the quality activities, including measurement, is often too narrow.

CATEGORY 2: INFORMATION AND ANALYSIS

STRENGTHS

- There is excellent advanced technological support of the information systems.
- The company has identified key quality measures which are tracked and often given high visibility.
- A lot of data, primarily financial/accounting data, are readily available.
- Informal benchmarking and other types of information acquisition and sharing are beginning to occur.
- Competitive comparisons are made against primary competitors.

AREAS FOR IMPROVEMENT

- The quality information is not well organized to support quality management. There is generally no coherent, articulated strategy for ensuring that the information needs of all organizational levels are met. Issues of what information is global, what is local, how local information is to be managed and analyzed, how local information is to be aggregated for higher level decision making, how aggregate information is to be analyzed, and how the results of aggregate analysis are to be disseminated, indexed, and otherwise made widely available are generally not adequately addressed.
- The data that are readily available are often developed to monitor results and assess achievement of goals. These measures tend to be downstream and financially oriented. They are often not well-suited either for managing operations or for maintaining customer focus (i.e., managing customer relationships and tracking satisfaction). In many cases, the cost data do not give an accurate picture of operations because they are based on inaccurate assumptions, such as arbitrary allocation of overhead, or because they merge costs from unrelated causes.
- The information systems are often inflexible and unable to support the kinds of change that are a part of both continuous improvement and evolving customer expectations.
- Competitive comparisons are often limited to immediate competitors only.
- Benchmarking is often confused with and limited to competitive comparisons. The purpose of benchmarking is to generate process innovation. Benchmarking is often most fruitful when similar processes or process steps are examined in companies in different industries. In addition, non-competitors are usually far more willing to share information.
- Analysis outside of technical functions and production areas is limited. Analysis at management levels is not based on management-by-fact. Rather, it is generally based almost exclusively on informal brainstorming. Effective problem-solving methods are not deployed at all levels.

CATEGORY 3: STRATEGIC QUALITY PLANNING

STRENGTHS

- Baldrige applicants usually develop some sort of written quality plan. This plan may be separate or part of the overall strategic or business plans.
- Quality-related goals are set in production-related areas of the company. Often quality goals are part of the management-by-objectives process.
- Many companies have adopted stretch goals (e.g., Six Sigma).

AREAS FOR IMPROVEMENT

- Few companies appear to have a well-developed strategic or corporate quality planning process. When plans do exist, they are seldom derived from systematic analysis of meaningful data and information, including customer, operational, and employee data and information.
- The plans generally stop at setting goals and objectives and developing the budget. They do not realistically address implementation issues or deployment of the plan throughout the organization. Even in companies with a fairly well-developed planning process, failure to realistically consider implementation issues is common and is a key reason the planning process is ineffective.
- The plans are often not effectively communicated to the organization. In many areas of the company, employees are either unaware of the plan or do not understand how the objectives and activities of their area relate to the overall plans. There is often no link between the overall company plans and either approaches to deployment (most commonly individual objective setting through an management-by-objectives process) or individual performance evaluation.
- Senior management believes that creating the right incentives is key to driving change.
- In many cases, too many top priorities are set. As a result, overall organizational focus is lost.

CATEGORY 4: HUMAN RESOURCE DEVELOPMENT AND MANAGEMENT

STRENGTHS

- There are a large number of teams focused on quality improvement projects. These teams are concentrated in production and the critical areas that directly support production. There are many examples of team projects that have been successful and have generated substantial improvements.
- There is usually a suggestion system with a required response time. A substantial percent of the employees submit suggestions.

- All employees receive basic quality training. Most employees receive a substantial amount of annual training. In the best companies, employees receive 40 to 80 hours of training per year with training expenditures around 3–5 percent of payroll.
- There is widespread employee recognition for various types of contributions, including quality.
- Substantial resources are devoted to safety.
- There are a lot of traditional benefits.
- An employee survey is used to assess employee morale.
- Human Resources measures such as turnover, absenteeism, and injuries show identifiable improvement trends and good levels in comparison to industry averages.

AREAS FOR IMPROVEMENT

- Most teams do not effectively use team processes such as problem-solving methods or quality tools, relying instead almost entirely on informal brainstorming. As a result, many teams are relatively ineffective. It is difficult to maintain momentum once the easy problems are solved.
- The concept of empowerment is poorly understood by management, even in cases where "empowerment" is an important part of a company's quality initiatives. In some cases, employees or teams are given authority that they are not comfortable exercising because either appropriate decision-making processes have not been developed or the employees have not been adequately trained. In other cases, decisions made by "empowered" teams are routinely reviewed by multiple levels of management prior to authorization. In other companies, empowerment is limited to giving the employee authority to act on behalf of the customer.
- Most employees have only received basic training. The effect of the training is primarily limited to awareness, either because the training is awareness training or because the employees do not successfully integrate the training into their work. In addition, there is little formal training given in company processes outside of the production area.
- The effectiveness of training is not directly measured. Measurement is limited to course evaluation forms and surveys and does not address how much was learned or how well the training is integrated into the employees' work.
- Much of the employee recognition is superficial and seems to be driven by the feeling that everyone should receive recognition (e.g., employee of the week). In other cases, it is results-oriented and substantially influenced by factors beyond the employee's direct control. In many cases, it

is unclear the extent to which the recognition reinforces quality relative to other considerations.

- Recognition of the work of quality improvement teams, such as competitions or presentations to senior management, which focuses on the team's improvement process is not common.
- The performance evaluation system is poorly aligned with the company's quality management system or overall plans and objectives. Performance evaluation emphasizes rewarding results which in many cases are primarily driven by factors beyond the individual employee's control.
- Safety and ergonomics are not part of quality improvement activities. This is often true even when there is substantial organizational focus on safety.

CATEGORY 5: MANAGEMENT OF PROCESS QUALITY

STRENGTHS

- Many manufacturing companies have vastly improved the design and introduction of new products and services. Approaches taken include increased customer focus, cross-functional teams, joint design with suppliers and customers, design simplification, process capability considerations, simultaneous engineering, experimental design, and Taguchi methods.
- In manufacturing companies, the concepts of variation and control are understood in the context of production. Many production processes are controlled using SPC. The production processes are reasonably in-control. For important processes, they are also demonstrably capable.[3]
- At least one specific approach to quality improvement has been implemented with tremendous improvement resulting. Examples of such improvement approaches include statistical process control, just-in-time production, employee involvement, work cells, self-managed teams, suggestion systems, and cycle-time reduction.

---

[3]The extent to which the production processes can be considered in-control depends on what technical definition of in-control is used. Experience suggests that many manufacturing processes that appear to be in-control using simple control charts fail to be in-control when more rigorous definitions of in-control are used such as those based on statistical models which take into account autocorrelation (e.g., see L.C. Alwan and H.V. Roberts, "Time-Series Modeling for Statistical Process Control," *Journal of Business and Economic Statistics,* 6 [1988]: 87–95). Many of the key manufacturing processes in the target group of very good companies are likely to fail the more rigorous definitions of in-control. Nevertheless, the key processes in these companies generally are quite stable and capable, usually appearing to be in-control according to simple control charts.

- In service companies, some degree of measurement of the service production processes has been developed. In particular, most easily quantifiable measures are made for key processes and exhibit some degree of stability.
- Production processes are improved by quality improvement teams consisting of either workers or staff employees. The levels of involvement in teams by the production workforce is high. Sometimes the improvement efforts are sophisticated, using tools such as experimental design.
- Some companies have a well-defined quality systems audit function for the production processes.
- Quality improvement teams are also active in repetitive service and business process areas.
- Many companies have extensive programs with their suppliers. These include supplier quality systems audits, supplier rating and qualification systems, training, joint design teams, joint quality improvement teams, and supplier (and supplier employee) recognition programs.

AREAS FOR IMPROVEMENT

- New product development is still primarily reactive (i.e., responds to, rather than anticipates, customer demands) and is driven by generally available technology improvements. Quality assurance of new product development and introduction is not prevention-based, relying instead primarily on inspection and testing. The new product development process is not well defined.
- Many companies, especially service companies, have very limited new product development activity. While they frequently change and augment the characteristics of their products, they do not view these changes as new product development and have no systematic approaches.
- Processes tend not to be very well defined except when they are naturally defined by the production processes, as is the case in many manufacturing and some repetitive service activities. As a result, processes are often not well defined in service companies and job shops, or in most companies outside of repetitive manufacturing and service activities.
- In many companies, the approaches taken to quality are limited to one or two approaches such as statistical process control or just-in-time production. Because the company has success with the specific approaches taken, management believes that they have a fully developed quality management system.
- In many cases, there is very little understanding of the idea of driving measurement of processes upstream, the importance of variables mea-

sures, or measurement qualification. Rather, management relies exclusively on end-of-process defect rates and customer complaints.

- There is often very little correlation of process measures with customer satisfaction, or of upstream measures with downstream measures. Identification of these relationships is based on the experience and intuition of management and technical staff.

- While many service companies collect the readily available quantifiable measures of their service processes, these measures are often not direct measures of the key attributes of the service processes. As a result, many service companies have very few direct process measures. Rather, they try to control their processes using customer feedback data. While customer satisfaction is clearly the goal, customer feedback generally cannot be used to effectively control processes because the cycle time for collecting customer feedback is too slow and the relationship between the process parameters and the customer's perceptions is often obscure.

- Many companies do not have a very broad scope of types of improvement teams such as workforce teams, management/technical teams, teams consisting of both management/technical staff and the workforce, and cross-functional teams. Many companies' TQM programs focus entirely on one type of team, usually workforce teams. As a result, the scope of improvement is limited.

- In many cases, improvement efforts are based on informal brainstorming and not on management-by-fact and systematic analysis. This is related to the failure of the quality improvement teams to effectively use a well-developed problem-solving process supported by analysis tools.

- Documentation of the improvement methods and activities and dissemination of the knowledge gained is often limited. Quality improvement teams do not make effective use of devices such as the QC Story.[4]

- The distinction between improvements that result from bringing a process into control and continuous improvement once the process is in-control is often not understood. As a result, while many problems are solved, a state of systematic, on-going refinement is not achieved. Because great improvement often occurs when the processes are brought into control, management believes prematurely that the company has

---

[4]A QC Story is a team problem-solving process which, together with QC Tools, both guides team problem solving and serves as a format for documenting team improvement activities and analysis (see H. Kume, *Statistical Methods for Quality Improvement*, The Association for Overseas Technical Scholarship, Tokyo [1985]). The term QC Story is also used to refer specifically to the story-board format Japanese QC Circles use to present the results of their improvement activities to management.

achieved a state of systematic on-going process refinement (i.e., continuous improvement).

- Systematic approaches to improving are less well developed in business processes and support services than in primary production areas. This is associated with the lack of well-defined processes in these areas. Repetitive service activities (e.g., billing) are sometimes an exception.
- Many companies have essentially no quality systems audits. In addition, audits originating from senior management or including senior management involvement are very rare.
- Many companies appear somewhat heavy-handed with their suppliers. A state of cooperation and appropriate integration does not exist.

CATEGORY 6: QUALITY AND OPERATIONAL RESULTS

STRENGTHS

- Very good companies can demonstrate high levels of quality in their products and services for a wide variety of measures relative to similar U.S. companies.
- Sustained improvement trends of at least a several-fold improvement over two to five years can be demonstrated for key product and operational areas. Sustained improvement results, but with weaker trends, can be demonstrated in most areas of the company.
- Quality results for key suppliers also show significant and sustained quality improvement.

AREAS FOR IMPROVEMENT

- For most companies, the scope of the data used by management to routinely track the results of their quality systems is inadequate. Key measures from all important processes are often not readily available. In addition, management often does not track in-process and upstream measures.
- In many companies, almost no variables-based measures are tracked. Instead the only measures are defect rates and customer complaints. Management is unaware of levels or trends in measures such as process capabilities.
- Linkage between operational measures and key customer requirements is not established.
- In many cases, sufficient data to establish trends are not readily available. Management is only aware of the most recent measures and may be unaware of adverse trends. Sustained improvement trends cannot be established.

- Even winners are not necessarily the best in the world.

CATEGORY 7: CUSTOMER FOCUS AND SATISFACTION

STRENGTHS

- Many companies use a large number of survey-type instruments to assess customer satisfaction and customer needs and expectations. Focus groups are also common.
- There is increasing emphasis on easy access for customers and quick response times.
- Some well-defined customer service standards are developed for such things as time to answer the telephone and response time to queries or complaints. These measures are often tracked.
- There is much motivational training for customer service representatives. There is also often extensive product training.
- Increasing attention is being given to formal complaint resolution. Complaints are aggregated by types and reported to management.
- Customer service representatives are being given increasing authority to satisfy the customer.
- Customer satisfaction levels are high in comparison to similar companies in the United States. Sustained customer satisfaction improvement trends can be established. Market share and repeat customer trends are favorable.

AREAS FOR IMPROVEMENT

- There is often little understanding of the technical issues relating to the accuracy of surveys (e.g., bias, variability, accuracy).
- There is also often little distinction between determining customer satisfaction and customer needs and expectations. The methods of extracting customer requirements or identifying latent desires from customer information are usually informal.
- There is no formal approach for integrating customer data with the (new) product development process. Product design relies on the designer's intuition and customer data collected primarily for other purposes.
- Often, only the company's current customers are surveyed. Appropriate information about lost customers, new customers, and competitor's customers is not obtained.
- Stratification of customer data is done by attributes important to the company (e.g., account size), not the customer. As a result, the data are of limited use for identifying patterns of satisfaction and dissatisfaction among customers with similar characteristics.

- In many cases, the sales force is used as a primary source of customer information. However, sales usually has no systematic, well-defined approach for gathering and aggregating customer data and no training in these activities. Other types of quality improvement activities in sales are also minimal.
- Customer service standards are not well defined except in cases where there are easy and obvious measures. Much customer service representative training is motivational and not specific. Methods for assessing customer service performance relative to standards are generally poor.
- Customers still have difficulty reaching someone with real authority to resolve their problems. The role of Customer Service is still to "protect" management.
- Companies still seem to think that customers should be completely satisfied with replacement guarantees.
- Usually, formal complaints are the only ones that are tracked. There is no operational definition of what a complaint is. As a result, informal or minor complaints are missed and thus are not aggregated or tracked and cannot be used for assessing customer requirements and satisfaction. In addition, complaint data are not effectively used to drive quality improvement.
- In many cases, customer satisfaction comparisons are left to third parties (e.g., industry associations) that do not use valid and reliable methods.

DISCUSSION: SOME CROSS-CUTTING THEMES

As the assessment above indicates, there are many important strengths in the approaches of leading TQM companies. In many cases, these approaches have produced impressive results. But there are also many important areas for improvement. Few, if any, U.S. companies have developed quality management systems with the levels of coherence, comprehensiveness, and integration of quality management in the best Japanese companies. Underlying many of the areas for improvement described above are a number of cross-cutting themes which appear to be limiting realization of TQM's full potential in the United States.

One of the most important cross-cutting themes is that the scope of the concept of "process" in TQM is not fully understood by most U.S. managers, even in companies that are committed to quality management. This is particularly true outside of structured, repetitive manufacturing and service activities where the basic production process is readily apparent and can be defined in specific detail. Thus, for many critical activities, processes are not defined. In fact, the higher-level or more abstract the activity, the less often an appropriately defined process has been developed. As a result, the approaches taken are created on-the-fly by the individuals responsible. Because there is no uniformity in approach, the activities cannot be stabilized or continuously improved.

This lack of understanding of process is related to the persistent results-oriented perspective of most managers. Because of this perspective, many companies' approach to management focuses on setting goals and objectives, on trying to create the right incentives, and on feedback based on after-the-fact measures. There is little before-the-fact emphasis on strategies, approaches, or methods—the process-oriented notions.

The planning process often exemplifies this problem. First, the planning process itself is often poorly defined. More importantly, planning often stops with the development of goals and budgets with little emphasis on developing strategies and methods for achieving the goals. In addition, there is often insufficient prevention-oriented analysis to anticipate barriers to implementation or to ensure sufficient flexibility to respond to problems as they occur. While an individual's goals may be reviewed by several levels of management, the methods to be used to achieve the goals often receive a cursory review at best. As a result, consensus concerning what strategies and methods to use is not developed in advance and the actual implementation is ad hoc, often developed at quite low levels of the organization. In summary, managers do not view the development and deployment of processes and methods as the fundamental management activities that drive achievement of the goals.

In many companies, the functioning of the quality improvement teams provides another important example of the limited development and deployment of the idea of a process. In the most common case, the improvement teams have been trained in a variation of the Shewart Plan-Do-Check-Act cycle together with a few basic quality tools. These, however, fail to be integrated into an effective team process. One reason is that the team process is not completely developed. This situation is often indicated by management having no clear concept of exactly how the teams are supposed to function. In many cases, there is no structure or method, such as documentation through a QC-story format, to guide deployment of the team process and ensure effective use of methods such as the quality tools. Effective use of the quality tools is difficult. As a result, the teams tend to rely almost exclusively on informal approaches such as brainstorming. The quality tools are seldom used, collection of data is avoided, and root cause analysis is not particularly effective.

A second cross-cutting theme is the lack of effective management-by-fact. In many cases, companies have relatively few direct operational and customer measures that can can be stratified for effective root-cause determination. Instead, as was discussed in Category 2, the measures focus on downstream results and after-the-fact assessment of the achievement of goals. The measures used are often indirect financial measures that aggregate effects from a variety of causes. They are difficult to disaggregate or stratify in meaningful ways that directly relate to planning and decision making.

The failure to consistently set clear priorities throughout the organization is another important cross-cutting theme. The principle of consistently developing a small number of key priorities is pervasive throughout TQM. In many companies, however, the key priorities are unclear to middle and front-line managers, and to the workforce. Sometimes this is because of unclear or inconsistent communication. But often a key contributing factor is that far too many top priorities are developed. As a result, departments and individuals pick and choose among the top priorities, and a consistent overall organizational focus is lost.

A final cross-cutting theme is that in many companies the primary focus of the quality effort is on the workforce. Consequently, roles for all levels of management and technical staff in TQM are not developed. As a result, management and staff tend to believe that TQM is primarily about attitude and that their role in TQM is to promote the importance of quality and to motivate the workforce. While there is often effort to involve all levels of management in promoting quality, the focus is nevertheless on supporting and encouraging the workforce as the primary generators of quality improvement. The workforce, however, cannot be the primary generators of improvement. While their contribution is very important, the vast majority of quality improvement must come from management and technical staff. Without well-defined roles for direct contribution by all levels, a company's TQM program is unlikely to achieve more than moderate success.

SUMMARY

So, what, then, is the current state of TQM in the United States? Overall, the assessment is generally favorable. An increasing number of companies are actively focused on quality as a key approach to improving their competitiveness. And as the assessment above indicates, U.S. companies that are committed to quality have a large number of areas of true strength. In many cases, they also demonstrate some exceptional management innovation. Further, their efforts are yielding clear results in terms of customer satisfaction, operational improvement, and employee involvement.

While the assessment is generally favorable, these companies also have a large number of important areas for improvement. These areas for improvement are not superficial or merely a matter of failure in execution. They are not just blemishes on conceptually well-developed management systems.

Rather, they are weaknesses in the fundamental approaches taken to management such as the lack of full understanding of process, the lack of emphasis on planning, the lack of effective systems to implement the plans, the reliance on incentives, failure to apply the principle of management-by-fact, focusing on results to the exclusion of processes or methods, focusing on financial measures to the exclusion of direct operational measures, and inadequate understanding of customer expectations. Senior management is not yet fully aware of the totality of its appropriate role in TQM and is often not even completely comfortable in its present role.

Thus, TQM in the United States is far from mature. It is important that TQM approaches continue to be developed, refined, and expanded, even in companies that have already achieved considerable success. Otherwise the competitive advantages that TQM promises will not be realized and many companies will be left struggling against competitive decline without any unified or coherent strategy for revitalization.

The Baldrige Award

This Appendix briefly describes the Baldrige Award and the process used to evaluate applicants for the Award. It is intended to provide some background information and context for the assessment of the state of U.S. TQM described in this article. For additional information, a copy of the Award Guidelines can be obtained by calling the Baldrige Award Office at (301) 975-2036.

THE BALDRIGE AWARD

The law creating the Malcolm Baldrige Award (Public Law 100-107) indicates a number of purposes of the Award. First, the Award is intended to increase the awareness of quality and quality management as a critical strategic issue in U.S. competitiveness. Second, the Award is intended to develop and promote an understanding of the requirements for excellent quality management systems. One way this is done is by establishing guidelines and criteria that can be used, not only in the evaluation of Award applicants, but also by business, governmental, and other organizations in evaluating their own quality systems. The Award is also intended to promote the sharing and dissemination of information about effective quality management strategies. Finally, the Award should identify companies with role-model quality management systems.

Companies apply for the Baldrige Award in one of three categories: manufacturing, service, and small business. The small business category is for companies, both service and manufacturing, with 500 or fewer employees. Up to two Awards can be given each year in each category, although none need be given if none of the applicants in that category meet the requirements for role-model status. In the first five years of the Award, only three Awards in the Service Category and four Awards in the Small Business Category have been given. Two Awards in the Manufacturing Category have been given every year. Previous winners of the Award are listed in Table 2.

Companies apply for the Baldrige Award by submitting a written application describing their quality management systems. These written applications must respond to approximately 90 "areas to address" organized into about 30 Items in seven major categories. The seven major categories are:

- Leadership
- Information and Analysis
- Strategic Quality Planning
- Human Resource Development and Management
- Management of Process Quality

TABLE 2	PREVIOUS WINNERS OF THE MALCOLM BALDRIGE NATIONAL QUALITY AWARD

YEAR	CATEGORY	COMPANY
1992	Manufacturing	AT&T Network Systems Group/Transmission Systems Business Units, Morristown N.J. Texas Instruments Defense Systems and Electronic Group, Dallas, TX
	Service	AT&T Universal Card Services, Jacksonville, FL Ritz-Carlton Hotel Co., Atlanta, GA
	Small Business	Granite Rock Co., Watsonville, CA
1991	Manufacturing	Solectron Corp., San Jose, CA Zytec Corp., Eden Prairie, MN
	Small Business	Marlow Industries, Dallas, TX
1990	Manufacturing	Cadillac Motor Car Co., Detroit, MI IBM Rochester, Rochester, MN
	Service	Federal Express Corp., Memphis, TN
	Small Business	Wallace Co., Houston, TX
1989	Manufacturing	Milliken & Co., Spartanburg, SC Xerox Business Products and Systems, Stamford, CT
1988	Manufacturing	Motorola, Inc., Spartanburg, SC Westinghouse Commercial Nuclear Fuel Division, Pittsburgh, PA
	Small Business	Globe Metallurgical, Inc., Cleveland, OH

- Quality and Operational Results
- Customer Focus and Satisfaction

The written applications must be no more than 75 pages (60 pages for small businesses).

THE SCORING PROCESS

The evaluation of the written company applications begins with independent scoring of each application by four to eight Examiners (in 1992, eight Examiners were

TABLE 3	SCORING GUIDELINES	
SCORE	**APPROACH/DEPLOYMENT**	**RESULTS**
0%	• anecdotal information; no system evident in information presented	• no data reported or anecdotal data only
10-30%	• beginning of a systematic approach to addressing the primary purposes of the Item • significant gaps still exist in deployment that would inhibit progress in achieving the major purposes of the Item • early stages of a transition from reacting to problems to preventing problems	• early stages of developing trend data • some improvement trend data or early good performance reported • data are not reported for many to most areas of importance to the Item requirements and to the company's key performance-related business factors
40-60%	• a sound, systematic approach responsive to the primary purposes of the Item • a fact-based improvement process in place in key areas addressed by the Item • no major gaps in deployment, though some areas may be in early stages of deployment • approach places more emphasis on problem prevention than on reaction to problems	• improvement or good performance trends reported in key areas of importance to the Item requirements and to the company's key performance-related business factors • some trends and/or current performance can be evaluated against relevant comparisons, benchmarks, or levels • no significant adverse trends or poor current performance in key areas of importance to the Item requirements and to the company's key performance-related business factors
70-90%	• a sound, systematic approach responsive to the overall purposes of the Item • a fact-based improvement process is a key management tool; clear evidence of refinement and improved integration as a result of improvement cycles and analysis • approach is well-deployed, with no significant gaps, although refinement, deployment, and integration may vary among work units or system activities	• good to excellent improvement trends in most key areas of importance to the Item requirements and to the company's key performance-related business factors or sustained good to excellent performance in those areas • many to most trends and current performance can be evaluated against relevant comparisons, benchmarks, or levels • current performance is good to excellent in most areas of importance to the Item requirements and to the company's key performance-related business factors
100%	• a sound, systematic approach, fully responsive to all the requirements of the Item • approach is fully deployed without weaknesses or gaps in any areas • very strong refinement an integration—backed by excellent analysis	• excellent improvement trends in most to all key areas of importance to the Item requirements and to the company's key performance-related business factors or sustained excellent performance in those areas • most to all trends and current performance can be evaluated against relevant comparisons, benchmarks, or levels • current performance is excellent in most areas of importance to the Item requirements and to the company's key performance-related business factors • strong evidence of industry and benchmark leadership demonstrated

Source: Malcolm Baldrige National Quality Award 1993 Award Criteria National Institute of Standards and Technology U.S. Department of Commerce, 1992

used). At the level of the Items (28 Items in 1992), each Examiner independently evaluates how well the company's quality management systems, as described in the application, address the issues contained in the Item. For each Item, the Examiner writes specific comments indicating, first, the strengths of the company's approach to that Item, and then the areas requiring improvement.

The evaluation of the Items is based on three dimensions: the company's approach to the issues in the Item, the extent to which the approach is fully and appropriately deployed within the organization, and the results that have been achieved. Not all three of the dimensions apply equally to each Item; the Examiners must make judgments about their importance based on the Item and the characteristics of the company being scored.

Once the Examiner has written comments for an Item, a percentage score is assigned. This percentage score must reflect the comments. In order to help calibrate the scores, Scoring Guidelines have been developed which outline characteristics of quality management systems at various scoring levels for each of the three dimensions—approach, deployment, and results (see Table 3). The percentage scores are ultimately multiplied by the points assigned to each Item in the Award Criteria and summed for the overall point score. The total point scale is from 0 to 1,000 points.

Based on the independent scoring of each of the applications by the Examiner teams, a panel of nine Judges selects the companies that will continue to the next stage of the evaluation process. For those applications which were not selected to continue, a Feedback Report is written. Every company that applies for the Award receives a written Feedback Report.

The next step for those applications continuing in the evaluation process is the development of consensus about the scoring within the team of Examiners assigned to the application. The approach used identifies Items for which there is too much variability among the Examiners' independent scores. The reasons for the divergence are then discussed. It is the responsibility of the Senior Examiner leading the consensus process to ensure that instantaneous majority rule does not occur. Rather, the underlying reasons for the divergence in scores should be uncovered, and their merits openly discussed and assessed.

The consensus process results in a modified set of scores and a Senior Examiner's Report which both synthesizes the written comments made by the members of the Examiner Team and indicates reasons for changes in the scores occurring as a result of the consensus process. Based on the consensus scores, the Judges then select the companies that will receive a Site Visit. In 1992, 90 companies applied for the award. Out of these, nine manufacturing, five service, and five small companies were selected for Site Visits.

The primary purpose of the Site Visit is to clarify and verify the content of the Company's written application. Typically, the Site Visit is performed by a team of seven Examiners which includes the members of the original consensus team. The Site Visit usually involves four days on site with the applicant company. To effectively conduct such a Site Visit requires extensive advanced planning in addition to the time actually spent with the applicant company. For small companies, both the number of Examiners involved and the length of time spent on site is likely to be somewhat less.

During the Site Visit, the Examiners conduct extensive interviews with employees at all levels of the company and examine company documentation. The objective is to verify the key information in the Company's application, assess the extent of deployment of the Company's approaches, clarify vague or confusing areas, and determine the appropriateness of the Company as a role model. The Site Visit is followed by a day during which the Team synthesizes the information collected during the Site Visit and develops a report which includes both an overall assessment of the company's status as a role model and a summary of key strengths and areas for improvement in each of the seven Categories.

The final step in the scoring process is the selection of the winners by the Judges. The Judges base their decision on the information contained in the Company's application, the original independent comments and scoring by the Examiner Team, the consensus comments and scoring, the reports generated by the Site Visit, and, finally, discussion with the Senior Examiner that led the Site Visit.

The scoring matrix mentioned above (Table 3) has been developed to aid in discrimination among the companies that achieve high scores. Examination of the scoring matrix will show that companies that score about 50 percent are really very good companies with quite well-developed quality management systems. In fact, the median score for companies that apply for the Award is below 500 out of the total 1,000 points. Figure 1 shows a histogram of the scores for the 1992 applicants.

FIGURE 1   HISTOGRAM OF THE SCORES OF THE 1992 APPLICANTS

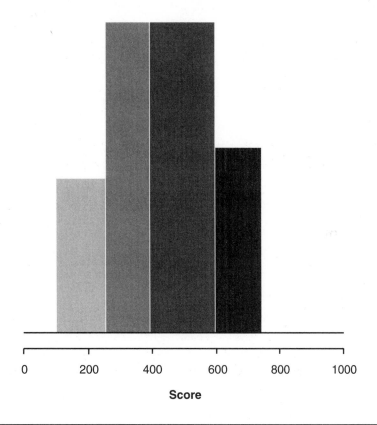

Source: Malcolm Baldrige National Quality Award Office.

PART SIX

CUSTOMER FOCUS

READING 12
COMMUNICATION AND CONTROL PROCESSES IN THE DELIVERY OF SERVICE QUALITY

AN ARTICLE ON THE SERVICE-PROFIT CHAIN (ALSO SEE READING 2) IN THE MARCH-APRIL 1994 *HARVARD BUSINESS REVIEW* SAYS, "ULTIMATELY, SERVICE QUALITY IS A FUNCTION OF THE GAP BETWEEN PERCEPTIONS OF THE ACTUAL SERVICE EXPERIENCED AND WHAT A CUSTOMER EXPECTED BEFORE RECEIVING THAT SERVICE." MORE SIMPLY STATED, SERVICE QUALITY EQUALS THE DIFFERENCE OF PERFORMANCE AND EXPECTATIONS. THIS READING EMPHASISES THE GAP MODEL OF SERVICE QUALITY, FIRST PRESENTED BY THE AUTHORS IN 1985 AND REVIEWED HERE IN SOME DETAIL. FOR A COMPLETE REPORT OF THEIR WORK IN THIS AREA, SEE *DELIVERING QUALITY SERVICE: BALANCING CUSTOMER PERCEPTIONS AND EXPECTATIONS* (NEW YORK: FREE PRESS, 1990).

THE GAP MODEL EXPLAINS THE CAUSES OF SERVICE QUALITY PROBLEMS AND SUGGESTS ACTIONS THAT ORGANIZATIONS CAN PURSUE TO IMPROVE QUALITY. AS YOU READ THIS WORK, KEEP THREE THINGS IN MIND. FIRST, ALTHOUGH DEVELOPED FOR THE SERVICE INDUSTRY, THE GAP MODEL OFFERS MUCH VALUABLE INSIGHT TO THOSE WITH MANUFACTURING INTERESTS. SECOND, THE CUSTOMER'S PERCEPTION OF THE SERVICE ENCOUNTER IS, FOR OUR PURPOSES, EQUIVALENT TO CUSTOMER SATISFACTION, SO YOU MAY INTERPRET THIS AS A MODEL FOR THE LATTER AS WELL. FINALLY, AS YOU REVIEW THE AUTHORS' RECOMMENDATIONS, NOTICE HOW OFTEN THEY CAN BE TIED BACK TO DEMING'S 14 POINTS FOR MANAGERS FROM READING 4.

READING 12
COMMUNICATION AND CONTROL PROCESSES IN THE DELIVERY OF SERVICE QUALITY

BY VALARIE A. ZEITHAML, LEONARD L. BERRY, AND A. PARASURAMAN

The delivery of quality in goods and services has become a marketing priority of the 1980s (Leonard and Sasser, 1982; Rabin, 1983). Though marketers of tangible goods have defined and measured quality with increasing levels of precision (Crosby, 1979; Garvin, 1983), marketers of services experience difficulty in understanding and controlling quality. Because services are performances rather than objects, precise manufacturing specifications for uniform quality rarely can be established and enforced by the firm. Quality in services is not engineered at the manufacturing plant, then delivered intact to the consumer. Most services cannot be counted, measured, inventoried, tested, and verified in advance of sale to ensure quality delivery. Furthermore, the performance of services—especially those with a high labor content— often differs among employees, among customers, and from day to day. In most services, quality occurs during service delivery, usually in an interaction between the customer and contact personnel of the service firm. For this reason, service quality is highly dependent on the performance of employees, an organizational resource that cannot be controlled to the degree that components of tangible goods can be engineered.

Research (Thompson, DeSouza, and Gale, 1985) and company experience (Rudie and Wansley, 1985) reveal that delivering high service quality produces measurable benefits in profit, cost savings, and market share. Therefore, an understanding of the nature of service quality and how it is achieved in organizations has become a priority for research. To that end, we previously

CREDIT: Valerie A. Zeithaml, Leonard L. Berry, and A. Parasuraman, "Communication and Control Progresses in the Delivery of Service Quality," *Journal of Marketing* (April, 1988) pp. 35–48.

developed a service quality model (Parasuraman, Zeithaml, and Berry, 1985) indicating that consumers' quality perceptions are influenced by a series of four distinct gaps occurring in organizations (see Figure 1). These gaps on the service provider's side, which can impede delivery of services that consumers perceive to be of high quality, are:

Gap 1: Difference between consumer expectations and management perceptions of consumer expectations.

| **FIGURE 1** | CONCEPTUAL MODEL OF SERVICE QUALITY |

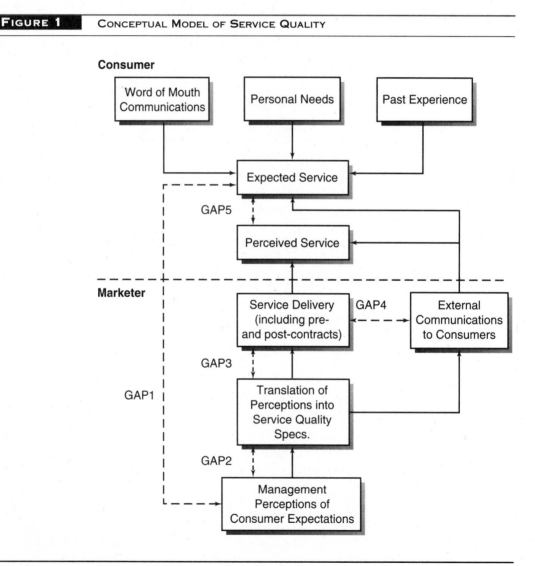

Gap 2: Difference between management perceptions of consumer expectations and service quality specifications.

Gap 3: Difference between service quality specifications and the service actually delivered.

Gap 4: Difference between service delivery and what is communicated about the service to consumers.

Perceived service quality is defined in the model as the difference between consumer expectations and perceptions (gap 5 in Figure 1), which in turn depends on the size and direction of the four gaps associated with the delivery of service quality on the marketer's side.

Delivering consistently good service quality is difficult, as organizations have discovered. Understanding why it is so difficult and how it might be facilitated is the purpose of our article. Our intent is to identify a reasonably exhaustive set of factors potentially affecting the magnitude and direction of the four gaps on the marketer's side. Most of these factors involve communication and control processes implemented in organizations to manage employees. Other factors involve consequences of these processes (e.g., role ambiguity and role conflict) that affect the delivery of service quality. Literature from the marketing and organizational behavior fields on these topics is reviewed and integrated with qualitative data from an exploratory study to help understand the way organizational processes affect service quality.

After describing the exploratory study, we examine gaps 1 through 4 in Figure 1. The theoretical constructs proposed to be responsible for each gap are delineated. In addition, specific organizational variables that can be used to operationalize these constructs in service organizations are itemized and explained. The result is a detailed conceptual explication of the service quality model that can be used as a blueprint for developing measures of the gaps. The steps necessary to develop these measures, and to test the model empirically, are discussed in the final section.

THE EXPLORATORY STUDY

The qualitative technique used to learn about service quality in organizations is what Mintzberg (1979) calls "direct research." Our study was not designed to test hypotheses because the literature on organizational processes involved in service quality delivery is not rich enough to suggest formal relationships among variables. Instead, we sought insights by collecting observations about service quality from managers and employees in actual service organizations. Observations were collected in three research stages. The approach used is consistent with procedures recommended for marketing theory development by several scholars (Deshpande, 1983; Peter and Olson, 1983; Zaltman, LeMasters, and Heffring, 1982).

In the first stage, in-depth personal interviews consisting of open-ended questions were conducted with three or four executives in each of four nationally recognized service organizations (a bank, a brokerage house, a repair and maintenance firm, and a credit card company). The executives were selected from marketing operations, senior management, and customer relations and held titles such as president, senior vice president, director of customer relations, and manager of consumer market research. These executives were interviewed about a broad range of service quality issues (e.g., consumer expectations about service quality, what steps they took to control or improve quality, and what problems they faced in delivering high quality services).

The second stage involved a comprehensive case study of a nationally known bank. Three of the bank's regions (each of which had at least 12 branches) were selected. Managers and employees at various levels of the bank were interviewed individually and in focus groups. Top and middle managers responded to open-ended questions about their perceptions of consume expectations of service quality (gap 1), service quality standards set in the organization to deliver quality (gap 2), and differences between standards set by management and the level of service actually delivered (gap 3). A total of seven focus group interviews with tellers, customer service representatives, lending personnel, and branch managers from within the three regions were held to identify factors contributing to gaps 3 and 4. Finally, managers associated with bank communication with customers (bank marketing, advertising, and consumer affairs executives, as well as the president and creative director of the bank's advertising agency) were interviewed to identify the factors responsible for gap 4.

The third stage of the exploratory study involved a systematic group interview with 11 senior managers of six nationally known service firms (two full service banks, two national insurance companies, and two national telephone companies) and was intended to verify and generalize the findings from the two earlier stages. We presented the conceptual framework, explained the four gaps, and questioned managers about the factors responsible for the gaps in their firms. Lists of factors derived from the first two phases were presented and discussed. Managers augmented the lists and evaluated the factors on the basis of experience in their industries and organizations.

In the following discussion, we combine insights from the three exploratory phases with those from relevant literature in marketing and organizational behavior to propose the main theoretical constructs and specific variables associated with the four service quality gaps that can be used to operationalize the constructs.

THE FOUR GAPS IN SERVICE QUALITY

GAP 1: DIFFERENCE BETWEEN CONSUMER EXPECTATIONS AND MANAGEMENT PERCEPTIONS OF CONSUMER EXPECTATIONS

Service firm executives may not always understand what features connote high quality to consumers, what attributes a service must have in order to meet consumer needs, and what levels of performance on those features are necessary to deliver high quality service (Langeard et al., 1981; Parasuraman and Zeithaml, 1983). Because there are few clearly defined and tangible cues for services, the gap between what consumers expect and what managers think they expect may be considerably larger than it is in firms that produce tangible goods (Gronroos, 1982; Zeithaml, 1981). As shown in Table 1, the size of gap 1 in any service firm is proposed to be a function of marketing research orientation, upward communication, and levels of management.

MARKETING RESEARCH ORIENTATION.

Evidence indicates that service firms lag behind goods firms in their use of marketing research and in other facets of customer orientation (George and Barksdale, 1974; Lovelock, 1981; Parasuraman, Berry, and Zeithaml, 1983). Service organizations also place less emphasis than goods firms on marketing in general (Lovelock, 1981), believing that the operations function is more critical. An operations orientation diverts focus from consumers and reduces efforts to understand their needs and expectations. Banks that close their branch lobbies in midafternoon to facilitate balancing the day's transactions and that issue monthly customer statements designed without input from customers exemplify an operations orientation.

Because marketing research is a key vehicle for understanding consumer expectations and perceptions of services, the size of gap 1 should depend greatly on the amount of marketing research conducted. Other research-related variables include the extent to which research data are used (i.e., read, understood, and applied) by managers in the organization and the degree to which the research focuses on service quality issues.

Another factor influencing degree of marketing research orientation is the extent to which top managers interact directly with consumers. In some service firms, especially ones that are small and localized, owners or managers may be in continual contact with consumers, thereby gaining firsthand knowledge of consumer expectations and perceptions. Even in large service organizations, top managers can spend time "on the line," interacting with consumers and experiencing service delivery. Radio Shack, for example, has a program called "Adopt a Store" through which senior managers spend time

TABLE 1	SERVICE QUALITY MANAGEMENT GAP 1	
THEORETICAL CONSTRUCTS	**SPECIFIC VARIABLES**	
Marketing research orientation	Amount of marketing research	
	Usage of marketing research	
	Degree to which marketing research focuses on service quality issues	
	Extent of direct interaction between managers and customers	
Upward communication	Extent of employee-to-manager communication	
	Extent to which inputs from contact personnel are sought	
	Quality of contact between top managers and contact personnel	
Levels of management	Number of layers between customer contact personnel and top managers	

in stores collecting information and interacting with the staff (Goyne, 1985). A major bank in the exploratory study required its managers to interact regularly with customers by telephone. As the degree of contact between top managers and consumers increases, top managers should understand the consumer better and the size of gap 1 should decrease.

UPWARD COMMUNICATION.

Though top managers may not have a firm grasp of consumer quality expectations, research suggests that customer-contact personnel can accurately predict consumer expectations and perceptions of the service (Schneider and Bowen, 1985). Therefore, top managers' understanding of the consumer may depend largely on the extent and types of communication received from customer-contact personnel and from noncompany personnel (e.g., independent insurance agents, retailers) who represent the company and its services. Upward communication typically provides information to upper level managers about activities and performances throughout the organization (Read, 1962). Specific types of communication that may be relevant are formal (e.g., reports of problems and exceptions in service delivery, performance reports on contact personnel, and financial and accounting information that would signal inferior or superior performance) and informal (e.g., discussions between contact personnel and upper level managers).

An important facet of upward communication is its quality or effectiveness, which in turn depends on the medium through which it occurs. Face-to-face communication, for example, is more effective than written communication because it uses several communication cues (verbal and visual) simultaneously. Face-to-face communication is preferred when the message is difficult or ambiguous, or when sender and receiver differ in background or opinions (Daft and Lengel, 1984). In these situations, media such as written reports do not provide sufficient richness. In service organizations, the types of messages that need to be conveyed are often complex and ambiguous (e.g., problems encountered in service delivery, how employees feel, morale and attitudes within the organization) and top managers often differ considerably in background from contact personnel (Berry, Zeithaml, and Parasuraman, 1985). Many successful service organizations (e.g., Marriott, Delta Airlines) pride themselves on using such rich communication channels as management by walking around (Clist, 1985; Peters and Waterman, 1982) and employee gripe sessions (Rout, 1981).

In the focus group interviews conducted in the second stage of the exploratory study, several bank employees clearly illustrated the lack of effective communication.

> *Branch Manager:* "I've been in this bank for 27 years and this is the first time I have had a regional VP that has never been in the branch." Another: "He never will." Another: "I haven't seen the man in a year and a half. That has a lot to do with our attitude. We're getting orders from someone we never see."
>
> *Customer service representative:* "We have three floors. Our manager, when he first got here, sat on the second floor. Now he is on the third floor in his enclosed office. He told us he doesn't want to be with the public. He needs time for himself. What are his priorities? He doesn't know what's going on on the first floor. I've had lots of customers ask for the manager. I say, 'I'm sorry, he's on a month's vacation.'"

We therefore propose that three specific variables influence the effectiveness of upward communication and hence the size of gap 1: extent of employees-to-managers communication, extent to which inputs from contact personnel are sought, and quality of contact between top managers and contact personnel.

LEVELS OF MANAGEMENT.

The number of layers of management between customer-contact personnel and top managers is expected to affect the size of gap 1. Layers of management inhibit communication and understanding because they place barriers between senders and receivers of messages. Therefore, the greater the number of layers between customer-contact personnel and top managers, the larger gap 1 is expected to be.

As shown in Table 1, the gap between consumer expectations and management perceptions of consumer expectations depends on the extent to which a company recognizes the importance of the consumer (marketing research orientation), receives accurate communication about consumers' needs (marketing research orientation, upward communication), and places barriers between contact personnel and top managers (levels of management).

P_1: The size of gap 1 is related to (a) extent of marketing research orientation (−), (b) extent and quality of upward communication (−), and (c) levels of management (+).

GAP 2: MANAGEMENT PERCEPTION—SERVICE QUALITY SPECIFICATION GAP

Managers of service firms often experience difficulty in attempting to match or exceed customer expectations. A variety of factors—resource constraints, short-term profit orientation, market conditions, management indifference—may account for the discrepancy between managers' perceptions of consumer expectations and the actual specifications established by management for a service. As shown in Table 2, the size of gap 2 in any service firm is proposed to be a function of management commitment to service quality, goal setting, task standardization, and perception of feasibility.

TABLE 2	SERVICE QUALITY MANAGEMENT GAP 2
THEORETICAL CONSTRUCTS	**SPECIFIC VARIABLES**
Management commitment to service quality	Resource commitment to quality
	Existence of internal quality programs
	Management perceptions of recognition for quality commitment
Goal-setting	Existence of a formal process for setting quality of service goals
Task standardization	Use of hard technology to standardize operations
	Use of soft technology to standardize operations
Perception of feasibility	Capabilities/systems for meeting specifications
	Extent to which managers believe consumer expectations can be met

MANAGEMENT COMMITMENT TO SERVICE QUALITY.

One explanation for gap 2 is the absence of total management commitment to service quality. Emphasis on other objectives such as cost reduction and short-term profit has outcomes that are more easily measured and tracked and may supercede emphasis on service quality. This tendency to emphasize other objectives is illustrated in the following statement.

> Most U.S. firms suffer significantly from the use of short-term, accounting-driven measures of performance to establish the reward mechanisms for high-level managers, who are mainly responsible for implementing strategic actions (Hax and Majluf 1984: 90).

Louis Gerstner, president of American Express, suggests the following reason for lack of management commitment to service quality.

> Because of the structure of most companies, the guy who puts in the service operation and bears the expense doesn't get the benefit. It'll show up in marketing, even in new product development. But the benefit never shows up in his own P&L statement (*Business Week* 1984).

Often, service firms take a product-based approach to quality rather than a user-based approach, which results in a de-emphasis on serving the customer (Garvin, 1983). In contrast, American Express illustrates a user-based approach to quality.

> Overriding all other values is our dedication to quality. We are a market-driven institution, committed to our customers in everything we do. We constantly seek improvement and we encourage the unusual, even the iconoclastic (*Business Week* 1981).

Specific variables related to management commitment to service quality include the proportion of resources committed to service quality (rather than to other goals), the existence of an internal quality program, and the extent to which managers believe their attempts to improve service quality will be recognized and rewarded in the organization.

GOAL-SETTING.

Research reveals that goal-setting not only improves both organizational performance and individual achievement, but also increases overall control of the organization (Ivancevich and McMahon, 1982: Latham and Locke, 1979; Locke et al., 1981; Sherwin, 1976). Companies that have been successful in delivering high service quality (e.g., American Express, McDonald's, Delta

Airlines) are noted for establishing formal goals relating to service quality. Because services are performances, the goals for service delivery usually are set and measured in terms of human or machine performance. American Express, after analyzing customer complaints, found that timeliness, accuracy, and responsiveness were the important outputs to be achieved. Management then identified 180 goals for different aspects of service quality provided to customers. After the formal goal-setting, they developed monitoring devices to evaluate the speed with which telephones were answered, complaints were handled, bills were mailed, and new applications were approved. The goals established by American Express illustrate many of the characteristics of effective goals (Locke et al., 1981): specific, accepted, cover important job dimensions, reviewed with appropriate feedback, measurable, challenging but realistic, and match individual characteristics.

The development of service goals involves defining service quality in ways that enable providers to understand what management wants to deliver. Existence of a formal quality program that includes identification and measurement of service quality standards is expected to be one variable that reduces the size of gap 2.

TASK STANDARDIZATION.

The effective translation of managerial perceptions into specific service quality standards depends on the degree to which tasks to be performed can be standardized or routinized. Efforts to conceptualize and measure the standardization of tasks in organizational research have focused on the construct of technology (Perrow, 1979; Reeves and Woodward, 1970; Woodward, 1965). This research suggests that the organization's technology can serve to standardize and regularize employee behavior. If jobs or tasks are routine (such as those needed for opening checking accounts or spraying lawns for pests), specific rules and standards can be established and effectively executed. If services are customized for individual consumers (e.g., investment portfolio management or estate planning), specific standards (such as those relating to time spent with the customer) are difficult to establish. Even in highly customized services, however, some aspects of service provision can be routinized. Physicians and dentists, for example, can standardize recurring and nontechnical aspects of the service such as checking patients in, collecting payment, weighing patients, and taking temperature.

According to Levitt (1976), standardization or (in his terms) industrialization of service can take three forms: (1) substitution of hard technology for personal contact and human effort, (2) improvement in work methods (soft technology), or (3) combinations of these two methods. Hard technology includes automatic teller machines, automatic car washes, and airport X-ray machines, all of which allow standardization of service provision by substituting machines for human effort. Soft technology is illustrated by restaurant salad bars, prepackaged travel tours, and the standardized training given to employees of organizations like McDonald's. Effective combination of these two methods is illustrated by Marshall Field's elimination of "task-interfering duties" for salespeople. The retail store automated check approval, implemented in-store telephone directories, reorganized wrapping stations, and simplified order forms, all of which resulted in faster checkout and more attention to the customer.

We propose that the more managers can standardize tasks for service delivery, the smaller gap 2 will be.

PERCEPTION OF FEASIBILITY.

The exploratory research revealed the size of gap 2 to be affected by the extent to which managers perceive that meeting customer expectations is feasible. Executives in the repair service firm participating in the exploratory study were fully aware that consumers view quick response to appliance breakdowns as a vital aspect of high quality service. However, they believed that establishing specifications to deliver a quick response consistently was not feasible for two reasons: (1) the time required to provide a specific repair service was difficult to forecast and (2) skilled service technicians were less available in peak season (the summer months) than at any other time. Therefore, the greater the management perception that consumer expectations cannot be fulfilled, the larger gap 2 will be. Variables related to this construct include the organizational capabilities and systems for meeting specifications and the degree to which managers believe expectations can be met economically.

> P_2: The size of gap 2 is related to (a) management commitment to service quality (−), (b) setting of goals relating to service quality (−), (c) task standardization (−), and (d) perception of feasibility for meeting customer expectations (−).

GAP 3: SERVICE QUALITY SPECIFICATION—SERVICE DELIVERY GAP

Gap 3 is the discrepancy between the specifications for the service and the actual delivery of the service. It can be referred to as the "service performance gap," that is, the extent to which service providers do not perform at the level expected by management. The service performance gap occurs when employees are unable and/or unwilling to perform the service at the desired level.

As shown in Table 3, the main theoretical constructs proposed to account for the size of gap 3 are teamwork, employee-job fit, technology-job fit, perceived control, supervisory control systems, role conflict, and role ambiguity.

TABLE 3	SERVICE QUALITY MANAGEMENT GAP 3
THEORETICAL CONSTRUCTS	**SPECIFIC VARIABLES**
Teamwork	Extent to which employees view other employees as customers Extent to which contact personnel feel upper level managers genuinely care for them Extent to which contact personnel feel they are cooperating (rather than competing) with others in the organization Extent to which employees feel personally involved and committed
Employee-job fit	Ability of employees to perform job Importance and effectiveness of selection processes
Technology-job fit	Appropriateness of tools and technology for performing job
Perceived control	Extent to which employees perceive they are in control of their jobs Extent to which customer-contact personnel feel they have flexibility in dealing with customers Predictability of demand
Supervisory control systems	Extent to which employees are evaluated on what they do (behaviors) rather than solely on output quantity
Role conflict	Perceived conflict between expectations of customers and expectations of organization • Amount of paperwork needed to complete service transactions • Number of internal contacts that customer-contact people must make to complete a service transaction or answer customer queries • Existence of management policy that conflicts with specifications
Role ambiguity	Perceived clarity of goals and expectations • Frequency and quality of downward communication • Extent of constructive feedback given to contact personnel Perceived level of competence and confidence • Product knowledge of contact personnel • Product-specific training provided to contact personnel • Training in communication skills provided to contact personnel

TEAMWORK.

As revealed in the following statements from the exploratory study, bank employees did not feel they were working together well.

> *Lending officer:* "I worked in the bank 13 years. There is a big difference in when I started and now in terms of how the employees feel about the bank. There used to be so much camaraderie. Now, it's like pulling teeth to get associates to help you."

Customer service representative: "We're not working as a family and as a group. We may all come together again but it hasn't happened yet."

Customer service representative: "Our cashier sits there and smokes cigarettes and drinks coffee. She doesn't help with any of our work. She says it isn't in her job description. She's a deadbeat."

The value of teamwork—employees and managers pulling together for a common goal—was emphasized throughout the exploratory interviews. The importance of this construct to achieving organizational goals also has been documented in studies on group cohesiveness (Davis, 1969; Shaw, 1976) and group commitment (Salancik, 1977). In high performing groups, people function as a team and accomplish their goals by allowing group members to participate in decisions and to share in the group's success (Lawler and Cammann, 1972).

Teamwork is the focus of service quality programs in several firms known for their outstanding customer service. Merrill Lynch, for example, has involved more than 2,500 operations personnel in quality teams of 8 to 15 employees each that work to improve customer service (McMurray, 1983). At American Express, employees are involved in setting standards and improving work procedures so that a sense of teamwork is fostered. Employees in various departments work together to analyze the work of each department, identify opportunities, and seek improvements.

We propose the following aspects as being critical to teamwork: the extent to which employees view other employees as customers, the extent to which employees feel management cares about them, the extent to which employees feel they are cooperating rather than competing with each other, and the extent to which employees feel personally involved and committed.

EMPLOYEE-JOB FIT.

The exploratory study indicated that service quality problems often occur because contact personnel are not well suited to their positions. Because customer-contact jobs tend to be situated at the lower levels of company organization charts (e.g., car rental agents, telephone operators, and repair technicians), personnel holding these jobs are frequently among the least educated and lowest paid employees in their companies. As a result, they may lack language, interpersonal, or other skills to serve customers effectively. Many service companies have high turnover among contact employees and are inclined to fill openings quickly, even if they must hire persons having background or skill deficiencies. Managers commonly do not give enough attention or devote sufficient resources to hiring and selection processes. We propose that emphasis on matching the employee to the job through selection processes and the consequent ability or skill of employees to perform the job well affect the size of gap 3.

TECHNOLOGY-JOB FIT.

Provision of high service quality also depends on the appropriateness of the tools or technology the employee uses to perform the job. Technology and equipment, such as bank computers and diagnostic equipment, can enhance the service employee's performance. Appropriate and reliable technology must be provided for high quality service delivery. Equipment failures can interfere with adequate employee performance.

Our exploratory study revealed several instances in which service quality shortfalls resulted from a lack of technology-job fit and/or employee-job fit. For example, a product repair executive, in bemoaning the proliferation of new high technology appliances, indicated problems stemming from a lack of both types of fit.

> We may not have all the [technical] specifications needed to train technicians before a new product is marketed [technology-job fit]. Some technicians may never be capable of being trained to service these new "high-tech" products [employee-job fit]. These products are coming too fast.

PERCEIVED CONTROL.

The notion of perceived control suggests that individuals' reactions to stressful situations depend on whether they can control those situations (Geer, Davidson, and Gatchel, 1970; Geer and Maisel, 1972; Glass and Singer, 1972; Straub, Tursky, and Schwartz, 1971). Averill (1973) has delineated three forms of control: behavioral, cognitive, and decisional. Behavioral control is the ability to make responses that influence threatening situations (Averill, 1973). Cognitive control is the ability to reduce stress by the way information is processed by an individual (Averill, 1973; Cromwell et al., 1971). Decisional control involves a choice in the selection of outcomes or goals (Averill, 1973). We propose that when service employees perceive themselves to be in control of situations they encounter in their jobs, they experience less stress. Lower levels of stress, in turn, lead to higher performance. When employees perceive that they can act flexibly rather than by rote in problem situations encountered in providing services, control increases and performance improves.

Perceived control can be a function of the degree to which organizational rules, procedures, and culture limit contact employee flexibility in serving customers. It can also be a consequence of the degree to which an employee's authority to achieve specific outcomes with customers lies elsewhere in the organization. Service companies commonly are organized internally in a way that makes providing fast service to the customer difficult for the service employee. When a contact person must get the approval of other departments in the organization before delivering a certain service, service quality is jeopardized. Though the contact person may be totally committed to serving the consumer, he or she cannot perform well because control over the service has been dispersed among multiple organizational units. Finally, perceived control can be a function of the predictability of demand, which is a major problem in service businesses (Zeithaml, Parasuraman, and Berry, 1985).

SUPERVISORY CONTROL SYSTEMS.

In some organizations, the performance of contact employees is measured by their output (e.g., the number of units produced per hour, the number or amount of sales per week). In these situations, the performance of individuals is monitored and controlled through what are termed "output control systems" (Ouchi, 1979; Ouchi and McGuire, 1975). Performance is based on written records that measure employee outputs. In many service organizations, however, output control systems may be inappropriate or insufficient for measuring employee performance relating to provision of quality service. For example, most bank customers want bank tellers to be accurate, fast, and friendly. Banks that measure teller performance strictly on output measures, such as end-of-the-day balancing of transactions, overlook key aspects of job performance that consumers factor into quality-of-service perceptions.

In these and other service situations, performance also can be monitored through behavioral control systems (Ouchi, 1979; Ouchi and McGuire, 1975), which consist largely of observations or other reports on the way the employee works or behaves rather than output measurements. The use of behavioral control systems is illustrated by an ongoing "tone-of-service" survey with customers who have recently opened accounts at The Friendly National Bank of Oklahoma City (Berry, 1986). Customers answer questions about the way they were treated by the customer service representative opening the account. Friendly also monitors customer service representatives' performance through ongoing "shopper" research (researchers pretending to be customers) and a cross-sales index. Each month, customer service representatives receive tone-of-service and shopper scores (behavioral measures) and a cross-sales score (output measure). The use of these types of behavioral measures encourages employee performance that is consistent with customer expectations of quality service.

ROLE CONFLICT.

The role attached to any position in an organization represents the set of behaviors and activities to be performed by the person occupying that position (Katz and Kahn, 1978). The role is defined through the expectations, demands, and pressures communicated to employees by individuals (e.g., top managers, immediate supervisors, customers) who have a vested interest in how employees perform their jobs (Katz and Kahn, 1978). When the expectations of these people are incompatible or too demanding, employees experience role conflict, the perception that they cannot satisfy all the demands of all these individuals (Belasco, 1966; Rizzo, House, and Lirtzman, 1970; Walker, Churchill, and Ford, 1977). Research has shown that perceived role conflict is related positively to feelings of job-related tension and anxiety and negatively to job satisfaction (Greene and Organ, 1973; Gross, Mason, and McEachem, 1957; Kahn et al., 1964).

Because contact employees are the links between the company and the consumer, they must satisfy the needs of both. Sometimes the expectations of the company and the expectations of the consumer conflict. For example, conflict occurs when an income tax firm expects staff members to process as many consumers as possible in a short time (i.e., limits the time with consumers) and consumers want personal attention from the staff (e.g., to discuss tax avoidance strategies for the future). Role conflict also may occur when employees are expected to cross-sell services to the consumer; the employees may feel they are pushing the services on the consumer and may be torn between the company's expectations and the desire to serve the consumer.

The managers of service organizations can inadvertently create role conflict for employees through excessive paperwork or unnecessary internal roadblocks. For example, new accounts personnel in banks who must complete separate forms for each service they sell to a customer may experience role conflict if other customers are waiting to be served. Does the new accounts employee take the time to cross-sell bank services to the customer at the desk or simply open the requested account and move on to the waiting customer? Complicating the issue is the reality that the new accounts employee may be measured—and rewarded—on the basis of cross-selling achievements.

Perceptions of role conflict are psychologically uncomfortable for the employee (Kahn et al., 1964; Walker, Churchill, and Ford, 1977), can have a negative effect on the employee's satisfaction and performance in the organization, and increase absenteeism and turnover. A service organization that recognizes inherent conflicts in the contact person's job will go far in eliminating the distress of role conflict. The result will be better employee performance and hence a reduction of gap 3. Use of performance measurement systems that focus on the consumer in addition to internal efficiency goals is one example of how role conflict can be reduced. Compensation tied to delivery of service quality (by measures of consumer satisfaction, loyalty, etc.) as well as sales is another.

ROLE AMBIGUITY.

When employees do not have the information necessary to perform their jobs adequately, they experience role ambiguity (Katz and Kahn, 1978; Walker,

Churchill, and Ford, 1977). Role ambiguity may occur because employees are uncertain about what managers or supervisors expect from them and how to satisfy those expectations or because they do not know how their performance will be evaluated and rewarded (Katz and Kahn, 1978; Walker, Churchill, and Ford, 1977).

Several organizational variables moderate the role ambiguity experienced by service employees. The frequency, quality, and accuracy of downward communication are likely to affect the service employee's role ambiguity. Downward communication involves messages used primarily by managers to direct and influence personnel at lower levels in the organization. It typically pertains to the goals, strategies, and objectives for the organization and its departments, job instruction and rationale, policy and procedures, and assessment and correction of performance (Katz and Kahn, 1978). The more frequently managers provide clear and unambiguous communication about these topics, the lower employees' role ambiguity will be.

The training provided by the organization can help employees gain an accurate understanding of what is expected and how they will be evaluated. Training that relates to specific services offered by the firm should help the contact person in dealing with the customer. Training in communication skills, especially in listening to customers and understanding what customers expect, also should give contact personnel greater role clarity. All such organizational training programs should affect the employee's perceived level of confidence or competence, which should result in greater role clarity.

P_3: The size of gap 3 is related to (a) extent of teamwork perceived by employees (−), (b) employee-job fit (−), (c) technology-job fit (−), (d) extent of perceived control experienced by customer-contact personnel (−), (e) extent to which behavioral control systems are used to supplement output control systems (−), (f) extent of role conflict experienced by customer-contact personnel (+), and (g) extent of role ambiguity experienced by customer-contact personnel (+).

GAP 4: DIFFERENCE BETWEEN SERVICE DELIVERY AND EXTERNAL COMMUNICATIONS

Media advertising and other communications by a firm can affect consumer expectations. Discrepancies between service delivery and external communications—in the form of exaggerated promises and/or the absence of information about service delivery aspects intended to serve consumers well—can affect consumer perceptions of service quality. As shown in Table 4, we propose that horizontal communication and propensity to overpromise within an organization affect the size of gap 4.

TABLE 4	**SERVICE QUALITY MANAGEMENT GAP 4**	
THEORETICAL CONSTRUCTS	**SPECIFIC VARIABLES**	
Horizontal communication	Extent of input by operations people in advertising planning and execution	
	Extent to which contact personnel are aware of external communications to customers before they occur	
	Communication between sales and operations people	
	Similarly of procedures across departments and branches	
Propensity to over promise	Extent to which firm feels pressure to generate new business	
	Extent to which firm perceives that competitors over promise	

HORIZONTAL COMMUNICATION.

Horizontal communications are the lateral information flows that occur both within and between departments of an organization (Daft and Steers, 1985). The basic purpose of horizontal communication is to coordinate people and departments so that the overall goals of the organization are achieved. If high service quality is to be perceived by the consumer, horizontal communication among departments is necessary.

One essential form of horizontal communication in service organizations involves the advertising department (and its agency) and contact personnel. When communication occurs between contact personnel and advertising personnel (e.g., the contact personnel provide input to the advertising department about the feasibility of what is being promised in advertising), consumers are led to expect what contact personnel can deliver. If communication is not present and advertising is developed independently, contact personnel may not be able to deliver service that matches the image presented in advertising. Such lack of communication is illustrated by Holiday Inn's unsuccessful "No Surprises" advertising campaign (George and Berry, 1981). Holiday Inn's agency used consumer research as the basis for a television campaign promising "no surprises" to customers. Top managers accepted the campaign in spite of opposition by operations executives who knew that surprises frequently occur in a complex service organization. When the campaign was aired, it raised consumer expectations, gave dissatisfied customers additional grounds on which to vent frustrations, and had to be discontinued.

In the focus group interviews in our exploratory study, contact personnel expressed the need to be aware of all company communications before they run as a basis for monitoring and responding to the consumer's advertising-induced expectations. They also believed their inputs to the campaign would result in more reasonable consumer expectations.

Service organizations that do not advertise also need horizontal communication, often between the salesforce and the service providers. Frequently salespeople promise more than can be delivered to obtain an order. Consumer expectations are raised and cannot be met by customer-contact personnel, resulting in an increase in the size of gap 4.

An important aspect of horizontal communication is the coordination or integration of departments in an organization to achieve strategic objectives (Anderson, 1984). One obvious form of coordination necessary in providing service quality is consistency in policies and procedures across departments and branches. If a service organization operates many outlets under the same name, consumers will expect similar performance across those outlets. If the company allows managers of individual branches significant autonomy in procedures and policies, consumers may not receive the same level of service quality across the branches. In this case, what they expect in a specific branch may be different from what is delivered and the size of gap 4 will increase.

PROPENSITY TO OVERPROMISE.

Because of the increasing deregulation and intensifying competition in the services sector, an intuitive explanation for gap 4 is that many service firms feel pressured to acquire new business and to meet or beat competition, and therefore tend to overpromise. Specifically, the greater the extent to which a service firm feels pressured to generate new customers, and perceives that the industry norm is to overpromise ("everyone else in our industry overpromises"), the greater is the firm's propensity to overpromise. We further propose that propensity to overpromise is related directly to the size of gap 4.

P_4: The size of gap 4 is related to (a) extent of horizontal communication $(-)$ and (b) propensity to overpromise $(+)$.

TESTING THE EXTENDED MODEL

The theoretical constructs we have derived from the organizational behavior and marketing literature are germane to an understanding of service quality shortfalls (i.e., gaps 1 through 4 in Figure 1) and in taking corrective action to ensure the delivery of high quality service. Figure 2 is an extended model of service quality, showing the various organizational constructs and their relationships to the service quality gaps. Tables 1 through 4 detail variables that can be used to operationalize and measure the theoretical constructs affecting the four gaps.

We previously developed a multiple-item scale called SERVQUAL (Parasuraman, Zeithaml, and Berry, 1986) to measure service quality as perceived by consumers (gap 5 in Figures 1 and 2). The SERVQUAL scale operationalizes and measures service quality along five distinct dimensions: tangibles, reliability, responsiveness, assurance, and empathy. SERVQUAL scores along these dimensions can be viewed as indicators of the construct of perceived service quality. Likewise, measures of the theoretical constructs affecting each gap can be viewed as indicators of that gap. Therefore, it is possible to recast the conceptual service quality model (Figure 1) in the form of a structural equations model wherein perceived service quality (gap 5) is the unobservable dependent variable and the four gaps on the marketer's side (gaps 1-4) are the unobservable independent variables. This model can be tested by collecting data on the indicators of the five gaps through a cross-sectional study of service organizations and analyzing the data with a technique such as LISREL.

In addition to testing the overall soundness of the service quality model, future research must address several specific questions about the model. Let us examine these questions and the research steps necessary to answer them.

Which of the four service quality gaps is (are) most critical in explaining service quality variation? Is one or more of the four managerial gaps more critical than the others in affecting perceived service quality? Can creating one favorable gap (e.g., making gap 4 favorable by employing effective external communications to create realistic consumer expectations and to enhance consumer perceptions) offset service quality problems stemming from other gaps? To answer this question, measures of each of the four service quality gaps must be developed. Gap 1, the difference between consumer expectations and management perceptions of consumer expectations, could be measured by administering the expectations section of the SERVQUAL scale to a set of top managers, then comparing the scores with those obtained from consumers on the same instrument. Gap 2, the difference between management perceptions of consumer expectations and service quality specifications, could be operationalized through questionnaires to top managers that measure the extent to which the organization sets standards to deliver to expectations. Gap 3, the difference between service quality specifications and service delivery, could be gauged through employee questionnaires that address their perceived ability to deliver to established standards. Gap 4, the difference between service delivery and what is communicated about delivery externally to consumers, also would involve employee perceptions of what they deliver in comparison with what external communication promises they will deliver.

As shown in Figure 1, service quality as perceived by consumers depends on the size and direction of an additional gap (gap 5 in Figure 1), which in turn depends on the nature of the gaps associated with the delivery of service

FIGURE 2   EXTENDED MODEL OF SERVICE QUALITY

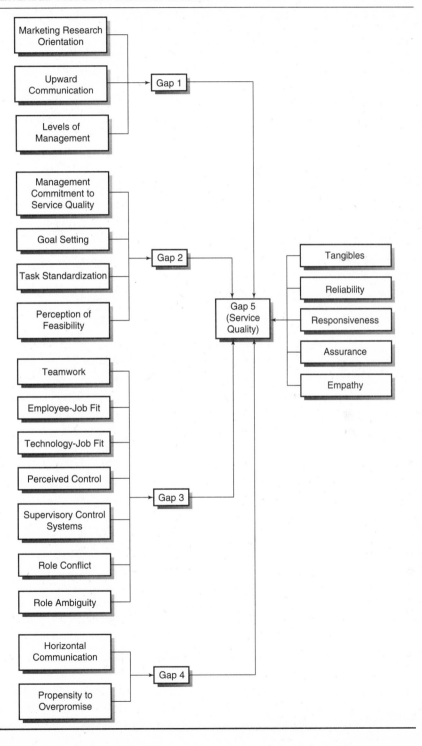

quality on the marketer's side. The SERVQUAL scale (or an adaptation of it) could be used to measure gap 5. Then the relative importance of the four managerial gaps could be examined empirically by means of a multiple regression model.

What are the main organizational factors responsible for the size of the four service quality gaps? A key managerial question involves the relative importance of the specific indicators in delivering high quality service to consumers. If a marketer could implement only a few of the many organizational strategies implied by the propositions, which ones should be undertaken? To answer this question, several measures are necessary: (1) overall measures of the four gaps and (2) measures of the organizational strategy variables detailed in Tables 1 through 4. Ways to measure the four gaps are discussed above. Measures of the other factors (e.g., amount of marketing research, extent of face-to-face contact between top managers and customers) must be developed and then can be related statistically (e.g., through regression analysis) to the measures of the four gaps.

SUMMARY

The intent of our study is to identify a reasonably exhaustive set of factors thought to effect the magnitude and direction of four gaps on the marketer's side of a service quality model (Figure 1). These factors, which mainly involve communication and control processes implemented in organizations to manage employees are reviewed and integrated with qualitative data from an exploratory study. Procedures for testing this extended model of service quality in a cross-sectional study are detailed.

REFERENCES

Anderson, Carl. *Management Skills, Functions, and Organizational Performance.* (Dubuque, IA: Wm. C. Brown Publishers, 1984).

Averill, J.R., "Personal Control Over Aversive Stimuli and Its Relationship to Stress." *Psychological Bulletin* (1973), 80 (4): 286–303.

Belasco, James A., "The Salesman's Role Revisited." *Journal of Marketing.* 30 (April 1966), 6–8.

Berry, Leonard L., "Reconciling and Coordinating Selling and Service." *American Banker,* (12 February 1986): 4–5.

————, Valarie A. Zeithaml, and A. Parasuraman, "Quality Counts in Services, Too." *Business Horizons.* 28 (May-June 1985): 44–52.

Business Week. "Boosting Productivity at American Express" (5 Oct. 1981): 62, 66.

————. "Making Service a Potent Marketing Tool" (11 June 1984):

164–70.

Clist, Todd. "Marriott Philosophies." In *Services Marketing in a Changing Environment,* Thomas Bloch, Gregory Upah, and Valarie Zeithaml, eds. Chicago: American Marketing Association, 1985: 13–14.

Cromwell, R.L., E.C. Butterfield, F.M. Bravfield. and J.J. Curry. *Acute Myocardial Infarction: Reaction and Recovery.* (St. Louis, MO: The C.V. Mosby Company, 1971).

Crosby, Phillip B., *Quality is Free.* (New York: New American Library, 1979).

Daft, Richard L. and Robert H. Lengel, "Information Richness: A New Approach to Managerial Behavior and Organization Design." In *Research in Organizational Behavior,* Vol. 6, Barry Staw and Larry L. Cummings, eds. Greenwich, CT: JAI Press, Inc., 1984: 191–233.

——————— and Richard Steers, *Organizations: A Micro/Macro Approach.* (Glenview, IL: Scott, Foresman, 1985).

Davis, J.H. *Group Performance.* (Reading, MA: Addison-Wesley Publishing Company, 1969: 78).

Deshpande, Rohit, "Paradigms Lost: On Theory and Method in Research in Marketing." *Journal of Marketing,* 47 (Fall, 1983): 101–10.

Ford, Neil M., Orville C. Walker, Jr., and Gilbert A. Churchill, Jr. "Expectation-Specific Measures of the Intersender Conflict and Role Ambiguity Experienced by Industrial Salesmen." *Journal of Business Research,* 3 (2), 1975: 95–111.

Garvin, David A., "Quality on the Line." *Harvard Business Review,* 61 (September-October 1983): 65–73.

Geer, J.H., G.C. Davidson, and R.J. Gatchel, "Reduction of Stress in Humans Through Nonveridical Perceived Control of Aversive Stimulation." *Journal of Personality and Social Psychology,* 16 (4), 1970: 731–8.

——————— and E. Maisel. "Evaluating the Effects of the Prediction-Control Confound." *Journal of Personality and Social Psychology,* 23 (8), 1972: 314–19.

George, William R. and Hiram C. Barksdale. "Marketing Activities in the Service Industries." *Journal of Marketing,* 38 (October, 1974): 65–70.

——————— and Leonard L. Berry. "Guidelines for the Advertising of Services." *Business Horizons,* 24 (May–June, 1981): 52–6.

Glass, D. C. and J. E. Singer. *Urban Stress.* (New York: Academic Press, Inc., 1972).

Goyne, David. "Customer Service in Retailing." presentation, Center for Retailing Studies Fall Conference (October 11), Houston, TX, 1985.

Greene, Charles and D. W. Organ. "An Evaluation of Causal Models Linkng Received Role and Job Satisfaction." *Administrative Science Quarterly,* 18 (March 1973): 95–103.

Gronroos, C. *Strategic Management and Marketing in the Service Sector.*

(Helsingfors: Swedish School of Economics and Business Administration, 1982).

Gross, Neal, W. S. Mason, and A. W. McEachern. *Expectations in Role Analysis. Studies of the School Superintendency Role.* (New York: John Wiley & Sons, Inc, 1957.)

Hax, Arnoldo and Nicolas S. Majluf. *Strategic Management: An Integrative Perspective.* (Englewood Cliffs, NJ: Prentice-Hall, 1984).

Ivancevich, J. M. and J. T. McMahon. "The Effects of Goal Setting, External Feedback, and Self-Generated Feedback on Outcome Variables: A Field Expenment." *Academy of Management Journal,* 25 (2), 1982: 359–72.

Kahn. R. L., D. M. Wolfe. R. P. Quinn. J. D. Snock. and R. A. Rosenthal. *Organizational Stress.* (New York: John Wiley & Sons, 1964).

Katz, B. and R. Kahn. *The Social Psychology of Organizations,* 2nd ed. (New York: John Wiley & Sons, 1978).

Langeard, Eric, John E. G. Bateson, Christopher H. Lovelock, and Pierre Eiglier. *Services Marketing: New Insights from Consumers and Managers.* (Cambridge, MA: Marketing Science Institute, 1981).

Latham. G. P. and E. A. Locke. "Goal Setting—A Motivational Technique That Works" *Organizational Dynamics,* 8 (Autumn 1971): 68–80.

Lawler, E. E. and C. Cammann. "What Makes a Work Group Successful?" In *The Failure of Success,* A. J. Marrow, ed. New York: AMACOM, 1972.

Leonard. Frank S. and W. Earl Sasser. "The Incline of Quality." *Harvard Business Review,* 60 (September–October 1982): 163–71.

Levitt, Ted. "Industrialization of Service." *Harvard Business Review,* 54 (September–October 1976): 63–74.

Locke, E. A., K. N. Shaw, L. M. Saari, and G. P. Latham. "Goal Setting and Task Performance, 1969–1980." *Psychological Bulletin,* 90 (1), 1981: 125–52.

Lovelock, Christopher H. "Why Marketing Management Needs to Be Different for Services." In *Marketing of Services,* J. H. Donnelly and W. R. George, eds., Chicago: American Marketing Association, 1981: 5–9.

McMurray, Scott. "Merrill Honors Quality Circles." *American Banker* (23 August 1983): 23.

Mintzberg, H. "An Emerging Strategy of 'Direct' Research," *Administrative Science Quarterly,* 24 (December 1979): 582–9.

Ouchi, William G. "A Conceptual Framework for the Design of Organizational Control Mechanisms." *Manageent Science,* 25 (September 1979): 833–48.

———— and Mary Ann McGuire. "Organizational Control: Two Functions." *Administrative Science Quarterly,* 20 (December 1975): 559–69.

Parasuraman, A., Leonard Berry, and Valerie Zeithaml. "Service Firms Need

Marketing Skills." *Business Horizons,* 26 (November 1983): 28–31.

————— and Valerie A. Zeithaml. "Different Perceptions of Suppliers and Clients of Industrial Services." In *Emerging Perspectives on Services Marketing.* L. Berry, G. L. Shostack, and G. Upah, eds. Chicago: American Marketing Association, 1983: 35–9.

—————, —————, and Leonard Berry. "A Conceptual Model of Service Quality and Its Implications for Future Research." *Journal of Marketing,* 49 (Fall 1985): 41–50.

—————, —————, and ————— "SERVQUAL: A Multiple-item Scale for Measuring Customer Perceptions of Service Quality Research." Report No. 86–108. Marketing Science Institute (August 1986).

Perrow, C. *Complex Organizations: A Critical Essay.* Glenview, IL: Scott, Foresman, 1979.

Peter, Paul and Jerry Olson. "Is Science Marketing?" *Journal of Marketing,* 17 (Fall), 1983: 111–25.

Peters, Thomas J. and Robert H. Waterman. Jr. *In Search of Excellence.* New York: Harper & Row, 1982.

Rabin, Joseph H. "Accent is on Quality in Consumer Services This Decade," *Marketing News,* 17 (4 March 1983): 12.

Read, W H. "Upward Communication in Industrial Hierarchies." *Human Relations,* 15 (February 1962): 3–15.

Reeves, T. K. and J. Woodward. "The Study of Managerial Control." In *Industrial Organizations: Behavior and Control,* J. Woodward, ed. London: Oxford University Press, 1970.

Rizzo, John, R. J. House. and S. I. Lirtzman, "Role Conflict and Ambiguity in Complex Organizations." *Administrative Science Quarterly,* 15, 1970: 150–63.

Rout, Lawrence. "Hyatt Hotel's Gripe Sessions Help Chief Maintain Communication With Workers." *Wall Street Journal* (16 July 1981): 27.

Rudie, Mary J. and H. Brant Wansley. "The Merrill Lynch Quality Program." In *Services Marketing in a Changing Environment.* T. M. Bloch, G. D. Upah. and V. A. Zeithaml, eds. Chicago: American Marketing Association, 1985: 7–9.

Salancik, Gerald R. "Commitment is Too Easy." *Organizational Dynamics,* 6 (Summer 1977): 62–80.

Schneider, Ben and David E. Bowen. "Employee and Customer Perceptions of Service in Banks: Replication and Extension." *Journal of Applied Psychology,* 70 (3), 1985: 423–33.

Shaw, M. E. *Group Dynamics: The Psychology of Small Group Behavior.* New York: McGraw-Hill, 1976.

Sherwin, D. S. "Management of Objectives." *Harvard Business Review.* 54 (May–June 1976): 149–60.

Straub, E., B. Tursky, and G. E. Schartz. "Self-Control and Predictability: Their Effects on Reactions to Aversive Stimulation." *Journal of Personality and Social Psychology,* 18, 157–62.

Thompson, Phillip, Glenn DeSouza, and Bradley T. Gale. *The Strategic Management of Service Quality.* Cambridge, MA: Strategic Planning Institute, PIMSLETTER, No. 33, 1985.

Walker, Orville C., Jr.. Gilbert A. Churchill, Jr., and Neil M. Ford. "Motivation and Performance in Industrial Selling: Present Knowledge and Needed Research." *Journal of Marketing Research,* 14 (May, 1977) 156–68.

Woodward, Joan. *Industrial Organization: Theory and Practice.* London: Oxford University Press, 1965.

Zaltman, Gerald, Karen LeMasters. and Michael Heffring. *Theory Construction in Marketing: Some Thought on Thinking.* New York: John Wiley & Sons, 1982.

Zeithaml, Valarie A. "How Consumer Evaluation Processes Differ Between Goods and Services," *Marketing of Services,* James Donnelly and William George, eds. Chicago: American Marketing Association. 1981: 186–90.

—————, A. Parasuraman and Leonard L. Berry "Problems and Strategies in Services Marketing," *Journal of Marketing,* 49 (Spring 1985): 33–46.

Valarie A. Zeithaml is Visiting Associate Professor of Marketing, Fuqua School of Business, Duke University. Leonard L. Berry is Foley's/Federated Professor of Retailing and Marketing Studies and Director of the Center for Retailing Studies, Texas A&M University. A. Parasuraman is Foley's/Federated Professor of Retailing and Marketing Studies, Texas A&M University. The authors thank the Marketing Science Institute and its corporate sponsors for the financial support and cooperation provided for the study.

READING 13
INSIDE THE BALDRIGE AWARD
GUIDELINES CATEGORY 7:
CUSTOMER FOCUS
AND SATISFACTION

THE BALDRIGE AWARD CRITERIA INDICATE THE IMPORTANCE OF CUSTOMER FOCUS AS AN ESSENTIAL ELEMENT OF A TOTAL QUALITY SYSTEM. CATEGORY 7: CUSTOMER FOCUS AND SATISFACTION OFFERS THE HIGHEST POTENTIAL SCORE OF ALL CATEGORIES—300 POINTS OUT OF A MAXIMUM OF 1,000. (THE NEXT MOST IMPORTANT OF THE SEVEN CATEGORIES CARRIES 180 POINTS.) CATEGORY 7 IS SUBDIVIDED INTO SIX MAJOR SEGMENTS. EACH OF THESE "EXAMINATION ITEMS," MUST BE ADDRESSED BY BALDRIGE APPLICANTS. THE SIX ITEMS FOR THE 1994 AWARD CRITERIA AND THEIR POINT VALUES ARE:

7.1 CUSTOMER EXPECTATIONS: CURRENT AND FUTURE . . 35
7.2 CUSTOMER RELATIONSHIP MANAGEMENT 65
7.3 COMMITMENT TO CUSTOMERS. 15
7.4 CUSTOMER SATISFACTION DETERMINATION 30
7.5 CUSTOMER SATISFACTION RESULTS 85
7.6 CUSTOMER SATISFACTION COMPARISON 70

ALTHOUGH THE ABOVE SHOW SOME CHANGE FROM THE 1992 CRITERIA REPORTED IN THE ARTICLE, NOTE THAT CUSTOMER SATISFACTION RESULTS (WHICH MEASURE CURRENT LEVELS AND TRENDS OF <u>COMPANY</u> INDICATORS) AND CUSTOMER SATISFACTION COMPARISON (WHICH MEASURES COMPANY RESULTS RELATIVE TO THOSE OF COMPETITORS) ARE STILL THE TWO HIGHEST-SCORING ITEMS. WE MIGHT ALSO NOTE THAT 1994 CRITERIA SPECIFICALLY REQUIRE INFORMATION ON CUSTOMER RETENTION (SEE READING 2).

CATEGORY 7, ALTHOUGH CONCERNED WITH THE KEY ELE-MENT OF CUSTOMER FOCUS, IS CLEARLY RELATED TO OTHER SUBJECTS REVIEWED IN THESE READINGS. FOR EXAMPLE, THERE IS AN OBVIOUS NEED FOR: <u>DATA</u> TO DESCRIBE THE CURRENT SITUATION AND DRIVE <u>CONTINUOUS</u> <u>IMPROVE-MENT,</u> <u>EMPOWERMENT</u> OF CUSTOMER-CONTACT EMPLOYEES, ORGANIZATIONAL <u>LEADERSHIP</u> THAT CREATES A CUSTOMER ORIENTATION AND FACILITATES CUSTOMER COMPLAINTS,.... AS NOTED, SUCCESSFUL ORGANIZATIONS UNDERSTAND THE INTEGRATED NATURE OF TQM (SEE READING 3).

READING 13
INSIDE THE BALDRIGE AWARD GUIDELINES CATEGORY 7: CUSTOMER FOCUS AND SATISFACTION

BY ROBERT L. DESATNICK

Category 7 of the Baldrige Award criteria is what total quality management is all about: customer satisfaction. Customer satisfaction can be defined as the degree of happiness a customer experiences with a company's product or service, resulting from the interaction and interrelationships of all people within that company.

The importance of Category 7 is illustrated by its relative weight in the point values. Category 7 carries more points than any other category–a total of 300 points out of a possible 1,000; the second highest point value is Category 6 (Quality and Operational Results) with a point total of 180.

Several of the core values and concepts discussed in the *1992 Award Criteria* booklet are of particular importance in customer relationships:[1]

CUSTOMER-DRIVEN QUALITY

Quality must be customer driven, meaning that the acceptable level of product or service quality is determined by the customer, not the provider.

LEADERSHIP

A company must be a leader in its market. Leadership is demonstrated in several ways, the first of which is competitive benchmarking. The most successful

---

[1]For more information on these core values and concepts, see the *1992 Award Criteria* booklet, pp.2–4.

CREDIT: Robert L. Desatnick "Inside the Baldrige Award Guidelines Category 7: Customer Focus and Satisfaction," *Quality Progress* (December, 1992).

organizations compare themselves with industry leaders and world-class organizations in many customer-related areas, such as cycle time and complaints.

Leadership is also demonstrated by a company's market share for each product or service in each market segment; conversely, closed accounts and lost business indicate leadership is lacking. Finally, leadership can be shown by the creation of new products and services.

CONTINUOUS IMPROVEMENT

This overriding theme must be in all that a company does, internally and externally. The question should be asked: Do we make our customers our partners in every sense of the word? Do they participate in our quality training?

FULL PARTICIPATION

All employees must work together to achieve quality and productivity objectives so that the product or service meets customer requirements. This working relationship must extend throughout a product's or service's life cycle, from initial design to prototype testing to delivery.

FAST RESPONSE

Responsiveness enables a company to command a premium price for its products or services in the competitive marketplace. One way to exceed customers' expectation of fast response is to have same-day shipment of a product.

MANAGEMENT BY FACT

Customer relationship management must be based on facts, not anecdotal evidence. It is not enough to say that customers are satisfied because they are still purchasing a product or service or because the company has not received any complaints. Objective data on customer satisfaction must be obtained from a variety of sources, including published surveys, third-party consultation, and customer satisfaction surveys. If a company asks the right questions, it will get the right answers.

LONG-RANGE OUTLOOK

Over the long haul, successful companies innovate–they anticipate changing, increasingly challenging customer needs and expectations. Those companies that are not innovative risk evaporation.

The *Customer Focus and Satisfaction* Category examines the company's relationships with customers and its knowledge of customer requirements and of the key quality factors that determine marketplace competitiveness. Also examined are the company's methods to determine customer satisfaction, current trends and levels of satisfaction, and these results relative to competitors.

7.1 Customer Relationship Management

(65 pts.)

Describe how the company provides effective management of its relationships with its customers and uses information gained from customers to improve customer relationship management strategies and practices.

AREAS TO ADDRESS

a. how the company determines the most important factors in maintaining and building relationships with customers and develops strategies and plans to address them. Describe these factors and how the strategies take into account: fulfillment of basic customer needs in the relationship; opportunities to enhance the relationships; provision of information to customers to ensure the proper setting of expectations regarding products, services, and relationships; and roles of all customer-contact employees, their technology needs, and their logistics support.

b. how the company provides information and easy access to enable customers to seek assistance, to comment, and to complain. Describe types of contact and how easy access is maintained for each type.

c. follow-up with customers on products, services, and recent transactions to help build relationships and to seek feedback for improvement.

d. how service standards that define reliability, responsiveness, and effectiveness of customer-contact employees' interactions with customers are set. Describe how standards requirements are deployed to other company units that support customer-contact employees, how the overall performance of the service standards system is monitored, and how it is improved using customer information.

e. how the company ensures that formal and informal complaints and feedback received by all company units are aggregated for overall evaluation and use throughout the company. Describe how the company ensures that complaints and problems are resolved promptly and effectively.

f. how the following are addressed for customer-contact employees: (1) selection factors; (2) career path; (3) special training to include: knowledge of products and services; listening to customers; soliciting comments from customers; how to anticipate and handle problems or failures ("recovery"), skills in customer retention, and how to manage expectations, (4) empowerment and decision making; (5) attitude and morale determination; (6) recognition and reward; and (7) attrition

g. how the company evaluates and improves its customer relationship management practices. Describe key indicators used in evaluations and how evaluations lead to improvements, such as in strategy, training, technology, and service standards.

Notes:

(1) Information on trends and levels in indicators of complaint response time and trends in percent of complaints resolved on first contact should be reported in Item 6.3.

(2) In addressing empowerment and decision making in 7.1f, indicate how the company ensures that there is a common vision or basis guiding customer-contact employee action.

7.2 Commitment to Customers

(15 pts.)

Describe the company's explicit and implicit commitments to customers regarding its products and services.

AREAS TO ADDRESS

a. types of commitments the company makes to promote trust and confidence in its products, services, and relationships. Describe how these commitments: (1) address the principal concerns of customers; and (2) are free from conditions that might weaken customer confidence.

b. how improvements in the quality of the company's products and services over the past three years have been translated into stronger commitments. Compare commitments with those of competitors.

c. how the company evaluates and improves its commitments, and the customers' understanding of them, to avoid gaps between expectations and delivery.

Note:

Commitments may include product and service guarantees, product warranties, and other understandings with the customer, expressed or implied.

7.3 Customer Satisfaction Determination
(35 pts.)
Describe the company's methods for determining customer satisfaction and customer satisfaction relative to competitors; describe how these methods are evaluated and improved.

AREAS TO ADDRESS

a. how the company determines customer satisfaction. Include: (1) a brief description of market segments and customer groups and the key customer satisfaction requirements for each segment or group; (2) how customer satisfaction measurements capture key information that reflects customers' likely market behavior; and (3) a brief description of the methods, processes, and scales used; frequency of determination, and how objectivity and validity are assured.

b. how customer satisfaction relative to that for competitors is determined. Describe: (1) company-based comparative studies; and (2) comparative studies or evaluations made by independent organizations, including customers. For (1) and (2) describe how objectivity and validity are assured.

c. how the company evaluates and improves its overall processes and measurement scales for determining customer satisfaction and customer satisfaction relative to that for competitors. Describe how other indicators (such as gains and losses of customers) and customer dissatisfaction indicators (such as complaints) are used in this improvement process.

Notes:
(1) Customer satisfaction measurements may include both a numerical rating scale and descriptors assigned to each unit in the scale. An effective customer satisfaction measurement system is one that provides the company with reliable information about customer views of specific product and service features and the relationship between these views or ratings and the customer's likely market behaviors.

(2) Indicators of customer dissatisfaction include complaints, claims, refunds, recalls, returns, repeat services, litigation, replacements, downgrades, repairs, warranty work, and warranty costs. If the company has received any sanctions under regulation or contract during the past three years, include such information in the item. Briefly summarize how sanctions were resolved or give current status.

(3) Company-based or independent organization comparative studies in 7.3b may take into account one or more indicators of customer dissatisfaction.

CATEGORY 7: CUSTOMER FOCUS AND SATISFACTION (300 PTS.) *(CONTINUED)*

7.4 Customer Satisfaction Results
(75 pts.)

Summarize trends in the company's customer satisfaction and trends in key indicators of dissatisfaction.

AREAS TO ADDRESS

a. trends and current levels in indicators of customer satisfaction, segmented as appropriate

b. trends and current levels in indicators of customer dissatisfaction. Address all indicators relevant to the company's products and services.

Notes:

(1) Results reported in this item derive from methods described in Item 7.3 and 7.1c and e.

(2) Indicators of customer dissatisfaction are listed in Item 7.3, Note 2.

7.5 Customer Satisfaction Comparison
(75 pts.)

Compare the company's customer satisfaction results with those of competitors.

AREAS TO ADDRESS

a. trends and current levels in indicators of customer satisfaction relative to that for competitors, based upon methods described in Item 7.3. Segment by customer group, as appropriate

b. trends in gaining or losing customers, or customer accounts, to competitors

c. trends in gaining or losing market share to competitors

Note:

Competitors include domestic and international ones in the company's markets, both domestic and international.

7.6 Future Requirements and Expectations of Customers
(35 pts.)

Describe how the company determines future requirements and expectations of customers.

AREAS TO ADDRESS

a. how the company addresses future requirements and expectations of customers. Describe: (1) the time horizon for the determination; (2) how data from current customers are projected; (3) how customers of competitors and other poten-

tial customers are considered; and (4) how important technological, competitive, societal, economic, and demographic
factors and trends that may bear upon customer requirements and expectations are considered.

b. how the company projects key product and service features and the relative importance of these features to customers and potential customers. Describe how potential
market segments and customer groups are considered.
Include considerations that address new product/service lines
as well as current products and services.

c. how the company evaluates and improves its processes
for determining future requirements and expectations of customers. Describe how the improvement process considers
new market opportunities and extension of the time horizon
for the determination of customer requirements and expectations.

In brief, a company with world-class quality in customer satisfaction
exhibits these types of characteristics:

- Several methods are used to determine customers' needs and expectations.
- Specific surveys are conducted to determine customers' satisfaction with
  the company's products or services.
- The company performs better than the competition in terms of accuracy
  and financial measurements.
- The company has a customer inquiry center with a toll-free telephone
  number.
- Survey results are used to initiate and implement positive changes.
- Formal processes exist to improve customer satisfaction.
- Customer-relationship management is highly visible.
- Employees who are in direct contact with customers are empowered to
  solve customers' problems promptly.
- Employees are involved in developing service quality standards.
- Audits, including mystery shoppers, are used to monitor service per-
  formance.
- Customer satisfaction standards are well-defined and objectively mea-
  surable.

- Complaint logs are used to analyze trends and develop quality improvement plans.
- Satisfaction data are correlated with increases in financial gains.
- The company surveys customers who close their accounts to determine the causes of their dissatisfaction. Plans are then implemented to correct the situations that caused the customers' dissatisfaction.
- The company is recognized for outstanding quality by other organizations.

A LEARNING TOOL

A company can learn much about itself by completing Category 7 and objectively using the scoring guidelines shown in Table 1. Initially, most organizations will score low, even if well-entrenched in the marketplace. While most companies perform many activities well, it is those activities they do not perform well that are of concern. For example, very few companies perform competitive benchmarking, and some do not even know their competitors. This self-scoring exercise also lets companies know how much more they can do to create perceptible differences between them and their competitors.

Most companies are good at solving problems but could improve through prevention- and fact-based management. As the management team members complete Category 7, their concepts about what really constitutes customer focus and satisfaction are considerably broadened. New opportunities become immediately visible, and cost-effective ideas are soon put into action. A real understanding of what constitutes commitment to customers is gleaned.

Perhaps the most beneficial lesson for companies completing Category 7 is that they learn they can do more with less by involving the entire organization in customer satisfaction. Companies learn how to more effectively integrate various efforts. Most companies informally gather information on customer satisfaction and give this information only to a handful of executives. This practice can result in fragmented efforts throughout the organization.

For example, in a recent customer satisfaction seminar I facilitated, I asked the operations personnel to form a team and write down what they were doing to enhance customer satisfaction. I asked the sales personnel to do the same. The team leaders then presented their extensive lists and explanations of what they were doing to exceed customers' expectations. Both teams were surprised to learn what the other was doing. This exercise fostered a closer working partnership between operations and sales.

TABLE 1	SCORING GUIDELINES		
SCORE	**APPROACH**	**DEPLOYMENT**	**RESULTS**
0%	• anecdotal, no system evident	• anecdotal	• anecdotal
10-40%	• beginnings of systematic prevention basis	• some to many major areas of business	• some positive trends in the areas deployed
50%	• sound, systematic prevention basis that includes evaluation/ improvement cycles • some evidence of integration	• most major areas of business • some support areas	• positive trend in most major areas • some evidence that results are caused by approach
60-90%	• sound, systematic prevention basis with evidence of refinement through evaluation cycles • good integration	• major areas of business • from some to many support areas	• good to excellent in major areas • positive trends–from some to many support areas • evidence that results are caused by approach
100%	• sound, systematic prevention basis refined through evaluation/ improvement cycles • excellent integration	• major areas and support areas • all operations	• excellent (world-class) results in major areas • good to excellent in support areas • sustained results • results clearly caused by approach

Source: 1992 Award Criteria, National Institute of Standards and Technology, Gaithersburg, MD.

COMMON SHORTFALLS

Low-scoring award applications reveal common shortfalls in customer satis-faction efforts. Most shortfalls deal with data gathering.

Some companies do not collect quantitative, measurable data on customer satisfaction (or at least their applications don't contain specific examples). Other companies possess a considerable amount of customer satisfaction data, but the information is not broken down by products, customers, or market seg-ments. Sometimes the data are diffused throughout the company; hence, there is no central source of competitive information on customer satisfaction.

In some instances, data are collected only from the sales and marketing functions, but other functions–such as management information systems, order entry, purchasing, engineering, operations, administrative, human resources, and accounting–can also offer valuable information. For example, human resources data on turnover and absenteeism can help determine whether customers are satisfied. High turnover and absenteeism means dissatisfied employees, which directly influences the company's ability to satisfy its customers. Thus, how the human resource function handles employee recruitment, orientation, training and development, and compensation affects customer satisfaction.

Information from accounting can also indicate the level of customer satisfaction. An increasing amount of receivables outstanding and an excessive time lapse between when customers get and pay their bills (e.g., more than 30 days) are direct, measurable indicators of customer dissatisfaction.

Another area in which shortfalls occur is in key indicators: Insufficient attention is paid to identifying and consolidating all indicators of customer satisfaction and dissatisfaction. This duty often tends to be within the purview of the complaint department–and there the information stays. It is not shared with sales, marketing, accounting, and administration. In other words, information deployment is limited. Thus, the information is not used to assess the current situation and plan improvements in customer satisfaction.

When addressing complaints, a company needs to note more than just their nature, frequency, and source. The company should also document how long it takes to resolve complaints, whether they are resolved to the customers' complete satisfaction, and the cost of their resolution.

In addition, trends in customer satisfaction comparisons are often treated too lightly. While overall complaints are usually tracked, specific gains and losses in products, services, market segment, and market share are not fully covered and integrated.

In summary, the data-gathering process tends to be incomplete in the low-scoring award applications. Not enough time and resources are devoted to factual, broad-based quantitative information and competitive comparisons.

SOME SUGGESTIONS

Here are some suggestions for completing Category 7:

1. Have the entire organization, level by level, provide appropriate input.
2. Allow enough time and resources to complete all six items (Items 7.1 to 7.6).
3. Integrate and interrelate all data gathered in a centralized location using appropriate hardware and software.
4. Make all information available to all employees to ensure comprehensive coverage and additional employee suggestions.

5. The entire management team, not just the sales force should talk to the customers. For example, each executive could personally call or visit five customers a week, asking them: Why did you start doing business with us? What do you like most about the relationship? Specifically, what do you dislike about doing business with us? If we had the ideal working relationship, what would be different from the way it is now? If you were to stop doing business with us and turn to a competitor, what would be your main reason?

This information should then be compiled into a composite report and analyzed. The analysis should highlight:

- The company's strengths as compared to those of its competitors
- The company's areas for improvement as compared to those of its competitors
- Problems that must be corrected immediately
- Future action plans containing specific assignments that ensure the company exceeds customers' expectations
- Plans to perform more competitive benchmarking using specific customer satisfaction measurements based on information from professional associations, published surveys, third-party consultants, market research, and the company's own surveys.
- Plans to emphasize total organization integration to ensure that the company practices prevention- and fact-based management, strives for continuous improvement, incorporates leadership in every facet of customer-relationship management, and anticipates future customers' needs and expectations.

EXCEEDING EXPECTATIONS

The ultimate objective of any organization–large or small, manufacturing or service, public or private–is to exceed customers' expectations. That is what Category 7 is about. If you believe that your company can better satisfy its customers, it will–if the appropriate actions are taken.

Robert L. Desatnick is on the board of examiners for the Malcolm Baldrige National Quality Award. He is the president of Creative Human Resource Consultants in Chicago, IL. Desatnick received a master's degree in business administration from Washington University in St. Louis, MO.

PART SEVEN

TEAMWORK/
PARTICIPATION/
EMPOWERMENT

READING 14
THE PAYOFF FROM TEAMWORK

THIS ARTICLE, A COVER STORY FROM *BUSINESS WEEK*, IS THE FIRST OF THREE READINGS DEALING WITH TEAMWORK/PARTICIPATION/EMPOWERMENT. THIS PIECE BEGINS, "CALL IT EMPLOYEE INVOLVEMENT (EI) OR WORKER PARTICIPATION OR LABOR-MANAGEMENT 'JOINTNESS'...." THE NEXT ARTICLE SAYS, "THOUGH WE WILL USE THE TERM 'PARTICIPATION' (OR 'EMPLOYEE INVOLVEMENT'), WORK ARRANGEMENTS WITH SUCH CHARACTERISTICS GO BY MANY NAMES, SUCH AS 'PARTICIPATIVE DECISION MAKING' AND 'EMPOWERMENT.' EACH HAS SOME DISTINCTIVE NUANCE, BUT FOR OUR PURPOSES THEY WILL BE TREATED AS THE SAME." THE THREE READINGS TOGETHER PROVIDE A SOUND INTRODUCTION TO THESE IDEAS AND THE VARIOUS FORMS THEY MAY TAKE IN ORGANIZATIONS.

PERHAPS WE SHOULD BEGIN BY NOTING THE SEVERAL DIFFERENT DEFINITIONS/INTERPRETATIONS OF THE WORD *TEAM*. *THE AMERICAN HERITAGE DICTIONARY* DEFINES *TEAM* FIRST AS "TWO OR MORE DRAFT ANIMALS HARNESSED TO A VEHICLE OR FARM IMPLEMENT." ALTHOUGH UNEXPECTED, SUCH A DEFINITION QUICKLY IMPLIES SOME BASIC IDEAS OF TEAMS: (1) THE ABILITY OF A TEAM TO PERFORM TASKS DIFFICULT OR IMPOSSIBLE FOR AN INDIVIDUAL WHEN/IF (2) THEY WORK TOGETHER, COOPERATIVELY (IN THIS CASE "ENCOURAGED" BY THE HARNESS). THE SECOND DICTIONARY DEFINITION ALSO DEALS WITH ANIMALS BUT THEN COMES "A GROUP OF PLAYERS ON THE SAME SIDE IN A GAME," AND THEN "ANY GROUP ORGANIZED TO WORK TOGETHER." NOTE THEN THAT "TEAMS" CAN COVER MANY POSSIBILITIES, AS THE READING REVEALS AS QUALITY CIRCLES, PROBLEM-SOLVING TEAMS, AND SELF-MANAGING TEAMS ARE DISCUSSED.

READING 14
THE PAYOFF FROM TEAMWORK

BY JOHN HOERR

What the company wants is for us to work like the Japanese. Everybody go
out and do jumping jacks in the morning and kiss each other when they go
home at night. You work as a team, rat on each other, and lose control of your
destiny. That's not going to work in this country.

—John Brodie, President
United Paperworkers Local 448
Chester, Pa.

Call it employee involvement (EI) or worker participation or labor-management
"jointness," as it is now known in the auto industry. Whatever the term, the concept is clearly troubling for many Americans. At one and the same time, it
promises workers autonomy over their jobs but also threatens their old ways of
working. It gives managers a powerful tool to improve productivity and quality
but could undermine their control. EI may be American industry's best hope
of competing with the Japanese and Europeans, as well as low-wage, Third
World producers. Yet for years, timid U.S. companies have merely sloshed a
thin coating of EI across an aging industrial base.

But now, there are signs that real employee involvement is sinking into
the core of Corporate America. While angry union officers such as the Paperworkers' Brodie still rail against participation, more and more workers and
labor leaders are willing to risk EI in hopes of making their employers more
competitive—and their jobs more secure. This message came across strongly
at the recent United Auto Workers convention in Anaheim, California. In
one of the most raucous debates in UAW history, critics made the rafters ring
with charges that "jointness" consisted of little more than "co-optation" and
a new form of the age-old "speedup." But delegates favoring cooperation

CREDIT: Reprinted from July 10, 1989 issue of *Business Week* by special permission,
copyright (c) 1989 by McGraw-Hill, Inc. John Hoerr, "The Payoff From Teamwork," *Business Week* (July 10, 1989) pp. 56–62.

overwhelmingly voted down the dissidents. And when the meeting ended on June 23, the UAW's leaders were more strongly committed than ever to EI programs at the Big Three auto makers. (See pg. 280.)

The UAW'S approval will make it easier for other unions to give more than lip service to EI. And there are comparable changes in management attitudes. So what had been a slow evolution of EI is turning into a revolution in the way work is organized and managed in the U.S. Companies that only a few years ago disdained participation are rushing to set up so-called self-managing work teams, the most advanced stage of EI (see table). The team concept is spreading rapidly in industries such as autos, aerospace, electrical equipment, electronics food processing, paper, steel, and even financial services.

Although work teams differ from company to company, they typically consist of 5 to 12 multiskilled workers who rotate jobs and produce an entire product or service with only minimal supervision. Adopting the team approach is no small matter; it means wiping out tiers of managers and tearing down bureaucratic barriers between departments. Yet companies are willing to undertake such radical changes to gain workers' knowledge and

THE EVOLUTION OF WORKER PARTICIPATION IN THE U.S.

PROBLEM-SOLVING TEAMS	SPECIAL-PURPOSE TEAMS	SELF-MANAGING TEAMS
Structure and function		
• Consist of 5 to 12 volunteers, hourly and salaried, drawn from different areas of a department. Meet one to two hours a week to discuss ways of improving quality, efficiency, and work environment. No power to implement ideas	• Duties may include designing and introducing work reforms and new technology, meeting with suppliers and customers, linking separate functions. In union shops, labor and management collaborate on operational decisions at all levels	• Usually 5 to 15 employees who produce an entire product instead of subunits. Members learn all tasks and rotate from job to job. Teams take over managerial duties, including work and vacation scheduling, ordering materials, etc.
Results		
• Can reduce costs and improve product quality. But do not organize work more efficiently or force managers to adopt a participatory style. Tend to fade away after a few years	• Involve workers and union representatives in decisions at ever-higher levels, creating atmosphere for quality and productivity improvements. Create a foundation for self-managing work teams	• Can increase productivity 30 percent or more and substantially raise quality. Fundamentally change how work is organized, giving employees control over their jobs. Create flatter organization by eliminating supervisors
When Introduced		
• Small-scale efforts in 1920s and 1930s. Widespread adoption in late 1970s based on Japanese Quality Circles	• Early-to-middle 1980s, growing out of problem-solving approach. Still spreading, especially in union sectors	• Used by a few companies in 1960s and 1970s. Began rapid spread in mid-to-late 1980s, and appear to be wave of future

commitment—along with productivity gains that exceed 30 percent in some cases.

Despite these recent signs of EI's growing acceptance, many workplace experts believe it is not spreading fast enough. "Participation is growing, but at an alarmingly slow rate considering the quality and productivity payouts," says Jerome M. Rosow, president of the Work in America Institute, a nonprofit research group that advocates employee involvement. He and others believe that the federal government now should actively promote EI. "We'll see some incremental growth in participation but not widespread diffusion unless it gets reinforced in public policy," says Thomas A. Kochan, a professor at Massachusetts Institute of Technology who has studied the EI movement for more than 10 years.

Resistance to further EI growth remains widespread. Many managers won't allow participation because it entails sharing power with employees. Low-level supervisors, whose interests often are ignored in the EI process, tend to fight it. For participation to become a way of life in industry, it also must over come Wall Street's insistence on short-term results. Managers who fear hostile takeovers think twice about investing in human-capital programs such as the continual training that's needed to help workers improve their technical and social skills. "Very few companies understand how deep the change must be, and really go after it," says W. Patrick Dolan, a St. Louis consultant who works with unions and employers on EI programs "Training is always a peripheral, secondary consideration, and when push comes to shove, it keeps sliding."

QUALITY CIRCLES

Although unions are declining in power, they still represent 24 percent of workers in the crucial manufacturing sector. Without their assent and help, instituting work reforms to boost efficiency simply is not possible. But many union leaders, veterans of a decade when management fought hard to avoid, oust, and beat down organized labor, are suspicious. Militant unionists see management proposals for work teams as union-busting ploys—and sometimes they are. Even union presidents who strongly advocate EI, such as Lynn R. Williams of the United Steelworkers, can't force their philosophy on local officers. At Inland Steel Co., for example, Mike Mezo, president of the 10,000 member USW Local 1010, flatly declares: "We don't think there's any benefit to cooperation. No way will we ever take part."

Despite this opposition, a broad array of employers practice some form of participation. Government employees are involved in EI efforts at many agencies, including the U.S. Postal Service and the New York City Sanitation

Department. Workers at the Philadelphia Zoo suggest ways to draw more visitors, and they get bonuses when attendance rises. A 1987 survey by the U.S. General Accounting Office found that 70 percent of 476 large companies had installed the most common EI form, problem-solving committees usually known as quality circles (QCs). But the coverage was spotty. At 70 percent of the companies studied, less than half of the work force was involved in EI activities.

A VOICE

But that constituted some progress over the 1970s, when the participation movement clung precariously to life at a few dozen leading-edge companies. Starting about 10 years ago, the trumpeting of Japan's success with participation induced hundreds of U.S. companies to copy the Japanese approach in setting up QCs. Recommendations made by quality circles can improve quality and cut costs. But QCs are merely "off-line" discussion groups and don't reorganize work or enlarge the role of workers in the production process.

Since the mid-1980s, however, participatory methods have advanced far beyond mere problem-solving techniques copied from the Japanese. It's at this point that American practices are beginning to diverge from those used in Japan. Work-reform experts say this is necessary to avoid imposing a foreign work culture on the U.S. workplace.

In American-style teamwork, for example, workers not only gain a more direct voice in shop-floor operations—as in Japan. They also take over managerial duties, such as work and vacation scheduling, ordering materials, and hiring new members. But there is no law that says this must happen, and plenty of U.S. companies install teams without corresponding participation. Increasingly, too, American union officials demand a consulting or decision-making role on plantwide issues such as production scheduling, capital expenditures, and introduction of new technology. After the A.O. Smith Corp. automotive parts plant in Milwaukee converted last year to the team approach, one proud worker, Albert Porter, exaggerated only slightly when he boasted: "They turned over control of the shops to us."

In fact, the EI movement has unleashed enormous energy and creativity stored up by the Albert Porters who like the idea of using their brains, as well as their bodies, on the job. It increases their feelings of dignity and self-worth. Opponents of cooperation may get more press, but pro-EI workers constitute a much larger portion of most work forces. Studies show that in many plants where participatory activities are not mandatory an average of about 25 percent of the workers volunteer to join problem-solving teams. Another 70 percent are passive supporters, while only 5 percent remain opposed.

This points up one of the ironies of the EI movement. Although unions introduced the idea of "industrial democracy" early in this century, it is now management that is pushing employees in both union and nonunion plants to accept more involvement—and not to make workers happy but to improve the company's bottom line.

About-Face

If the U.S. is to become a world-class manufacturing nation, companies must be able to produce in small lots, customizing products to increasing demands. This calls for flexible work practices and workers who are willing to move from job to job. Teamwork makes this possible because the employees usually are "cross-trained" to perform all tasks. They can fill in for absent co-workers and respond quickly to changes in models and production runs. A General Electric Company plant in Salisbury, North Carolina, typically changes product models a dozen times a day by using a team system to produce lighting panelboards. This plant has increased productivity by a remarkable 250 percent compared with GE plants that produced the same products in 1985. It combines teamwork with "flexible automation" and other computerized systems.

Salisbury's success convinced even GE's typically hardheaded managers that participation can boost profits. As recently as the early 1980s, when many companies succumbed to the quality-circle fad, GE hung on to its traditional management style. But in the past few years, GE's top management has done an about-face. Of its 120,000 U.S. employees, nearly 20 percent now work under the team concept. GE doesn't dictate what human-resource practices each plant must adopt, but it encourages innovation. The corporate goal is to have 35 percent of the work force in teams by the end of 1989. "We're trying radically to reduce the work cycle needed to produce a product," says Robert Erskine, manager of production resources. "When you combine automation with new systems and work teams, you get a 40 percent to 50 percent improvement in productivity."

But teamwork plants are by no means workplace Utopias. For two years after GE's Salisbury plant converted to team-based production in late 1985, it had a 14 percent turnover rate; many workers quit rather than accept more responsibility and face constant movement from job to job. "It's not all wonderful stuff," warns plant manager Roger Gasaway. "But we've found that when you treat people like adults, 95 percent act like adults." And teamwork can provide exceptional opportunities for self-development. In Salisbury's pay-for-knowledge plan, employees can raise their salaries by completing company-funded courses in technical, economic, and behavioral subjects.

The team idea is mushrooming throughout manufacturing (see table). It's also gaining a toehold at banks insurance firms, and other companies specializing in financial services. In Morristown, N.J., for example, AT&T Credit Corp. uses teams of employees to process applications from companies that want to lease computer equipment. (See box on pages 285–286.) But teamwork is rare in the service industries, which account for more than 70 percent of employment in the U.S. In other words, the most productive form of participation hasn't spread to many millions of employees.

SOME BIG COMPANIES THAT USE WORK TEAMS

COMPANY	WHEN STARTED
BOEING	1987
CATERPILLAR	1986
CHAMPION INTERNATIONAL	1985
CUMMINS ENGINE	1973
DIGITAL EQUIPMENT	1982
FORD	1982
GENERAL ELECTRIC	1985
GENERAL MOTORS	1975
LTV STEEL	1985
PROCTOR & GAMBLE	1962
A. O. SMITH	1987
TEKTRONIX	1983

DATA: WORK IN AMERICA INSTITUTE, BW

HUMAN FACTOR

At the same time, economists are beginning to see marked evidence of EI's impact on efficiency. In a newly released report for the Brookings Institution, Steve Levine and Laura D'Andrea Tyson of the University of California reviewed all major studies of employee involvement. "If you sum it all up, meaningful participation has a positive effect on productivity. It's almost never negative or neutral," Tyson says. Moreover, studies of employee-owned companies show that stock ownership alone doesn't motivate employees to work harder, while ownership combined with participation does.

Indeed, the "human factor" emerges as the critical element in efforts to make auto plants more competitive, according to a study of 65 plants around the world by the International Motor Vehicle Program at MIT. Plants that combined computer-based technology with advanced work

BENEFITS FOR THE BACK OFFICE, TOO

It's not only Rust Belt America that needs to overhaul the way work is organized. Millions of clerical employees toil in the back offices of financial companies, processing applications, claims, and customer accounts on what amount to electronic assembly lines. The jobs are dull and repetitive and efficiency gains minuscule—when they come at all.

That was the case with AT&T Credit Corp. (ATTCC) when it opened shop in 1985 as a newly created subsidiary of American Telephone & Telegraph Co. Based in Morristown, N.J., ATTCC provides financing for customers who lease equipment from AT&T and other companies. A bank initially retained by ATTCC to process lease applications couldn't keep up with the volume of new business.

ATTCC President Thomas C. Wajnert saw that the fault lay in the bank's method of dividing labor into narrow tasks and organizing work by function. One department handled applications and checked the customer's credit standing, a second drew up contracts, and a third collected payments. So no one person or group had responsibility for providing full service to a customer. "The employees had no sense of how their jobs contributed to the final solution for the customer," Wajnert says.

UNEXPECTED BONUS. Wajnert decided to hire his own employees and give them "ownership and accountability." His first concern was to increase efficiency, not to provide more rewarding jobs. But in the end, he did both.

In 1986, ATTCC set up 11 teams of 10 to 15 newly hired workers in a high-volume division serving small businesses. The three major lease-processing functions were combined in each team. No longer were calls from customers shunted from department to department. The company also divided its national staff of field agents into seven regions and assigned two or three teams to handle business from each region. That way, the same teams always worked with the same sales staff, establishing a personal relationship with them and their customers. Above all, team members took responsibility for solving customers' problems. ATTCC's new slogan: "Whoever gets the call owns the problem."

The teams largely manage themselves. Members make most decisions on how to deal with customers, schedule their own time off, reassign work when people are absent, and interview prospective new employees The only supervisors are seven regional managers who advise the team members, rather than give orders. The result: The teams process up to 800 lease applications a day vs. 400 under the old system. Instead of taking several days to give a final yes or no, the teams do it in 24 to 48 hours. As a result, ATTCC is growing at a 40%-to-50% compound annual rate, Wajnert says.

EXTRA CASH. The teams also have economic incentives for providing good service. A bonus plan tied to each team's costs and profits can produce extra cash. The employees, most of whom are young college graduates, can add $1,500 a year to average salaries of $28,000, and pay rises as employees learn new skills. "It's a phenomenal learning opportunity," says 24-year-old team member Michael LoCastro.

But LoCastro and others complain that promotions are rare because there are few managerial positions. And everyone comes under intense pressure from co-workers to produce more. The annual turnover rate is high: Some 20 percent of ATTCC employees either quit or transfer to other parts of AT&T. Still, the team experiment has been so successful that ATTCC is involving employees in planning to extend the concept throughout the company. "They will probably come up with as good an organizational design as management could," Wajnert says, "and it will work a lot better because the employees will take ownership for it."

innovations outperformed all others. Automated plants with no work reforms were the poorest performers. But teams are "no panacea unless they are integrated in a whole new approach to the production system," says John Paul MacDuffie, an MIT research associate.

This growing body of evidence suggests strongly that the old system of assumptions, beliefs, and practices relating to work has been disproved as a pattern for modern factory and office jobs. Based on principles developed by Frederick W. Taylor, the old paradigm involved the division of production work into simple, repetitive tasks performed by unskilled workers under close supervisory control.

LABOR WELFARE

In the new paradigm, workers will be multiskilled and to some degree will manage themselves through teamwork. Management will train workers, share business information with them, and develop specialized "gainsharing"—or bonus—plans to allow workers to cash in on the gains of increased productivity. Jobs will be protected by long-term security plans.

American companies are now discovering what the Japanese learned long ago: that people—not technology alone or marketing ploys—are the keys to success in global competition. Indeed, American workers can be just as productive as Japanese workers. This has been demonstrated conclusively by the success of Honda, Toyota, and Nissan using American labor in U S. plants. The keys to Japanese competitive superiority are their management and production systems, not some unique feature in Japan's group-oriented culture.

But the growth of participation in Japan wasn't snarled by the kind of implacable labor-management warfare that exists in many U.S. industries. (See box on pages 288–290.) Moreover, the "no cooperation" slogan of diehard EI opponents is understandable to foreign labor experts such as Haruo Shimada, an economics professor at Keio University in Tokyo who has studied Japanese and American labor systems. "If American unions give in to American management, they run the risk of being destroyed because management always wants to destroy them," he says. Japanese unions aren't threatened this way, he says.

For these reasons, militant unionists contend that management can never be trusted. In using work teams, charges Don G. Douglas, president of United Auto Workers Local 594 in Pontiac Michigan, "the company has a hidden agenda to erode the collective bargaining system, to lessen resistance to changes that are more favorable to the company than they are to the employees."

And the militants' position seems validated by hardball company tactics to force acceptance of EI. For example, UAW members complain that General Motors Corp. has threatened to shut down plants unless the union accepts the team concept. In the pulp and paper industry, the United Paperworkers International Union at Mobile, Alabama, and Chester, Pennsylvania, waged long—and losing—strikes in 1986 and 1987 against demands by Scott Paper Co. for contract changes that would allow establishment of work teams. The UPW's Brodie contends that the company demanded the new provision without explaining why. At both Chester and Mobile, the union caved in when Scott threatened to hire permanent replacements. Scott won these battles, but at the cost of embittering the workers. Perhaps belatedly understanding this, the company hasn't tried to force the locals to accept teamwork.

Brodie's criticism of teamwork as a Japanese import is echoed by other unionists who claim that management is really trying to "Japanize" the U.S. industrial-relations system. Actually, the work-team concept was developed and used in Britain, Sweden, and the U.S. long before Japanese auto makers

FOR AUTO WORKERS, IT'S TEAM SPIRIT VS. SUSPICION

After years of wavering on the issue, leaders of the United Auto Workers have now dispelled all doubts about their commitment to employee involvement (EI). In a showdown with EI critics at the UAW'S convention in late June, President Owen F. Bieber rallied a large majority of the 2,100 delegates to the cause of labor-management "jointness," as it's called in the auto industry, and defeated the dissidents. Most important, he put himself squarely on the line in support of joint programs to help the Big Three auto makers in their do-or-die fight against Japanese competitors.

Bieber and other UAW officers may now move more confidently in pressing for greater worker involvement on the shop floor. That's good news for General Motors, Ford Motor, and Chrysler. They contend that cooperation is necessary to match the quality and productivity of Japanese producers, which threaten to glut the market with vehicles made in their new North American plants. U.S. companies want to convert conventional plants to the team concept—a more productive way of organizing work that calls for dramatic changes in job classifications and seniority rights.

Although the UAW has been involved in EI activities since 1973, the leadership often has been divided on how strongly the concept should be pushed. Ironically, the complaints of dissidents forced Bieber—who has been hesitant on the issue—to take a strong stand. In a convention speech, he declared: "I think those who say that workers don't want change in the workplace—who insist that the old ways were always the best ways—are insulting the intelligence of UAW members."

But translating convention-floor rhetoric into shop-floor reality will be tough. Recalcitrant managers often undermine the EI process, and the sharp slowdown in car sales is threatening the job security on which cooperation is based. As a result, many workers are afraid of changes in traditional work practices. A dissident group, which dubs itself "New Directions," tapped this discontent to win the support of an estimated 10% of the delegates at the Anaheim (Calif.) convention. Even EI supporters concede that the dissidents cannot be easily dismissed. They point to the victories of New Directions delegates at major plants with team systems, including several at General Motors Corp.

But GM isn't the only company struggling with work teams. In the first union election at a new Flat Rock (Mich.) plant owned by Mazda

Motor Manufacturing (USA) Corp., workers dumped UAW-appointed leaders in favor of opponents who promised to challenge management abuses of the team concept. Debbie S. Cornelius, a former reception-ist who is now an assembly line worker and team leader at Mazda, says initial training sessions prepared workers for unprecedented involve-ment in shop-floor decisions. "But when we started mass-producing cars, there was no such thing as teamwork," she says. "All of a sudden, you were just another factory rat."

Cornelius says that workers were pressured to keep the assembly line moving even though they were told they had the right to stop pro-duction to solve quality problems. Mazda officials blame typical startup glitches and, sometimes, poor communication.

Many believe that the troubles at Mazda and elsewhere can be traced to poor management. "This is not a union problem. It's a management problem," says UAW Director Bruce A. Lee. He helped to establish suc-cessful Japanese-style teams at GM'S carmaking venture with Toyota Motor Corp. in Fremont, Calif. Managers "have to bite that bullet to give up power," he says. After five years of experience with teams at GM's Orion Township (Mich.) plant, Robert D. Wilson—a New Direc-tions supporter—is still skeptical about the concept. "I'd like to have input into my job," he says, "but when that work-group manager said, "I've got 51% of the decision-making," that was the end of that."

At other plants, however, participation activists say cooperation is working well. "We're finding that jointness is the best way to do busi-ness," says Michael S. Knox, who works at a GM plant in Flint, Mich. "I wish we could have started doing this a long time ago." Knox was named by the chairman of Local 326 to a new job as "hourly adviser" to the superintendent of a 150 worker department that makes door hinges. "We make all decisions jointly," he says, including scheduling production, choosing suppliers, and analyzing the competition.

SAVING JOBS? Nonetheless, UAW dissidents see the team con-cept as inherently flawed. Their central resolution in Anaheim—which was overwhelmingly defeated—argued that the team concept pits worker against worker and eliminates jobs, all in the name of "com-petitiveness." Local unions often agree to such changes under the threat of plant closings, they charged, and are pressured to keep the joint systems by an army of union appointees.

But UAW leaders point to the benefits that flow from cooperation. The union's most dramatic victory is the slowdown of GM'S efforts to buy more of its components from non-GM plants. Indeed, the auto maker credits joint programs with saving some 8,000 jobs so far in its long-threatened components operations.

Although they were defeated at the convention, New Directions leaders promise to continue the fight against jointness. And a recent union commission discovered that anxieties about joint programs are widespread, even though only a third of UAW members in the auto sector are involved in some form of team system. Clearly, Bieber and the auto makers have a long way to go before jointness becomes a reality in the only place that counts.

By Wendy Zellner in Anaheim, Calif.

introduced their own, highly efficient model on a wide scale. Now that Japanese companies operate many plants in the U.S., American management and labor are beginning to see that worker participation means quite different things in the two countries. To American unionists, real participation means not only problem-solving on the shop floor but also gaining a voice in higher-level decisions.

But that is precisely what the Japanese-style team concept does not do. The "team concept is not intended to increase workers' autonomy but to help them find out the problems in the production line so that no defective goods will be produced," says Keio University's Shimada. "In the U.S.," he adds, "workers tend to take participation as having a voice in all kinds of things that in Japan are determined by management and engineers." The Japanese system seems to work well at their auto plants in the U.S., but most of them employ nonunion workers with few expectations about sharing power with managers.

In union auto plants, however, the method of organizing work on an assembly line is a burning issue. The UAW seems to prefer the approach that is evolving in Sweden. At two Volvo plants, teams assemble large units of a car—indeed, an entire car in the case of Volvo's new plant at Uddevalla—without much supervision at all. Some GM plants, however, are adopting the Japanese method used at New United Motors Manufacturing Inc. (NUMMI), the joint venture between GM and Toyota Motor Corp. in Fremont, California. Japanese-style teams work on conventionally organized lines, performing minutely subdivided tasks. Team members have a lot of discretion in improving quality, but they work under first-line supervisors.

TRUST

American-style teams force significant changes in work practices, and unions are still struggling to find a new role on the shop floor in teamwork plants. With only one or two classifications for production jobs, employees have to learn a wide variety of tasks and move with the flow of work. They typically can't use their seniority, the bedrock of American unionism, to bid for better or easier jobs. In some nonunion plants, team members are expected to rate each other's performance and sometimes even fire shirkers—though most unions refuse to let their members get involved in disciplinary decisions. And teamwork also can reduce the influence of the union on traditional matters such as seniority and the grievance procedure.

"There's no question managers in Japan can get away with doing some things, because of a more compliant labor force, that would not be accepted in America," says Robert E. Cole, a U.S. authority on Japanese labor practices at the University of Michigan. But American unions can protect their members by aggressively monitoring EI programs. At A. O. Smith in Milwaukee, the president of the A. O. Smith Steelworkers Union, Paul Blackman, insisted on setting up work teams so that his members could have more influence in operations. Moreover, Blackman has a voice in all major decisions made by company officers. But it is hard to write this kind of participation into a contract, and U.S. unionists are wary of giving up one kind of power in the mere hope of gaining another.

NATIONAL STRATEGY

Cole points out an important reason why employee involvement has spread more quickly in Japan and Sweden than in the United States. In both countries, national organizations that promoted participation had the respect and support of top corporate management. The Japanese Union of Scientists & Engineers not only advocated the quality-circle approach but actually helped companies install QCs. In Sweden, the Employers' Federation acted as a consultant for companies introducing participation. And the powerful Swedish labor movement, which is closely allied with the dominant Social Democratic Labor Party, has pushed participation as a means of gaining a voice in corporate decisions.

No comparable organizations exist in the United States. Nor is there a large federal presence. The Labor Department's Bureau of Labor-Management Relations & Cooperative Programs gathers and disseminates information about employee involvement. But most of its $6 million annual budget must be spent on other programs. Although Sweden's work force is less than a tenth the size of America's, the government-financed Center for Working Life spends $6.5 million a year on programs "to help democratize working life."

In the United States, states such as Massachusetts, Ohio, New York, Pennsylvania, and Indiana also promote EI and provide funds and technical help to companies and unions. But as helpful as these programs are, says MIT'S Kochan, they can't substitute for the central role that the federal government could play in building networks of professionals across the nation. What is needed, Kochan adds, is "a statement that the government recognizes the centrality of these innovations to its long-term economic strategy." The government could encourage participation—just as it has capital investment—through a tax-credit system, Kochan says.

ALIENATED?

Richard E. Walton, a top EI theorist at Harvard University, says participation should be at the heart of a national competitiveness strategy. This means investing in human capital, as well as technology, to boost productivity. "People must see the interrelationship between social performance and economic performance," Walton says. "To have world-class quality and costs and the ability to assimilate new technology, we must have the world's best ability to develop human capabilities."

The United States is moving in that direction. Participation has permanently altered the old industrial relations system, based on the idea that efficient mass-production inevitably breeds alienated workers who must be bought off with high pay. The EI movement puts the lie to that assumption. When jobs are challenging, workers are committed and perform superbly. But participation will remain only a beachhead in hostile territory—unless management, labor, and government join forces to foster the revolution in the way Americans work.

READING 15
QUALITY, PARTICIPATION,
AND COMPETITIVENESS

THIS ARTICLE ASKS WHY, DESPITE YEARS OF ADVOCACY FROM ACADEMIC CIRCLES, HAVE PARTICIPATION/EMPLOYEE INVOLVEMENT (EI) PRACTICES NOT BEEN WIDELY ADOPTED BY AMERICAN MANAGEMENT? THE AUTHORS REVIEW THE STRENGTHS AND WEAKNESSES OF PARTICIPATION AND CONCLUDE THAT ITS DEFICIENCIES ARE PRIMARILY FOUND AT THE ORGANIZATIONAL LEVEL. PARTICULARLY, THEY FOCUS ON (1) FLABBINESS AND (2) A LACK OF STRATEGIC CONTEXT. FLABBINESS REFERS TO AN INADEQUATE SUBSTANCE, STRUCTURE, OR SYSTEMATIC METHODOLOGY, THAT, IN THE SUBSEQUENT UNCERTAINTY, MAKES PARTICIPATION BECOME HOLLOW. (IT IS PROBABLY NOT A COINCIDENCE THAT A *HARVARD BUSINESS REVIEW* ARTICLE RELATING A HONEYWELL UNIT'S EI EXPERIENCE WAS TITLED "WRESTLING WITH JELLYFISH.") A LACK OF STRATEGIC CONTEXT FOR EI MEANS THAT IT IS NOT TIED TO WORK OR CUSTOMERS, AND THUS EVENTUALLY WILL BE VIEWED AS "FEEL-GOOD" PERIPHERAL ACTIVITY. THESE TWO PROBLEMS MEAN THAT, LACKING CLEAR ORGANIZATIONAL BENEFITS, "MANAGERIAL SUPPORT FOR PARTICIPATION IS UNLIKELY TO BE FORTHCOMING, AND IF IT IS FORTHCOMING, UNLIKELY TO BE SUBSTAINED."

THE AUTHORS SUGGEST THAT THE STRENGTHS OF EI CAN BE KEPT AND THE DEFICIENCIES ADDRESSED IF PARTICIPATION IS INTRODUCED AS AN INTEGRAL PART OF A QUALITY INITIATIVE. TQM BRINGS A WELL-DEFINED METHODOLOGY FOR PROBLEM-SOLVING, ADVOCATES COOPERATION AND A PROCESS FOCUS, AND EMPHASIZES BOTH INTERNAL AND EXTERNAL CUSTOMER SATISFACTION. THE AUTHORS WRITE, "TO PURSUE PARTICIPATION WITHOUT QUALITY HAS PROVED INEFFECTIVE, A RECIPE FOR FAILURE IN TODAY'S COMPETITIVE MARKETS."

READING 15
QUALITY, PARTICIPATION, AND COMPETITIVENESS

BY ROBERT E. COLE, PAUL BACDAYAN, AND B. JOSEPH WHITE

Despite years of preaching from academics and repeated assertions of the benefits associated with participatory work practices, managers have been slow to embrace and incorporate these practices into everyday work routines in American corporations.[1] Why is this the case? Once we identify the obstacles, we can examine the role that a modern quality improvement focus plays in eliminating these obstacles.[2]

There are many different forms of employee participation.[3] By participation, we mean employee involvement in decision making that has three characteristics:

- It is *relatively formal*. It is part of official role behavior.
- It is *direct*. It involves individuals instead of, or in addition to, elected representatives.
- It is *relatively local and moderately open regarding decision-making access*. Workers have a strong input into most operational decisions directly affecting their work and will be delegated authority for some aspects of that work.

Though we will use the term "participation" (or "employee involvement"), work arrangements with such characteristics go by many names, such as "participative decision making" and "empowerment." Each has some distinctive nuance, but for our purposes they will be treated as the same.

The central puzzle is: "Why don't managers fully embrace participation?" Despite extensive exposure to ideas about participation and its alleged benefits, surveys of American firms show rather superficial participation: participatory techniques, while used in many companies, rarely affect large numbers of employees in any single company.[4] Comprehensive reviews of the effects of participatory practices often reveal modest short-run improvements with "a positive, often small effect on productivity, sometimes a zero or statistically insignificant effect, and almost never a negative effect."[5] These are modest claims indeed. Historical accounts suggest a long but on-again-off-again pattern of experimentation with participation. Thus, Tom Bailey's recent overview of employee participation in the United States concludes:

> There are many positive, even enthusiastic reports of the benefits of work reform and employee participation practices and to some extent these examples are supported by systematic research that also shows positive effects. Nevertheless, the diffusion of these practices has been slow and frustrating, and many efforts do not last.[6]

A variety of possible explanations may account for these outcomes. David Levine argues that the external environment of the firm is hostile to participation in the United States and it leads the market to discourage participation as well as related practices (e.g., encouraging employment security), "suggesting the need for public policies to overcome the current penalties suffered by initial adopters."[7] While these arguments may well be valid, they interact with internal inhibitors. Our own analysis of these internal factors attributes the low level of acceptance to the low level of managerial support—and that, in turn, to managers' perceptions of a weak connection between participation and improved productivity (or other desirable organization-level outcomes). Furthermore, an understanding of the internal factors leading managers not to support participation also can shed light on why workers don't give stronger support to participatory initiatives.

By examining the integration of participatory work practices with the modern quality paradigm, we highlight theoretically important and previously ignored relationships. These relationships promote desirable organization-level results, thereby heightening managerial support.

STRENGTHS AND WEAKNESSES OF THE PARTICIPATION TRADITION

Table 1 provides an overview of the strengths and weaknesses of the participation tradition in terms of its contributions to individuals and groups on the

TABLE 1	STENGTHS AND WEAKNESSES OF THE PARTICIPATIVE TRADITION BY LEVEL OF ANALYSIS		
LEVEL OF ANALYSIS	**STRENGTHS**	**WEAKNESSES**	
Individual/Small Group	• focus on motivation • opportunity for goal agreement • emphasis on interpersonal process • human capital development • integrating interdependent tasks	• lack of employee rewards • motivational emphasis diverts attention from process improvement	
Department/ Managers	• release for higher level activities	• absence of managerial rewards • absence of role for lower managers	
System/ Organization/ Society	• potential competitive advantage • democratization	• flabbiness • absence of strategic context for group activities	

one hand and to overall organizational objectives on the other. The extensive literature on participation treats its strengths (which are primarily at the individual and small group level) in great depth and can be summarized as follows:

- *Motivational*—The participation theme highlights the important relationship between human motivation and organizational outcomes. Its premise is that participation yields its best results when it is based on a voluntary act. The enactment of participation is said to lead to self-realization and human dignity.
- *Opportunity for Goal Agreement*—Participation provides a way of aligning individual and organizational objectives.
- *Emphasis on Inter-Personal Processes*—Participation provides a heavy emphasis on human process skills like communications, teamwork, and conflict resolution, skills that improve the quality of decision making and enhance employee "buy-in."
- *Human Capital Development*—Participation stresses the importance of building individual and team competency through training. It thus encourages the development of human capital.
- *Integrating Interdependent Tasks*—Participation through team activity provides a strategy for integrating work involving highly interdependent tasks.

- *Release for Higher-Level Activities*—Participation releases managerial and technical personnel from firefighting activities by making lower-level employees responsible for maintaining and improving their work processes.
- *Potential Competitive Advantage*—Participation has the potential to unleash a great force through allowing all employees to make substantial contributions to improving work performance.
- *Democratization*—Notions of self-governance and self-determination underlie approaches to participation. Some individuals, particularly scholars and labor activists, see participation as a strong democratizing force that finally brings the benefits of political democracy to the workplace.

By contrast, the weaknesses of the participation tradition are primarily at the organization level. They are less commonly discussed, but they are critical because they diminish managerial and worker support for participation. The weaknesses can be summarized as follows:

- *Lack of Employee Rewards*—Employee rewards, including non-monetary enhancements such as employment security, are seldom specified. Without such assurances, individuals often will withhold commitment because they see participatory initiatives which lead to productivity gains threatening their economic security by lowering the demand for labor.
- *Myopic Emphasis on Motivation*—The overwhelming stress on the motivational benefits of participation tends to crowd out other necessary conditions for organizational success such as the improvement of operational processes. The simplistic idea that "if we could just get people motivated everything would turn out all right" is an implicit assumption of much American academic literature (perhaps a function of the domination of this literature by psychologists), not to speak of many American managers.
- *Absence of Managerial Rewards*—Managerial rewards (including power and status) for supporting participative work practices are seldom well-defined. Lower-level supervisors, and middle managers in particular, often see participatory initiatives as a threat to their traditional roles and prerogatives; they see little personal benefit in supporting them. Managerial promotion criteria typically have not been tied to success in introducing and leading participatory activities.
- *Absence of Role for Lower-Level Managers*—Looking at both the scholarly literature and practitioner experience, there is a lack of clarity about the operational requirements (integrating groups and participation into the existing managerial structure). As a consequence,

participatory initiatives experience high resistance from supervisors and middle managers because their role is unclear.

- *"Flabbiness"*—Participation advocates are typically unclear about the nature of participative activities as they relate to actual work operations; the emphasis is on the process of participation per se, not the elements of a systematic work improvement methodology. It is often unclear just what one is supposed to be participating in. Consequently, firms tend not to sustain participatory efforts since managers do not see participation as tied to important organizational objectives. Participation comes to be seen as an end in itself.[8] Workers also perceive the irrelevance and similarly withhold their support. Under these conditions, the agenda of issues in which people can participate tends to dry up.

- *Absence of Strategic Context for Group Activities*—This is the final and critical factor. The workteam is portrayed as "context-less"—that is, not embedded in the work flow and not tied to a customer. Given the lack of linkage to the work process, managerial support for participation fades because participation is seen as a peripheral activity, not linked to strategic objectives. In this context, participation comes to be seen more as a philosophy, a parallel work process (conducted apart from the main business activities of the enterprise), and as an end in itself rather than as a means to the end of increasing organizational effectiveness.

This list of weaknesses focuses heavily on what we believe are the major organizational forces driving change or inhibiting it. As can be seen in Table 1, the potential advantages identified as strengths of the participative tradition are canceled out at the organization level by the participatory tradition's flabbiness and the absence of strategic context for group activities. While the weaknesses are the sort of reasons that managers might give for not starting or for abandoning participation, and therefore merit attention, they are unfortunately not the reasons that researchers in the participatory tradition typically have addressed.

The majority of these weaknesses focus on manager's support for participation. Our intent in emphasizing this support is not to deny the need for employee cooperation and support (or union support, where relevant) in implementing participatory work practices. Rather, our intent is to assert that in most cases it is management, and only management, which can initiate such activities and command resources to consistently support them. Moreover, it is managers who are in a position to provide the resources that can secure worker commitment through providing such things as job security, recognition, and wages. But without benefits to managers and the organization as a whole, managerial support for participation is unlikely to be forthcoming, and if it is forthcoming, it is unlikely to be sustained.

A Brief Historical and Comparative Note

We can contrast Japan on the one hand with America and Europe on the other in terms of the historical relationship of participation to quality. Whereas the two traditions developed separately in America and Europe, they emerged after World War II as integrated practices in Japan. Known as total quality control (TQC), this approach stresses quality improvement through the efforts of all employees and all departments. This approach is distinctive and original in philosophy and scope.

The Japanese integration of quality and participation provides important organization-level benefits which, when coupled with individual- and group-level benefits, foster managerial support for participation. By the same token, the historic separation of the two traditions in America and Europe has weakened managerial support for participation and has stunted the development of both the quality and the participation movements. While the reasons for these different historical trajectories lie beyond the scope of this article, it relates to the unique development of Taylorism in the United States, driven in part by a large relatively uneducated immigrant labor force in the early 20th century. While Taylorism spread to both Europe and Japan, in Japan the participatory theme received an early hearing.[9]

Key Characteristics
of the Modern Quality Paradigm

Table 2 lists the key characteristics of the modern quality approach as developed by the Japanese. Following is a brief overview of these characteristics:

- *The "Market-In" Principle*—"Market-in" is a major focus in Japanese quality improvement activities. It means bringing customer needs into every possible part of the organization, thereby heightening uncertainty. These activities include informing production workers or front-line service employees of warranty claims relevant to their work, informing a broad range of employees how customers use products and services, and educating as many employees as possible on customer-desired product and service features. The market-in approach contrasts sharply with the reliance on specialized organization experts to process information about the environment and solve specific problems.
- *Quality as an Umbrella Theme*—Quality provides an overall theme for change in the organization, one that is more intrinsically appealing and less threatening than competing themes such as cost reduction or productivity improvement. It is hard to find anyone who is against

TABLE 2	CHARACTERISTICS OF THE MODERN QUALITY MOVEMENT AS IT EVOLVED IN JAPAN

- "Market-In" approach provides strong external customer orientation and uses internal customer chain as connection to final user
- Quality as an umbrella theme for organizing work
- Improved quality seen as strategy to strong competitive strategy
- All-employee, all-department involvement a pivotal strategy for improving quality of every business process
- Upstream prevention activities key to quality improvement
- Well-defined problem-solving methodology and training activities tied to continuous quality improvement
- Integration into control system of goals, plans and actions for continuous quality improvement
- Focus on cross-functional cooperation and information sharing

quality, but cost reduction and productivity improvement often evoke fears of displacement. Quality by contrast is positive, unifying, and constructive.

- *Quality's Relationship to Costs and Productivity*—Japanese manufacturers (by which we especially mean large- and medium-sized firms) saw improved quality as flowing from the elimination of waste and rework in every business process; this definition contrasts with the traditional American view of improved quality through adding more product attributes and/or additional inspectors, thereby leading to added cost.

- *All-Employee, All-Department Involvement*—The Japanese extended the concept of quality improvement to include business processes beyond the shop floor (e.g., purchasing and design), thus broadening the scope of participation to include all employees and departments. In the typical manufacturing firm, employee involvement means that all employees, individually and in teams, are trained to engage in designing and redesigning their own work processes.

- *Upstream Prevention*—The Japanese also recognized that upstream prevention activities, particularly in the design phase, were the primary place where large-scale quality breakthroughs could take place. While to some extent this devalued the contributions of lower-level employees, it also made it clear that traditional efforts to blame lower-level personnel for poor quality were misplaced.

- *Problem-Solving Methodology*—Japanese firms developed a simple yet powerful problem-solving methodology that was usable by workers with high school and even junior high school educations. This methodology is based on application of Shewhart's Plan, Do, Check, Act cycle

(PDCA) and is used to improve the employees' own work processes. The methodology is backed up with training in a variety of problem-solving tools, including the Pareto and cause-and-effect diagrams. The solution to many problems was no longer the domain of the industrial engineering department. Simplified statistical tools became widely used among workers in all departments.

- *Integration with Control System*—The deployment of quality improvement efforts is carefully cascaded down through the organization, starting from a long-term plan, moving to the annual plan and then having each level (from managers down through worker quality circles) formulate quality improvement objectives that tie into these plans. Progress toward these plans is checked regularly through personal audits by top executives. By integrating quality into the control system in this way, middle managers and workers are made central to the execution of quality improvement and implicitly told that what they are doing is important. As Prof. Kano has shown in his article in the Spring 1993 issue of *California Management Review,* this policy management approach contrasts sharply with the traditional operation of MBO in the United States.

- *Cross-Functional Cooperation and Information Sharing*—Information about customer needs and expectations is critical to successful quality improvement because this information drives important processes such as goal setting, problem identification and problem solving. Japanese firms are less inclined to assign customer research to one highly specialized group and they tend to widely deploy the resultant information to as many organizational actors and departments as possible. Consider the example of Quality Function Deployment (QFD). QFD is a system for translating consumer requirements into appropriate company requirements at each stage from research and development through the intermediate stages to marketing/sales and distribution. From our point of view, however, QFD is important and successful because it involves a matrix of specified activities that brings members of different departments together regularly to solve problems. Through these discussions, customer needs and competitor information are widely shared throughout the organization. Key targets for quality, cost, and delivery (QCD) are typically set by cross-functional groups.

In sum, large Japanese firms—through wide sharing of customer information and the empowerment of decentralized work teams to act on that information—have implemented a system of broad-based, task-focused participation that yields quality gains.

INDIVIDUAL AND GROUP LEVEL BENEFITS OF QUALITY-PARTICIPATION INTEGRATION

At the same time, the Japanese have realized important individual and group-level benefits from the integration of quality with participation which we can frame as improved *information processing* and improved *motivation*. These individual and group-level outcomes contribute indirectly to the organization-level outcomes of managerial support for participation.

First, from an information processing standpoint, comprehensive and grass-roots participation in problem solving allows firms to move the "distribution of intelligence" downward in the organization. Participation brings to bear increased information and capability in local problem solving without involving costly middle managers who often contribute to information distortion. As a consequence, participation can improve information processing and decision making, thereby increasing organizational effectiveness.[10]

Second, from an employee motivation standpoint, the market-in approach makes sense for two reasons. First, the process activities for meeting market requirements are based on the sound behavioral principle that those involved in work processes will more enthusiastically implement changes that they themselves have designed. In addition, quality—the act of satisfying the customer and therefore the market—provides a powerful motivational theme around which to build employee involvement and commitment.

ORGANIZATION-LEVEL BENEFITS OF QUALITY-PARTICIPATION INTEGRATION

The organization-level interpretation of the benefits of merging quality with participation is the cornerstone of our answer to our original question about why managers haven't supported participation. Managers at all levels (and, to a lesser extent, workers) have lacked motivation to support extensive employee participation, particularly in the redesign of the routines that guide work. As we suggested earlier, the lack of organization-level benefits partly explains the low managerial support.

Just how does the Japanese approach of merging quality improvement with participation decrease the fear of changing routines and increase managerial support for participatory work practices? The answer requires a closer look at the synergy between participation and the "market-in" principle.

The idea that organizations might try to bring the market into the organization, and thus heighten uncertainty for many employees, runs counter to most social science (especially business strategy) thinking about organizations. Such thinking stresses uncertainty reduction as the normal criterion for organizational decision making. Buffers, which include inventories and specialized units to pre-process information from the environment, shield the bulk of organizational members from the direct forces of the environment.

The buffering approach to dealing with uncertainty probably captured a good deal of how Western firms have operated in the post-World War II period (and how many still do). Beyond the United States, buffering has been a common theme in the Swedish and German approach to group activity. Here, the strategy has been to buffer individual tasks from upstream and downstream pressures (with commensurate and expensive increases of in-process inventory). The idea was to avoid shutdowns when blockages occurred and/or to obtain a humane pace of work that gave workers more control and autonomy over their work environment. While the short-term benefits to workers and managers are clear, the long-term benefits to management and organization-level objectives are less obvious. Recognition of these problems is increasingly leading to the redesign of major Northern European companies. The model in Sweden for example is no longer Volvo with its buffered semi-autonomous work groups but Asea Brown Boveri (ABB) with its Project T50, which stresses decentralization, customer satisfaction, a learning organization, and reduced cycle time.[11]

In contrast to the traditional Western managerial approach to uncertainty, the modern Japanese manufacturer seeks to heighten the pressure for change that the environment exerts on all parts of the organization. The just-in-time system represents the most visible symbol of bringing market pressures into the firm, but the scope and depth of the market-in principle goes far beyond JIT. The "pull system" driving JIT initiates production as a reaction to present demand. But market-in provides far more comprehensive coverage of market characteristics, including anticipation of future demand and of multi-dimensional aspects of customer needs and expectations. Similarly, it widely distributes throughout the firm knowledge about other dynamic aspects of the firm's environment such as raw materials, suppliers, labor markets, regulatory environment, and so on.

The heightening of uncertainty associated with this approach is linked directly to a motivational strategy of involving all employees in the change process. The amount of business information on performance and environment that Japanese manufacturing firms distribute to employees, including those at the lowest levels, is staggeringly high compared to what occurs at most American firms. American managers often restrict sharing even elementary information on a unit's performance and environment.

Moreover, Japanese firms provide the necessary training to insure that employees understand the information being provided. Finally, Japanese managers empower employees to act on such information. By providing this framework in which employees are part of the improvement process, fear of changing existing routines is reduced. "Fearlessness" becomes an extraordinary asset as organizational environments become more uncertain in industry after industry. If the firm can better align itself with its environment and therefore better cope with rapidly changing circumstances, higher-level managers will be more inclined to support participation. One of the authors saw a dramatic visual representation of these themes at the Mazda Hiroshima transmission plant in 1988. A large banner hanging over the assembly line read: "Fear Established Concepts" (Kyōfu Kisei Gainen).

The Japanese focus on the customer and "market-in" ties work improvement efforts directly into internal and external customer satisfaction in a way that clearly benefits the company. But what about the workers? The reduced buffers certainly can contribute to more stressful work conditions. Janice Klein reports that when buffers were removed between and within work teams, American workers complained about their loss of team identity and individual freedom.[12]

The reduced buffers and the resultant tightened linkages, however, also have benefits for both workers and the firm. On the positive side, from the company's viewpoint, these practices make error more readily visible and subject to accountability. From the workers' side, customer satisfaction themes provide challenges to which they can relate, thereby reducing the seemingly arbitrary nature of managerial decision making. The emphasis on customer satisfaction tightens perceived connections among quality, job security and employee motivation. In short, employees can see a connection between their own job security and company goals like customer satisfaction and increased market share. These connections also provide an avenue for union cooperation in quality improvement initiatives.

Let us look now at the impact of market-in on management. Market-in increases managers' willingness to support participation in at least three ways. First, it increases participation's perceived utility to managers. The quality improvement methodology involves cascading customer satisfaction and other improvement goals down through the organization, assuring managers and executives that participation is controlled and directed towards important organizational outcomes (thereby also reducing management's fear of changing routines). Because market-in imposes customer requirements on the organization, it underscores the strategic importance of participation for the firm's prosperity and survival. Market-in also speeds response times and helps pinpoint quality problems, thereby reducing throughput time for business processes and insuring prompt delivery for internal and external customers. Managers are only too happy to reap the benefits associated with these activities.

A second way market-in promotes managerial support is by decreasing internal factionalism and increasing cohesion by focusing organizational activity on customer demands and competitor threats.

Third, market-in can enhance managerial commitment to participation through the creation of a common language of customer needs as well as methods and techniques designed to satisfy those needs. Given a common language, all employees regardless of status and department are better able to communicate with one another, and it becomes more credible for everyone to believe that all employees have valuable contributions to make. In the most fundamental sense, it is a common language that creates and sustains the existence of effective social groups and organizations.

The belief that all employees have a valuable contribution to make is important because the market-in approach depends on management's decentralization of decision making and problem-solving activities. Without an ability to make rapid on-the-spot decisions by those involved in the work process, market-in would be an organizational nightmare. There is no time for moving decisions up to higher-level superiors.

Notwithstanding the synergy between market-in and participation, there is no doubt that the focus on using the market as a driver, if not managed in a balanced fashion, can lead to excessive pressure on workers in the name of satisfying customers. Indeed, just this theme has emerged in Japan in recent years, particularly in the auto industry where long working hours have been associated with an excessive emphasis on meeting customer needs. In a rare example of joint positions, both the normally acquiescent Japan Autoworkers Union and the Chairman of the Japan Automobile Dealers Association, Kenichiro Ueno, recently attributed the current economic problems of the Japanese domestic auto industry to the "excessive desire by manufacturers to maximize customer satisfaction." In particular, an overabundance of model and option variation greatly complicated the work process and created stressful work conditions.

BRINGING IT ALL TOGETHER

Let us return now to the weaknesses of the Western participation tradition (noted in Table 1), to show how a blending of participation with quality improvement addresses those weaknesses. The responses to the items below overcome the weaknesses at the system/organization level referred to in Table 1. In addition to providing employee rewards (described above), the blending secures managerial support providing an organizational context and focus for participation.

- *Addressing Flabbiness*—Recall that employees are typically unclear about the nature of participative activities as they relate to the work process, and they lack a systematic work improvement methodology. Linking participation to quality addresses all of these issues. The modern quality movement stresses continual quality improvement through better-designed work processes, and it has a well-defined problem-solving methodology. Participation is tied to the achievement of a publicly identified organizational objective: quality. This umbrella theme has intrinsic appeal to employees. At the same time, it has content and concreteness as opposed to the vagueness of the term "participation."

- ***Addressing Absence of Strategic Context for Group Activities***—The second major problem with the participation tradition is that the work team is portrayed as context-less; the team is not embedded in the work flow and not linked to a customer. The linkage of participation with quality through a market-in approach insures a strong internal and external customer focus. It is possible to flowchart every work process and identify the process's immediate and/or ultimate customer. By giving the work team the responsibility for job design, the teams become an integral part of the work flow.

In sum, what the Japanese have shown us is that, taken separately, quality and participation are weak concepts with limited potential to transform the firm. But wedded, they are powerful in concept and consequences.

CONCLUSION

It is our contention that powerful interactive properties exist between a modern approach to quality and participation. This interaction arises because using quality as an umbrella theme for broad-based participation provides a plausible route to improving organizational performance. The connection of participation with organizational Performance through quality can attract managerial support for participation, whereas participation alone attracts little support. To pursue participation without quality has proved ineffective, a recipe for failure in today's competitive markets. The most notable example in the U.S. were the failure of many quality circle programs in the early 1980s. These failures resulted from the lack of strong management support, which in turn derived from the flabbiness of the conventional participation concept and the absence of a linkage to the achievement of core business objectives. The linkage of participation with quality not only solves this problem, but the linking of the two can also operate as a significant motivating force for workers. Workers can benefit directly in terms of expanded responsibilities and skills and indirectly in union situations through negotiations to secure their fair share of organizational success.

Japanese and leading Western companies such as Motorola have demonstrated that participation, when framed as an avenue to the highly ranked corporate objectives of quality and waste reduction, becomes a credible organizational approach. This is not to say that we must precisely follow the Japanese formula nor that the particular Japanese way of combining quality with participation is without its problems. To the contrary, customer satisfaction, taken to an extreme, can be coercive and counterproductive. Indeed, in response to such problems some leaders in the Japanese quality movement recently have added to their traditional calls for customer satisfaction (CS), the new slogan CS + ES. That is to say, customer satisfaction must be combined with employee satisfaction. Such adjustments remind us that we should learn from the mistakes of the Japanese as well as their successes.

Finally, preliminary data analysis supports the view that the quality movement has become the major driving force for the participative movement in the United States. In their analysis of the 1987 national survey conducted by GAO, Lawler and associates found that quality accounted for the biggest reason that respondents (72 percent) gave for adopting employee involvement.[13] Moreover in analyzing this finding, Levine and Kruse discovered that those companies reporting that improving quality was their reason for initiating employee involvement had more success with employee involvement practices than those giving other reasons.[14] Quality was the most consistent correlate of organizational success as measured by increased productivity, worker satisfaction, customer service, competitiveness, employee quality of worklife, profitability and lower turnover and absenteeism. In short, initial data analysis supports our interpretation that linking employee participation initiatives to the quality initiative can yield strong positive results for the firm. We enhance managerial and worker acceptance by using quality to refocus participatory initiatives towards more organizational-level outcomes. In so doing, we increase the probability of bottom-line results for the firm. This, in turn, further increases managerial and worker acceptance thereby creating a "virtuous cycle."

REFERENCES

1. See, for example, Thomas Bailey, "Discretionary Effort and the Organization of Work: Employee Participation and Work Reform Since Hawthorne," paper prepared for the Sloan Foundation, August 1992.
2. For descriptions of the new quality paradigm, see Kaoru Ishikawa, *What is Quality Control* (Englewood Cliffs, N.J.: Prentice-Hall, 1985); Joseph Juran, *Juran on Leadership for Quality* (New York, NY: Free Press, 1989); and Shigeru Mizuno, *Company-Wide Total Quality Control* (Tokyo: Asian Productivity Organization, 1988).
3. For an overview of the various characteristics, see Peter Dachler and

Bernhard Wilpert, "Conceptual Dimensions and Boundaries of Participation in Organizations: A Critical Evaluation," *Administrative Science Quarterly,* 23 (1978): 1–39.

4. Edward Lawler III, Gerald Ledford, Jr., and Susan Mohrman, *Employee Involvement in America* (Houston, TX: American Productivity and Quality Center, 1989).

5. David Levine and Laura Tyson, "Participation, Productivity, and the Firm's Environment," in *Paying for Productivity* (Washington, DC: Brookings Institution, 1990): 203–204.

6. Bailey, p.51.

7. David Levine, "Public Policy Implications of Imperfections in the Market for Worker Participation," *Economic and Industrial Democracy,* 13 (1992): 183–206.

8. Edwin Locke and David Schweiger, "Participation in Decision-making: One More Look," in Barry Staw, ed., *Research in Organizational Behavior,* 1 (Greenwich, CT: JAI Press, 1979): 265–339.

9. Robert E. Cole, *Work, Mobility & Participation* (Berkeley, CA: University of California Press, 1979): 101–113.

10. Masahiko Aoki, *Information, Incentives, and Bargaining in the Japanese Economy* (Cambridge: Cambridge University Press, 1988).

11. John Stinesen, "T50 Seminarium med ABB: Kompetensutveckling Nyckelord For Ny Industriell Revolution," [T50 Seminar with ABB: Competence Development, a Key term for the New Industrial Revolution] *Nya Verkstads Forum,* 1 (February 1992): 11–12.

12. Janice Klein "The Human Costs of Manufacturing Reform," *Harvard Business Review,* 67 (1981): 60–66.

13. Klein; Lawler et al.

14. David Levine and Douglas Kruse, "Employee Involvement Efforts: Incidence, Correlates and Effects," unpublished manuscript, University of California, Berkeley, 1990.

READING 16
THE EMPOWERMENT OF
SERVICE WORKERS: WHAT, WHY,
HOW, AND WHEN

THIS ARTICLE FROM THE *SLOAN MANAGEMENT REVIEW* (SPRING 1992) PRESENTS A CONTINGENCY APPROACH TO EMPOWERMENT—THAT IS, ONE SIZE DOES <u>NOT</u> FIT ALL. THE AUTHORS BEGIN BY CONTRASTING THE "INDUSTRIALIZATION OF SERVICE" WITH THE EMPOWERMENT APPROACH. THE FORMER OFFERS LITTLE DISCRETION TO EMPLOYEES WHILE THE LATTER "IN MANY WAYS IS THE REVERSE OF DOING THINGS BY THE BOOK." THEY NOTE THAT SUCCESSFUL ILLUSTRATIONS CAN BE FOUND THAT FOLLOW EACH MODEL—FOR EXAMPLE, UPS AND DISNEY VERSUS FEDERAL EXPRESS AND CLUB MED. IS THERE A "BEST APPROACH"? NO, IT DEPENDS ON SEVERAL ORGANIZATIONAL FACTORS. BOWEN AND LAWLER REVIEW THE BENEFITS AND COSTS OF EMPOWERING SERVICE EMPLOYEES, AND THEY CAUTION MANAGERS TO "USE EMPOWERMENT KNOWLEDGEABLY, NOT JUST BECAUSE IT IS A FAD." THEY REVIEW THREE LEVELS OR DEGREES OF EMPOWERMENT, AND DISCUSS THE FIVE FAC-TORS/CONTINGENCIES THAT DETERMINE WHICH LEVEL WOULD BE OPTIMAL FOR A GIVEN ORGANIZATION AND ITS CUSTOMERS.

IN A 1992 *BUSINESS WEEK* ARTICLE ON "MANAGEMENT'S NEW GURUS," THEY REPORT THAT "MUCH CURRENT MAN-AGEMENT THINKING SOUNDS SUSPICIOUSLY RECYCLED AND REPACKAGED. 'HIGH INVOLVEMENT,' FOR EXAMPLE, IS ONLY THE LATEST ITERATION OF 'EMPOWERMENT,' WHICH IN TURN WAS JUST ANOTHER NAME FOR AN OLDER NOTION." "'THE IDEA HAS BEEN RENAMED MORE TIMES THAN ELIZABETH TAYLOR,' LAUGHS LAWLER, ONE OF THE FOREMOST

THINKERS IN THE ARENA OF EMPLOYEE PARTICIPATION (AND RECOGNIZED AS ONE OF THE NEW GURUS). 'IT ALL GOES TO THE SAME BASIC ISSUE: HOW DO YOU MOVE POWER, KNOWLEDGE, INFORMATION, AND REWARDS DOWNWARD IN AN ORGANIZATION?'"

READING 16
THE EMPOWERMENT OF SERVICE WORKERS: WHAT, WHY, HOW, AND WHEN

BY DAVID E. BOWEN AND EDWARD E. LAWLER III

Empowering service workers has acquired almost a "born again" religious fervor. Tom Peters calls it "purposeful chaos." Robert Waterman dubs it "directed autonomy." It has also been called the "art of improvisation."

Yet in the mid-1970s, the production-line approach to service was the darling child of service gurus. They advocated facing the customer with standardized, procedurally driven operations. Should we now abandon this approach in favor of empowerment?

Unfortunately, there is no simple, clear-cut answer. In this article we try to help managers think about the question of whether to empower by clarifying its advantages and disadvantages, describing three forms that empower employees to different degrees, and presenting five contingencies that managers can use to determine which approach best fits their situation. We do not intend to debunk empowerment; rather we hope to clarify why to empower (there are costs, as well as benefits), how to empower (there are alternatives), and when to empower (it really does depend on the situation).

THE PRODUCTION-LINE APPROACH

In two classic articles, the "Production-Line Approach to Service" and the "Industrialization of Service." Theodore Levitt described how service operations can be made more efficient by applying manufacturing logic and tactics[1] He argued:

Manufacturing thinks technocratically, and that explains its success.... By contrast, service looks for solutions in the performer of the task. This is the paralyzing legacy of our inherited attitudes: the solution to improved service is viewed as being dependent on improvements in the skills and attitudes of the performers of that service.

While it may pain and offend us to say so, thinking in humanistic rather than technocratic terms ensures that the service sector will be forever inefficient and that our satisfactions will be forever marginal.[2]

He recommended 1) simplification of tasks, 2) clear division of labor, 3) substitution of equipment and systems for employees, and 4) little decision-making discretion afforded to employees. In short, management designs the system, and employees execute it.

McDonald's is a good example. Workers are taught how to greet customers and ask for their order, including a script for suggesting additional items. They learn a set procedure for assembling the order (for example, cold drinks first, then hot ones), placing items on the tray, and placing the tray where customers need not reach for it. There is a script and a procedure for collecting money and giving change. Finally, there is a script for saying thank you and asking the customer to come again.[3] This production-line approach makes customer-service interactions uniform and gives the organization control over them. It is easily learned; workers can be quickly trained and put to work.

What are the gains from a production-line approach? Efficient, low-cost, high-volume service operations, with satisfied customers.

THE EMPOWERMENT APPROACH

Ron Zemke and Dick Schaaf, in *The Service Edge: 101 Companies That Profit from Customer Care*, note that empowerment is a common theme running through many, even most, of their excellent service businesses, such as American Airlines, Marriott, American Express, and Federal Express. To Zemke and Schaaf, empowerment means "turning the front line loose," encouraging and rewarding employees to exercise initiative and imagination: "Empowerment in many ways is the reverse of doing things by the book."[4]

The humanistic flavor of empowerment pervades the words of advocates such as Tom Peters:

It is necessary to "dehumiliate" work by eliminating the policies and procedures (almost always tiny) of the organization that demean and belittle human dignity. It is impossible to get people's best efforts, involvement, and caring concern for things you believe important to your customers and the long-term interest of your organization when we write policies and procedures that treat them like thieves and bandits.[5]

And from Jan Carlzon, CEO of Scandinavian Airlines Systems (SAS):

To free someone from rigorous control by instructions, policies, and orders and to give that person freedom to take responsibility for his ideas, decisions, and actions is to release hidden resources that would otherwise remain inaccessible to both the individual and the organization.[6]

In contrast to the industrialization of service, empowerment very much looks to the "performer of the tasks" for solutions to service problems. Workers are asked to suggest new services and products and to solve problems creatively and effectively.

What, then, does it really mean—beyond the catchy slogans—to empower employees? We define empowerment as sharing with frontline employees four organizational ingredients: 1) information about the organization's performance, 2) rewards based on the organization's performance, 3) knowledge that enables employees to understand and contribute to organizational performance, and 4) power to make decisions that influence organizational direction and performance. We will say more about these features later. For now, we can say that with a production-line approach, these features tend to be concentrated in the hands of senior management; with an empowerment approach, they tend to be moved downward to frontline employees.

WHICH APPROACH IS BETTER?

In 1990, Federal Express became the first service organization to win the Malcolm Baldrige National Quality Award. The company's motto is "people, service, and profits." Behind its blue, white, and red planes and uniforms are self-managing work teams, gainsharing plans, and empowered employees seemingly consumed with providing flexible and creative service to customers with varying needs.

At UPS, referred to as "Big Brown" by its employees, the philosophy was stated by founder Jim Casey: "Best service at low rates." Here, too, we find turned-on people and profits. But we do not find empowerment. Instead we find controls, rules, a detailed union contract, and carefully studied work methods. Nor do we find a promise to do all things for customers, such as handling off-schedule pickups and packages that don't fit size and weight limitations. In fact, rigid operational guidelines help guarantee the customer reliable, low-cost service.

Federal Express and UPS present two different faces to the customer, and behind these faces are different management philosophies and organizational cultures. Federal Express is a high-involvement, horizontally coordinated organization that encourages employees to use their judgment above and beyond the rulebook. UPS is a top-down, traditionally controlled organization, in which employees are directed by policies and procedures based on industrial engineering studies of how all service delivery aspects should be carried out and how long they should take.

Similarly, at Disney theme parks, ride operators are thoroughly scripted on what to say to "guests," including a list of preapproved "ad libs"! At Club Med, however, CEO Jacques Giraud fervently believes that guests must experience *real* magic, and the resorts' GOs (*gentils organisateurs,* "congenial hosts") are set free to spontaneously create this feeling for their guests. Which is the better approach? Federal Express or UPS? Club Med or Disney?

At a recent executive education seminar on customer service, one of us asked. "Who thinks that it is important for their business to empower their service personnel as a tool for improving customer service?" All 27 participants enthusiastically raised their hands. Although they represented diverse services, banking, travel, utilities, airlines, and shipping—and they disagreed on most points, they all agreed that empowerment is key to customer satisfaction. But is it?

EMPOWERING SERVICE EMPLOYEES: WHY, HOW, AND WHEN

WHY TO EMPOWER: THE BENEFITS

What gains are possible from empowering service employees?

- **Quicker On-Line Responses to Customer Needs during Service Delivery:** Check-in time at the hotel begins at 2 p.m., but a guest asks the desk clerk if she can check in at 1:30 p.m. An airline passenger arrives at the gate at 7:30 a.m., Friday, for a 7:45 a.m. departure and wants to board the plane with a travel coupon good Monday through Thursday, and there are empty seats on the plane. The waitress is taking an order in a modestly priced family restaurant; the menu says no substitutions, but the customer requests one anyway.

  The customer wants a quick response. And the employee would often like to be able to respond with something other than "No, it is against our rules," or "I will have to check with my supervisor." Empowering employees in these situations can lead to the sort of spontaneous, creative rule-breaking that can turn a potentially frustrated or angry customer into a satisfied one. This is particularly valuable when there is little time to refer to a higher authority, as when the plane is leaving in fifteen minutes. Even before greeting customers, empowered employees are confident that they have all the necessary resources at their command to provide customers with what they need.

- **Quicker On-Line Responses to Dissatisfied Customers during Service Recovery.** Customer service involves both delivering the service, such as checking a guest into a hotel room, and recovering from poor service, such as relocating him from a smoking floor to the nonsmoking room he originally requested. Although delivering good service may mean different things to different customers, all customers feel that service businesses ought to fix things when service is delivered improperly. Figure 1 depicts the relationships among service delivery, recovery, and customer satisfaction.

  Fixing something after doing it wrong the first time can turn a dissatisfied customer into a satisfied, even loyal, customer. But service businesses frequently fail in the act of recovery because service employees are not empowered to make the necessary amends with customers. Instead, customers hear employees saying. "Gee, I wish there was something I could do, but I can't," "It's not my fault," or "I could check with my boss, but she's not here today." These employees lack the power and knowledge to recover, and customers remain dissatisfied.

FIGURE 1 POSSIBLE OUTCOMES DURING SERVICE DELIVERY AND RECOVERY

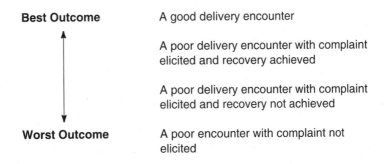

From *Service Breakthroughs: Changing the Rules of the Game* by James L. Heskett, W. Earl Sasser, Jr., and Christopher W. L. Hart. Copyright © 1990 by James L. Heskett, W. Earl Sasser, Jr., and Christopher W. L. Hart. Adapted with permission of The Free Press, a Division of Macmillan, Inc.

- **Employees Feel Better about Their Jobs and Themselves.** Earlier we mentioned Tom Peters' thinking on how strict rules can belittle human dignity. Letting employees call the shots allows them to feel "ownership" of the job; they feel responsible for it and find the work meaningful. Think of how you treat your car as opposed to a rented one. Have you ever washed a rental car? Decades of job design research show that when employees have a sense of control and of doing meaningful work they are more satisfied. This leads to lower turnover, less absenteeism, and fewer union organizing drives.

- **Employees Will Interact with Customers with More Warmth and Enthusiasm.** Research now supports our long-standing intuition that customers' perceptions of service quality are shaped by the courtesy, empathy, and responsiveness of service employees.[7] Customers want employees to appear concerned about their needs. Can empowerment help create this? One of us has done customer service research in branch banks that showed that when the tellers reported feeling good about how they were supervised, trained, and rewarded, customers thought more highly of the service they received.[8] In short, when employees felt that management was looking after their needs, they took better care of the customer.

  In service encounters, employees' feelings about their jobs will spill over to affect how customers feel about the service they get. This is particularly important when employee attitudes are a key part of the service package. In banking, where the customer receives no tangible benefits in the exchange other than a savings deposit slip, a sour teller can really blemish a customer's feelings about the encounter.

- **Empowered Employees Can Be a Great Source of Service Ideas.** Giving frontline employees a voice in "how we do things around here" can lead to improved service delivery and ideas for new services. The bank study showed that the tellers could accurately report how customers viewed overall service quality and how they saw the branches' service climate (e.g., adequacy of staff and appearance of facilities).[9]

  Frontline employees are often ready and willing to offer their opinion. When it comes to market research, imagine the difference in response rates from surveying your employees and surveying your customers.

- **Great Word-of-Mouth Advertising and Customer Retention.** Nordstrom's advertising budget is 1.5 percent of sales, whereas the industry average is 5 percent. Why? Their satisfied-no-matter-what customers spread the word about their service and become repeat customers.

THE COSTS

What are the costs of empowerment?

- **A Greater Dollar Investment in Selection and Training.** You cannot hire effective, creative problem solvers on the basis of chance or mere intuition. Too bad, because the systematic methods necessary to screen out those who are not good candidates for empowerment are expensive. For example, Federal Express selects customer agents and couriers on the basis of well-researched profiles of successful performers in those jobs.

  Training is an even greater cost. The production-line approach trains workers easily and puts them right to work. In contrast, new hires at SAS are formally assigned a mentor to help them learn the ropes; Nordstrom department managers take responsibility for orienting and training new members of the sales team; customer service representatives at Lands' End and L.L. Bean spend a week in training before handling their first call. They receive far more information and knowledge about their company and its products than is the norm.

  The more labor intensive the service, the higher these costs. Retail banking, department stores, and convenience stores are labor intensive, and their training and selection costs can run high. Utilities and airlines are far less labor intensive.

- **Higher Labor Costs.** Many consumer service organizations, such as department stores, convenience stores, restaurants, and banks, rely on large numbers of part-time and seasonal workers to meet their highly variable staffing needs. These employees typically work for short periods of time at low wages. To empower these workers, a company would have to invest heavily in training to try to quickly inculcate the organization's culture and values. This training would probably be unsuccessful, and the employees wouldn't be around long enough to provide a return on the investment. Alternatively, the organization could pay higher wages to full-time, permanent employees, but they would be idle when business was slow.

- **Slower or Inconsistent Service Delivery.** Remember the hotel guest wanting to check in early and the airline passenger requesting special treatment at the gate? True, there is a benefit to empowering the employee to bend the rules, but only for the person at the front of the line! Customers at the back of the line are grumbling and checking their watches. They may have the satisfaction of knowing that they too may receive creative problem solving when and if they reach the counter, but it is small consolation if the plane has already left.

  Based on our experiences as both researchers and customers, we believe that customers will increasingly value speed in service delivery.

Purposeful chaos may work against this. We also believe that many customers value "no surprises" in service delivery. They like to know what to expect when they revisit a service business or patronize different outlets of a franchise. When service delivery is left to employee discretion, it may be inconsistent.

The research data show that customers perceive reliability—"doing it right the first time"—as the most important dimension of service quality. It matters more than employees' responsiveness, courtesy, or competency, or the attractiveness of the service setting.[10] Unfortunately, in the same research, a sample of large, well-known firms was more deficient on reliability than on these other dimensions. Much of the touted appeal of the production-line approach was that procedurally and technocratically driven operations could deliver service more reliably and consistently than service operations heavily dependent upon the skills and attitudes of employees. The production-line approach was intended to routinize service so that customers would receive the "best outcome" possible from their service encounters—service delivery with no glitches in the first place.

We feel that service managers need to guard against being seduced into too great a focus on recovery, at the expense of service delivery reliability. We say "seduced" because it is possible to confuse good service with inspiring stories about empowered employees excelling at the art of recovery. Recovery has more sex appeal than the nitty-gritty detail of building quality into every seemingly mundane aspect of the service delivery system, but an organization that relies on recovery may end up losing out to firms that do it right the first time.

- **Violations of "Fair Play."** A recent study of how service businesses handle customer complaints revealed that customers associate sticking to procedures with being treated fairly.[11] Customers may be more likely to return to a business if they believe that their complaint was handled effectively because of company policies rather than because they were lucky enough to get a particular employee. In other words, customers may prefer procedurally driven acts of recovery. We suspect that customers' notions of fairness may be violated when they see employees cutting special deals with other customers.

- **Giveaways and Bad Decisions.** Managers are often reluctant to empower their employees for fear they will give too much away to the customer. Perhaps they have heard the story of Willie, the doorman at a Four Seasons Hotel, who left work and took a flight to return a briefcase left behind by a guest. Or they have heard of too many giveaways by empowered Nordstrom employees. For some services, the costs of giveaways are far outweighed by enhanced customer loyalty, but not for others.

Sometimes creative rule breaking can cause a major problem for an organization. There may be a good reason why no substitutions are allowed or why a coupon cannot be used on a certain day (e.g., an international airfare agreement). If so, having an empowered employee break a rule may cause the organization serious problems, of which the employee may not even be aware.

These are some of the costs and benefits of empowerment. We hope this discussion will help service businesses use empowerment knowledgeably, not just because it is a fad. But we must add one more caveat: There is still precious little research on the consequences of empowerment. We have used anecdotal evidence, related research (e.g., in job design), and our work on service. More systematic research must assess whether this array of costs and benefits fully captures the "whys" (and "why nots") of empowerment.

HOW TO EMPOWER: THREE OPTIONS

Empowering service employees is less understood than industrializing service delivery. This is largely because the production-line approach is an example of the well-developed control model of organization design and management, whereas empowerment is part of the still evolving "commitment" or "involvement" model. The latter assumes that most employees can make good decisions if they are properly socialized, trained, and informed. They can be internally motivated to perform effectively, and they are capable of self-control and self-direction. This approach also assumes that most employees can produce good ideas for operating the business.[12]

The control and involvement models differ in that four key features are concentrated at the top of the organization in the former and pushed down in the organization in the latter. As we have discussed above, these features are the following: 1) information about organizational performance, (e.g., operating results and competitor performance); 2) rewards based on organizational performance (e.g., profit sharing and stock ownership); 3) knowledge that enables employees to understand and contribute to organizational performance (e.g., problem-solving skills); and 4) power to make decisions that influence work procedures and organizational direction (e.g., through quality circles and self-managing teams).

Three approaches to empowering employees can be identified (see Figure 2).[13] They represent increasing degrees of empowerment as additional knowledge, information, power, and rewards are pushed down to the front line. Empowerment, then, is not an either/or alternative, but rather a choice of three options:

1. Suggestion Involvement represents a small shift away from the control model. Employees are encouraged to contribute ideas through formal suggestion programs or quality circles, but their day-to-day work activities do not really change. Also, they are only empowered to recommend; management typically retains the power to decide whether or not to implement.

Suggestion involvement can produce some empowerment without altering the basic production-line approach. McDonald's, for example, listens closely to the front line. The Big Mac, Egg McMuffin, and McDLT all were invented by employees, as was the system of wrapping burgers that avoids leaving a thumbprint in the bun. As another example, Florida Power and Light, which won the Deming quality award, defines empowerment in suggestion involvement terms.

2. Job Involvement represents a significant departure from the control model because of its dramatic "opening up" of job content. Jobs are redesigned so that employees use a variety of skills. Employees believe their tasks are significant, they have considerable freedom in deciding how to do the work, they get more feedback, and they handle a whole, identifiable piece of work. Research shows that many employees find enriched work more motivating and satisfying, and they do higher-quality work.[14]

Often job involvement is accomplished through extensive use of teams. Teams are often appropriate in complex service organizations such as hospi-

---

FIGURE 2   LEVELS OF EMPOWERMENT

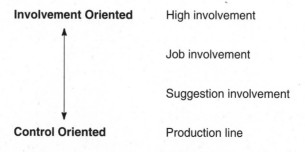

Involvement Oriented   High involvement

Job involvement

Suggestion involvement

Control Oriented   Production line

tals and airlines because individuals cannot offer a whole service or handle a customer from beginning to end of service delivery. Teams can empower back-office workers in banks and insurance companies as well.

Employees in this environment require training to deal with the added complexity. Supervisors, who now have fewer shots to call, need to be reoriented toward supporting the front line, rather than directing it. Despite the heightened level of empowerment it brings, the job involvement approach does not change higher-level strategic decisions concerning organization structure, power, and the allocation of rewards. These remain the responsibility of senior management.

3. High-Involvement organizations give their lowest-level employees a sense of involvement not just in how they do their jobs or how effectively their group performs, but in the total organization's performance. Virtually every aspect of the organization is different from that of a control-oriented organization. Business performance information is shared. Employees develop skills in teamwork, problem solving, and business operations. They participate in work-unit management decisions. There is profit sharing and employee ownership.

High-involvement designs may be expensive to implement. Perhaps most troublesome is that these management techniques are relatively undeveloped and untested. People Express tried to operate as a high-involvement airline, and the ongoing struggle to learn and develop this new organizational design contributed to its operating problems.

Today, America West is trying to make the high-involvement design work. New hires spend 25 percent of their first year's salary on company stock. All employees receive annual stock options. Flight attendants and pilots develop their own work procedures and schedules. Employees are extensively cross-trained to work where they are needed. Only time will tell if America West can make high-involvement work as it struggles with its financial crisis stemming from high fuel costs and rapid growth.

Federal Express displays many high-involvement features. A couple of years ago, it began a companywide push to convert to teams, including the back office. It organized its 1,000 clerical workers in Memphis into superteams of 5 to 10 people and gave them the authority and training to manage themselves. These teams helped the company cut customer service problems, such as incorrect bills and lost packages, by 13 percent in 1989.

WHEN TO EMPOWER: A CONTINGENCY APPROACH

Management thought and practice frequently have been seduced by the search for the "one best way to manage." Unfortunately, business does not lend itself to universal truths, only to "contingency theories" of management. For example, early job enrichment efforts in the 1960s assumed that all employees would prefer more challenging work and more autonomy. By the 1970s it was clear that only those employees who felt the need to grow at work responded positively to job enrichment.[15] As the research on it is still thin, it is at least possible that empowerment is a universal truth, but historical evidence weighs against its being the best way to manage in all situations.

We believe that both the empowerment and production-line approaches have their advantages, and that each fits certain situations. The key is to choose the management approach that best meets the needs of both employees and customers.

Table 1 presents five contingencies that determine which approach to adopt. Each contingency can be rated on a scale of 1 to 5 to diagnose the quality of fit between the overall situation and the alternative approaches. The following propositions suggest how to match situations and approaches. Matching is not an exact science, but the propositions suggest reasonable rules of thumb.

Proposition 1: The higher the rating of each contingency (5 being the highest), the better the fit with an empowerment approach; the lower the rating (1 being the lowest), the better the fit with a production-line approach.

Proposition 2: The higher the total score from all five contingencies, the better the fit with an empowerment approach; the lower the total score, the better the fit with a production-line approach. A production-line approach is a good fit with situations that score in the range of 5 to 10. For empowerment approaches, suggestion involvement is a good fit with situations that score in the range of 11 to 15, job involvement with scores

TABLE 1	THE CONTINGENCIES OF EMPOWERMENT		
CONTINGENCY	**PRODUCTION LINE APPROACH**		**EMPOWERMENT**
Basic business strategy	Low cost, high volume	1 2 3 4 5	Differentiation, customized, personalized
Tie to customer	Transaction, short time period	1 2 3 4 5	Relationship, long time period
Technology	Routine, simple	1 2 3 4 5	Nonroutine, complex
Business environment	Predictable, few surprises	1 2 3 4 5	Unpredictable, many surprises
Types of people	Theory X managers, employees with low growth needs, low social needs, and weak interpersonal skills	1 2 3 4 5	Theory Y managers, employees with high growth needs, high social needs, and strong interpersonal skills

that range from 16 to 20, and high involvement with scores that range from 21 to 25.

Proposition 3: The higher the total score, the more the benefits of increasing empowerment will outweigh the costs.

In what follows, we describe each contingency's implications for a production-line or empowerment approach.

BASIC BUSINESS STRATEGY.

A production-line approach makes the most sense if your core mission is to offer high-volume service at the lowest cost. "Industrializing" service certainly leverages volume. The question is: what is the value-added from spending the additional dollars on employee selection, training, and retention necessary for empowerment? This question is especially compelling in labor-intensive services (e.g., fast food, grocery stores, and convenience stores) and those that require part-time or temporary employees.

The answer depends on what customers want from the service firm, and what they are willing to pay for. Certain customer segments are just looking for cheap, quick, reliable service. They do want quality—a warm hamburger rather than a cold one. But they are not necessarily expecting tender loving care. Even if they wanted it, they wouldn't pay for it.

These customers prefer a production-line approach. A recent study of convenience stores actually found a negative relationship between store sales and clerks being friendly with customers.[16] Customers wanted speed, and friendly clerks slowed things down. The point is that customers themselves may prefer to be served by a nonempowered employee.

At Taco Bell, counter attendants are expected to be civil, but they are not expected or encouraged to be creative problem solvers. Taco Bell wants to serve customers who want low-cost, good quality, fast food. Interestingly, the company believes that as more chains move to customized, service-oriented operations, it has more opportunities in the fast, low-price market niche.

The production-line approach does not rule out suggestion involvement. As mentioned earlier, employees often have ideas even when much of their work is routinized. Quality circles and other approaches can capture and develop them.

An empowerment approach works best with a market segment that wants the tender loving care dimension more than speed and cost. For example, SAS targets frequent business travellers (who do not pay their own way). The SAS strategy was to differentiate itself from other airlines on the basis of personalized service. Consequently, the company looked at every ingredient of its service package to see if it fit this segment's definition of service quality, and, if so, whether or not customers would pay for it.

TIE TO THE CUSTOMER.

Empowerment is the best approach when service delivery involves managing a relationship, as opposed to simply performing a transaction. The service firm may want to establish relationships with customers to build loyalty or to get ideas for improving the service delivery system or offering new services. A flexible, customized approach can help establish the relationship and get the ideas flowing.

The returns on empowerment and relationship-building are higher with more sophisticated services and delivery systems. An employee in the international air freight industry is more likely to learn from a customer relationship than is a gasoline station attendant.

The relationship itself can be the principle valued commodity that is delivered in many services. When no tangibles are delivered, as in estate planning or management consulting, the service provider often is the service to the customer, and empowerment allows the employee to customize the service to fit the customer's needs.

The more enduring the relationship, and the more important it is in the service package, the stronger the case for empowerment. Remember the earlier comparison between Disney, which tightly scripts its ride operators, and Club Med, which encourages its GOs to be spontaneous? Giraud, Club Med's CEO, explains that Disney employees relate to their guests in thousands of brief encounters; GOs have week-long close relationships with a limited number of guests. The valuable service they sell is "time."

TECHNOLOGY.

It is very difficult to build challenge, feedback, and autonomy into a telephone operator's job, given the way the delivery technology has been designed. The same is true of many fast-food operations. In these situations, the technology limits empowerment to only suggestion involvement and ultimately may almost completely remove individuals from the service delivery process, as has happened with ATMs.

When technology constrains empowerment, service managers can still support frontline employees in ways that enhance their satisfaction and the service quality they provide. For example, managers can show employees how much their jobs matter to the organization's success and express more appreciation for the work they do. In other words, managers can do a better job of making the old management model work!

Routine work can be engaging if employees are convinced that it matters. Volunteers will spend hours licking envelopes in a fundraising campaign for their favorite charity. Disney theme park employees do an admirable job of performing repetitive work, partly because they believe in the values, mission, and show business magic of Disney.

BUSINESS ENVIRONMENT.

Businesses that operate in unpredictable environments benefit from empowerment. Airlines face many challenges to their operations: bad weather, mechanical breakdowns, and competitors' actions. They serve passengers who make a wide variety of special requests. It is simply impossible to anticipate many of the situations that will arise and to "program" employees to respond to them. Employees trained in purposeful chaos are appropriate for unpredictable environments.

Fast-food restaurants, however, operate in stable environments. Operations are fairly fail-safe; customer expectations are simple and predictable. In this environment, the service business can use a production-line approach. The stability allows, even encourages, management with policies and procedures, because managers can predict most events and identify the best responses.

TYPES OF PEOPLE.

Empowerment and production-line approaches demand different types of managers and employees. For empowerment to work, particularly in the high-involvement form, the company needs to have Theory Y managers who believe that their employees can act independently to benefit both the organization and its customers. If the management ranks are filled with Theory X types who believe that employees only do their best work when closely supervised, then the production-line approach may be the only feasible option unless the organization changes its managers. Good service can still be the outcome. For example, most industry observers would agree that Delta and American Airlines are managed with a control orientation rather than a strong empowerment approach.

Employees will respond positively to empowerment only if they have strong needs to grow and to deepen and test their abilities—at work. Again, a checkered history of job enrichment efforts has taught us not to assume that everyone wants more autonomy, challenge, and responsibility at work. Some employees simply prefer a production-line approach.

Lastly, empowerment that involves teamwork requires employees who are interested in meeting their social and affiliative needs at work. It also requires that employees have good interpersonal and group process skills.

THE FUTURE OF SERVICE WORK

How likely is it that more and more service businesses will choose to face the customer with empowered employees? We would guess that far more service organizations operate at the production-line end of our continuum than their business situations call for. A recent survey of companies in the "Fortune 1000" offers some support for this view.[17] This survey revealed that manufacturing firms tend to use significantly more employee-involvement practices than do service firms. Manufacturing firms use quality circles, participation groups, and self-managing work teams far more than service firms.

Why is this so? We think that the intense pressure on the manufacturing sector from global competition has created more dissatisfaction with the old control-oriented way of doing things. Also, it can be easier to see the payoffs from different management practices in manufacturing than in service. Objective measures of productivity can more clearly show profitability than can measures of customer perceptions of service quality. However, these differences are now blurring as service competition increases and service companies become more sophisticated in tracking the benefits of customer service quality.

As service businesses consider empowerment, they can look at high-involvement manufacturing organizations as labs in which the various empowerment approaches have been tested and developed. Many lessons have been learned in manufacturing about how to best use quality circles, enriched jobs, and so on. And the added good news is that many service businesses are ideally suited to applying and refining these lessons. Multisite, relatively autonomous service operations afford their managers an opportunity to customize empowerment programs and then evaluate them.

In summary, the newest approaches to managing the production line can serve as role models for many service businesses, but perhaps not all. Before service organizations rush into empowerment programs, they need to determine whether and how empowerment fits their situation.

REFERENCE

1. T. Levitt, "Production-Line Approach to Service," *Harvard Business Review* (September-October 1972): 41–52; T. Levitt, "Industrialization of Service," *Harvard Business Review* (September-October 1976): 63–74.
2. Levitt (1972).
3. D. Tansik. "Managing Human Resource Issues for High-Contact Service Personnel," in *Service Management Effectiveness,* eds. D. Bowen, R. Chase, and T. Cummings (San Francisco: Jossey-Bass. 1990).
4. R. Zemke and D. Schaaf, *The Service Edge: 101 Companies That Profit from Customer Care* (New York: New American Library, 1989): 68.
5. As quoted in Zemke and Schaaf (1989): 68.
6. J. Carlzon, *Moments of Truth* (New York: Ballinger, 1987).
7. V. Zeithaml, A. Parasuraman, and L.L. Berry, *Delivering Quality Service: Balancing Customer Perceptions and Expectations* (New York: Free Press,

1990). See also: B. Schneider and D. Bowen, "Employee and Customer Perceptions of Service in Banks: Replication and Extension," *Journal of Applied Psychology 70* (1985): 423–433.

8. Schneider and Bowen (1985).

9. Schneider and Bowen (1985).

10. Zeithaml, Parasuraman, and Berry (1990).

11. C. Goodwin and I. Ross, "Consumer Evaluations of Responses To Complaints: What's Fair and Why," *Journal of Services Marketing 4* (1990): 53–61.

12. See E.E. Lawler III *High-Involvement Management* (San Francisco: Jossey-Bass, 1986).

13. See E.E. Lawler III, "Choosing an Involvement Strategy," *Academy of Management Executive 2* (1988): 197–204.

14. See for example J.R. Hackman and G.R. Oldham, *Work Redesign* (Reading, Massachusetts: Addison-Wesley, 1980).

15. Hackman and Oldham (1980).

16. R.J. Sutton and A. Rafaeli, "Untangling the Relationship between Displayed Emotions and Organizational Sales: The Case of Convenience Stores," *Academy of Management Journal 31* (1988): 461–487.

17. E.E. Lawler III, G.E. Ledford, Jr., and S.A. Mohrman, *Employee Involvement in America: A Study of Contemporary Practice* (Houston: American Productivity & Quality Center, 1989).

David E. Bowen is associate professor of management, business programs, Arizona State University, West. Edward E. Lawler III is director of the Center for Effective Organizations. Graduate School of Business Administration, University of Southern California.

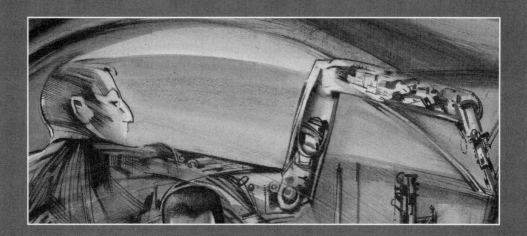

PART EIGHT

LEADERSHIP

READING 17
QUALITY LEADERSHIP
AND CHANGE

THIS ARTICLE DEALS WITH THE ACTIONS LEADERS CAN TAKE
TO CREATE AN ENVIRONMENT THAT FOSTERS DESIRED ORGA-
NIZATIONAL CHANGE—FOR EXAMPLE, THE TRANSFORMATION
TO A TOTAL QUALITY MANAGEMENT SYSTEM. TWO BROAD
ASPECTS OF LEADING CHANGE ARE REVIEWED. FIRST, "THE
ORGANIZATION MUST PUT INTO PLACE THE SYSTEMS, PRAC-
TICES, CULTURE, AND REWARDS THAT WILL ENCOURAGE PEO-
PLE TO BE ENTERPRISING"—THAT IS, TO BECOME MORE
AWARE AND RESPONSIVE TO PROBLEMS/OPPORTUNITIES. THE
SECOND ASPECT IS TO MAKE PEOPLE CAPABLE OF ACTING ON
THEIR IDEAS: "THAT'S A MATTER OF EMPOWERMENT"—MAK-
ING SURE PEOPLE HAVE ACCESS TO WHAT I CONSIDER THE
THREE KEY POWER TOOLS IN ANY ORGANIZATION: INFORMA-
TION, SUPPORT, AND RESOURCES." COMPANIES THAT CANNOT
MAKE THE TRANSFORMATION ARE <u>SEGMENTALIST</u>, WITH NAR-
ROW DEPARTMENTAL/FUNCTIONAL PERSPECTIVES THAT
ENCOURAGE PROBLEM DISAVOWAL AND SUBOPTIMIZATION.

THE AUTHOR, ROSABETH MOSS KANTER, HOLDS AN
ENDOWED CHAIR AT THE HARVARD BUSINESS SCHOOL AND
IS A FORMER EDITOR OF THE *HARVARD BUSINESS REVIEW.*
SHE HAS WRITTEN NUMEROUS BOOKS AND ARTICLES. FOR
MORE OF HER WORK ON ORGANIZATIONAL CHANGE, CONSULT
THE CHANGE MASTERS (1983), *WHEN GIANTS LEARN TO
DANCE* (1989), AND *THE CHALLENGE OF ORGANIZATIONAL
CHANGE* (1992), THE LATTER CO-AUTHORED WITH TODD
JICK AND BARRY STEIN.

READING 17
QUALITY LEADERSHIP
AND CHANGE

BY ROSABETH MOSS KANTER

I would like to put the issues of quality and leadership for quality in a slightly larger perspective. We are under siege as a nation, and many of our companies are under siege, because we're playing a very new game today. One thing I enjoy as I travel around the country, reminding people that the future is unfolding very differently from how we had imagined, is asking executives what game they think best describes their business today. We use many sports metaphors in business, so I've asked people to think about the right metaphor. The answers have been very interesting and very revealing.

At Apple Computer last summer, somebody said roller derby. At Bell South Corporation, an executive said he thought they were playing badminton in a hurricane. It's delicate, and they thought they had the skills, but storms were brewing all around them. In fact, another executive in the same company said he feared that he didn't even know what game they were playing. He was afraid his team would show up with five players and a big ball and the other team would show up fielding nine players and a little ball, and they wouldn't be able to win because they were playing the wrong game.

In considering the relationship of the environment to the dramatic need for quality, innovation, and better management in American corporations, I think the game that best describes most businesses today is the croquet game in *Alice In Wonderland*. In that game nothing remains stable for very long. Everything is changing around the players. Alice goes to hit the ball, but her mallet is a flamingo. Just as she's about to hit the ball, the flamingo lifts its head and looks in another direction. That's just like technology and the tools

CREDIT: Used by permission of the author. Rosabeth Moss Kanter, "Quality Leadership and Change," *Quality Progress* (February, 1987) pp. 45-51. Rosabeth Moss Kanter holds the class of 1960 chair as Professor at the Harvard Business School.

we use. Just when employees have mastered them, they seem to change, requiring different learning and competence.

When Alice finally thinks she's mastered the flamingo and goes to hit the ball, the ball becomes a hedgehog. It walks to another part of the court. That's just like our employees and customers, who are no longer waiting for us to whack them. Instead, they have minds of their own and will in fact walk off to another part of the court to choose another option in a heightened competitive environment.

And finally in that croquet game, the wickets are the card soldiers being ordered around by the Red Queen. This is perhaps a great metaphor for government. Just as Alice thinks she understands the tools, her employees, and her customers, the Red Queen barks out another order and the wickets reposition themselves. The very structure of industry, the structure of regulation, the structure of international competition, are changing at the same time that we're trying to get people to do a better job. That, to me, is the ultimate quality challenge. It's not only to improve what we're already doing, but it's to build into our organizations the capacity to improve and change direction as conditions change all around us.

That means paying attention not only to the visible mistakes, but also to the invisible mistakes. Randall Meyer, president of EXXON U.S.A., pointed this out to his people as an important distinction. He said most of what American industry pays attention to are the visible mistakes—solving problems and taking care of the processes that are under our control. What worries him for the future of industry and competitiveness are the invisible mistakes—missed opportunities. I was delighted to see in Westinghouse's statement of quality principles the statement that an important source of waste is the failure to exploit a technological opportunity or use a new tool or technique. I'm concerned with teaching organizations not only to avoid visible mistakes, waste, and failures, but also to avoid invisible mistakes. There are times when people have an idea about how to do something differently or better, to respond to a rapidly changing competitive environment, but they don't act on it.

ENCOURAGE PEOPLE TO BE ENTERPRISING

I'd like to talk about the kind of people who do act on opportunities for change; in fact, have confidence in change. I call them *change masters*. These are the people who can see the need for, and lead, productive change. It could be the employees in a quality circle, it could be a hidden entrepreneur in middle management, it could be the chief executive or a staff department, or a customer-company coalition. There are certain aspects of culture, structure, and organization that allow people to lead productive change—to make the improvements needed to win at the game of *Alice in Wonderland* croquet.

First, the organization must put in place the systems, practices, culture, and rewards that will encourage people to be enterprising—to solve problems and to see and take advantage of opportunities.

ORGANIZATION

The first key is in how we define and organize around jobs. There's more initiative and enterprise in organizations that define jobs in broad, rather than narrow, terms. This idea is almost a cliche of modern management theory, yet it's a relatively newer idea for most organizations. The old wisdom about the best way to design jobs was that they should be as narrow and as specialized as possible, to avoid human error. People could do the same thing over and over again, getting better and better, and avoiding mistakes. Exceptions or problems were sent upward for management to take care of, or to another department.

The new wisdom says that people work better when they get bigger pieces to do or are connected more broadly to goals. The new wisdom about defining jobs says that there should be bigger pieces, clearer knowledge of goals, and measurement on results, not on rules. That's hard for very old organizations to do. In fact, it's much easier to put in a quality circle that takes people off the job than it is to change the definition of the job. Sometimes that's because of constraints built into the system. One concession that GM had to get from the UAW when they started New United Motors Manufacturing Inc., a joint venture with Toyota, concerned job classifications. In one major area, when GM ran that plant, they had over 35 job classifications. The Japanese had only three—all bigger, all broader, all tapping people's enterprise, by giving them a bigger piece of the picture to pay attention to.

One of our leading consumer goods manufacturers, one that gets high marks on quality from consumer, has been very successful with a new work design system that involves one job classification. Now, almost 50 percent of their plants have systems in which jobs and responsibilities are enlarged and broadened. Employee teams manage their piece of the business as if they owned it. In the most advanced example of that system, costs are about 50 percent of what they are in a conventional plant, quality is much higher, and they have reduced the need for supervision down to 17 managers for about 350 people. They really need only four managers—one plant manager and one product manager for each of the three product lines. They still have 17 because the employees don't want to see the middle managers done out of a job. But in fact, the plant could run effectively with just employees in teams who have mastered all of the jobs. They're on a pay-for-knowledge system; as people master each job, their pay goes up. Seventy-five percent of the people are at the highest pay rate already because they've learned it all.

Some high-tech companies take this notion of broad job definition to an extreme. In some computer companies the typical job definition is, "Do the right thing." People are given no more guidelines than that. "We'll aim you in the right direction, but it's up to you to figure out how to get results." That's extreme—but the worst thing you could hear any employee say in any company is, "That's not my job." Many companies suffer because jobs are defined too narrowly, and people don't have any sense of the reasons for what they're doing.

TEAMS

The second characteristic of change master companies is that they have a structure that's built around small working teams. The teams have autonomy to act in local areas and are functionally complete. That is, they have representatives from every function, every discipline, required to get the end job done. It's the opposite of dividing the process into infinite numbers of departments and specialists, each with a territory to manage.

This is why, for a long time, Hewlett-Packard's classic growth strategy was "small is beautiful." As soon as a division grew to more than 2,000 people or reached $100 million in sales, they would break it into two divisions. That would produce a smaller business unit where integration across specialties and the ability to act locally were fostered. In that kind of structure, people take ownership for results. They can see the customer firsthand. In fact, there's a famous example of an engine plant that makes truck engines, built around cross-functional teams. Whenever there's an accident involving a truck that uses their engines, representatives of the team responsible for that product visit the truck driver and his or her family. They take personal responsibility for the failures, as well as personal responsibility for the end product, because they're part of an integrated team.

CULTURE OF PRIDE

The third noteworthy aspect of change master companies is in their culture. Those organizations that tap people's problem-solving abilities and enterprising skills have what I call a culture of pride, rather than a culture of mediocrity or inferiority. A culture of pride has several aspects. First is a myth that says, "Our people are the best people and they're always getting better." I say it's a myth because the number of high-tech companies, all in the same industry, each of which swears that it hires only from the top 5 percent of the class, tells me that it must be statistical impossibility. But they all believe that they have only the best.

I contrast that with the attitude I see in companies that are not as good at innovation and are scrambling to keep up. In the results from employee opinion surveys, in response to the statement "We hire only the best people," fewer than 20 percent of the employees show even weak agreement with that statement. That's a culture of inferiority or mediocrity. The belief is that if you've worked there for more than two years, you must be a real turkey.

In such companies, the attitude is that all wisdom comes from the outside, not from the inside. If you want to make a change, hire an outsider. In one insurance company, for example, the whole top management team had turned over within three years, and six out of the nine players were new to the company within two years. Every time they wanted a new function or a new department, they'd bring in somebody from Citicorp or IBM or GE, rather than look for people from the inside. They didn't believe they had the best people. They used consultants freely, and for trivia. I am not against using consultants—I should make that clear. But they should not substitute for things that people inside could do perfectly well. That insurance company actually hired consultants to figure out how to speed up the photocopying of procedures manuals. Wouldn't that have been a wonderful opportunity for a team of their own employees to become heros by solving a problem?

We also recognize cultures of pride by their expenditures. High-innovation, flexible companies that are better at adapting to change spend more on human resource programs, on career development, and education in particular. Low-innovation companies—and by the way, this is based on statistical comparisons that were part of my research—do not necessarily avoid spending. Instead, they tend to spend on recruitment and replacement costs because of high turnover. On the other hand, high-innovation companies invest in things that will make their employees better over time. Increasingly, those investments, which tell people that they're valued and are getting better, are not done just at the point of promotion, which is the classical system. It's done simply to improve people's ability to take action in their current position, whether or not they were groomed for anything more. It assumes that people can always do more, regardless of whether they're moving up in the official hierarchy. Another aspect of the culture of pride is in the abundant praise, recognition, awards, trophies, and wall plaques all of which populates high-innovation companies. Like many of you, I greeted these at first with skepticism. I said, "What does this rah-rah culture really do for motivation? How many of us really work for a trophy or a plaque or a pat on the back?" I realized that the impact is not on the people who actually get the award, but on the others who view it. It's the publicity value from which the high-innovation companies benefit—the fact that everybody sees what our people are capable of. That raises the esteem of the whole organization.

My firm did an innovation audit on a company that wanted to know whether it had the systems and practices that would allow it to compete in the new game. We told them that among all the reasons why their product development was slow and not particularly exciting, was the fact that they didn't have much in the way of recognition systems. And they said, "But wait a minute, didn't we show you? Sure we do." It turned out that they did have a lot of awards, but they were all secret. People would get a little cash stuffed in the paycheck or the boss would do something in private. It defeated the whole purpose. It's the publicity value that creates a culture of pride in which everybody feels they must live up to the level of achievement set by the people who were singled out as role models.

REWARDS

And finally, we found that high-innovation companies have a different attitude toward reward. They not only have rewards that pay people after they do a good job, but they also have what I call investment-oriented rewards. These are rewards before the fact—investments in the fact that somebody will perform later. It might take the form of a budget for a special project, or a pool of cash that employees can tap if they write proposals and show that they had something good to do with it. Data General Corporation became famous through the bestseller, *Soul of a New Machine*. It described how a manager, Tom West, got teams of young engineers to perform miracles. They did in one year what the experts said would take five years or could never be done at all. They built a totally new computer from scratch—a computer, by the way, that along with its following generations is responsible for more than half of the company's total revenues. He did it by extraordinary teamwork in an atmosphere where rewards seemed to be investment oriented.

When the young engineers were asked, "What was in it for you? Why did you kill yourself for this product when you didn't even get stock options at the end?"

The answer was "Pinball."

Pinball? "Yes," they said, "it's like playing pinball. If you win, you get a free game. You get a chance to do it again on your own terms. The reward comes from being singled out and invested in." That's a very different attitude toward rewards. Challenge—opportunity—is one of the greatest untapped potential rewards that most organizations have. It doesn't cost anything to give people opportunities, and yet it often pays off in problems solved and innovations developed.

EMPOWERMENT

While the first feature of change master companies is encouraging people to be enterprising in the first place, the second is making sure they have the tools to act on their ideas. That's a matter of empowerment—making sure that people have access to what I consider the three key power tools in any organization: information, support, and resources.

INFORMATION

Change master companies tend to make more information more available to more people at more levels through more devices. These devices include oral and written communication. I'm amused by some of the examples in *In Search of Excellence,* which talks about the famous one-page memo that one company developed to reduce paperwork. Behind the scenes, managers spend weeks and weeks perfecting the one-page memo. One senior executive sent back a memo 17 times to be rewritten so that it would be in perfect one-page form. Why didn't he just go and talk to the person to whom the memo was being sent?

High-innovation companies emphasize immediate, direct communication in real time, to give people the information they need to act. This is why many leading manufacturing companies, like the consumer products company I mentioned earlier, invest heavily in microcomputers to make sure that people on the shop floor can get immediate product data. In fact, in one division of that company, the workers on the shop floor have product data that the brand managers themselves don't have. By the way, that is a flaw in their system—the brand managers should probably have it too. But they emphasize people getting timely information about what they're doing. For this reason, there will likely be more meetings in high-innovation, high-quality, change master companies, more groups convening to share information and compare notes.

I happen to be a fan of *USA Today.* I particularly like their color-coded weather map, on which you can see instantly what the weather is like in any part of the country. I was going to propose that they do a similar map of meeting density, so that on any day you could see where meetings are taking place around the country. My guess would be that you'd find most on Route 128 in Boston, Silicon Valley, Austin, and maybe Pittsburgh, now that I know so much about what Westinghouse is doing. The map would be densest in places where there is an emphasis on adjustment, improvement, and change—because wherever there's change, there's a need to share information.

The attitude toward open information that exists in high-innovation companies sometimes astonishes even me. For example, some organizations have open meeting policies, which say that anybody can attend any meeting, unless particular individuals are being discussed. Now, most people hate meetings and would be unlikely to take advantage of that policy. But the point is, they don't want to limit access. A "need-to-know" policy is counterproductive during change. Instead, those organizations emphasize access—not forcing information on people, but access.

There was a classic story at Wang Laboratories of a new executive who had an office on the executive floor. All of the offices had glass walls, although they also had doors. The new executive was sitting in his office one day, trying to interview somebody that he wanted to hire. It was a little noisy out in the hall, so he closed his door. Dr. Wang himself came by and started walking back and forth, peering through the glass wall. After that happened six or seven times, the fellow finally got the idea. He got up and opened his door, and Dr. Wang stopped walking by. It was important there that everybody be able to hear everything. In fact, at one HP division that we studied, people who were working on budgets found that the library was the only place where there wouldn't be people peering over the shoulder-height partitions at what was on their desks.

This attitude is very different from those in low-innovation companies that are not adapting to change and are having problems competing on quality and productivity. In those companies, the attitude was that information was a weapon to be hoarded by departments who felt that they were excluded from information about what was happening in the organization. At one telephone company, for example—predivestiture—the field people complained that they couldn't get certain data from headquarters that they needed to run their operation. So they paid somebody to go out and get that data for them. And they made sure that headquarters could never see their data, thereby diminishing the total value of that information to the system.

Finally, another necessary kind of communication is information on company goals, strategies, and plans. One area that tends to get low marks on employee attitude surveys in manufacturing companies involves knowledge of company direction. Until people feel informed about where they're heading overall, they don't feel capable of taking the initiative to solve a problem. They don't feel empowered to act, because they're not sure that the direction in which they're headed will fit with the decisions being made at the top.

COLLABORATION

Another aspect of empowering people to act on their ideas is to make sure the organization permits collaboration so that people can build problem-solving coalitions. One aspect of building such an environment is sheer mobility. People must be able to move freely across areas and functions. What used to be called "unusual career moves" are common in high-innovation companies. That is, people's careers often take them across many different functions rather than up in one direction. They acquire more knowledge and contact with people all over the organization.

The mobility doesn't have to be career or job mobility. It also involves the movement of people to gather and solve problems together. High-innovation companies also seem to have more conferences, more councils, more reasons to be gathering people together. In fact, those of you who fly through Boston's Logan airport, the next time you do, look at the board that lists commuter airlines as you enter the airport. There's a very interesting anomaly on the list. It's called Digital Helicopters, and that's not a new commuter airline. It's DEC's own in-house helicopter service that flies between 17 New England facilities on a regular basis. DEC people can get out and collaborate on solving problems that may go beyond the local area. Contrast that with the usual corporate jet that costs $2,000 an hour and is available only to the top 20 people. It's a very different attitude toward who needs to move easily to collaborate.

In fact, at one point DEC was worried about its travel costs, naturally, so it installed an elaborate teleconferencing facility to reduce the need to travel. What do you think happened to travel costs? They went up, because as more people could communicate, they found even more reasons why they should be getting together.

It's also true that there's more total collaboration where there's more employment security. It's hard for people to be enterprising or to support each other in changes when they're not sure who's going to last. Having a sense that there's a future makes it easier for people to invest in and plan for that future. People must feel they have a future if you want them to take responsibility for creating it.

In addition, an organization has more innovation and support when its people work well together and where there's more access up, down, and around the hierarchy. Several companies in Silicon Valley have Friday afternoon beer parties around the company swimming pool. That's the kind of thing they do out there. It serves an important function for companies that must be innovative and have everyone constantly collaborating on problem solving. When everyone's around the swimming pool in bathing suits, it's hard to stand on rank. Paunch is a great leveler! People at all levels are mixing. That's the issue—that people have access to each other, regardless of rank or status.

This is why one major bank was seriously considering eliminating titles. Eliminate titles in a bank—35 levels of vice presidents. They felt that those status distinctions interfere with mobilizing groups to solve problems, and with someone who has an idea to get support for it. The whole bank hasn't eliminated officer titles yet, but its credit card division has, in favor of very broad functional titles. The titles describe the person's "home," but don't make rank or status such a barrier to access.

Contrast that again to a company that's struggling to change its culture. Every time a task force is formed, each department makes sure that the team has a representative of equal rank from each department, or they won't play. That game inhibits the people who want to recruit talent, because instead they have to recruit status. It used to be impossible in some companies to get more than two levels of the hierarchy together in the same room at the same time. I've been in meetings where we'd start talking about what was going on at another level, and I'd say something innocent like, "Why don't we invite them in?" And people would say, "No, no, we can't do that."

This still happens in the best companies. When we plan conferences for the top 50 or 100 people to go play golf in Florida and talk about new goals and culture changes, we often recommend the presence of people from many levels below. That would provide first-hand contact with key issues. But people would say, "No, that violates protocol," or "We're nervous about it." Several years ago, one of these companies innovated skip-level meetings. Level A could skip Level B and meet directly with Level C to find out what was going on. But since Level B wasn't present, it all ended up being Level B's fault, which was the squeezed middle manager again. And that still got only two levels of the organization in the same room at the same time.

Clearly, flattening hierarchies and removing barriers to access are important to improving people's problem-solving capacities.

RESOURCES

Finally, high-innovation companies also tend to decentralize resources to make them more available for local problem solving. This means more general managers through smaller business units; more project teams that have budgets; special resource pools at lower levels, like internal venture capital banks; and internal pools of unallocated funds that people can tap to solve problems. In short, they make it easier for people to tap locally what they need to get things done.

Again, a division of one leading bank began experimenting to make resources available locally, and also to give people incentives to solve problems. Their smart idea was to let employees keep a portion of the cost savings, to invest in their department's activities. This was not gainsharing, so they could not take it home and buy VCRs. It was not money to take out of the company—it was invested in the company. Any department that saved money for the company got to keep a portion of it in its budget, as long as it was invested in a productive new activity. That was another way to make resources more available locally.

CHANGING THE CULTURE

To do these things in many companies, the culture must be changed. The first requirement is a shared vision. Before improving quality or changing the culture or business direction, people at every level must understand and buy into the vision. Consider, for example, the Stanley Works, a 150-year-old tool manufacturer. It's always been known for high quality and high profitability. Now it's meeting the Pacific Rim challenge in many basic product lines. At Stanley Tools, every worker on the shop floor can tell you why they're moving in the direction in which they're moving. They understand the rationale and what it means to them. The vision is real for them and they buy into it. It's not just another set of marching orders from the top.

Second, there must be a management structure in place. One doesn't simply announce "We want to change." Rather, you manage changes, and make a clearly identifiable set of people responsible for them.

A third factor is education and action tools. Having a management structure and the education are the two easiest things for companies to do, and they're very important.

Fourth is the need to encourage local innovations and experiments, rather than imposing a discipline on everyone. Let local units decide for themselves what it means to operate with high quality and high performance, and to innovate in ways that might serve as models for the rest of the organization. At the same time, the people at the top must be continually reviewing other policies, strategies, structures, and systems in the organization to make sure they're all compatible with the direction.

There must be good communication in all directions to assure that people learn from what's happening locally and that the policy decisions made at the top quickly reach the people who are taking action locally. And there must be new signals, symbols, and rewards that tell people, "We're serious and we're going to prove it by signalling it in a different way, such as who gets promoted or which new plant gets the business."

LEADERSHIP

This kind of management of a total change effort takes leadership. There are at least four important leadership competencies that we must encourage in the people who run our enterprises, to make sure they're doing these things.

First, like all change masters, they must be tuned into the environment and connected with sources of data and problems, so that they know what and when to change.

Second, they must be able to use a style of thinking that I call kaleidoscopic thinking. This is the ability to challenge traditional beliefs, assumptions, and practices, to see whether things should be done differently today. Change masters think the way a kaleidoscope works. A kaleidoscope is just a device for seeing patterns. When you look through it, a set of fragments forms a pattern. But if you twist it, shake it, or change direction, the same fragments form an entirely different pattern. It's not reality that's fixed, but often our views of reality. Change masters can shake up and shuffle the pieces of the business, the array of departments, the systems we use, in many different ways. They can challenge their own beliefs and assumptions to move toward something new.

Third, change masters have a clear vision and communicate it. They actively believe in it and are committed to it.

Fourth, change master leaders build coalitions. They know how to create partnerships across areas, between suppliers and the company, with customers as joint ventures, and with the union. They reach out to embrace many parties because they realize that every change must be sold—because people can say no to it.

Overall, the kind of environment that drives change master companies can be called integrated. The culture and structure are integrative. Jobs are broad so territories overlap. People tend to be linked together in cross-functional teams, oriented toward the same end product. Communication flows freely and knits people together. Groups can form and reform with access to any part of the organization if that's what's needed to solve a problem. These organizations are flexible, but they're also connected by a shared vision that's set at the top.

SEGMENTALISM

The opposite environment, which destroys the ability to be competitive, is what I call segmentalism. Such systems chop the world into tiny pieces. The philosophy is, "Stay on your piece, learn that job and nothing else, take no responsibility for anything else." Department doesn't talk to department, level doesn't talk to level. There are systemic roadblocks to innovation, change, and problem solving. This could be called the elevator mentality. Elevators go up and down in narrow vertical channels. That's the mentality, instead of just saying to the guy in the next office, "Can we get together to form a team or solve this problem?" Departments act as fortresses rather than collaborators. Internal competition nearly killed our auto industry. Buick thought Cadillac was the enemy, not that they were knit together by common purpose and a need to collaborate. GM's new structure says they're no longer divided by product.

Unfortunately, even in this day of searching for excellence and questing for quality, too many companies still operate the old way. I predict that the biggest limitation many of you will have in implementing your quality goals will come from organizational structures and practices that segment people. It will come from the inter-departmental issues that can't be solved through quality circles at one level. It will come from the barriers that exist between areas—not from a lack of teamwork or a failure of the processes. You can establish excellent participative processes and statistical process controls and then fail because the weight of the whole organization is still too divisive.

In the interest of equal time, I wrote a corporate philosophy for the company that prefers mediocrity and stagnation. This is my guide to *stifling innovation* for those who *do not* want to be change masters:

- Be suspicious of any new idea from below—because it's new and because it's from below. If the idea were any good, the people at the top would have thought of it already.

- Insist that people who need your approval to act go through many other levels of the hierarchy first—it doesn't matter in which direction. The point is to slow them down, because you don't want radical changes. A variant is to have departments challenge and criticize each other's proposals and then just pick the winner, thereby guaranteeing they'll never collaborate on anything again.

- If you don't want innovation, high performance and quality, then withhold praise, express criticism freely, and instill job insecurity. That keeps people on their toes. How else would they know that you have standards? With all due respect—I know he's written a book and he's mellowed, but he's retired now—I used to call this the Harold Geneen macho school of management. It said that people do their best work when terrified. If you don't have strong standards, they just won't perform.

- Change policies in secret and reorganize unexpectedly and often. If you don't want people taking initiative to solve problems, then you must keep them in suspended animation, never knowing when another directive from corporate is going to cut things to ribbons again. Some of our old-style manufacturing plants found that the best way to close the facility was to announce it on the radio that morning as people were driving to work. That way, they didn't lose productivity and they avoided anxiety that might slow things down.

- Be control conscious. Count everything that can be counted as often as possible. If you don't want people to take initiatives and solve problems, you want to have more measurements than you need. You want to measure so much that all behavior will go only to the measures. To stamp out initiative, make sure there is no spare change that people could ever invest in a special project that's not in a budget somewhere. Make sure that so much time is taken up just meeting the measures that nobody would be able to think about investing in the future or solving a problem.

- The attitude at the top should be, "We already know everything important there is to know about this business. We've been in business a long time, and we've been successful, so we'll just keep doing what we've been doing."

THE NEW RULES

A good place to start in changing the culture is to reverse the old rules.

Increase receptivity to and forums for new ideas. Many companies are already doing this through quality processes. What about other processes? How many people are reached? What about ideas for things that can't be done right the first time because they've never been done before? That is one of the slight contradictions in "Do it right the first time." You have to have done it once before to know what right is. Make sure those kinds of quality standards aren't a barrier to experimentation and to trying new things.

Faster approval and less red tape are required. Do things really have to go through so many levels of signatures? Increase praise, recognition for achievements, and open communication—especially advance warning of changes in plans.

Maintain an attitude that you're always learning and can learn from any source. This helps convert change from being a threat to being an opportunity. Change is always a threat when it's done to me or imposed on me, like it or not. But it's an opportunity if it's done by me. It's my chance to contribute and be recognized. That's the simple key to all of this: make it an opportunity for people and reward them for it. Throughout every rank of American organizations, we must think about problem solving as entrepreneurs do. They think of every problem as an opportunity to do it better. This is the kind of attitude we need.

Rosabeth Moss Kanter is the class of 1960 professor at Harvard Business School. She also founded Goodmeasure, Inc., a management consulting firm. Her latest best selling book is *The Change Masters,* published in 1983 by Simon & Schuster.

READING 18
A CONVERSATION WITH
ROBERT W. GALVIN

FORTUNE (APRIL 19, 1994) REPORTED THAT "CHIEF EXEC-
UTIVES OF THE ELITE BUSINESS ROUNDTABLE RANK
MOTOROLA THE COUNTRY'S TOP PRACTITIONER OF TOTAL
QUALITY MANAGEMENT." ROSABETH MOSS KANTER, AUTHOR
OF READING 17, SAYS "MOTOROLA IS ONE OF THE FEW GEN-
UINE ROLE MODELS OF INDUSTRY TRANSFORMATION." THE
QUALITY OF THE COMPANY'S PRODUCTS HAVE HELPED IT
ACHIEVE NOTABLE SUCCESS IN GLOBAL MARKETS: 45 PER-
CENT SHARE OF THE WORLDWIDE CELLULAR PHONE MAR-
KET, $6 BILLION IN SEMICONDUCTOR SALES (RANKING IT
THIRD WORLDWIDE BEHIND INTEL AND NEC), AND 85 PER-
CENT OF THE GLOBAL MARKET FOR PAGERS. ONE INDIVIDUAL
MOST CLEARLY ASSOCIATED WITH THE QUALITY MOVEMENT
AT MOTOROLA IS ITS FORMER CEO AND CHAIRMAN, ROBERT
W. GALVIN.

GALVIN SAYS QUALITY BECAME A MOTOROLA FOCUS FOL-
LOWING A MEETING OF TOP CORPORATE EXECUTIVES IN
CHICAGO IN 1979. AT THIS MEETING SALES EXECUTIVE
ARTHUR SUNDRY, THEN WITH MOTOROLA'S TWO-WAY RADIO
OPERATIONS, SAID, "OUR QUALITY STINKS AND WE OUGHT TO
DO SOMETHING ABOUT IT." AND, INDEED, THEY DID. SIX
SIGMA QUALITY—A DEFECT RATE OF 3.4 PARTS PER MIL-
LION—BECAME A MANUFACTURING GOAL. TEAMWORK WAS
EMPHASIZED. EDUCATION WAS INCREASED SO THAT ALL
EMPLOYEES RECEIVE AT LEAST FORTY HOURS OF TRAINING
PER YEAR, AND TRAINING COSTS ARE NOW 4 PERCENT OF
PAYROLL (OVER $100 MILLION PER YEAR). AND QUALITY
CONCERNS EXTEND FAR BEYOND THE MANUFACTURING
FLOOR. FOR EXAMPLE, A TEAM OF ENGINEERS AND LAWYERS
WORKED ON IMPROVING THE PROCESS FOR FILING PATENTS,

AND <u>ACCOUNTANTS</u> IMPROVED THE YEAR-END BOOK-CLOS-
ING FROM SIX WEEKS TO FOUR DAYS. GALVIN'S LEADERSHIP
WAS A MAJOR FACTOR IN THE RECOGNITION OF MOTOROLA AS
A NATIONAL QUALITY LEADER WHEN THEY RECEIVED THE
BALDRIGE AWARD IN 1988 (THE FIRST YEAR THE AWARD
WAS GIVEN.)

READING 18
A CONVERSATION WITH
ROBERT W. GALVIN

BY KENNETH R. THOMPSON

What more appropriate conversation piece for a special issue on quality than a talk with Robert W. Galvin. In recent years, Motorola has become closely associated with the renewed emphasis on quality products and service worldwide. And, of course, Bob Galvin is the widely recognized architect of the Motorola quality effort—a driving force behind Motorola's capture of a 1988 Malcolm Baldrige National Quality Award.

Bob Galvin started with Motorola at the young age of seven, when he accompanied his father, Paul V. Galvin, founder of Motorola, on business trips. In 1940, Bob Galvin began full-time employment for Motorola, holding jobs such as stock boy and production-line troubleshooter. Bob was promoted to executive vice president in 1948, became president in 1956, and chairman and chief executive officer in 1964. In 1986, he moved into the position of chairman of the board of directors. Now in the role of elder statesman, Galvin is active in a number of strategic, educational, and advisory capacities. He has been elected to the National Business Hall of Fame and received the 1991 National Medal of Technology. Robert W. Galvin has shared his philosophy of management in a book entitled *The Idea of Ideas* (Motorola University Press, 1991).

I was struck with Galvin's concern for the individual and his quiet passion for quality. During this conversation, as in my other experiences with people at Motorola, I found a spirit that I have encountered only once before, and that was when I was working with the people at Wal-Mart. Here, as at Wal-Mart, is an organization that cares about its people, and the people care about reaching the organization's goals. Whether this is the result of visionaries such as Paul and Robert Galvin, a simple consequence of total quality management done correctly, or the result of some other force, I am not sure.

I believe, however, that an organization can only be as strong as the guidance it receives from someone at the top who cares. Bob Galvin is that sort of person.

Former Motorola CEO and chairman Robert W. Galvin has been closely associated with the quality movement.

The following interview was conducted at Motorola's headquarters in Schaumburg, Illinois. My goal was to learn more about how Motorola moved into total quality management and what led to the company's strong commitment to employee development. A clear signal of that commitment was visible during the interview. Across the parking lot, workmen were finishing the new addition to the Galvin Center, a 88,000 square foot training facility that houses Motorola University.

THOMPSON
    What led you to recognize the need for change at Motorola?

GALVIN
    The driving thrust of our company, from the day it was founded, was renewal. So we've never had to rediscover the need to change. My father started the company just to start a company, and within 18 months he knew he'd be out of business. The battery eliminator, the founding product, was on its way to total obsolescence, and so he had to have a new product within a year or two after he started. This was in 1928. And that's been the pattern ever since. We just constantly have to renew ourselves. That's the nature of the industry.

THOMPSON
    Obviously there was some concern, in the '60s or '70s, with the encroachment of Japanese competition.

GALVIN

That was certainly one of the stimulations. We recognized that the world really was getting bigger, and that the Japanese were becoming a market and becoming serious competitors. The more we learned, the more we realized that Japan was the greater of all the competitive threats to our industry. And yes, then we started to focus an immense amount of attention on countering that threat.

THOMPSON

How did total quality come on board?

GALVIN

Total quality came aboard from a variety of stimulations. First off, we noticed that the Japanese truly had made a transition to a high-quality supply base in the 1970s. That was an attention-getter unto itself. But we finally focused on quality when a sales executive [Arthur Sundry] at a 1979 meeting of top corporate executives interrupted the meeting, in a gracious way, and said we really weren't on the most important subject. He said, in effect, "Our quality stinks and we ought to do something about it." And this man happened to have extraordinary credentials, because he was the sales manager of our largest, fastest growing, and most profitable product line—which happened to be two-way radios. And here he is, telling us that he is immensely dissatisfied with our quality. With those credentials, all of us looked in the mirror and said, "If Art thinks that's true, it must be true. We'd better do something about it." So you look at the competitive threat, and you look closely at what you can offer, and you decide you better really renew your organization on the subject of quality.

THOMPSON

Would you attribute the Japanese stress on quality to [W. Edwards] Deming or to something else—just their own sense of how to be competitive, for example?

GALVIN

I think the Deming influence is most significant. Whether or not the Japanese would have gotten there without Deming..., I would guess they would have—but not near as well, and not near as fast. I think it was the nature of the Japanese to be willing to admit they had to change, and they found an excellent guide in the Deming thesis.

THOMPSON

What do you mean by total quality management (TQM)? Obviously, meeting the needs of the customer is the central core in the concept, but at Motorola it seems to be much more a part of the organization's being and existence.

GALVIN

The paramount idiom in our company (and it's not different than in a lot of other companies) is *total customer satisfaction*. The words take on very special meanings in institutions. And *total* in our case means *total*. It doesn't mean *a lot*, it doesn't mean *best in class*. It means *everything*. Just like the phone call I made this morning [to one of the company's officers]. It didn't take a lot of words. He and I know that the first thing I'll do any day is to work on behalf of seeing that a given single customer is totally satisfied before the next few hours are over. And so he knows what to do. And if he gave me the assignment, I'd know what to do. So total customer satisfaction is the paramount of the quality situation. Now, organizations have to *institutionalize* what they do. They do this with language, with understanding, or with procedures and processes, principles and standards, etc. We have put into our company every imaginable means that can fall under those particular words, that give us both the culture and the mechanism to accomplish this total customer satisfaction. It starts with better design. It starts with the intention of having teams of people work to accomplish a job in a very short cycle time to meet the delivery needs of the customer—which, in the case of this morning's phone call from a customer, we apparently *weren't* doing, but *will* be doing between now and tonight. So it's everything, and we measure to make sure that we're understanding that we're getting the job done, or looking for first causes so we won't repeat the same problem tomorrow. It's the totality of everything.

THOMPSON

Let's take a look at that call. It happened to be about a pager. Now, there will be follow up; that exec will call, and so on. Will there be some way to determine if this problem was just a fluke, or something within the system that needs correcting?

GALVIN

We will get every relevant department involved in correcting the problem. If the problem is in the design—a bug that the customer has discovered—the design people will be working on that today, if they're not already working on it. If it's a supply problem, people will work an extra hour tonight and fly some more pagers to the customer overnight to meet the service needs. Whatever it takes, this will become what we call *a cycle of learning*. What we learn from this experience will revise how we conduct our business, in general, with a lot of other customers—because this problem could affect five other customers somewhere along the line.

THOMPSON

This implies that there's a good information flow in the organization, and that the information is available to all decision makers.

GALVIN

Customers give us good data and we can often interpolate the data. We correlate that with other data from other customers. Maybe we've had two other customers that I didn't know about, who have had this problem. Well, somebody else knows that, and they honestly look at the data. We don't kid ourselves. We admit our mistake if there is one, and we'll correct it. And we're always going back to first causes...going through cycles of learning, looking for first causes so that we don't have this kind of problem very often again, or never again after we solve the problem. You ask, what is our total quality? It's a culture of intending that we never do anything that would dissatisfy the customer.

THOMPSON

But how do you create that? It wasn't here in the '50s, was it?

GALVIN

No, we thought we had it. A lot of American industries thought they had it in the '50s and even in the '60s. Some companies think they have it today and don't. You're a teacher. And although this is a poor analogy, you will probably give certain of your students a 95, and that will be looked upon as a very high grade. Well, it's not *quite* the same—I don't think we decided to come to work and say, "If we can get 95s all the time, we'll do a good job." But there has been a little bit of that. And people have said, "Gee, 99 percent that's pretty good." But when 1 percent, 1 out of 100, has something wrong, and we're dealing in thousands and millions of projects, then customers may not be happy. For example, in a car with a thousand parts, a 99 percent quality rate would mean that 10 things are wrong with that car. The customers have higher expectations than that. Expectation levels are very important. The answer to your question is, when you finally get the attention of all of us in our institution (or in yours) and have us say, "It's fun to be perfect," then it is possible to be perfect, and it is satisfying to be perfect. And we've discovered that we can do an immense number of things perfectly. It doesn't mean that we're afraid to fail as we try, but having tried we can employ processes and principles that can finally cause that repetitive action to be perfect. And people like to do that. Because of that, we win in the marketplace and we get more business. With more business, we lower our unit costs. All the other things that are thought about business all finally come to pass as a derivative of quality.

THOMPSON

In your writings, you talk about total quality actually lowering costs. What you were doing this morning—handling a complaint yourself and asking other people to take the time to get involved in handling that one complaint—some people would say that's not a good use of your time.

GALVIN

To the extent that we allow the company to perform in a fashion that too many customers feel the need to call me, it absolutely manifests that there's a lot of ineffective use of people's time throughout the company. I'm merely one example of that. But if the problem exists, then it absolutely is the *best* use of my time until we solve it. Now, if all I (and all those others) do is paper over the issue, and we don't go back to first causes, and we don't go through a cycle of learning—if we don't learn from this experience and prevent the problem from occurring again or very often—yes, *then what a terrible way to run a business.* One of the idioms in business is "fire fighting." I guess it happens in all institutions. It's kind of fun to be a fire fighter. Little children grow up thinking, "I'd like to be a fire fighter." It's glamorous, and in business there is something heroic about having a problem dumped on your desk and then solving it. Well, if you allow the *conditions* of allowing a lot of problems to exist just so you can have the fun of solving them, *that's a terrible way to waste your time.*

THOMPSON

Implied in this is measurement. Somewhere in that process there has to be some documentation or measurement as to what we mean by effectiveness and efficiency.

GALVIN

We measure everything in this company—well, virtually everything. All kinds of data will be taken on this experience that you witnessed today. They'll find out how many pagers were shipped and how many defects they had and what was the cause of those defects, and we'll analyze some products in the lab, and so on. And as I said, this is a cycle of learning and we'll learn everything we can from the data. We'll plot charts, and so on. All this will look like it would be rather costly, but what it provides (and scholars know this very well) is that when you finally synthesize your data, now you can discover what you need to do to correct the problem.

THOMPSON

Let's take new product development as an example. You talk about teams trying to reduce the cycle time on new product development. Who are on those teams?

GALVIN

We call this the *contract book process*. And what we do is to cause people with relevant inputs to come together. These can be marketing people, sales people, maybe a couple of company leaders who have an insight into this particular business, engineers who know about products and applications, the factory people who are going to have to produce it, the accounting people who are going to have to keep accounts for it, purchasing people—all the relevant people are brought together, literally, in one room. These people in effect design on paper (with occasionally lots of computers in the act) and in as much detail as possible what they think the customer needs and wants, because they've learned a lot about customers also. So here's a team of people who write a contract with each other. It's a book and it will describe the specifications and the parts and how they make it and so on and so forth. At the end of the sessions, they finally all look at the book, and they agree with each other, "That's what we want to do." Incidentally, that takes time. Some people will say, "Well, in the meantime you could have been actually working on the designs." Well, in this process we're *thinking out what the design needs to be*. That saves an immense amount of time, because now the whole team knows what the play is. From there on we can design and prepare the factory, and prepare the suppliers concurrently, and we move very rapidly.

THOMPSON

Who decides that a group should form and start a new product design?

GALVIN

Teams of creative people are in constant effervescence on these kinds of subjects. In other words, it is our "natural way of being" in this class of company. All technology companies are the same; some do it a little better than others. We have, for example, a road map, and all these things that we think of are all on road maps. We have thousands of road maps and we know how to integrate them and collate them and keep most of them in mind. Lots of people review these road maps. So we already know that we're going a certain way, and then creative teams of people keep saying, "Oh, but there's a variation or an addition or a new trend" or "I just learned that this would be related to that." Again, teams of people each contribute some piece, and once in a while, your brilliant idea, mine, or somebody else's may be the stimulating force. We're constantly thinking about this. This is not something that is created in a vacuum. Somebody says, "Let's now create a new rose," and then we start all over. We've been developing roses all the time. And now we arrive into the next event. Occasionally, there are major discontinuities. But the history of our kind of company is a history of derivations. Yes, we renewed. Our renewal follows a path. Mostly of derivation. In other words, we made a car radio and then the car radio could be made into a home radio, and a radio receiver could have a transmitter put with it to make a two-way radio, and then we could have video communications on top of audio, which gives us a television set. And then there was a discontinuity where we needed a new kind of part called a transistor. Well, Bell Telephone laboratories invented that, and we said, "Gee, we're going to have to learn a whole new way of cooking...recipes, parts." That was a big discontinuity. But once we were in that, it led us to microprocessors and all manner of very sophisticated componentry—atomic structure of materials, for example. Everything is derived from something else. So we're following this path, this road map, and there are probably 2,000 creative people over in that building across the way from us who have got all kinds of minority ideas as to how to go ahead. We're also very big on wondering what the minority report is. Some big shot has made the decision to do something or other. But there's a guy over here who says, "Yeah, but there's another way of doing it." He's a minority. What's he got to say about it? We want to know.

THOMPSON

Does somebody assign the teams?

GALVIN

Yes. Assignments are made. One of the jobs of a manager is allocating resources. But that doesn't mean just slicing pies up. It's knowing that someone's really good on two-way radio technology, or very good on buying parts for two-way radios, etc. So whatever that skill is, as soon as the road map says we ought to be doing something in a new kind of two-way radio, then the resource manager in effect says to these people, "We've got to break you loose. We've got to get you on that team, half time or full time. Finish up what you're doing, and do it well. But we need you over here." It's like a coach on the sidelines deciding who goes in to play tackle. We have a lot of players on the bench, and most of them are doing something very useful, but we keep shifting people into different places.

THOMPSON

Now what happens if, say, I'm in accounting and have this great idea to reduce response time to customer needs, or maybe billings. How would I get that sold to a creative team?

GALVIN

Again, in our case the culture now exists, and you can keep stirring until the culture is finally inculcated. But the culture exists and you go to one of your peers—or your boss—and say, "I've got an idea." Let's take one that was a real-life situation in accounting. Lots of us, over the decades, have said, "Why can't we close the books in less time?" Families close books at the end of the month, businesses close books at the end of a something. Well, at the end of the year it used to take us maybe six weeks to close the books. So what difference does it make? All you're doing is putting some data on a piece of paper, and finally in February you know that your actual sales were so much and your profits were so much, and you already knew it pretty close, so we excuse ourselves. But we kept saying, "Can't you do it in less than six weeks?" Well, finally, at a given stage within renewal, certain of our very bright accounting people said, "It's taking us 16 days to close a company that's doing $7 to $9 billion in revenues this year. We're going to do about $12 billion next year, and we should be able to close the books in a lot less time if we PERT chart the whole process again, lay out this whole diagram of every single step, and ask ourselves where we have all kinds of waiting time. Or maybe we'll find a step we don't need anymore." Finally, after these people made the suggestions and their peers were receptive and teams went to work on it (some of whom were in the factory because the data from the factory had to get to the accountants), last year we closed the basics in four days. Actually, we did that by evolution over a couple of years. That saved the company well over $10 million a year, because things were getting done that weren't needed, or we were waiting or taking too much time. Within a year or two we'll close the books in two days, and on the road map of the objectives of the accounting people, who must tie in with everybody else in the company, is "close the books of the whole corporation in hours." So some time in this decade, before January 1st is over, we will have closed the books on the prior year. It's all possible. We know that we've learned how to do it. We just have to put all the little pieces in place. And that will save a lot of money, and when you have information earlier you often can do something with it.

THOMPSON

How do you create the sort of culture that you seem to have at Motorola, i.e., a passion to reduce the cycle time, a passion for quality?

GALVIN

By first pointing out that it is possible to run the four-minute mile. As soon as somebody shows us that one can achieve more at whatever one is doing, then we all discover we can do the same thing. Accountants like to do things superiorly, and public relations people like to do things superiorly, and personnel people like to do things superiorly, and so all of us like to achieve. It's fun to achieve and fun to win. In our company, we have learned how to measure how each of these functions is doing its job. We have, for example, a quality systems review. That's different from measuring quality itself. It's the *system of having good quality* that we measure. That becomes, in effect, another benchmark within the company. We have learned how to come to your department and measure *your* quality system. Incidentally, we will know the actual quality measure of your output, but we are first interested in your *system*. Because if your system is good, you are eventually going to have outstanding output. If you're in the personnel department, and I'm in the accounting department, and she is in the engineering department, and if we give you a grade of 2500 on your system, and I've got a grade of 3500, and she's got a grade of 4500, then we have a measure of the quality of your system. We have learned to integrate these data to where you can't say, "But the data from personnel is different from the data from accounting." We've now convinced everybody that the numbers have almost the same meaning. But you don't like to be measured lower than another group. You're a part of a pretty good company called Motorola, and you'd like to be as good as anybody else around the joint. You're going to have lunch or meet with people from other units everyday, and the word's out that your department's quality system only rates a 2500, and everybody else's is 3500 to 4000 points....well, you're going to think about the quality of your unit. So the culture drives you to say, "I'm going to really spend time on my quality system." Incidentally, I really do believe now that the system produces the end product itself. Procedures and systems are very important if we teach ourselves how to use them. So the culture is competitive. The culture is achievement-oriented.

THOMPSON

So this is a standardized evaluation system that could be superimposed on accounting, purchasing, production, etc.

GALVIN

Always, exactly! And the data are analogous. It's not apples and oranges.

THOMPSON

And this approach, called the quality system review, evaluates the unit's quality system, not the end products.

GALVIN

When you get all through, you will happily find that the output does equate the system. But we separate them for the sake of at least a given point of analysis. Just look at the system. And after looking at the system, if your grade is 2500, we're pretty darn sure the quality output isn't good enough either.

THOMPSON

So it's not a standard evaluation done by an accounting audit team.

GALVIN

We professionals, in effect, audit our peers. I'm from accounting, you're from personnel, she's from engineering, and we're taken off our jobs for about four or five weeks, and we just go through a heck of a lot of organizations in the company. We spend two or three days and say, "Tell us about your system." And we look at that system, and we collectively say "2500 for this department."

THOMPSON

But don't you have an engineer saying "You're an accountant; you can't evaluate my unit"?

GALVIN

They used to. They don't say it anymore.

THOMPSON

Now a Fred Taylor type would say, "Well, you've taken that person off what she's good at (let's say purchasing), put her out in the field to evaluate for five weeks. You've moved her away from where she can make her best contribution to this organization, and that's going to hurt the organization."

GALVIN

Technically, that's correct. But we get a lot more back because the whole company lifts its quality level. All of us learn when a person goes out on the evaluation team. For example, while I'm evaluating that system of yours at 2500, I've discovered that something you're doing is really dumb, so I'm not going to do that in my department, and I'm going to tell everybody else not to do what you're doing. Or I might find that there is a brilliant thing that you are doing, and I am going to think, "Why don't we pass that around to all of us." And bingo. Now we amplify the excellence of your system through-out the rest of the corporation. We have two or three other mechanisms for accomplishing that sharing of good ideas, but the evaluation system mecha-nism is one of the good ones. So here's six of us out there looking with a microscope at these brilliant, creative ideas in your department. Now I'm going to tell you that you're a 4500 guy. Boy, is it fun to look at you! You get 4500. We say to everybody, "Why don't you do what they're doing."

Everybody's eyes light up and say, "That's a great idea."

THOMPSON

Part of your concern, I believe, is eliminating some of the functional silo thinking.

GALVIN

You people use terms like "functional silo" better than we do. We've learned that from academia....that there can be pockets of functional excellence in any institution, and that excellence should not be husbanded to the exclusive benefit of just that group. So the group may be very proud to say, "We're so good we'd like to keep some of our secrets to ourselves." There is a propensity to that in a human institution... to think my office is being run a little better than some of the other folks up and down the hall. But even more, I'd like to think that you'd listen to me, and maybe because of that your office would run as well as mine would. So my little silo can make all silos better. Here's a relevant anecdote, a very fundamental anecdote. Institutions have all kinds of hierarchical meetings. We have in our company a thing called *operating and policy committee meetings*. And that's a bunch of big shots who meet every month and try to see things from the top. It used to be that the principal time was devoted to the analysis of forecasts, budgets, expenditures, detailed operating results, and so on. When we were getting very enthusiastic about the subject of quality, we switched things around and said quality must be the first subject on every agenda. First thing in these meetings, there is a general report that gives everybody the picture of how the company is doing on quality—lots of statistics on some things, lots of phenomena, and some major anecdotes are recorded. Then *you,* as the head of a given business, are given the privilege of telling what's going on in quality in your business. And you can tell us anything you want about what's going on in quality. And you'll admit a couple of failures, if you have them, and tell what you're doing about them. But what happens is we can hardly get you off the platform, because you have so many success stories that you'd like to share with your peers. You are not trying to present yourself as superior, but you would like to be a contributor. So you go on and on and we listen because we're hearing things that every once in a while sparks something in us. So whereas the semiconductor sector of the company, which is a good silo of excellence, could be rather exclusive, it delights now in knowing that maybe it has helped me by telling me some things that I could use in my business. Then I'm up next week or next month, and I tell you about my things. We hardly have time in these meetings to talk about budgets, forecasts, and costs because we're getting so much out of the quality discussion that drives lower costs or improves profits, so we're getting back to first causes versus dealing with symptoms.

THOMPSON

And you can do this without people jealously guarding their ideas?

GALVIN

That's correct. The culture, mostly, is one of delighting in sharing with each other our success stories. People are obliged, occasionally, *not* to get up—cases where we may have a very unique proprietary right and we wouldn't like to have that leak out to a competitor someplace along the line. But those cases are few and far between. The basic processes are such that we love to share them among ourselves. And we trust each other that we will keep it within the company until we can present it to the customer.

THOMPSON

Which raises a good point. When you include suppliers and customers in the initial design stages of a new product, isn't there a risk that somebody would expose a competitive advantage?

GALVIN

Yes, there is. And, incidentally, it's a reciprocal risk. I presume we pick up rumors that a supplier is retooling, and that gives us a hint that someone is trying for a smaller radio or a higher powered product of some kind. However, in the natural communications of an industry there are all kinds of little tidbits that float around. But there is also honor and discipline to a substantial degree. When Ford Motor Company, for example, wishes us to do some very special work for them on a new engine control, we have a security system to prevent anyone who doesn't need to know what we're doing from knowing. These are manageable circumstances, and it is important for us to keep that close to our vest, so that when Ford announces a car that has a new engine control, they have their advantage for having put their research and our work together. We can also do that with some of our suppliers. We can go to one or two suppliers and say we want you to tool this for us. It's perfectly obvious that we're going to have a new and better product, and they know that they must not let anybody else know. And they're honorable. They don't tell us what they're doing for somebody else as well. And that happens very nicely in a lot of businesses. So there is honor, and there is discipline in the system—to a very substantial degree.

THOMPSON

It must be tough. If I'm working on one project, I may get excited about a particular design innovation or way of approaching a problem, and I'd love to apply it to perhaps another product.

GALVIN

Remember, we're here to serve a customer. So, to serve that particular customer best, we have to limit access to a piece of knowledge. Ironically, in an awful lot of things, we're an open book. For example, on the subject that started our dialogue, quality, people come to us—competitors, customers, suppliers, and academics—looking to learn something from us. We hold nothing back on quality systems. The thesis is very simple, the stronger America becomes with quality, the greater will be the platform from which all business can grow. If we have something to share on quality systems and processes and principles, we'll tell that to anybody.

THOMPSON

Are you going to run into what I call the Bobby Knight effect? As his methods get copied by his competitors, the other teams, it becomes much harder to compete, to make the dramatic changes that excite people—you reach a kind of ceiling. Are you going to experience that?

GALVIN

Well, if such a prospect happens to be a likelihood, it is so far away that my grandchildren will still be reaching for the horizon. But I doubt that we'll ever reach that stage. The reason is that it almost doesn't make any difference what our standards are today, and they're far off the mark across the entire industry. I don't know about academia, but it will take us a few generations just getting things up to a uniform high standard. For example, we were dealing with issues some years ago about quality on the level of percentage out of a hundred. So now we're measuring everything in terms of millions. And already we're experimenting with how we're going to measure things as parts per billion. That's a thousand times greater. And then there is so much renewal going on in nature. Man is taking nature and solving problems—learning how to code genes in the body, and doing something about it honorably and ethically. We're learning so much about materials. The atom was the big thing two decades ago, and then the proton, and then the electron and the sub-parts. As we learn those things, we discover that in the handling of them we have all new lessons to learn about how to deal with them in quality. But we haven't invented everything yet. I remember that my father, who was very progressive and a visionary, would occasionally lapse back just to muse for an hour and say, "Well, when we get this business established, or that building set, or this process going, we'll really have things pretty well set for a while." Well, the next morning he'd come to work and realize he shouldn't have said that, because somebody opened a whole new Pandora's box—invented the transistor, created the laser, discovered there was a thing called fiber optic cable, or now there's a microprocessor. The patent office is not closed. Whatever we were doing yesterday is so far away from what we will be doing tomorrow that we must apply these principles for the tomorrows. There's no danger of this rising to a ceiling, and there we're capped. There is no ceiling.

THOMPSON

You've mentioned the importance of a visionary in leading the organization. Is this a matter of one person who can put spark into the entire company?

GALVIN

No, it doesn't come just from one person. To begin with, it came from my father. And he enabled other people to contribute their pieces of the vision. He may have synthesized it, or kicked it down the pike a little faster than someone else for a while, and therefore he gets all the early credit. Some others of us have made an incremental kick to the ball, moving it down the field a little faster at times. Daniel Noble was, at one point, our senior visionary, along with my father, and he got us going on some things. He was the one who pointed out to my father the significance of the transistor. He enlightened my father on that subject, and my father was bright enough to see it and then support it. I helped a little bit on a piece of that puzzle; so did a few others. Once you decide you're going to do something with transistors, for example, then thousands of people get into the act. Remember I talked earlier about the importance of minority reports. How many of us are saying to ourselves, "If I were the president, this is what I would do?" People in Motorola are the same way. They have an opinion and we listen to those opinions and sometimes they're pretty good.

THOMPSON

But there has to be that visionary who creates the climate that makes people believe that their ideas can be shared and will be heard.

GALVIN

There has to be an atmosphere where a large number of people say, "I am welcome to contribute my part of the vision for the company." We have a development, now in the process of being promulgated, that is a dramatic example of that. Have you heard of Iridium? Iridium is a name that we give to a new satellite communication system. You and I will be able to carry portable radios not much bigger than cellular telephones anywhere in the world and talk up to the satellites, into the telephone systems and across the oceans. That's an immensely creative idea, and I'll say maybe up to twelve people were the catalysts in our government electronics division to extend their thinking and say, "If we have this technology and this kind of function we can perform, wouldn't it be possible to have a series of satellites flying in orbits 400 miles above earth, and couldn't we do this, etc." Sounds pretty simple now, but it was very creative about 10 years ago. They gradually combed this out on the back of an envelope. Then they went to their peers and their bosses and said, "Hey, we've got an idea." And nobody turned them down. Everybody said, "Hey, not bad. Keep working on it." Finally, this minority of people said they had [a good grasp of the] idea. The organization told them, "Why don't you go try it?" So now we are proposing a $4 billion investment in a system that we may or may not get off the ground. But it's because these folks knew that they were in an environment where people would listen to them that they committed the energy and time to think through their ideas. Now that's spectacular. If this gets going, it will be a $5 billion annual business for somebody. But there are all manner of creative experiences going on here every day. Where somebody says, "Why don't we make a pager that has different colors to it than black? How about pagers that are red, green, and blue?" It's not a very clever idea, but I want to go from the very sophisticated to the sublime. So we make lots of fancy colors of pagers. Not a big deal. Some guy buys a pager because he likes red. There's a question. Is anybody listening? In this company people listen. There's a culture of listeners.

THOMPSON

But how do you institutionalize this?

GALVIN

By role modeling.

THOMPSON

So that gets back to the visionary.

GALVIN

We shouldn't personalize these things, but it play-acts easier if you personalize. If I listen and the people I come in contact with say, "Hey, that is the way the people at the top act and therefore expect others to act," then others start to listen.

THOMPSON

You made quite a substantial commitment to training. How does that fit with developing the organizational culture?

GALVIN

It's very simple. It wasn't simple to come to the idea, but the idea is simplicity itself. Folks like myself, and there are hundreds of us in this company, are constantly being challenged with generic questions. What's a generic question? "How do you become more competitive?" So at a given point in time, circa the time we were getting interested in quality in an extraordinary way, that was a question that I would occasionally go home with. And finally, as I sorted out all kinds of creative ideas about it, I found myself pursuing the question, "How is an individual competitive?" And then I personalized it and said, "How can I be competitive with Mr. Kobayashi of NEC?" And out of that came a very simple prophecy. If Motorola is going to be competitive, each person must be competitive to his or her counterpart. At that point, everything falls in place because now I can say, like a coach preparing for the next game, "What do I need to know about my competitor? What does he know that I don't know?" And I could guess, or I could get some mentors to come in and say, "I think Mr. Kobayashi knows more about this than you do, Bob." So now I know that I've got to know that. So then I come to you and say, "Teach me something about that." So the essence of our training program is that we intend that every individual at Motorola will be as good or better than his best counterpart. The vice president will be as good as the vice president of Texas Instruments, etc. It's very personal. If it is very personal, it means that I have to be taught something. To facilitate that, you need a school.

THOMPSON

You made a conscious decision to create a school, Motorola University, on your property. Does that mean you felt Motorola could do it better than if you subcontracted the work to academics?

GALVIN

Yes. But we use everything. All manner of our people go to DePaul. I made a commencement address to an MBA class at Northwestern. Two of our people were in the class. So our people are going to Northern Illinois, Northwestern, DePaul, Arizona State, University of Texas, community colleges, etc. We'll put them anyplace that we need to put them. But our facilitating agent is Motorola University.

THOMPSON

From what you have said before, it would seem that somewhere along the line there are individualized learning programs established for your professional staff. Is that right?

GALVIN

Absolutely. We have professionals who are saying that we've got to teach everybody statistical quality control so that they could engage in problem solving and knowing what was going on, etc. So, we send thirty people to class so that individually they are as smart as their counterparts at Intel or NEC. For officers, we do something else; for middle managers, we do some other things. For Ph.D.'s in engineering, we teach them how to design experiments.

THOMPSON

Is your major educational emphasis on developing technical skills or on behavioral skills?

GALVIN

Everything. I would say the majority of the programs emphasize pragmatic education to help develop needed tools. They're vocational things. To me, the most important thing our people are going to have to learn is creativity. I find that people's expectation level on creativity is too low. Most people don't know that there are vocational processes that improve creativity. I trained myself from the book that I'll give you. There are twenty-five other books just as good, but this one works. So we're going to train tens of thousands of people at Motorola in the vocational skill of how to be creative. And people who think they're creative will become ten times as creative—not just 10 percent more. We always think in terms of multiple changes, and we always achieve them. Every time we go for a cost-cutting or time change, we try to cut it at least 50 percent—not 5 percent, not 1 percent. And it always happens. Continuous improvement is emphasized. So, on creativity, I consider it a trainable vocational skill and one which you people literally have avoided teaching since the beginning of time. Father Theodore Hesburgh, former President of Notre Dame, said to me, "Bob, you can't train people to be creative." I said, "How come? I learned it. How come I taught myself? Why aren't you more creative?" But you people have been avoiding it. I'm causing (through Motorola's efforts) some universities to teach creativity. If you'd teach it, then we wouldn't have to fill that gap. I am guessing that I wouldn't want to compete with our company in the year 2005 once our people are ten times more creative than our competitors.

THOMPSON

Doesn't that put a greater burden on the company, in that you're creating the expectation that someone will listen to their ideas?

GALVIN

Oh, absolutely. But look how we would grow. Motorola is a thousand times bigger than when I came in as a kid. Not because I'm here. We all made it happen. I helped a little.

Kenneth R. Thompson, is chairman of the management department at Depaul University and a member of the editorial board of *Organizational Dynamics*.

PART NINE

ORGANIZATIONAL LEARNING

READING 19
BUILDING LEARNING
ORGANIZATIONS

PETER SENGE, THE AUTHOR OF THIS ARTICLE, POPULARIZED THE IDEA OF LEARNING ORGANIZATIONS IN HIS 1990 BOOK *THE FIFTH DISCIPLINE*. HE SAYS, "I BELIEVE THAT THE QUALITY MOVEMENT AS WE HAVE KNOWN IT UP TO NOW IN THE U.S. IS IN FACT THE FIRST WAVE IN BUILDING LEARNING ORGANIZATIONS—ORGANIZATIONS THAT CONTINUALLY EXPAND THEIR ABILITY TO SHAPE THEIR FUTURE." OF COURSE, IF ORGANIZATIONS ARE TO FACILITATE CONTINUOUS IMPROVEMENT, THEY MUST PROMOTE ORGANIZATIONAL LEARNING; THE TWO ARE LINKED, AND THE LINK SHOULD BE RECOGNIZED AND STRENGTHENED THROUGH MANAGERIAL ACTION. IN A SIMILAR VEIN THE 1993 BOOK *A NEW AMERICAN TQM* HAS A CHAPTER ON "TQM AS A LEARNING SYSTEM" THAT NOTES "THE REAL QUALITY BEING TOTALLY MANAGED IS THE QUALITY OF HUMAN CAPABILITIES. THE REAL IMPROVEMENT ACTIVITY TAKING PLACE IS IMPROVING SKILLS AND THE ABILITY TO LEARN. THROUGH TQM EVERY SIZE OF UNIT, FROM INDIVIDUAL TO TEAM TO COMPANY TO REGION OR NATION, CAN LEARN HOW TO LEARN."

SENGE IS DIRECTOR OF THE SYSTEM THINKING AND ORGANIZATIONAL LEARNING PROGRAM AT THE MASSACHUSETTS INSTITUTE OF TECHNOLOGY'S SLOAN SCHOOL OF MANAGEMENT. HE ALSO CO-FOUNDED THE MANAGEMENT CONSULTING FIRM, INNOVATION ASSOCIATES AND WAS RECOGNIZED AS ONE OF "MANAGEMENT'S NEW GURUS" IN THE AUGUST 31, 1992 ISSUE OF *BUSINESS WEEK*. HIS CLIENTS HAVE INCLUDED FEDERAL EXPRESS, FORD, AND HANOVER INSURANCE CO.

READING 19
BUILDING LEARNING
ORGANIZATIONS

BY PETER SENGE

Without a unifying conceptual framework, the quality movement in the U.S. risks being fragmented into isolated initiatives and slogans. *The voice of the customer, fix the process not the people, competitive benchmarking, continuous improvement, policy deployment, leadership*—the more we hear, the less we understand.

"Trying to put together the alphabet soup coming out of Japan of SPC, JIT, QIP, QFD, and so on can be hopelessly confusing without a unifying theme," says Analog Devices CEO Ray Stata.

It is not surprising that, for many, it doesn't add up to much more than management's latest *flavor of the month* that must be endured until the next fad comes along.

Even those firms where there has been significant commitment to quality management for several years are encountering slowing rates of improvement. "We've picked all the low hanging fruit," as one Detroit executive put it recently. "Now, the difficult changes are what's left."

The "difficult changes" are unlikely without a coherent picture of where we are trying to take our organizations through the quality management process.

OUR GLOBAL COMPETITORS

Equally troubling, the best of our international competitors are not fragmenting, they are building—steadily advancing an approach to improving

CREDIT: Peter Senge, "Building Learning Organizations," *Journal for Quality and Participation,* (March, 1992). Reprinted with permission of the Association for Quality and Participation from the March, 1992 issue of the *Journal for Quality and Participation.*

quality, productivity, and profitability that differs fundamentally from the traditional authoritarian, mechanical management model.

"Total quality [TQ] is not a closed-ended methodology; its an open-ended methodology," says Shoji Shiba, of Japan's Tsukuba University. "TQ continues to develop according to the needs of society."

The tools American corporations are racing to master today, the frontier of the quality movement in Japan in the 1960s, are no longer the frontier. The "thought revolution in management," as quality pioneer Ishikawa called it, is still evolving.

LEARNING ORGANIZATIONS

I believe that the quality movement as we have known it up to now in the U.S. is in fact the first wave in building *learning organizations*—organizations that continually expand their ability to shape their future.

The roots of the quality movement lie in assumptions about people, organizations, and management that have one unifying theme: to make continual learning a way of organizational life, especially improving the performance of the organization as a total system. This can only be achieved by breaking with the traditional authoritarian, command and control hierarchy where the top thinks and the local acts, to merge thinking and acting at all levels.

This represents a profound re-orientation in the concerns of management—a shift from a predominant concern with controlling to a predominant concern with learning. Failure to come to grips with this shift plagues the efforts of many U.S. firms eager to jump on the quality bandwagon.

LEARNING ORGANIZATIONS IN JAPAN

Our Japanese competitors have no trouble with this shift. "Japan's greatest long-term comparative advantage is not its management system, Japan Inc., or quality," says C. Jackson Grayson Jr., of the American Productivity and Quality Center in Houston. "It's the Japanese commitment to learning."

More specifically, as management practices in Japan have evolved over the past 40 years, there has been a steady spread of the commitment to learning—starting with statistical process control (SPC) for small groups of quality experts, to teaching quality improvement tools to frontline workers throughout the organization, to developing and disseminating tools for managerial learning.

LEARNING WAVES

The evolution of learning organizations can be best understood as a series of waves. What most managers think of as quality management focuses on improving tangible work processes. This is the first wave.

THE FIRST WAVE OF QUALITY

In the first wave, the primary focus of change was frontline workers. Management's job was to:

- Champion continual improvement
- Remove impediments (like quality control experts and unnecessary bureaucracy) that disempowered local personnel.
- Support new practices like quality training and competitive benchmarking that drive process improvement.

THE SECOND WAVE OF QUALITY

In the second wave, the focus shifts from improving work processes to improving how we work—fostering ways of thinking and interacting conducive to continual learning about the dynamic, complex, conflicting issues that determine system wide performance. In the second wave, the primary focus of change is the managers themselves.

THE THIRD WAVE OF QUALITY

These two ways will, I believe, gradually merge into a third, in which learning becomes *institutionalized* as an inescapable way of life for managers and workers alike (if we even bother maintaining that distinction).

WE ARE STILL IN THE FIRST WAVE

American industry is, with a few exceptions, primarily operating in the first wave. "Despite all our improvements, the basic behavior of our managers, especially our senior managers, hasn't really changed much," laments the head of a major corporation's quality office.

JAPAN AND THE SECOND WAVE

By contrast, the second wave is well under way in Japan, driven by their *seven new tools for management,* as distinct from their traditional *seven quality tools* that drove the first wave.

AMERICA'S CHALLENGE

The challenge today, as American companies endeavor to master the basic tools and philosophy of quality management, is not to be caught shortsighted with mechanical "quality programs."

If we fail to grasp the deeper messages of the quality movement, we will one day awaken to discover ourselves chasing a receding target.

THE ROOTS OF THE QUALITY MOVEMENT

A close look at the roots of the quality movement shows that it has always been about learning.

"The prevailing system of management has destroyed our people," says Dr. Deming. "People are born with intrinsic motivation, self-esteem, dignity, curiosity to learn, joy in learning."

INTRINSIC VERSUS EXTRINSIC MOTIVATION

Intrinsic motivation lies at the heart of Deming's management philosophy. By contrast, extrinsic motivation is the bread and butter of Western management.

The holiest of holy for the American manager, "People do what they are rewarded for," is actually antithetical to the spirit of quality management. This doesn't imply that rewards are irrelevant. Rather, it implies that no set of rewards, neither carrots nor sticks, can ever substitute for intrinsic motivation to learn. A corporate commitment to quality that is not based on intrinsic motivation is a house built on sand.

MOTIVATE THEM OR LOOSE THEIR OWN MOTIVATION?

Consider, for example the goal of continuous improvement, which remains an elusive target for most American corporations.

MOTIVATE THEM

From an extrinsic perspective, the only way to get continuous improvement is to find ways to continually motivate people to improve, because people only modify their behavior when there is some external motivation to do so. Otherwise, they will just sit there—or worse, slide backwards. This leads to what workers perceive as management continually raising the bar to manipulate more effort from them.

LOOSE THEIR MOTIVATION WITH INFORMATION AND APPROPRIATE TOOLS

However, from an intrinsic perspective, there is nothing mysterious at all about continuous improvement. If left to their own devices, people will naturally look for ways to do things better. What they need is adequate information and appropriate tools.

From the intrinsic perspective, people's innate curiosity and desire to experiment, if unleashed, creates an engine for improvement that can never be matched by external rewards.

LEARNING AND INTRINSIC MOTIVATION TO LEARN HAVE ALWAYS BEEN THE ROOTS OF QUALITY

A management system based on intrinsic motivation to learn is as befuddling to Western economists as it is to Western managers.

Princeton economist Alan Blinder recently cited an impressive list of Japanese "violations" of economic orthodoxy—tolerated monopolies and cartels, single suppliers, salary scales that do not differentiate adequately between ranks, keeping promising young managers waiting too long for promotion and "almost nothing gets you fired."

"We did the opposite of what American economists said." Blinder quotes a top Ministry of International Trade & Industry (MITI) official. "We violated all the normal rules." But the puzzle of how a nation that does so many things *wrong* can get so many things right dissolves when we realize that Western economic theories, from Adam Smith on, are based solely on extrinsic motivation.

THE WAY WE THOUGHT IT WAS

Adam Smith's *homo economicus* is presumed to maximize his income, not his learning. The following are some maxims of U.S. homo economicus:

- If there is no opportunity for significant salary increase by climbing the corporate ladder, he will have little motivation to do his best or to improve.
- If there is no fear of dismissal, there will be nothing to drive him to be productive.
- If his company, made up of lots of greedy little buggers just like him, does not have to compete against other companies, they will have no motivation to continually lower costs of production, nor to improve their products.

In short, no competition, no innovation. But, if the drive to innovate comes from within, all this changes—especially if a management system can nurture and harness this drive.

SHEWHART'S AND DEWEY'S ROOTS TO QUALITY

But we don't have to look just to subtleties like intrinsic motivation to see that the quality movement has always been about learning.

PDCA

The famous PDCA cycle is evidence enough. No one ever gets far into any introduction to total quality management without learning about

Plan–Do–Check–Act, the never-ending cycle of experimentation that structures all quality improvement efforts.

Deming called it the *Shewhart cycle* when he introduced it to the Japanese in 1950, in honor of his mentor Walter Shewhart of Bell Labs. Eventually the Japanese called it the *Deming cycle.*

OF JOHN DEWEY, LEARNING AND QUALITY

But the roots of the PDCA cycle go back further than Deming or Shewhart, at least as far as the educator, John Dewey.

Dewey posited that all learning involves a cycle between four basic stages:

- Discover: the discovery of new insights.
- Invent: creating new options.
- Produce: producing new actions.
- Observe: seeing the consequences of those actions, which leads to new discoveries, continuing the cycle.

This is how we learned to walk, talk, to ride a bicycle, to act skillfully wherever we have achieved some proficiency. The young child first must discover that they want to walk, invent ways of getting started, act, and observe the consequences of her or his action.

Interrupting the cycle interrupts learning. If the toddler is supported so they do not fall, they also do not learn.

LEARNING IS MOVING FROM THOUGHT TO ACTION

In effect, Dewey canonized the simple fact that all real learning occurs over time, as we move between the world of thought and the world of action. Learning is never simply an intellectual exercise. Nor is it a matter of changing behavior. It is an interactive process linking the two, in a spiral of continually expanding our capabilities.

It is not altogether irrelevant that this is a far cry from the image of learning inculcated in the schoolroom, where most of us conclude that learning is synonymous with *taking in information* and being able to produce the *right answer* on cue—little wonder that for most adults, the word *learning* does not quicken the pulse.

The PDCA cycle takes Dewey's theory of learning one step further, saying, in effect, that in an organization it is often wise to distinguish *small actions* from wide-spread adoption of new practices.

The *do* stage then becomes pilot tests from which new data can be collected and analyzed *(checked)*. Gradually, a series of such pilots results in more general learnings and the act stage moves to broader and broader application of new practices.

PDCA AMERICAN STYLE

While simple in concept, the PDCA cycle is often practiced quite differently in the U.S. and in Japan.

Impatient for quick results, American managers often jump from plan to act.

THE RUSH TO ACT UNDERMINES EFFORT

We conceive new programs and then begin rolling them out throughout the organization. In fact, that's exactly what many U.S. firms are doing with their total quality programs.

While rolling out new programs makes us feel good about doing something (*acting*) to improve things in our business, in fact we are actually undermining possibilities for learning. Who can learn from an experiment involving thousands of people that is only run one time?

PDCA JAPANESE STYLE

By contrast the Japanese are masters of organizational experimentation. They meticulously design and study pilot tests, often with many corporations participating cooperatively.

Through repeated cycles, new knowledge gradually accumulates. By the time for organization-wide changes, people adopt new practices more rapidly because so many more have been involved in the learning.

For Americans, this whole process often seems unnecessarily time consuming and costly. As one manager pointed out to me recently, the statement "I'm running an experiment" in most American companies is a code word for "Don't hold me accountable for the results." Consequently, while we may go through the motions of quality improvement, we often get the facade without the substance. At best, we get limited bursts of learning.

IMPROVING HOW WE WORK

THE FIRST WAVE

Improving tangible work processes (from the production line to order entry, to responding to customer inquiries or coordinating the typing queue) was the predominant theme of the first wave in building learning organizations.

The initial tools were derived primarily from statistics, including SPC, and related methods for diagraming, analyzing, and redesigning work processes to reduce variability and enable systematic improvement.

As the first wave has unfolded, the focus has broadened to include more complex processes like product development. By and large, the customer was outside the system of production and the system was designed to meet customer needs.

FIRST WAVE STRENGTH

The strength of the first wave lay in achieving measurable improvements in cost, quality, and customer satisfaction through rigorous and reproducible processes of improvement.

FIRST WAVE LIMITATION

The limitation lay in the relatively passive role of management and the limited impact on the larger systems whereby processes interact—for example, how sales, order entry, manufacturing and customer satisfaction interact.

THE SECOND WAVE UNFOLDS

The initial profile of the second wave could be seen in Japan as early as the 1960s when leading firms began to undertake mass deployment of quality tools. Previously, only small groups of quality control experts learned how to analyze work processes, reduce variation, and improve quality and cost.

JAPANESE QUALITY CIRCLES AND LEARNING

"Beginning with quality circles," says Massachusetts Institute of Technology's Alan Graham. "that changed. Everyone began to participate in quality improvement." This was the time when *kaizen* (organization-wide commitment to continuous improvement) was born. This also was the time when Japanese organizations began extensive training in team learning skills, to develop the norms and capabilities needed if quality circles were to be effective.

U.S. QUALITY CIRCLES AND A LACK OF EMPHASIS ON LEARNING

Interestingly, when U.S. firms began to organize production workers in quality circles, 10 to 15 years later, the emphasis was on forming teams, not on developing team learning skills. Consequently, "The skills and practices, both among workers and managers, necessary for QC circles to be effective," according to Graham, "were not present in the introduction of QC circles in the US. This has been typical of the general underemphasis here on skills and practices, as opposed to official programs and management goals."

The result was that many initial efforts at quality control circles in the U.S. failed to generate lasting commitment or significant improvement. "Mid-level managers," says USC's Ed Lawler. "saw QC circles as a threat to their authority, and workers saw them as a gimmick to elicit increased effort and undermine union influence."

THE SECOND WAVE ARRIVES

In Japan, the second wave arrived in full force with the introduction of the *seven new tools for management* in 1979

THE SEVEN NEW TOOLS

These tools, the work of a committee of the Society for QC Technique Development that operated from 1972 to 1979, focus specifically on how managers think and interact. They particularly emphasize developing better communication and common understandings of complex issues, and relating that understanding to operational planning.

"There are a lot of methodologies for measuring, analyzing, and testing quantitative data." says the leader of the group that developed the new tools. Professor Shiba. "but the area of qualitative methodologies, how to create hypotheses, is very weak. Professor Jiro Kawakita, a Japanese anthropologist, developed methods for analyzing non-numerical data and making sense of that data."

For example, the KJ method or affinity diagram, as taught by Professor Shiba and other experts on the *seven management tools,* help teams gather large amounts of non-quantitative data and organize it into groupings based on natural relationships or affinities. Other tools help to clarify interrelationships, establish priorities. and think through and plan the complex tasks required for accomplishing an agreed upon goal.

A NEW PERSPECTIVE OF THE CUSTOMER

Along with these new tools for thinking and interacting, a new orientation toward the customer has gradually emerged. The new perspective moved from *satisfying the customer's expressed requirements to meeting the latent needs of the customer.*

THE MIATA AS A SECOND WAVE EXAMPLE

As one Detroit executive put it, "you could never produce the Mazda Miata from market research. You have to understand what the customer would value if he experienced it." In the second wave, the customer becomes part of the system. There's an interplay between what the firm seeks to produce and what the customer desires.

THE SECOND WAVE IN AMERICA

Today, a small number of American companies are starting to experiment with the seven new management tools.

They are discovering a whole new territory for increasing organizational capabilities—how we think and interact around complex, potentially conflicting issues. This is the real message of the second wave—leverage ultimately lies in improving us, not just improving our work processes.

ENGELBART'S A, B AND C WORK

"There are three levels of work in organizations," says computer pioneer and inventor of the *mouse* Douglas Engelbart, who has spent the better part of 20 years studying the nature of collaborative work.

The most obvious level, *A work*, involves the development, production, and sale of a firm's products and services. Most of a company's people and resources are focused at this level.

Effective *A work* would be impossible, however, without the next level, *B work*, which involves designing the systems and processes that enable a company to develop, produce, and sell its products and services.

But, the subtlest and potentially most influential level is *C work*, improving how we think and interact. Ultimately. the quality of *C work* determines the quality of systems and processes we design and the products and services we provide.

THE FIRST WAVE AND B WORK

The major contribution of quality management in the first wave was to focus time and energy systematically on Engelbart's *B work*, especially on improving processes, and to provide tools for the task.

THE SECOND WAVE AND C WORK

The major contribution of the second wave will be to systematically focus on Engelbart's *C work*. This, too, will require appropriate tools. But, before such tools can be developed, we must understand the *core competencies of learning organizations*, those distinctive capabilities in thinking and interacting which will enable us to "continually improve the total behavior of organizations."

CORE COMPETENCIES FOR LEARNING ORGANIZATIONS

The seven new tools point in the right direction. But, our work suggests that they are only a start to developing an organization's capabilities in:

> *Building shared vision*—There is no substitution for organizational resolve, conviction, commitment, and clarity of intent. They create the need for learning and the collective will to learn. Without shared visions, significant learning occurs only when there are crises, and the learning ends when the crises end.

Personal mastery—Shared vision comes from personal visions. Collective commitment to learning comes from individual commitment to learning. An organization that is continually learning how to create its future must be made up of individuals who are continually learning how to create more of what truly matters to them in their own lives.

Working with mental models—Organizations become frozen in inaccurate and disempowering views of reality because we lack the capability to *see our assumptions,* and to continually challenge and improve those assumptions. This requires fostering managerial skills in *balancing inquiry and advocacy* in organizations that have been traditionally dominated by advocacy.

Team learning—Ultimately, the learning that matters is the learning of *groups of people who need one another to act* (the real meaning of team). The only problem is that we've lost the ability to talk with one another. Most of the time we are limited to *discussion,* which comes from the same roots as *percussion* and *concussion* and literally means *to heave one's views at the other.* What is needed also is dialogue, which comes from the Greek *dialogos* and literally means when a group of people talk with one another such that the meaning (logos) moves through (dial) them.

Systems thinking—it's not just how we learn, but what we learn. The most important learning in contemporary organizations concerns gaining shared insight into complexity and how we can shape change. But, since early in life we've been taught to break apart problems.

The resulting fragmentation has left us unable to see the consequences of our own actions, creating an illusion that we are victims of forces outside our control and that the only type of learning that is possible is learning to react more quickly. Systems thinking is about understanding wholes, not parts, and learning how our actions shape our reality.

CREATING AN ORGANIZATIONAL SYMPHONY

The intrinsic limitations to each of these capabilities is only overcome if they are developed in concert:

- Empowering people (an organization-wide commitment to personal mastery) empowers the organization, but only if individuals are deeply aligned around a common sense of purpose and shared vision.
- Shared vision will energize and sustain an organization through thick and thin, but only if people think systemically. Once people are able to

see how their actions shape their reality, they begin to understand how alternative actions could create a different reality.

- Individual skills in reflection and inquiry mean little if they cannot be practiced when groups of people confront controversial issues.
- Systems thinking will become the province of a small set of *systems experts* unless it is tied to an organization wide commitment to improving mental models, and even then nothing much will change without shared visions.
- A commitment to seeing the larger system only matters when there is a commitment to the long-term. In the short run, everyone can just fix their piece. Only with a long term view can an organization see that optimizing the parts, one at a time, can lead to sub-optimizing the whole.

A Short Study on Learning As a Way of Organizational life

In 1970, Royal/Dutch Shell was arguably the weakest of the *big seven* oil companies. Today, it is one of the strongest. A key to Shell's ascent has been reconceiving *planning as learning,* a conscious process of bringing operating managers' mental models to the surface and challenging those models.

Shell's Scenario Planning

This conceptual shift has been operationalized by tools like scenario planning. Through its use of scenarios, Shell's planners help managers continually think through how they would manage under multiple possible futures. Today, it is hard for a Shell manager to do business planning without engaging in a conscious learning process.

Shell has become perhaps the first global corporation to realize the leverage of institutionalizing learning as the most effective approach to strategy in a turbulent world. "The corporate one-track mind." says former planning chief Arie deGeus, "is the single primary reason why so many once successful corporations fail to survive beyond their infancy."

From a Foreboding View to a New Form of Planning

Shell's innovations in institutional learning were driven by necessity. As early as 1971, Shell's planners became convinced that major shocks in supply and price were becoming a possibility in world oil markets. But, they were unable to convince managers conditioned by the stability of world markets in the 50s and 60s.

This led the planners to develop scenario planning *exercises,* wherein managers thought how they would manage if there were shift from a buyer's market to seller's market, where sudden changes in price would be a part of life, regardless of whether or not they expected such a change.

PREPARED FOR CHANGE IN THE 70S

When OPEC did become a reality and the first oil shocks hit in the winter of 1973 and 1974. Shell responded differently than any other big oil company. It increased local operating company control rather than increasing corporate control. It accelerated development of reserves, especially in its North Sea fields. While the other major oil companies saw a sudden unexpected crisis and acted accordingly, Shell's managers perceived a sea change in the basic nature of the business, and acted differently.

SHELL'S SCENARIO PLANNING AND THE 80S

The discipline of thinking in terms of alternative futures served Shell equally well in the 80s. Shell planners created a $15 a barrel oil scenario in 1983, at a time when prices averaged around $30. They considered two alternative futures:

> *Alternative future one:* As managers considered how they would manage in a depressed price world, they quickly concluded that many of their present production processes would have to be shut down because they were too costly.
>
> *Alternative future two:* A few engineers suggested that radical redesign of their oil platforms using new miniaturization technologies could make them operable at prices as low as $11 per barrel.

As they considered the plan, it soon became obvious that such a redesign was in fact more desirable under any possible scenario!

Their production people went ahead with the new design concepts. And when prices did fall, hitting an unbelievable $8 per barrel in 1984, Shell was, once again, one step ahead of its competitors.

ORGANIZATIONAL LEARNING ALTERNATIVES

Institutionalizing learning as part of the planning process is one of many possible approaches. It's clear that many Japanese companies have institutionalized learning around quality improvement teams and related innovations.

There is no shortage of ways by which learning may become an inescapable aspect of organizational life, once the nature of the commitment to learning is understood, and once appropriate tools are available.

INSTITUTIONALIZED EXPERIMENTATION

"Institutionalizing experimentation can make an enormous difference," says Harvard's Dave Garvin. "For example. Allegheny Ludlum, one of the most profitable American steel companies, treats its entire production process as a laboratory for experimenting with new processes and technologies. Production managers can designate experiments they want to conduct and an entirely different set of measures and standards are used to evaluate their efforts."

MANAGERIAL MICROWORLDS

Another means to institutionalizing learning, the focus of our research at MIT, involves developing *managerial microworlds,* practice fields for management teams.

A FINANCIAL SERVICES MICROWORLD

For example, in a microworld designed for a leading property and liability insurance company, managers discover how many of their most trusted practices, when they interact in the larger systems of which they are a part, actually contribute to runaway settlement and litigation costs.

Using a computerized *management flight simulator,* they are then able to freely experiment, in ways that would be difficult in real insurance offices, with a wide range of alternative personnel, workflow and quality management practices to find where there may be leverage in reversing the growing insurance crisis.

Eventually, we envision such microworlds being as common place in organizations as meeting rooms. There will be places where we gather to think through complex issues and learn through experimentation when trial and error learning is impossible in the real system.

ACTIVITY-BASED COST ACCOUNTING

Another potential breakthrough lies in changing managerial accounting practices to reinforce learning rather than controlling.

"Managers and manufacturing engineers," says Harvard's Robert Kaplan "frequently comment that considerable operating improvements they achieve go unrecognized in their financial results."

If the emphasis is on continuous, system wide improvement, how can we have accounting practices based on historically determined standards? "Traditional cost accounting measures fail when they focus on small, local (but not system wide) measures of efficiency and productivity."

WHY BECOMING A LEARNING ORGANIZATION MATTERS

Seeing quality management as part of a deeper and even more far reaching shift leads to several realizations into why the unfolding changes in American management practices may not produce an enduring transformation.

First Wave Quality Is Still Not Well Understood in the U.S.

Despite enormous attention, public commitment by prominent corporations, and even a national award, there is a distinct possibility that American management still does not understand what the quality movement is really all about.

Specifically, we lack understanding of what is required for even first wave quality management practices to take root, and why they often fail to take root in American firms.

Confusion over the Connections between Learning, Teams, Standards, Motivations and Innovation

The total quality management task force at one of America's most successful high-tech manufacturing firms recently came unglued around a question of standards.

The external consultant brought in to help develop and implement the TQM strategy argued that standards and standardization were vital to gain better control of the organization's production processes, so that they could be improved. But, to some of the firm's managers, standardization meant rigidity, and a loss of freedom and respect for workers creativity and individuality.

"Everything becomes vanilla," argued one manager. "We will kill the spark of individual creativity that has made this company what it is."

"If you're not operating in a learning orientation," observed MIT's Dan Kim, "you hear *standardization* differently than if you are. People internalize the need to improve as, *I must be deficient*. Naturally, they then resist what they perceive as an effort to make their deficiencies public and *fix them*."

Confusion over the Meaning of Continuous and Control

The same happens with continuous improvement. Within a learning culture, continuous improvement is a natural by-product of people's commitment and empowerment. Within a controlling culture it is an admission of deficiency. "Why must I improve, unless I'm not good enough now?"

From such a view point, continuous improvement is about becoming less deficient. It is not about learning. This is why it is so deeply resisted by workers in many U.S. companies.

In response to this resistance, managers with good intentions resort to exhortation and to driving *highly mechanized* quality programs through their organizations. This creates a vicious cycle of increasing exhortation and increasing resistance. What is needed is understanding and changing the source of the resistance, which stems from bringing tools for learning into a managerial system based on controlling.

WE STILL BELIEVE CONTROLLING PEOPLE IS MORE IMPORTANT THAN CREATING A LEARNING ENVIRONMENT

The second realization is that there is nothing in the American bag of quality tools today that will cause the shift to a learning orientation. And causing such a shift is exactly what is needed in most American corporations. Without a shift of mind from controlling to learning, or as Kim puts it, from "protect and defend" to "create and learn," we "get the tools for quality management without the substance."

LEARNING CANNOT BE SWITCHED ON

Creating such a shift is an organic process, not a mechanical one. It demands penetrating to deep levels of the corporate psyche and unearthing and examining deep fears.

WHAT WILL IT TAKE TO CHANGE?

To put it bluntly, the shift will not occur if it is not within us. It cannot be faked. It cannot be achieved by public declarations. If at some basic level, we do not genuinely value and truly desire to live life as learners, it will not happen.

My experience is that it can only be caused by small groups of thoughtful leaders who truly desire to build an organization where people are committed to a larger purpose and to thinking for themselves.

Such thoughtful groups then must be willing to become models of continually learning, with all the vulnerability and uncertainty that implies. They become lead users of new learning tools and approaches.

PUBLIC AND ORGANIZATIONAL LEARNING/EDUCATION ARE LINKED

The last, and potentially most important. realization is that the transformation in corporate and public education may be linked.

"Humans are the learning organism *par excellence*" according to anthropologist Edward T. Hall. "The drive to learn is as strong as the sexual drive— it begins earlier and lasts longer."

IF THE DRIVE TO LEARN IS SO STRONG, WHY IS IT SO WEAK IN OUR CORPORATIONS?

What happened to our "intrinsic joy in learning," as Dr. Deming puts it. The answer according to Deming, Hall, and many educators lies, surprisingly, as much in the classroom as on the factory floor. "The forces of destruction begin with toddlers," says Deming, "...a prize for the best Halloween costume, grades in school, gold stars—and on up through the university."

PERFORMING VERSUS LEARNING

The young child in school quickly learns that the name of the game is not learning, it is performing. Mistakes are punished, correct answers rewarded. If you don't have the right answer, keep your mouth shut.

If we had operated under that system as two-year olds, none of us would have ever learned to walk. Is it any wonder the manager or worker shows little intrinsic motivation to *learn*—that is, to experiment and discover new insights from *mistakes,* outcomes that don't turn out according to plan.

If the conditioning toward performing for others rather than learning is so deeply established in schools, it may not be possible to reverse it on the job. If knowledge is always something somebody else has and I don't, then learning becomes embedded in deep instincts of self-protection not free experimentation.

If the identification of *boss* with *teacher,* the authority figure who has the answers and is the arbiter of our performance is so firmly anchored, we may never be able to roll up our sleeves and all become learners together.

Today, there is no lack of corporate concern for the erosion in our public education. But, there is a lack of vision as to what is truly needed. It is not enough to go back to the 3 R's. We must revolutionize the school experience so that it nurtures and deepens our love of learning, develops new skills of integrative or systemic thinking, and helps us learn how to learn, especially together.

FINAL THOUGHTS

I recently asked Dr. Deming if he thougnt it was possible to fully implement his philosophy of management without radical reform in our schools. as well as in our corporations. "No" was his answer.

However, if we come to a deeper understanding of the linkage between school and work in the 21st century, we may be able to generate a wholly new vision and commitment to the vital task of rethinking both. This may be the real promise of the *learning organization.*

READING 20
MANAGING THE DREAM:
THE LEARNING ORGANIZATION

IN HIS BOOK *THE AGE OF UNREASON,* CHARLES HANDY NOTES, "THE LEARNING ORGANIZATION CAN MEAN TWO THINGS, IT CAN MEAN AN ORGANIZATION WHICH LEARNS AND/OR AN ORGANIZATION WHICH ENCOURAGES LEARNING IN ITS PEOPLE. IT SHOULD MEAN BOTH." HANDY'S BOOK, AS WELL AS THIS ARTICLE, MAKES A POINT OF EQUATING CHANGING WITH LEARNING. HERE HE SAYS THE LEARNING ORGANIZATION IS RENEWING, REINVENTING, REINVIGORATING ITSELF. "RATHER THAN CHANT CHANGE, IT IS MORE ACCURATE TO SAY THAT WE—ALL INDIVIDUALS AND ORGANIZATIONS—MUST ACQUIRE THE LEARNING HABIT...."

HANDY'S WHEEL OF LEARNING (NOT UNRELATED TO THE SHEWHART/DEMING PDCA CYCLE) IS MORE EASILY TURNED WHEN LUBRICATED BY SUBSIDIARITY AND INCIDENTAL LEARNING. THE FORMER MEANS "ENCOURAGING INDIVIDUALS AND GROUPS TO HAVE AS MUCH POWER AS THEY ARE COMPETENT TO HANDLE.... POWER IS GIVEN TO THOSE CLOSEST TO THE ACTION." (RECALL EMPOWERMENT.) INCIDENTAL LEARNING MEANS LEARNING FROM THE INCIDENTS OR CASES THAT ARE EXPERIENCED BY THE INDIVIDUAL OR ORGANIZATION. FOR SUCH EXPERIENCES TO BE SHARED ACROSS THE ORGANIZATION, THERE MUST EXIST FORGIVENESS, TRUST, A SPIRIT OF EXPERIMENTATION, AND AN ASSUMPTION OF COMPETENCE. HANDY SAYS, "DISAPPOINTMENT AND MISTAKES ARE PART OF CHANGE AND ESSENTIAL TO LEARNING.... [A] LEARNING ORGANIZATION WILL TRY TO TURN THOSE MISTAKES INTO LEARNING OPPORTUNITIES, NOT BY USING THEM AS STICKS TO BEAT WITH BUT AS CASE STUDIES FOR DISCUSSION." AS A QUALITY AXIOM HAS IT, "FIX THE PROCESS, NOT THE BLAME."

READING 20
MANAGING THE DREAM:
THE LEARNING ORGANIZATION

BY CHARLES HANDY

In an uncertain world, where all we know for sure is that nothing is sure, we are going to need organizations that are continually renewing themselves, reinventing themselves, reinvigorating themselves. These are the learning organizations, the ones with the learning habit.

Just as the world has changed, so too has the process of learning. When the future was an extension of the present, it was reasonable to assume that what worked today would also work next year. That assumption must now be tossed out. During times of discontinuous change, it can almost be guaranteed that what used to work well in the past will not work at all next time around. The old approaches to change are simply too incremental. More than that, they are too slow.

Today we are hearing so much about change that the word is becoming a cliché. Rather than chant change, it is more accurate to say that we all—individuals and organizations—must acquire the learning habit, the new learning habit. It is a habit that changes many of the old assumptions about management. The learning organization is a different sort of place. But it is an exciting one.

CHARACTERISTICS OF THE LEARNING ORGANIZATION

The learning organization is built upon an *assumption of competence* that is supported by four other qualities or characteristics: *curiosity, forgiveness, trust* and *togetherness*. The assumption of competence means that each

CREDIT: Charles Handy, "Managing the Dream: Learning Organization," reprinted from the Spring, 1993 issue of *Benchmark Magazine*, a publication of the Xerox Corporation.

individual can be expected to perform to the limit of his or her competence, with the minimum of supervision.

For too long, organizations have operated on an assumption of incompetence. The characteristics of this assumption are controls and directives, rules and procedures, layers of management and pyramids of power—all very costly. By contrast, the assumption of competence promotes flat organizations, with fewer checkers checking checkers. Flat organizations are far more responsive, efficient and cost-effective. They put a high premium on early training, on acculturation in their ways and values and on some form of vetting or qualification before an individual is allowed to operate. In these organizations the learning habit starts early.

Competence alone, despite all the prior learning it implies, is not enough to foster the learning habit. It must be accompanied by curiosity. Watch a small child learning. The questions are endless, the curiosity insatiable. But curiosity does not end with the questions. Questions beg answers, and the truly curious go in search of the right answers. This often requires experimentation. This process is encouraged in the learning organization, provided there is an assumption of competence and a license to experiment within the boundaries of a person's authority.

Because experiments can fail, forgiveness is essential. Instead of failures, unsuccessful experiments must be viewed as part of the learning process, as lessons learned. One can also learn from successful experiments. That form of learning needs not to be forgiven but to be celebrated.

None of these things—competence, curiosity, forgiveness or celebration—can foster a learning organization if there is no trust. While people may be highly competent, you will not allow them to be competent unless you trust them. Of course, it is difficult to trust someone you don't know or have never seen in action. A person you know only by name from a memo is not a person to take a risk with. For the learning organization, the implications of this simple human fact are enormous. How many people can one person know well enough to trust them? On the answer to that question hangs the whole design and structure of the corporation.

One solution is togetherness. Few, if any, of the problems businesses face nowadays can be handled by one person acting alone. That is fortunate in a way, because curiosity, experimentation and forgiveness need to be shared. Lonely learners are often slow and poor learners, whereas people who collaborate learn from each other and create synergy.

Today we are seeing an increasing number of organizations made up of shifting "clusters," or teams, that share a common purpose. The need for togetherness, both to get things done and to encourage the kind of exploration that is essential to any growing organization, creates the conditions for trust. Trust, in turn, improves togetherness.

Despite the presence of trust and togetherness, the learning organization is not a comfortable place for its leaders. It is an upside-down sort of place, with much of the power residing at the organization's edge. In this culture, imposed authority no longer works. Instead, authority must be earned from those over whom it is exercised. This organization is held together by shared beliefs and values, by people who are committed to each other and to common goals—a rather tenuous method of control.

Such an upside-down way of running an organization requires a powerful theory to justify it: in this case, a theory of learning. Real learning is not what many of us grew up thinking it was. It is not simply memorizing facts, learning drills or soaking up traditional wisdom.

THE WHEEL OF LEARNING

This process can best be described as a wheel—a wheel of learning. The wheel has four quadrants that, ideally, rotate in sequence as the wheel moves. The first quadrant consists of the *questions,* which may be triggered by problems or needs that require solutions. The questions prompt a search for possible answers or *ideas,* which must pass rigorous *tests* to see if they work. The results are then subjected to *reflection,* until we are certain we have identified the best solution. Only when the entire process is complete can we truly say that we have learned something. There are no shortcuts.

This process lies at the heart of individual growth and of corporate success. Too simple, some would say. They should try putting it into practice.

Organizations that have acquired the learning habit are endlessly questioning the status quo, are forever seeking new methods or new products, forever testing and then reflecting, consciously or unconsciously pushing round that wheel.

KEEPING THE WHEEL MOVING

Maintaining constant movement of the wheel is not as easy as it sounds. There are two key concepts which can help to keep it turning: *subsidiarity* and *incidental learning.*

SUBSIDIARITY

The word itself is rather ugly, but the concept is important. Subsidiarity means encouraging individuals and groups to have as much power as they are competent to handle. It is an old idea in political theory, an idea central to democracy and an idea which, today, is at the heart of the learning organization. Power is given to those closest to the action.

Subsidiarity is managed, organizationally, by defining the boundaries of the job. There are two boundaries. The inner boundary defines the essential core of the job, be it an individual's job, a team's or a function's. This part of the job is defined, the roles and responsibilities made clear. If these things are not done, then one is seen to have failed. The outer boundary defines the limits of discretion. In between lies the scope for initiative and for personal responsibility.

W. L. Gore, creator of the well-known "Gore Tex" fabric, whose company does its best to foster the learning habit, makes a nice distinction between the two boundaries. There are experiments above the water-line, which do little harm if they go wrong, Gore pointed out, and there are experiments below the water-line, which might sink the ship. The former are encouraged; the latter are outlawed.

In good organizations, the mistakes are rare because the people are good; and they are good because they know that they will be entrusted with big responsibilities, including the chance to make mistakes. Subsidiarity is self-fulfilling.

In traditional organizations, the space for initiative is limited. Many jobs are all core and no space. The water-line is set very high. Control is tight. There is no initiative without prior permission. In the flexible, responsive organizations that are needed today, the space has to be larger because the center cannot define in advance the details of every job. Control then has to be after the event—with forgiveness if necessary. This means that each individual or team must understand very clearly which types of initiatives are acceptable and which are not. Everyone has to agree on the definition of success. Control depends more on a common understanding than on budgets and procedures. Shared values reinforce constant and effective communications, all of which are essential if subsidiarity is going to work. The organization that talks together works together.

INCIDENTAL LEARNING

Subsidiarity by itself will not move the wheel of learning. It needs to be bolstered by incidental learning. Incidental learning means treating every incident as a case study from which we can learn.

This learning does not occur automatically; opportunities must be created for it to develop. For example, regular meetings of one's group or cluster can be arranged to review recent critical events. This is, in fact, the time-honored way in which doctors, social workers and other professionals help each other to learn from their experiences. It requires honesty with oneself and with others, a sense of togetherness and trust. Incidental learning is the organization's way to build in time for reflection, the final segment of the wheel. A mentor from outside the organization or group can enhance the process by encouraging a free and frank exchange without acrimony.

Incidental learning is most appropriate when one is dealing with divergent problems. It was E. Schumacher, author of *Small Is Beautiful,* who first distinguished between convergent and divergent problems. Convergent problems have right answers: "This is the shortest route to Boston." Divergent problems, such as "Why do you want to go to Boston?" have answers that are only right for a particular person, time and place.

Once we have moved beyond the basics, all the problems of organizations are divergent, to be solved only by the process of the wheel. This is what makes organizations so endlessly fascinating, and also so difficult.

THERE IS NO ALTERNATIVE

People once believed that there was a science and a theory of organizations which, like the laws of motion, would allow us to predict and determine the future. We now know that this is impossible. We have learned that chance happenings will trigger chain reactions, that the past will be a poor guide to the future and that we shall forever be dealing with unanticipated events.

Given that scenario, organizations have no choice but to reinvent themselves almost every year. To succeed, they will need individuals who delight in the unknown. The wise organization will devote considerable time to identifying and recruiting such people and to ensuring job satisfaction. Being a "preferred" organization will become increasingly important. Preferred organizations will be learning organizations. They will provide opportunities to exercise responsibility, to learn from experience, to take risks and to gain satisfaction from results achieved and lessons learned.

Such organizations will continue to defy conventional wisdom. They will be organizations of consent, not of control. They will be able to maintain a feeling of togetherness despite their size and far-flung locations. They will make many mistakes, but will have learned from them before others realize they occurred. They will invest hugely in their people and trust them hugely and save the salaries of ranks of inspectors. Above all, they will see learning not as a confession of ignorance but as the only way to live. It has been said that people who stop learning stop living. This is also true of organizations.

Charles Handy is the author of *The Age of Unreason,* (published by Harvard Business School Press, as well as by Business Books in the U.K.) and is visiting professor at the London Business School. He is currently writing a new book called *The Age of Paradox,* to be published next year by HBSB.

PART TEN

SUCCESS STORIES

READING 21
HOW RITZ-CARLTON
APPLIES "TQM"

THE RITZ-CARLTON HOTEL COMPANY WON THE BALDRIGE AWARD (SEE READINGS 10, 11, AND 13) IN 1992. THIS WAS A PARTICULARLY NOTABLE ACHIEVEMENT FOR A SERVICE FIRM BECAUSE, FROM THE INITIAL AWARDS IN 1988 THROUGH 1993, ONLY TWO OTHER BALDRIGE WINNERS HAD BEEN SELECTED FROM THE SERVICE INDUSTRY, FEDERAL EXPRESS (1990) AND AT&T UNIVERSAL CARD SERVICES (1992). THIS PRIVATELY-OWNED COMPANY OWNS BUT THREE OF THE RITZ-CARLTONS, BUT ITS 11,500 EMPLOYEES MANAGE AND OPERATE TWENTY-SEVEN RITZ-CARLTON PROPERTIES WORLDWIDE.

THIS ARTICLE REVIEWS HOW TOTAL QUALITY MANAGEMENT IS PRACTICED AT THE RITZ, AND YOU CAN ANTICIPATE THE BROAD THEMES INVOLVED BEFORE READING THE RITZ' PARTICULAR IMPLEMENTATIONS. TOP-MANAGEMENT <u>LEADERSHIP</u>, FOR EXAMPLE, WHERE THE SENIOR QUALITY-MANAGEMENT TEAM (THE PRESIDENT AND 13 OTHER SENIOR EXECUTIVES) MEET <u>WEEKLY</u> TO REVIEW SERVICE-QUALITY MEASURES, GUEST SATISFACTION, ETC. THE TOP MANAGERS ALSO PARTICIPATE IN THE TWO-DAY ORIENTATION FOR NEW EMPLOYEES AND HELP INCULCATE THE RITZ' CULTURE AND CREATE A SHARED VISION AMONG ITS EMPLOYEES. YOU WILL ALSO NOTE AN AWARENESS OF THE <u>ECONOMICS OF CUSTOMER RETENTION</u> (SEE READING 2), AND THE NEED FOR AND USE OF <u>CUSTOMER-INFORMATION SYSTEMS/DATA</u>. IN FACT, THE RITZ' ABILITY TO GATHER, DIGEST, AND COMMUNICATE GUEST INFORMATION TO PROPERTIES WORLDWIDE IS SAID TO BE UNMATCHED IN THE INDUSTRY. TEAMWORK, EMPOWERMENT, EMPLOYEE TRAINING, AND SUPPLIER PARTNERSHIPS ARE AMONG OTHER THEMES INCORPORATED IN THE RITZ MODEL OF TQM.

READING 21
HOW RITZ-CARLTON
APPLIES "TQM"

BY CHARLES G. PARTLOW

The search for sustained, competitive advantage in the hotel industry has become focused to a large degree on product and service quality. Achieving this quality on a consistent and low-cost basis, however, has proven to be an elusive target. In the past, managers have been provided with such techniques and programs as management by objectives (MBO), quality circles (QC), and organizational development (OD). Most recently, total quality management (TQM) has become a focus in many manufacturing and service industries, including the hotel industry.

The drive for quality improvement has become a nationally recognized goal. To that end, the Malcolm Baldrige National Quality Award, established by Congress in 1987, recognizes U.S. companies that have achieved excellence through adherence to quality-improvement programs. Named for the late Secretary of Commerce, the award is administered by the Commerce Department's National Institute of Standards and Technology. The goals of the award are to promote quality awareness, recognize quality achievement of U.S. companies, and publicize successful quality strategies.

Companies participating in the award application process must submit comprehensive information on the quality-improvement programs they have implemented. The seven categories on which applicants are evaluated are leadership, information analysis, strategic quality planning, human-resource development and management, quality assurance, quality operating results, and customer satisfaction. Applications are graded on a 1,000-point scale, and companies with the highest scores are visited by a team of quality examiners. The examiners submit their findings to a board of nine judges, who then provide feedback reports to applicants and select award recipients. Two awards

CREDIT: Charles G. Partlow, "How Ritz-Carlton Applies 'TQM'", *The Cornell H.R.A. Quarterly*, (August, 1993) pp. 16–24. (c) Cornell University, used by permission. All rights reserved.

may be granted yearly to companies in each of three categories: manufacturing, service, and small business. While award recipients are allowed to publicize and advertise their awards, they are also expected to share information about their successful quality strategies with other U.S. companies.[1]

In the first four years of its existence, 12 firms won the Malcolm Baldrige National Quality Award: eight came from manufacturing, three were in the small-business category; and only one, Federal Express, hailed from the service sector. Certain aspects of the service encounter that are endemic to the hotel industry may make it difficult but not impossible to apply many of the management principles from other industries. Those aspects include the intangibility and perishability of the product, variability of delivery, simultaneous production and consumption of the service, and the changing needs and expectations of providers and users.[2] In a seminar held at the 1991 Annual CHRIE Conference in Houston, hospitality educators and industry professionals stated their belief that the hotel industry could successfully apply Baldrige award criteria and achieve performance levels needed to win the award.[3] That belief was substantiated on October 14, 1992, when the Ritz-Carlton Hotel Company was named a winner of the 1992 Baldrige award, making it the first hotel company to win this coveted honor.

In this article, I will relate the lessons of the Ritz-Carlton experience, based on an extensive interview with Patrick Mene, Ritz-Carlton's corporate director of quality. At the conclusion, I will discuss some of the issues relative to implementation of TQM in the hotel industry.

THE CONTEMPORARY RITZ-CARLTON

The Ritz-Carlton Hotel Company is a management firm that develops and operates luxury hotels worldwide. It was formed in 1983 when Atlanta-based W.B. Johnson Properties purchased exclusive U.S. rights to the Ritz-Carlton trademark along with the Boston Ritz-Carlton Hotel. Today, under the leadership of William B. Johnson (CEO) and Horst Schulze (COO), the privately-owned company operates 27 hotels and resorts in the United States

---

[1]Most of the information presented here is adapted from the 1992 Award Criteria: Malcolm Baldrige National Quality Award. To obtain a copy at no cost, contact: Malcolm Baldrige National Quality Award, National Institute of Standards and Technology, Gaithersburg, MD 20899 (telephone: 301-975-2036).

[2]Robert C. Lewis and Richard E. Chambers, *Marketing Leadership in Hospitality: Foundations and Practices* (New York; Van Nostrand Reinhold, 1989), pp.39–49.

[3]R. Dan Reid and Melvin Sandler, "An Evaluation of the Baldrige Award and Its Implications for the Hotel Industry," abstracted in 1991 *Annual CHRIE Conference Proceedings* (Washington, DC), pp. 256–257.

and Australia.[4] Its future international expansion plans include adding hotels in Hong Kong, Barcelona, and Cancun. Ritz-Carlton also has nine international sales offices and employs 11,500 people.

QUALITY-MANAGEMENT PROGRAM

Quality management begins with president and chief operating officer Schulze and the other 13 senior executives who make up the corporate steering committee and the senior quality-management team. They meet weekly to review product- and service-quality measures, guest satisfaction, market growth and development, organizational indicators, profits, and competitive status. Approximately one-fourth of each executive's time is devoted to quality-related matters.

GOLD STANDARDS

Key product and service requirements of the travel consumer have been translated into Ritz-Carlton Gold Standards, which include a credo, motto, three steps of service, and the "Ritz-Carlton Basics" (see next page). Each employee is expected to understand and adhere to these standards, which describe processes for solving problems guests may have as well as detailed grooming, housekeeping, and safety and efficiency standards.

To provide superior service, Ritz-Carlton created its targeted selection process to ensure a successful match of potential employees to employment. Upon being selected, new employees are versed on the corporate culture through a two-day orientation, followed by extensive on-the-job training, then job certification. Ritz-Carlton values are reinforced continuously by daily "line ups," frequent recognition for extraordinary achievement, and a performance appraisal based on expectations explained during the orientation, training, and certification processes.

To ensure guests' problems are resolved quickly, workers are required to act at first notice—regardless of the type of problem or customer complaint. All employees are empowered to do whatever it takes to provide "instant pacification." No matter what their normal duties are, other employees must assist if aid is requested by a fellow worker who is responding to a guest's complaint or wish.

---

[4]For comments from Horst Schulze, see: Kenneth R. Greger and Glenn R. Whithiam, "The View from the Helm: Hotel Execs Examine the Industry," *The Cornell Hotel and Restaurant Administration Quarterly,* 32, No. 3 (October 1991), pp. 18–36.

THE RITZ-CARLTON "GOLD STANDARDS"

The Ritz-Carlton Credo

The Ritz-Carlton is a place where the genuine care and comfort of our guests is our highest mission. We pledge to provide the best service and facilities for our guests who will always enjoy a warm, relaxed yet refined ambience. The Ritz-Carlton experience enlivens the senses, instills well-being, and fulfills even the unexpressed wishes and needs of our guests.

The Ritz-Carlton Motto

"We are Ladies and Gentlemen serving Ladies and Gentlemen." Practice teamwork and "lateral service" (i.e., employee-to-employee contact) to create a positive work environment.

Three Steps of Service

1. A warm and sincere greeting. Use the guest's name, if and when possible.
2. Anticipation and compliance with guest needs.
3. Fond farewell. Give guests a warm good-bye and use their names, if and when possible.

The Ritz-Carlton "Basics"

1. The Credo will be known, owned, and energized by all employees.
2. The three steps of service shall be practiced by all employees.
3. All employees will successfully complete Training Certification to ensure they understand how to perform to The Ritz-Carlton standards in their position.
4. Each employee will understand their work area and hotel goals as established in each strategic plan.
5. All employees will know the needs of their internal and external customers (guests and fellow employees) so that we may deliver the products and services they expect. Use guest preference pads to record specific needs.
6. Each employee will continuously identify defects ("Mr. BIV": Mistakes, Rework, Breakdowns, Inefficiencies, and Variations) throughout the hotel.
7. Any employee who receives a customer complaint "owns" the complaint.
8. Instant guest pacification will be ensured by all. React quickly to correct the problem immediately. Follow-up with a telephone call within 20 minutes to verify that the problem has been resolved to the customer's satisfaction. Do everything you possibly can to never lose a guest.

9. Guest-incident action forms are used to record and communicate every incident of guest dissatisfaction. Every employee is empowered to resolve the problem and to prevent a repeat occurrence.
10. Uncompromising levels of cleanliness are the responsibility of every employee.
11. "Smile. We are on stage." Always maintain positive eye contact. Use the proper vocabulary with our guests. (Use words like: "good morning," "certainly,", "I'll be happy to", and "my pleasure.")
12. Be an ambassador of your hotel in and outside of the work place. Always talk positively. No negative comments.
13. Escort guests rather than pointing out directions to another area of the hotel.
14. Be knowledgeable of hotel information (hours of operation, etc.) to answer guests' inquiries. Always recommend the hotel's retail and food and beverage outlets prior to facilities outside the hotel.
15. Use proper telephone etiquette. Answer within three rings and with a "smile." When necessary, ask the caller, "May I place you on hold." Do not screen calls. Eliminate call transfers when possible.
16. Uniforms are to be immaculate; wear proper and safe footwear (clean and polished), and your correct name tag. Take pride and care in your personal appearance (adhering to all grooming standards).
17. Be certain of your role during emergency situations and be aware of fire and life-safety response processes.
18. Notify your supervisor immediately of hazards or injuries and of equipment or assistance that you need. Practice energy conservation and proper maintenance and repair of hotel property and equipment.
19. Protecting the assets of a Ritz-Carlton Hotel is the responsibility of every employee.

The responsibility for ensuring high-quality guest services and accommodations rests primarily with employees. Surveyed annually to ascertain their levels of satisfaction and understanding of quality standards, workers are keenly aware that excellence in guest services is a top hotel and personal priority. A full 96 percent of all employees surveyed in 1991 singled out this priority—even though the company had added 3,000 new employees in the previous three years.

DETAILED PLANNING

At each level of the company—from corporate leaders to managers and employees in the individual work areas—teams are charged with setting objectives and devising action plans, which are reviewed by the corporate steering committee. In addition, each hotel has a designated quality leader, who serves as a resource and advocate as teams and workers develop and implement their quality plans. To cultivate employee commitment further, each work area is covered by three teams responsible for problem solving, strategic planning, and setting quality-certification standards for each position.

The benefits of detailed planning and the hands-on involvement of executives are evident during the seven days leading up to the opening of a new hotel. Rather than opening a hotel in phases, as is the practice in the industry, Ritz-Carlton aims to have everything right when the door opens to the first customer. A "seven-day-countdown control plan" synchronizes all steps leading to the opening.[5] The company president and other senior leaders personally instruct new employees on the gold standards and quality management during a two-day orientation, and a specially selected start-up team composed of staff from the company's other hotels ensures that all work areas, processes, and equipment are ready.

QUALITY DATA

Daily quality production reports, derived from data submitted from each of the 720 work areas in the hotel, serve as an early warning system for identifying problems that can impede progress toward meeting quality and customer-satisfaction goals. Coupled with quarterly summaries of guest and meeting-planner reactions, the combined data are compared with predetermined customer expectations to improve services. Among the data gathered and tracked over time are annual guest-room preventive-maintenance cycles, percentage of check-ins with no queuing, time spent to achieve industry-best clean-room appearance, and time to service an occupied guest room.

From automated building and safety systems to computerized reservation systems, Ritz-Carlton uses advanced technology to full advantage. For example,

---

[5]See: William E. Kent, "Putting Up the Ritz: Using Culture to Open a Hotel," *The Cornell Hotel and Restaurant Administration Quarterly,* 31, No. 3 (November 1990), pp. 16–24.

each employee is trained to note a guest's likes and dislikes. Those data are entered in a computerized guest-history profile that provides information on the preferences of 240,000 repeat guests, resulting in more personalized service.

QUALITY RESULTS

The aim of these and other customer-focused measures is not simply to meet the expectations of guests but to provide them with a memorable visit. According to surveys conducted for Ritz-Carlton by an independent research firm, 92 to 97 percent of the company's guests leave with that impression. As a result of its quality program, Ritz-Carlton received 121 quality awards from the travel industry in 1991 alone, including: "Best Hotel Chain in the United States," by Zagat Travel Survey; "Index Award of Excellence," by *Hotel and Travel Index;* "Alred Award" for Best Hotel Chain, by *Corporate Travel;* and "Top Hotel Chain in Ability to Service Meetings," by *Successful Meetings.*

PATRICK MENE AND TQM

Patrick Mene joined the Ritz-Carlton Hotel Company three years ago as corporate director of quality to coordinate and spearhead the company's TQM program. Prior to joining Ritz-Carlton, he was with L'Hermitage Hotels in Los Angeles and served as general manager of the Le Bel-Age. He has also been associated with Hyatt Hotels, Westin International, and Omni Hotels. He brings to his position a comprehensive knowledge of all aspects of the hotel industry, from operations to food and beverage and management training.

In Mene's view, Ritz-Carlton's approach to the Baldrige award began long before the award was established and before anyone had heard of TQM. "About eight years ago Ritz-Carlton set out to be a single supplier of luxury properties that met Mobil's and AAA's highest standards. Six years later, we had achieved recognition from those independent rating organizations as the only hotel company that consistently met their highest standards," he said. Now, Ritz-Carlton is the benchmark used by AAA and Mobil in rating lodging properties.

"At that point, company president Horst Schulze shook us to our foundations one day when he told us, 'You know what? We're a lucky, bloody six, on a scale of one to ten.' What he was saying was that all of our customers were still not being satisfied all the time," Mene said.

He said that despite a desire to find areas of improvement and a strong quality-based culture, the company had run out of ideas for how to improve.

FIVE TENETS OF TQM

While the following five principles are not the only tenets of Total Quality Management, by concentrating on these principles, employees will realize that TQM is not just another "program" that will almost certainly vanish. The key is that TQM is an integrated system of techniques and training.

(1) Commit to Quality. Making quality a number-one priority requires an organizational culture to support it, and only top leadership can foster a TQM culture. Thus, the first step toward TQM must involve active support and direction from top-level managers, especially the CEO.

(2) Focus on Customer Satisfaction. Customers are concerned about quality and, in fact, define it for the organization. Successful TQM companies are acutely aware of the market. They know what their customers really want and invariably meet and exceed their expectations.

(3) Assess Organizational Culture. A select group of top managers and employees from different parts of the company should examine the organization with a focus on its culture, and assess the fit between that culture and TQM's principles. This assessment, which may take several months to complete, will help management build on strengths, identify weaknesses and set priorities.

(4) Empower Employees and Teams. Although TQM is led from the top, the real work occurs "bottom-up." Empowering employees and teams requires training them to use their authority effectively. It may also require redesigning some jobs to facilitate a team approach and modifying policies and practices that support rewards for results and other cultural elements that empower employees.

(5) Measure Quality Efforts. The ability to gauge your efforts toward superior employee performance, streamlined decision-making, supplier responsiveness and improved customer satisfaction is endemic to the TQM process. Information gathering and analysis techniques should help identify causes of work-process problems and be well-designed, timely, and straightforward. In the end, TQM is based mostly on rational thinking and problem solving, not on sophisticated statistics and other measurement techniques.—C.G.P.

"We went to several of our main customers and independent quality-rating organizations," Mene recalled. "They suggested turning to the Baldrige criteria for guidance. Those criteria were hard to understand, and at first we didn't think they were relevant to our business. We gradually realized the award criteria could serve as a road map for quality improvement."

"I think it is important that everyone understands we were not a classic TQM company to begin with," Mene added. "Despite our culture and obsession with quality improvement, we were not a classic TQM company and I don't even know to this day if we are, although we certainly apply many of the principles. We aren't as statistically controlled as some of the more traditional TQM companies, but we are beginning to move more and more in that direction."

EMPOWERMENT

One of the planks of TQM, empowerment, was an easy step for Ritz-Carlton, Mene said. "To us, empowerment means giving employees the responsibility for solving guests' problems. We found that happens in two stages if you're staying at a hotel and you encounter a problem or something is wrong. In stage one, the employee will have to break away from his or her normal routine to take an immediate positive action, to investigate what went wrong, and straighten it out."

Breaking away is not exactly the proper term, since solving guests' problems is a major consideration in guest service. Mene explained, "We would rather have a guestroom attendant, for example, deal with fixing a guest's problem on the spot rather than having the director of marketing fix it later. It's the 1-10-100 rule that we believe in: What costs you a dollar to fix today will cost $10 to fix tomorrow and $100 to fix downstream."

TEAMWORK

Building a team approach did occasion some resistance from managers, because of its novelty. Employees met as teams to spot problem patterns, prioritize problems, and develop measures to prevent their recurrence. " This was the phase that was completely new to us," Mene said. "The way we addressed managerial concerns was by involving all the managers in a review process. Later, we went on to create strategic planning teams where every level of the organization was charged with the responsibility to set goals and action plans. We allowed the managers to sit in on review boards and study each team's objectives and plans. Of course, they had some training on what to look for. The managers came to see their role as still responsible for objectives and solutions and to ensure they were adequately researched and funded, but with input and involvement from employees."

Mene said the company has learned that not everyone wants the responsibility of being on a strategic-planning team and that some managers are better suited to a team approach—particularly as facilitator or coach—than others. "We use screening methods in hiring to determine who shares in our values, and we use predictive instruments to tell if people are well suited to teamwork. That's a breakthrough," he said. "We also spent more time building the relationship of the team. We took for granted that if you were already a good Ritz-Carlton employee, you already understood our concept of lateral service. So when we put a group of cross-functional people together in a team, we figured they would just naturally work together as a team and go forward. But what we found was that we had to spend more time to allow the team members to get to know each other and learn how to build and maintain support before they could really get the kind of improvement we wanted. Let's just say that we learned how to better build and maintain our teams."

FEEDBACK

Winning the Baldrige award turns out to be a "good-news, bad-news" situation. A month or two after winning the award, Ritz-Carlton received a feedback report suggesting 75 areas of improvement. The next step, Mene said, was to go right back after defects. "We announced to the employees that by 1996, and this one really shook them, we wanted to reduce the cycle time (the time between identifying a guest's need and satisfying that need) by 50 percent, and we also wanted to set an objective of 100-percent customer retention. So, we actually set goals of enormous magnitude right on the heels of winning the Baldrige, long-range quality goals. What I think got people's attention was that not only did we have new high-quality goals, but we weren't stopping at Baldrige. We wanted the highest level of quality." Ritz-Carlton did not target such traditional goals as occupancy rate because the company expects the focus on quality goals will develop quality production that will drive the financial outcome. "That was a real shock to our employees," Mene said. "Whether we end up with the highest average rate and occupancy I don't know, but we will have the most efficient system to satisfy customers."

SUPPLIERS, TOO

Ritz-Carlton is now working with its suppliers for quality management. The firm has developed supplier certification, by which the company not only measures how often suppliers meet specifications on time, but how well they improve their cycle time from order to delivery. "If they don't have the willingness to do that we can no longer do business with them," Mene warned. "We want to see which suppliers are best able to meet our quantity needs, and which will meet our quality needs by doing an internal assessment or by applying for the Baldrige award themselves."

The internal assessment involves a rigorous 100-question internal audit of suppliers' capabilities, plus a survey of the people who use their products and services, including purchasing agents, accounting personnel, sales persons, and hotel guests, who also rate the quality of those suppliers' products and services. Ritz-Carlton ranks the suppliers based on a score developed from the supplier audits and user surveys. The goal is to get suppliers to advance through a certification program to become a fully integrated partner.

"Most of our suppliers are already involved in this approach and they're happy to share with us their capabilities, but we have all sorts of other suppliers showing up and saying, 'Look at me, look at what I can do.' So I think the response to our program has been good," Mene said.

HUMAN RESOURCES

Ritz-Carlton completely integrates human resources and operations, so that an outside observer might be hard pressed to figure out who were the human-resources people and who were the operations people, Mene observed. Human resources and operations personnel work together to select, orient, train, and certify employees. They also ensure that the employees remain deeply involved in running the business, since every level of the organization is charged with the responsibility of setting goals and objectives.

APPRAISAL

"Our quality performance standards are also established by employees through their work teams in each area of the hotel," Mene said. "This leads me to our performance appraisal system, in which we hold our people responsible only for the things they can control. Appraisal is based on the things that we told employees were important during their orientation—the gold standards. Once our employees become certified, performance appraisals are nothing more than a recertification, so that training can become a continuous process. We also ask our people to contribute to the process by identifying problems and working to solve them."

ADVICE FOR EDUCATORS

Mene had the following thoughts for educators: "The education establishment needs to recognize that quality is a whole new branch of knowledge, and it has to be taught to the students as an entirely separate concept. I don't even know if it should be a separate course or something that is inculcated throughout the curriculum. I really believe the manager of the future must be a generalist. I don't think we teach students enough about interpersonal relationships or how to build and maintain a team approach.[6]

"I think we should teach them less about finances and more about quality. We've got to get them off the financial agenda. You cannot improve a company's financial performance merely by focusing on finances. So, we can no longer say to human-resources people that they be responsible for personnel, and to controllers that they be responsible for finances. Future managers, and employees to a different extent, have to know and be responsible for quality, relationships, and finances."

ADVICE FOR INDUSTRY

To make quality work successfully, the president and senior leaders must initiate and drive the process, Mene believes. "The quality culture has got to be there, and top leaders help to set that. It's also important to understand the criteria before starting, because it may seem irrelevant to the typical hotel. Guidebooks and TQM seminars can be helpful. An application committee should be formed to assess the current situation and implement the TQM process. Our committee was divided into seven subcommittees based on the seven examination areas in the Baldrige application, with a senior manager as leader for each area. Developing a detailed plan or work flow similar to opening a new hotel is extremely important for the purpose of completing the Baldrige application itself. The application process of drafting the report and then reviewing, editing, publishing, printing, and defending it is a major undertaking. I recommend using a professional editing team, because you are publishing a book, make no mistake about it. I also suggest editing the final document in a business-center environment, like a retreat, where you get your editing team together for a week to lock yourself down and just go through the iterations. The editing process is bigger than one might imagine. Finally, I believe you ought

---

[6]These statements are congruent with the findings of the stakeholder survey discussed by Cathy Enz, Leo Renaghan, and A. Neal Geller in "Graduate-Level Education: A Survey of Stakeholders," in this issue's Educator's Forum.

to challenge your organization with an extraordinary goal. The goal to improve by using the application as a guide for self-assessment and developing a quality program should outweigh the goal of wanting to win the Baldrige award.

IMPLICATIONS OF THE RITZ-CARLTON EXPERIENCE

The Ritz-Carlton case demonstrates that the hotel industry can apply Baldrige-award criteria to develop a successful quality program just like other firms in the manufacturing and service industries. The chief mechanism for ensuring the steady quality improvement required by the Baldrige award is empowering employees, which means giving them the authority to identify and solve customer problems on the spot and to improve work processes. A corollary of empowerment is that employees should be able to make modest changes in normal procedures, especially in resolving a guest's complaint. Ritz-Carlton, for instance, allows each individual employee to spend up to $2,000 to satisfy a guest. As Patrick Mene so aptly put it, "Ritz-Carlton employees know that from day one they are empowered to break away from their normal routines whenever they see a problem to bring that problem under control." For empowerment to have a positive effect, however, employees must also have the knowledge and skills to use their authority well. That requires training not only in quality concepts and quality control tools and techniques, but also in how to do the job and how to work together as a team.[7]

Another lesson learned from Ritz-Carlton's quality effort is that hotel companies can achieve excellence in quality improvement without using the sophisticated statistical techniques normally associated with manufacturing companies. Although many persons feel that the precisely measured Baldrige criteria favor manufacturing, the award does not require companies to use computer-generated statistical techniques. Companies are required, however, to collect and analyze information related to customer satisfaction, quality of products and services, cycle-time reduction, and financial and employee-related performance, and to make comparisons with competitors and industry benchmarks.

In fact, measuring quality is one spot where Ritz-Carlton encountered problems. In our conversation, Patrick Mene expressed how difficult it was to find quality-related information on the industry. Except for financial data, neither single competitors nor the industry as a whole was tracking

---

[7]For empowerment to be effective, employees must also be enabled. That is why Deming emphasized the need for training and education in his principles of TQM. Demings ideas are presented in: Mary Walton, *The Deming Management Model* (New York: Putnam/Perigee, 1986).

TQM FROM THE SUPPLIER'S VIEWPOINT

Six years ago, McDevitt Street Bovis, a construction firm based in Charlotte, North Carolina, adopted Total Quality Management. The decision didn't take long to make. There was no lengthy study or cost-benefit analysis. As CEO Luther Cochrane told the story, company executives had barely even heard of TQM at the time ("Not Just Another Quality Snow Job," *The Wall Street Journal,* May 24, 1993, p. A10). The reason for adopting TQM was that a major client, Hospital Corporation of America, had announced that a commitment to TQM would be a substantial factor in the award of future contracts.

To its credit, the McDevitt firm did more than adopt TQM in name; it has "taken TQM to another level," as Cochrane put it. "Instead of trying to find one set of quality indicators that fit every job, we decided to create a total quality plan for each new job, working together with the architects, engineers, and major sub-contractors." McDevitt has used the procedure, Jobsite Quality Planning (JQP), on more than 40 projects, including Independence Square in Washington, D.C.

Cochrane wrote that the results have been positive in more than one way: the firm has won repeat business from most clients with whom it has used JQP; the firm has had no construction-related lawsuits on JQP projects; the company has been profitable, despite the construction industry's turmoil; and, most important, clients agree that JQP results in a better job.

JQP is not inexpensive. McDevitt spends some $500,000 per year on developing quality standards. Cochrane stated that that investment has been "more than returned through increased market share and decreased mistakes." Moreover, the JQP approach initially made architects uncomfortable, because they were concerned that McDevitt would interfere with the architects' relationship with the client. The architects, too, became believers when they saw how JQP could benefit all parties.

Cochrane also told about how resistance within the company was gradually broken down. "Initially, resistance ranged from division managers who saw huge expenditures with no payback, to job-site workers who just didn't understand," he wrote. By giving strong support to early adopters, McDevitt was able to win over doubters. In fact, Cochrane stated, some of the long-term veterans are now the

> strongest advocates of the JQP procedure. In a recent presentation, a potential client interrupted to ask whether this "stuff" really works. As Cochrane told the story: "The presentation team included a 40-year veteran of the industry, a construction worker as crusty as a cement-finisher's boots. Without a moment's hesitation, this superintendent replied in the affirmative, with language a bit too spicy to print."—G.W.

quality-assessment information. The need to change current systems of information gathering and analysis to focus more on quality and data related to customer satisfaction will be a challenge to other hotel companies in planning their quality programs. Ritz-Carlton's lesson was that it needed immediate responses throughout the system and accessible to all employees, just to keep pace with ever-changing customer demands.

The Ritz-Carlton experience also offers lessons for other hotel companies interested in pursuing the Malcolm Baldrige National Quality Award. For the Ritz-Carlton, winning the Baldrige has been a double-edged sword. On the one hand, the award is a crowning achievement for employees on their successful development and implementation of TQM. It has also been effective in solidifying the company's position as a leader in the luxury hotel market and in generating business from companies interested in doing business with a Baldrige award winner. On the other hand, the number of requests for presentations, appearances, tours, and general information being placed on Ritz-Carlton's executives and staff has been staggering—over 600 in the first three months of 1993 alone. Patrick Mene admitted to spending more than 50 percent of his time traveling and making presentations on Ritz-Carlton's quality program and the Baldrige experience. Although the award winners are not required to respond to such demands, they are expected to support the quality movement by sharing what they have learned with others.

Mene would change nothing, though. The chain's representatives no longer have to convince prospective clients that its properties offer a high-quality guest experience. "People need to understand the economics of quality," Mene warned. "When you don't satisfy all the customers all the time it can cost you a fortune. So we found the benefits more than outweighed any problems. A quality approach to running a business is the most cost-effective, least capital-intensive path to profitability. I have nothing but positive things to say, and I've spent several years of my life on this."

In light of the substantial effort and actual costs involved in competing for the Baldrige award, not to mention a hefty up-front application fee ($4,000), hotel companies may want to consider whether they really want to try for the award itself. Companies that seek the award merely to gain publicity or prestige will find that such pursuits usually do not withstand the scrutiny that examiners give each applicant.[8] The real danger lies in becoming more concerned with winning the award than with quality improvement.[9] Today, Baldrige-award winners typically spend several years working on TQM before even applying for the award, and on that score, Ritz-Carlton's "born at birth" philosophy to quality appears to be prescient.

Ritz-Carlton's experience with TQM and the Malcolm Baldrige National Quality Award provides valuable lessons for any hotel company. The hotel industry today is being challenged by a sluggish economy, increased multinational competition, and a more-sophisticated and demanding customer. How these issues are addressed may very well determine the difference between success and failure. While approaches to TQM can vary depending on an organization's unique circumstances and characteristics, the Baldrige-award criteria serve as a useful guide for setting up and monitoring a quality-improvement program.

If the Ritz-Carlton experience teaches us anything, it's that a focus on customer satisfaction must be built into the management processes of the organization and supported through an integrated system of information analysis, total employee participation, training, and the continuous effort to improve service and product quality.

---

[8]Marshall Saskin and Kenneth J. Kiser, *Total Quality Management* (Seabrook, Maryland: Ducochon Press, 1991), pp. 159–167.
[9]Jeremy Main, "Is the Baldrige Overblown?," *Fortune*, July 1, 1991, pp. 62–65.

Charles G. Partlow, PhD., is associate professor and Director of Graduate Studies in the School of Motel, Restaurant and Tourism Administration at the University of South Carolina.

READING 22
DISCOVERING NEW PERSPECTIVES

THIS LAST READING IS THE FIRST CHAPTER FROM A RECENT BOOK ON THE EVOLUTION OF QUALITY MANAGEMENT AT XEROX TITLED *A WORLD OF QUALITY: THE TIMELESS PASSPORT*. THIS CHAPTER DEALS WITH AN HISTORICAL OVERVIEW OF THE XEROX QUALITY JOURNEY. ITS SEVEN OTHER CHAPTERS DEAL WITH FUJI XEROX (A JOINT VENTURE OF XEROX AND FUJI PHOTO FILM CO., AND WINNER OF THE DEMING PRIZE IN 1980), THE LEADERSHIP SECTION OF THE XEROX APPLICATION FOR THE BALDRIGE AWARD (XEROX IS THE ONLY BALDRIGE WINNER TO HAVE MADE THEIR SUBMISSION AVAILABLE TO THE PUBLIC), SUBSIDIARY RANK XEROX AND THE EUROPEAN QUALITY AWARD, AND LESSONS LEARNED AND THE CHALLENGES YET AHEAD FOR THE ORGANIZATION. JOSEPH JURAN SAYS OF THE BOOK, "IT IS A REWARDING BOOK FOR THOSE WHO FACE THE NEED TO LAUNCH A MAJOR QUALITY INITIATIVE."

LIKE MANY OTHERS, THE JAPANESE PLAYED A SIGNIFICANT ROLE IN XEROX'S DISCOVERY OF "NEW PERSPECTIVES." THE CHAPTER REPORTS DEFECT LEVELS FOR XEROX EQUIPMENT ONCE WERE ABOUT SEVEN TIMES THAT OF ITS JAPANESE COMPETITORS (RECALL AIR-CONDITIONER COMPARISONS BY GARVIN IN READING 1). FURTHER, AT ONE POINT, THE JAPANESE COULD PROFITABLY <u>SELL</u> EQUIPMENT FOR WHAT XEROX CALCULATED WERE ITS INTERNAL <u>COSTS</u>. FOR MORE DETAIL ON XEROX' SUCCESSFUL RESPONSE TO THESE PROBLEMS, I ALSO RECOMMEND *PROPHETS IN THE DARK* BY DAVID KEARNS (XEROX CEO FROM 1982 TO 1990) AND DAVID NADLER (PRESIDENT OF A MANAGEMENT CONSULTING GROUP AND A KEY KEARNS' ADVISOR). THIS BOOK, WITH ITS RICH PERSONAL DETAIL, IS A PERFECT COMPANION TO *A WORLD OF QUALITY*.

READING 22
DISCOVERING NEW PERSPECTIVES

Many in the business world know something of the Xerox quality story: Xerox had serious business problems in the mid-1970s through the early 1980s but then improved the quality of its products to recapture a portion of the market share that had been lost to the Japanese. What is not quite as well known, however, are the details behind this turnaround, specifically:

- Why Xerox came so close to catastrophe
- How Xerox changed its business using Total Quality Management
- How Xerox developed its focus for the future

The problems Xerox faced did not happen overnight; they built up over a long time. Likewise, the answers did not magically appear. Not all elements of the Xerox quality program, as it exists today, were created at one point in time. Although some elements were part of the original strategy, many were developed in response to a specific event or circumstance. As Xerox progressed on its quality journey and gained additional insights, it modified its strategy to reflect what it had learned. The advantage of this strategy: 100,000 people were trained in a common language and in the quality process, and were encouraged to use these tools to improve and produce an astounding array of business changes and innovations.

THE MODEL OF BUSINESS SUCCESS: THE LATE 1960S AND EARLY 1970S

During the early days, Xerox experienced very rapid growth. This growth resulted from the introduction of the 914—the first plain paper copier—

CREDIT: Richard C. Palermo and Gregory H. Watson, Editors, "Discovering New Perspectives," chapter from *A World of Quality: The Timeless Passport* (1993). *A World of Quality: The Timeless Passport* is available from ASQC/Quality Press, 611 East Wisconsin Avenue, P.O. Box 3005, Milwaukee, Wisconsin 53201-3005, (414) 272-8575.

which was based on a new technology, xerography. It was a product customers were waiting in line to use. With the introduction of the 914, Xerox created a new industry.

By the time the competition entered the marketplace in the early 1970s, Xerox was generating record levels of profit and revenue. In the mid-1970s, the return on assets (ROA) generated by Xerox averaged in the low twenty percent range. This high level of profitability focused much attention on the Xerox business. Competition became only one of several major business issues that demanded the company's attention.

- In the early 1970s, IBM and Kodak entered the copier business and went after the same lucrative segments of the market created by Xerox. Xerox wrongly believed these two giants were the main competitive threat.
- The Japanese entered the market with low-volume machines that delivered reliable, high-quality equipment in a market segment Xerox had virtually ignored. Their performance allowed them to build a stronghold and later move upmarket into the heartland of the Xerox business.
- A number of antitrust lawsuits kept the Xerox management team distracted from the business end of company operations.
- In the 1970s, Xerox was caught off guard by the Federal Trade Commission (FTC), which accused Xerox of illegally monopolizing the office copier business. After negotiations with the FTC, Xerox agreed to open approximately 1,700 patents to its competitors. Later, Xerox agreed to limit some pricing practices and patent licensing arrangements as well. Xerox also agreed to provide technical assistance to those organizations that wanted to use these patents.

The cumulative effect of these issues caused the Xerox market share to fall from approximately 85 percent in the late 1970s to approximately 40 percent over the next several years. However, even during these turbulent times, Xerox continued to report strong revenues and profits. As a result, it was difficult to recognize the impact these changes had upon the company, because the profits masked the actual business performance.

FUJI XEROX AND THE NEW XEROX MOVEMENT

These adverse business trends had already been detected in Japan at the Xerox subsidiary, Fuji Xerox. Fuji Xerox was a joint venture created by Fuji Photo Film and Rank Xerox in 1962. In the early 1970s, Fuji Xerox had begun to experience the onslaught of competition in their home markets and had conducted several studies of its competitive position. At that time, Fuji Xerox estimated it was approximately 25 percent off the mark of its Japanese competitors for manufacturing costs.

To address this issue, Fuji Xerox began implementing its quality journey, the principles of Total Quality Management (TQM), in 1976. Fuji Xerox called this journey the New Xerox Movement. This effort resulted in Fuji Xerox receiving the Deming Prize and making substantial improvements of its business position.

In the late 1970s, Yotaro "Tony" Kobayashi, President of Fuji Xerox, encouraged Xerox executives to look at their comparative cost analysis and take action. After examining the Fuji Xerox comparative studies, Xerox believed that comparing its United States operations to those of Fuji Xerox and its Japanese competitors would provide an excellent assessment of its current competitive position. This study was conducted by internal engineers from both the design and manufacturing functions, and it provided Xerox with a baseline for comparison of its low volume copier products against their Japanese competition. The results of this pioneering benchmarking effort, which took place in 1979, were met with dismay and disbelief:

- The ratio of indirect workers to direct workers at the United States operations was twice that of the best Japanese competitor.
- Xerox used almost double the number of workers to develop a new product.
- It took Xerox twice as long to develop new products.
- It took Xerox nearly three times longer to deliver new products to the marketplace.

The benchmarking provided additional insights about Japanese competitors. These included:

- Defect levels of Xerox equipment were approximately seven times higher than those of its Japanese competitors.
- On average, the Japanese selling price of equipment in the United States almost equaled the Xerox Unit Manufacturing Cost (UMC), and the Japanese were making a profit.

From 1980 to 1983, evidence that Xerox was in trouble continued to mount:

- Market share continued to decline.
- The Xerox ROA slipped from nineteen percent in 1980 to below ten percent by the end of 1982.

- Over 20,000 positions were eliminated worldwide through initiatives such as early retirement programs and both voluntary and involuntary reductions in force (RIF).
- Levels of management were removed and promotional opportunities diminished.
- Wages were frozen in 1983.
- The decline in ROA greatly reduced employee profit sharing.
- New product delivery stagnated.
- Employee satisfaction began to slip as people lost confidence in the abilities of senior management.

Xerox was not completely taken by surprise, however, and it had already taken actions to counter this reversal in business fortune. For instance, in 1980, the union representing the Xerox production work force, the Amalgamated Clothing and Textile Workers Union (ACTWU), recognized that in order to protect its constituents, Xerox must remain competitive. The union had witnessed the demise of the clothing industry in America and knew that the problems Xerox was experiencing could result in the same negative outcome.

During the 1980 contract negotiations, the union and Xerox forged an agreement regarding employee involvement, which was called Quality of Work Life. This followed several years of research into Japanese Quality Circles and other employee involvement strategies and techniques. This concept of employee involvement became an important catalyst for turning the business around.

In 1981, Xerox combined the concepts of benchmarking and employee involvement into a productivity initiative called Business Effectiveness. This effort focused on reducing costs and improving the financial picture of the company. The phrase, "do it once and do it right," became the slogan, although no enablers were provided that would allow people to work smarter. In fact, most employees felt they were already working hard, and as a result, they became increasingly frustrated by the demands to do more. All of these efforts—Quality of Work Life, employee involvement, and benchmarking of product costing—were not enough to counter the competitive challenge.

Meanwhile, in 1982, David Kearns, the newly appointed chief executive officer of Xerox, had been witnessing firsthand the implementation of TQM at Fuji Xerox. During one of his return trips from Japan, Kearns began listing the factors that made the Japanese better than their American counterparts. After eliminating those factors that he felt were not significant, three elements remained: cost, quality, and expectations. Moreover, Kearns noticed that the Japanese set much higher expectations for their performance and output than the United States operations did—not by a little, but by a lot!

At about the same time, Kearns was approached by a few Xerox employees who urged the use of a TQM approach to address these business needs. To put these findings into action, Kearns commissioned eleven people to explore and outline a TQM approach for Xerox. This design team would draft a "vision book" that would outline how the company would look if TQM efforts were successful. The intent was to construct a strategy that would be broad enough and deep enough to turn the competitive tide.

THE BIRTH OF LEADERSHIP THROUGH QUALITY

As the design team developed its quality vision book over the next several months, it became apparent that operational changes alone would not be enough for success. For Xerox to reach the improvement objective, changes in behaviors and attitudes throughout the entire company would also be required. This realization prompted the team to recommend retaining an expert in the field of behavioral change. David Nadler, President of Delta Consulting, was selected to assist the team through organizational change issues and to help communicate these issues to senior management. This was the beginning of an enduring relationship which continues today.

Nadler coached management to understand that they should expect resistance to the recommended changes. This resistance, he said, would not be driven by technological issues but by behavioral issues. Nadler believed that it was critical to support the desired behavioral and cultural changes through a variety of approaches. Thus, the design team focused on what was often referred to as the six "levels of change." These were:

- Senior management behavior
- Communication
- Training
- Reward and recognition
- Standards and measures
- Transition team

Unless all of these factors were addressed together, any attempt at basic change would have been isolated and subsequently rejected by the old system.

The efforts of the design team resulted in a draft notebook that was shared with the top 25 Xerox executives attending a meeting at the Xerox Training Center in Leesburg, Virginia. The purpose of this February 1983 meeting was to engage the worldwide Xerox senior management team in developing a change strategy that was specific to the Xerox culture and needs.

By Kearns' direction, there were three absolutes of this quality strategy:

- Xerox was going to initiate a TQM approach.
- Xerox would take the time to design it right the first time.
- It would involve all employees.

A set of discussion-provoking questions was developed by the design team. These questions would help direct the progress of the management team in developing the details of its commitment to quality. This discussion aid included such questions as:

- Is there agreement on the principles, tools, and management actions on which the definition of quality is based?
- Is the proposed problem-solving process accepted as basic to the concept and part of the definition?
- Do we believe that five years is a realistic time period in which to achieve a state of maturity?
- Is there agreement on the need to provide quality training for all Xerox employees?
- How will quality be incorporated into the management process?
- By what name should the Xerox total quality strategy be known?

The resulting output of this team's work included the Xerox Quality Policy.

Xerox is a quality company. Quality is the basic business principle for Xerox. Quality means providing our external and internal customers with innovative products and services that fully satisfy their requirements. Quality improvement is the job of every Xerox employee.

The quality policy established during this 1983 meeting has not been changed and still guides the operating philosophy of Xerox today.

THE DEVELOPMENT OF LEADERSHIP THROUGH QUALITY

After the first Leesburg meeting, the senior management team personally took responsibility for communicating the quality direction and serving as the role model for deployment of Leadership Through Quality. Leadership Through Quality became the agreed upon strategy that would be used to turn around the three most significant business challenges which Xerox faced in 1983:

- No true customer focus—Customer satisfaction and customer opinions were not actively pursued in order to include their requirements for running the business.
- Costs—Product production costs were too high.
- Lack of market-connectedness—Product development was based on capability rather than marketplace need.

Leadership Through Quality was also the strategy for changing the Xerox culture which would focus and empower employees to:

- Meet customer requirements
- Drive business priorities
- Continuously improve

The development of Leadership Through Quality was an intensive effort. Three major efforts were identified to make Leadership Through Quality fully operational.

First, it was essential for the quality initiative to fit into the unique Xerox environment. To coordinate the deployment of Leadership Through Quality, management decided that the corporation needed a quality focal point within each organizational unit, as well as a focal point for the entire company. Quality was not going to be a separate department or function. Management also thought that the individuals selected for these quality positions would send a strong signal to employees of how serious management really was. To this end, management appointed high growth potential individuals as quality officers in each operating unit and a corporate vice president of quality. Together, these individuals formed the Quality Implementation Team (QIT) that was charged with researching and designing the implementation specifics of the Xerox approach to quality.

The QIT worked for approximately six months on its assignment. As part of their research effort, QIT members consulted renowned quality experts such as W. Edwards Deming, Joseph M. Juran, and Philip B. Crosby. They benchmarked companies with quality initiatives in effect, including Corning, Ford Motor Company, Hewlett-Packard and IBM. Pieces of each were adapted to fit into a quality mosaic that was specific to Xerox, and complemented its strengths and important areas of need.

During this research and design phase, the team members reviewed their progress with unit management and solicited input for strengthening the quality strategy. This input was then shared with management as a whole. This approach helped to ensure a wider acceptance of the final strategy throughout the management ranks. The output created was the Xerox Green

Book, which outlined all of the elements of Leadership Through Quality and set the goals and expectations for the quality journey.

Second, because Xerox management understood that training was critical to the success of the quality effort, it formed a 12-member Quality Education and Training Council. The council, whose members came from the various Xerox training organizations around the world, spent several months designing the supporting training program which would provide employees with the quality skills and tools that they needed to use for addressing the business issues.

Since its introduction in the first quarter of 1984, the Leadership Through Quality training program has been translated into fourteen languages to ensure a common approach to quality training at all Xerox facilities world-wide. The only exception was Fuji Xerox, which had its own materials prepared and deployed in the late 1970s as part of the New Xerox Movement. The widespread use of common Leadership Through Quality training has proven to be one of the most important aspects of the Leadership Through Quality implementation strategy.

Third, management needed to extend its commitment to Leadership Through Quality. To achieve this, Xerox leaders met again in Leesburg in August 1983. This time, approximately 120 people, including the original 25 team members plus the next two levels of the upper management team, convened to review and obtain support for the final strategy. After reaching consensus on the overall approach, each unit finalized its own implementation plans. Kearns set the example of active involvement of management in the support of the Leadership Through Quality deployment effort. He initiated the training cascade by leading his family group (his seven direct reports) through six and a half days of Leadership Through Quality training. After the completion of this training, they were required to participate in an on-the-job improvement project within their family group to apply the newly learned tools, thus reinforcing these new skills and techniques of quality.

THE DEPLOYMENT JOURNEY

Although Leadership Through Quality took eighteen months to develop, the training of 100,000 Xerox employees took over four years to complete. To deploy Leadership Through Quality, an innovative strategy to cascade the training by family group through the organization, level by level, was used. This model was called the Learn-Use-Teach-Inspect (LUTI) model of training. This proved to be effective in deploying the training and practicing of Leadership Through Quality without losing the substance of the methods. Figure 1.1 illustrates this training strategy.

FIGURE 1.1 THE LEARN-USE-TEACH-INSPECT (LUTI) MODEL

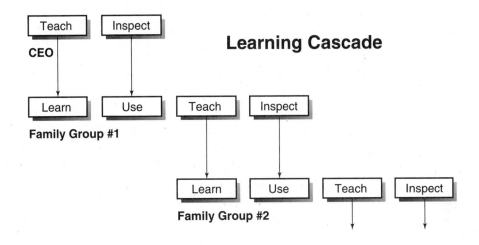

Following the LUTI model, a team is first trained by its manager in the principles, methods, and tools of Leadership Through Quality. Xerox training professionals assist the manager in delivering the training. The second step is to use the training to address business challenges immediately after the training is provided. Team members use what they have learned in training to attack a problem within their own area. In the third step, each manager, now experienced in the use of the tools, trains his or her direct reports using the standard Leadership Through Quality materials. In the final step, the manager inspects each of the direct report's application projects. (In Xerox, the term "inspection" means to monitor, assess, and coach rather than the traditional meaning of measuring against a fixed standard of goodness.)

During this four-year deployment period, Xerox had to weather continued downward trends and business pressures. However, the effort paid off. In addition to being a strategy for change within Xerox, Leadership Through Quality also proved to be a tool for measuring progress in business improvement. By 1987, the people of Xerox had reversed the decline in market share and ROA. The majority of Xerox employees had been trained—and were using—Leadership Through Quality in their daily work processes.

THE 1987 QUALITY ASSESSMENT AND THE
BALDRIGE AWARD

Xerox came to understand the importance of periodic assessments in order to provide an opportunity for reflection and to stimulate future initiatives. The key to business success, after all, was in the reinforcement of both the commitment and the pursuit of continuous improvement.

The first assessment at Xerox was conducted in 1987 shortly after Paul A. Allaire became president of the company. The purpose of this assessment was to evaluate the progress in deployment of Leadership Through Quality and to compare the quality results against the goals established in 1983. The objective was to measure and define gaps in quality implementation against the plan and to gain insight into why progress was not being achieved at a faster pace.

To complete the data collection phase of the assessment, the Corporate Quality Office engaged Delta Consulting to help design a survey that would be distributed to a cross section of managers; numerous interviews were conducted throughout Xerox, and employee feedback results were gathered. The analysis of this data yielded both strengths and areas for improvement.

Strengths of the 1987 assessment were:

- The strategy was fundamentally sound.
- There was worldwide support for the strategy.
- Meetings, teamwork, and group effectiveness showed the most improvement.
- Success and areas of excellence contributed to employee satisfaction.

There were many examples of individual managers, across a wide range of functions and on a worldwide basis, who were making a difference in the business by using the principles and tools of quality. These people helped disprove the argument that while quality could be made to work in Japan, it might not work elsewhere. They became the role models that others sought to emulate.

Xerox also had made good progress on what it needed most: teamwork. Xerox people were beginning to listen a lot better—especially to customers. This behavior change, combined with the disciplined use of quality tools, was helping to solve problems faster and more effectively by getting to the root cause of the issues. The advertising theme "Team Xerox" was originally used to describe groupings of new products. It was later adapted to Leadership Through Quality as an accurate characterization of the way Xerox employees were beginning to behave by mid-1987. Since then, "Team Xerox" has become more widely recognized as a call for Xerox people to exercise the quality methods through participative team efforts to improve processes and increase customer satisfaction.

Areas for improvement uncovered during the 1987 assessment included the following:

- Quality was not integrated into the basic business process. It was still a management topic rather than the way things were done.
- Pressure for near-term financial results was overriding the quality focus.
- Specific weaknesses were identified in the following categories:
  - Role models—not many were apparent
  - Inspection and coaching—not enough
  - Recognition, reward, and penalties—often weighted against old values
  - Use of the Leadership Through Quality tools and processes—not deployed sufficiently
  - Benchmarking—not universally used

In addition, there were not enough examples of line managers who were improving business results by using the quality process. When business pressures for profit performance increased, quality principles sometimes became secondary considerations. This was especially true in the trade-off between financial performance and customer satisfaction. All three corporate priorities—return on assets (ROA), market share, and customer satisfaction—supposedly had equal importance. In reality, management was emphasizing ROA as the primary goal and priority. This finding in itself justified the assessment effort and resulted in a customer satisfaction white paper, which was prepared by a cross-functional team using the standard six-step problem-solving process deployed in the Leadership Through Quality training.

In response to this assessment, senior management prioritized the three fundamental corporate goals to reflect the objectives of Leadership Through Quality:

1. Customer satisfaction
2. ROA
3. Market Share

Senior management believed that a stronger customer focus would build market share and profits over time. Putting customer satisfaction first was a major symbolic change for Xerox, and it set the stage for a change in ongoing business operations reviews. The reviews would become the forum for "in-process" assessments of quality progress at Xerox, and they would be conducted from a customer-focused perspective.

The timing of this renewed focus on the customer coincided with the celebration of the fiftieth anniversary of the invention of xerography on October 22, 1988. This was particularly fitting because the founders had established a tradition that focused on delivering value to the customer. This was also the first year companies could apply for the Malcolm Baldrige National Quality Award—an award that recognizes excellence in delivering customer satisfaction. Xerox management seriously considered its readiness to apply for the Baldrige Award during the first year of competition. However, management recognized that the true value of the application submission was in its effect as a stimulant for "tuning up" the Xerox quality system during the preparation process. There was not enough time to prepare an application during the first Baldrige Award cycle, so management postponed the application decision for review during the second Baldrige Award cycle.

Why apply for a quality award? Xerox managers came to understand that some periodic interventions were required to stimulate and to refocus an organization. Management had evidence that the experience of applying for quality awards, and having to respond to each part of the award criteria, would help Xerox continue to address the quality issues identified in the 1987 assessment. The assessment process, as laid out by the various criteria for the different quality awards, proved to be an excellent business improvement tool. For instance, in applying for the Deming Prize, Fuji Xerox had gained critical insights. Other Xerox units have similarly benefited through their pursuit of various quality awards. By the end of 1988, Xerox had been successful in its pursuit of five national quality awards (the Netherlands, France, two in Britain, and Japan). Management believed that Xerox would achieve similar benefits from an external evaluation as conducted by the Baldrige examiners. The application process would provide the vehicle necessary for improvement.

In December 1988, Xerox senior management decided that the company would complete a Baldrige application, but submit it only if Xerox had adequately responded to the award criteria. If the application did not meet the Xerox quality standard, management reasoned, the process of answering the award criteria would still be a useful self-assessment activity. Senior management selected a team that would gather information and write the application. As it generated the application document and coordinated the site visits, the Xerox National Quality Award (NQA) Team kept a record of the problem areas it discovered. The team eventually identified 513 opportunities in the Xerox quality system. These "warts," as they were called, were not eliminated during the process of drafting the application but served as the basis for directing Xerox to the next level of its quality journey once the application was complete.

Business results continued to improve as a result of the deployment of Leadership Through Quality, and the renewed focus on quality and customer satisfaction in the 1987 to 1989 period paid off. Business improvement resulted in return on assets over 10 percent for the first time since 1981, and customer satisfaction reached slightly higher than 86 percent—up from approximately 48 percent in 1985, but still 14 percent from the desired state. (Note: In the Xerox system for scoring customer satisfaction, a neutral response is counted with negative responses so this fourteen percent is the sum of neutral and negative responses.)

BEYOND THE BALDRIGE

The problem areas in the company's performance that were identified during the Baldrige application process formed the basis for the next stage of the quality improvement effort—Intensification. Quality Intensification occurred between 1989 and 1993. It focused on the development and company-wide expansion of two major initiatives: internal quality assessment and more rigorous use of policy deployment. These were deployed in the operating units. In 1992, Rank Xerox demonstrated how these initiatives were integrated with the basic elements of Leadership Through Quality through its successful application for the European Quality Award. Rank Xerox became the first winner of this award.

In 1993, as Xerox reflects back upon the 10-year journey for Leadership Through Quality, the success is evident. Customer satisfaction was up to 92 percent and ROA reached almost 15 percent for 1992 year-end results. Figure 1.2 shows how the journey positively influenced the company's profitability during this decade.

Today, Xerox holds a respected position in American industry and is recognized as "world-class" in many of its operations. Xerox is the only company in the world to have been recognized as a quality leader by the award of the Deming Prize, the Malcolm Baldrige National Quality Award, and the European Quality Award. Xerox is also one of the few companies to regain market share lost to the Japanese without the assistance of government support in the form of subsidies, quotas or tariffs. However, Xerox is not satisfied with its achievements; it still seeks selected "breakthrough" improvements combined with general constantly evolving improvements to maintain its leadership position.

LOOKING TO THE FUTURE

During the pursuit of the Baldrige Award, Allaire had challenged all Xerox units to apply for each of the quality awards for which they were eligible. He

---

FIGURE 1.2 | **XEROX CORPORATE-WIDE BUSINESS PERFORMANCE**

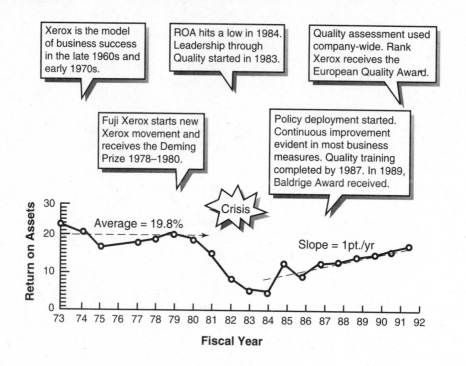

Xerox is the model of business success in the late 1960s and early 1970s.

ROA hits a low in 1984. Leadership through Quality started in 1983.

Quality assessment used company-wide. Rank Xerox receives the European Quality Award.

Fuji Xerox starts new Xerox movement and receives the Deming Prize 1978–1980.

Policy deployment started. Continuous improvement evident in most business measures. Quality training completed by 1987. In 1989, Baldrige Award received.

Crisis

Average = 19.8%

Slope = 1pt./yr

Return on Assets

30 · 20 · 10 · 0

73 74 75 76 77 78 79 80 81 82 83 84 85 86 87 88 89 90 91 92

Fiscal Year

---

further challenged the operating managers to support the development of quality awards in countries that did not currently have them. This is the type of practice that stimulates quality awareness and improvement within Xerox, while externally supporting the improvement of quality and productivity as an international imperative.

To date, Xerox has been successful in applications for fourteen national quality awards throughout the world. It is not the attainment of these awards that makes the difference, rather, it is the preparation and the stimulus from exposure to eternal review that causes each business unit to excel. In the end, the winner is the customer, both in terms of higher quality products and services and a heightened responsiveness by Xerox to their needs.

Making breakthrough improvements in business performance over the past 10 years—doubling the level of customer satisfaction, return on assets, and market share while satisfying Xerox employees—is one result of Leadership Through Quality. This balanced improvement of all four Xerox priorities indicates that quality does not need to be considered a trade-off with business profitability or performance. The Xerox experience shows that quality is the enabler for business success. For Xerox, increased productivity and an improved competitive position will be achieved using ever-improved methods and practices of Leadership Through Quality in a renewed commitment to continuous business improvement.

Index